THE NATIONAL QUESTION

BERCH BERBEROGLU

Editor

THE NATIONAL

QUESTION □ □

Nationalism, Ethnic Conflict,

and Self-Determination

in the 20th Century

TEMPLE UNIVERSITY PRESS

Philadelphia

Temple University Press, Philadelphia 19122

Text design by Adrianne Onderdonk Dudden

Library of Congress Cataloging-in-Publication Data
The national question : nationalism, ethnic conflict, and
   self-determination in the 20th century / Berch Berberoglu, editor.
     p.   cm.
   Includes bibliographical references.
   ISBN 1-56639-342-6 (cl.).—ISBN 1-56639-343-4 (pb.)
   1. Nationalism and communism.   2. Nationalism and socialism.
   3. Nationalism.   I. Berberoglu, Berch.
   HX550.N3N327   1995
   320.5′4—dc20   95-11672

◻ Contents ◻

PART III
Socialism and the Nationalities Question

❐ Preface ❑

Today, on the threshold of the twenty-first century, the world community is confronted by an ironic twist in its centuries-long development across geographic boundaries—the emergence of nationalism, ethnic conflicts, and struggles for national self-determination in an age of internationalism. At a time when the internationalization of capital has torn down national boundaries erected in an earlier age during the transition to capitalism, thereby setting the stage for transnational economic, social, and political relations between states, the current upsurge in national movements and struggles for national autonomy in many parts of the world has brought into focus the national question in places where it has not yet been fully resolved.

Although the nature and class content of national movements often differ from one another with respect to their historical origins and development, their underlying common logic has been remarkably similar—the striving toward national autonomy and independence, free from control and domination by an alien central state. Herein lies the importance of movements for national self-determination, for the primary objective of these movements has been to demand the resolution of a question that was ''solved'' by the advanced capitalist societies long ago, but remains unresolved for a number of groups in countries across the globe—the establishment of an independent nation-state.

It seems clear that progress at the international level will not be fully achieved until the national question is resolved in places where it remains a major problem. Resolving this question on a world scale is therefore necessary before we can move ahead on the most fundamental of all struggles: the class struggle.

The examination of some of the most important national movements and struggles for self-determination around the world presented in this book will, I hope, contribute to our understanding of this explosive issue. While an expanded understanding of the dynamics of nationalism and ethnic conflict may in some modest way contribute to a successful resolution of the national question and help bring about an end to the continuing civil wars across the globe—from Palestine, Kurdistan, and South Africa, to Spain and Northern Ireland, to Armenia, Azerbaijan, and the former Yugoslavia—it may, one hopes, also provide some lessons on the nature and pitfalls of nationalism and ethnic conflict so that we may be able to rise above these (national) phenomena once and for all, and begin to address the emerging, indeed central, questions of our time—class, class struggle, and social revolution, which we will soon confront in global proportions.

Although the national question has been a major concern of mine for more than two decades, this volume was inspired by the coalescence of a number of events in recent years—the Palestinian uprising in the West Bank and Gaza, the intensification of the struggle against apartheid in South Africa, the turn of events in Northern Ireland and Quebec, ethnic conflicts in the Transcaucasus and Central Asia, continuing civil war in the former Yugoslavia, and, most recently, the repression of Kurds in Iraq and Turkey. These and similarly important developments in Puerto Rico, the Basque Country, India, China, and elsewhere have brought the issues of nationalism, ethnic conflict, and the national question in general to the forefront of discussion and debate throughout the world.

I would like to thank, first and foremost, all the contributors to this volume. My thanks go to Martin Murray, Juan Manuel Carrión, and Gordon Welty for their prompt work and patience through the various stages of the publication process; to Dipankar Gupta, Martin Orr, Gerry Postiglione, Ona Alston Dosunmu, and M. Bahati Kuumba for producing quality work and making my job as editor much easier; and to Levon Chorbajian and Jasminka Udovički for tackling some very important and difficult problems that are still unfolding. Gilles Bourque, Ferhad Ibrahim, and Francisco Letamendía wrote their chapters in French, German, and Spanish, respectively; I am grateful to them for overcoming linguistic, cultural, and geographic barriers to take part in this project. The contributions of all the authors to making this such a successful collective undertaking is much appreciated.

I would also like to thank Lisa Corcostegui for translating the chapter on Basque nationalism from the Spanish original; Jennifer Beeman for translating the chapter on Quebec nationalism from the French original; and Philip Ziess-Lawrence for translating the chapter on the Kurdish national question from the German original.

I am also grateful to Doris Braendel, my editor at Temple University Press, for her interest and confidence in this book and for seeing to it that it receives the attention that such a work so urgently deserves. My thanks also go to Elizabeth Johns for her superb copy-editing skills and for doing an excellent job in shaping the manuscript to its final form. I would also like to thank Debby Stuart at Temple University Press for seeing through the final steps of the publication process in an efficient and professional manner.

Finally, I would like to thank my wife, Suzan, and my sons, Michael and Stephen, for their continuous and much needed appreciation and support of my work for all these years. It is through such understanding and support that I have been able to devote myself to the analysis of some of the central issues of our time—nationalism, ethnic conflict, and struggles for national self-determination.

❏ THE NATIONAL QUESTION ❏

❐ Introduction ❐

Nationalism, once thought of as a historical phenomenon emerging along with capitalism and the nation-state in Europe during the eighteenth century, has resurfaced in this century as part of the struggles for national liberation and self-determination in countries and regions of the Third World dominated by colonialism and imperialism.[1] Today, in the final decade of the twentieth century, it has become a worldwide phenomenon, spreading to every corner of the globe—from the Middle East to South Africa, to Europe, to North America, and to the former Soviet Union. That such nationalist fervor should develop in an age when the internationalization of capital has torn down national and geographic boundaries and ushered in a global political economy is hardly surprising, since issues of national liberation and self-determination, regardless of political form or class content, remain unresolved for a number of groups.[2]

Originating in Europe in the eighteenth century, when the rising bourgeoisies found it necessary to establish nation-states to protect their economic interests and thus consolidate their class rule,[3] nationalism became the preferred form of political expression for rival capitalist powers engaged in a life-and-death struggle for world domination during the eighteenth and nineteenth centuries. In the twentieth century, nationalism and national movements emerged throughout the world in the context of the struggle against European colonialism and imperialism.[4] National struggles against foreign domination in Asia, Africa, and the Middle East, for example, took the form of anticolonial or anti-imperialist liberation struggles—as in India and China in the 1940s, in Algeria and Cuba in the 1950s, and in much of sub-Saharan Africa in the 1960s.[5] In these and other countries and regions of the Third World subjected to external domination, the yearning for national independence and self-determination took the form of political struggles to establish sovereign national states with jurisdiction over a national territory based on self-rule.

Such movements took various forms: secular political struggles for a homeland (as in Palestine), struggles for regional and cultural autonomy and self-rule across several states (as in Kurdistan), struggles to end racism and national oppression (as in apartheid South Africa), and a multitude of national, ethnic, and religious conflicts (as in India, Nigeria, and Rwanda), which have led to continued social strife.

Elsewhere, the advanced capitalist countries have experienced movements of previously colonized peoples and territories (such as Puerto Rico) or of oppressed groups and nationalities (as in Northern Ireland, the Basque Country, and Quebec), especially during the past several decades.

In the socialist countries, especially in the former Soviet Union, where the opening accorded by glasnost and perestroika reforms and the subsequent crisis of Soviet society provided an opportunity for nationalist forces, such movements have sprung up in the Baltics, the Transcaucasus, and Central Asia, as they have in Eastern Europe, particularly in the former Yugoslavia, where a civil war between the Serbs, the Croats, and the Bosnians has torn that country apart. In China, on the other hand, the conflicts in Tibet and more recently in Xinjiang have given way to peaceful relations between the Han majority and the more than fifty-five minority nationalities that live in various autonomous regions and provinces throughout the country.[6]

Nationalism and national movements are phenomena that cannot be studied in isolation from the social and class structure of the society in which they arise. A class analysis of such movements, therefore, is imperative for a better understanding of the dynamics of social change that these movements entail. We contend in this book that class conflicts and class struggles are manifestations of social and political divisions that are, at base, a reflection of relations of production.[7] Such production relations (i.e., class relations) come to inform the nature and content of political relations, which at the *inter*national level take the form of *national* struggles. Thus, on the national level, exploitative relations between two contending classes within a national boundary take the form of an internal class struggle; a similar relationship at the international level manifests itself in the form of a national struggle—a struggle that, in essence, is the national expression of an international class struggle that is often based on an alliance of a number of classes unified for a single, most immediate goal—national liberation.[8]

These struggles for self-determination, which as I have described them are characteristic of Third World anti-imperialist national liberation struggles, take quite a different form in the advanced-capitalist imperial centers of Europe and North America. Here the struggles waged by national minorities against the central state—as in Quebec and the Basque Country, as well as among Native Americans in the United States and Canada—tend to be demands for limited autonomy, self-rule, or similar such status within the boundaries of the larger federal structure, demands that fall short of full national independence and statehood.

In the context of the socialist states, we find an entirely different dynamic at work. In some cases, as in China, the nationalities question and nationalities policy may be framed as an issue of national integration, of finding a way to recognize cultural diversity and allow regional autonomy to various ethnic and nationality groups. In other cases, as in the former Soviet Union, where the center fails to deal with deep-seated national antagonisms inherited from an earlier period, some national groups may come to play a disproportionately dominant role; the resulting hostilities may in time give rise to the disintegration of the central state along national lines. It is important to remember, however, that while long-suppressed national aspirations within an apparently cooperative federated state may give rise to national movements that *appear* to be "above class," here too an analysis of the class nature of national movements is necessary for a clear understanding of the dynamics of such movements.

The primary aim of this book is to provide a comparative-historical perspective on nationalism through case studies of nationalism, ethnic conflict, and struggles for national self-determination. By this means, the volume traces the historical development of some of the most important national movements of this century situated in different geographic and sociopolitical settings. No attempt is made to engage in theoretical discussion or debate on the nature of nationalism or the national question in general, or to develop a general theory of nationalism and self-determination based on the experiences of the various national movements examined here.[9]

The unique histories, cultural characteristics, class nature, and political forms of the struggles of peoples for national liberation around the world examined in these pages can themselves give us insight into these movements. In order to understand these movements fully, however, we must also look at a few key substantive questions that lie at the heart of the phenomenon of nationalism (and the national question) in order to sort out their class nature.[10] The central question we must raise in all of these cases is: Why should we take a *class analysis approach* to the study of nationalism, ethnic conflict, and movements for national self-determination?

Nationalism, writes Albert Szymanski in his book *Class Structure*, "is the ideology that members of a nation, people, ethnic group, or 'racial' minority have more in common with each other than the various constituent classes of the group have with other people in similar class positions."[11] He continues his definition by saying:

> "Nationalism" dictates that because of their postulated overriding common interest, all classes within the ethnic group, people, or "racial" minority should work together economically and politically to advance their collective interests *against* other "nations", "races", ethnic groups, or peoples (even against those who are in the *same* classes). Nationalism is the advocacy of ethnic or "national" solidarity and action over class consciousness and action. It is, thus, the opposite of class consciousness that argues solidarity should occur and political alliances be formed primarily along *class* lines (even against the relatively privileged groups within one's subordinate ethnic group). Nationalism and class consciousness are, thus, alternative strategies of political action for gaining improvement in one's life.[12]

"In fact," adds Szymanski, "nationalism is a product of class forces. Although different kinds of nationalism differ qualitatively in their effects, *all* serve some classes within a given racial or ethnic group as opposed to others."[13]

Adopting a class-analysis approach for the study of nationalism would entail analyzing the class base of a particular national movement, the balance of class forces within it, and the class forces leading the movement. On this basis, we can determine the nature and future course of development of a national movement and see whether it is progressive or reactionary. Once the class character of the movement and its leadership is established, we can differentiate politically among various types of national movements. This differentiation can in turn provide us with clues to the movement's social and political character.[14]

Understanding the class nature of a given national movement may also help us understand the nature of the class forces that that movement is struggling *against*, and hence the nature and forms of the struggle itself. The class content of a struggle against imperialism, for example, may transform it from a national struggle into a class struggle being fought at the national and international levels; that is, although the struggle takes the form of a national struggle, it is, in essence, a struggle for state power.[15]

If, as James Blaut points out, national struggle is class struggle, that is, "one very important form of the struggle for state power," then we need to ask "which classes make use of it, in which historical epochs, and for which purposes?"[16] Looking at the struggle in this way, we can expect a relationship between the class character of a national movement, its class leadership, its political goals, and, if it is successful, the nature and direction of the postindependence state. Thus, the ideology of a national movement led by a national or petty bourgeoisie, which can be characterized as "bourgeois nationalism," will lead to the creation of a national *capitalist* state; an anti-imperialist national movement led by the working class in alliance with the peasantry, on the other hand, will give rise to a popular *socialist* state.[17]

Because the settings in which these struggles take place are so diverse, we must look carefully at the relationship between class, nation, and state in order to understand the social relevance of nationalism (and the national question) as manifested in different spatial, temporal, and political contexts.[18] Consequently, the three parts of this book look separately at nationalism, ethnic conflict, and struggles for national self-determination in the Third World (Part I), the advanced capitalist countries (Part II), and the socialist states (Part III). Specifically, Part I examines the Palestinian, Kurdish, South African, and Indian movements, as well as the role of women in national liberation movements in Africa, the Middle East, and Central America. Part II looks at nationalism and national movements in Puerto Rico, Northern Ireland, the Basque Country, and Quebec. Finally, Part III takes up the nationalities question in the former Soviet Union, China, and the former Yugoslavia. Together, the twelve chapters provide a wide-ranging comparative-historical analysis of some of the most important national movements and struggles for national self-determination in the world today.

In the first chapter, on the Palestinian national question, Gordon Welty traces the progress of Palestinian nationalism from the social, economic, and political structure of Palestinian society under Ottoman rule, through the popular opposition to Zionist colonization that emerged even before the British Mandatory period, to its awakening after 1947, when Zionist war plans led to the emergence within Israel and especially in the diaspora of such political movements as Pan-Arabism and "pragmatic" nationalism, and eventually to the founding of the Palestine Liberation Organization (PLO) in 1964. Since 1967, Israeli attempts to control the Palestinian population through violence (exercised by the military and paramilitary apparatus) and through political, economic, legal, and social institutions have resulted in a deepening and maturing of the nationalist movement. The political mobilization of the Palestinian diaspora in the 1960s, Welty points out, was reflected back into the Occupied Territories after 1967, giving rise to the popular resistance, which led, in turn, to the Israeli military debacle in Lebanon after 1982—all of which has come together and found dialectical expression in massive Palestinian unrest and finally, in December 1987, in the uprising known as the Intifada, which represents the coming to full maturity of the Palestinian nationalist movement. Clearly, the various political tendencies within the Palestinian national movement reflect the class forces that exist in Palestinian society. The movement's success stems from the willingness of these class forces to effect a popular alliance to achieve their national goal of independence and self-rule. The future of the Palestinian movement and the nature of the new society that it is now building will depend on how these forces interact and which class(es) emerge as leaders in charting the development path for the Palestinian people in the years ahead.

In Chapter 2, Ferhad Ibrahim examines the Kurdish national question as it is played out in several states in the Middle East (mainly Turkey, Iraq, Iran, and Syria). Not unlike the PLO, the Workers' Party of Kurdistan (PKK), the leading force confronting the Turkish state in the most recent period of nationalist upsurge among the Kurds in Turkey, has, according to Ibrahim, served as a catalyst to reinvigorate and mobilize the Kurdish national movement and renew its demands for national self-determination. Certainly, given developments across the border in Iraq in the aftermath of the Gulf War in 1991, and the crushing defeat suffered by the Kurds there at the hands of Saddam Hussein's regime, the future of the Kurdish national movement and the struggle of Kurds for self-rule is far from certain. But, like the Palestinian cause, the resistance of the Kurds against their oppressors is gaining them growing attention in the world community and may eventually lead to the establishment of a national homeland. Certainly, as in other cases of nationalism and national movements, the Kurdish movement will undergo internal struggles over leadership and political direction that will reflect class struggles lodged in the social structure of the society, and the direction that the movement takes will thus depend on the nature and composition of these forces and how they come to define the movement and the new society it creates.

In his chapter on apartheid in South Africa, Martin Murray argues that the national question in South Africa has been a bone of contention among political organizations committed to eliminating racial oppression and class exploitation in that country. Despite common opposition to white minority rule, he writes, there is no shared agreement over what defines the "nation" among such political organizations as the African National Congress, the South African Communist Party, and the Pan Africanist Congress. Indeed, Murray concludes that the definition of the national question prefigures the "imagined community" of postapartheid South Africa.

In Chapter 4, Dipankar Gupta takes up the question of the interplay of religion, ethnic conflict, and national politics in India, and particularly the role of the central state in confronting linguistic, nativist, and regional movements to keep the Indian nation-state intact. Gupta argues that the acceptance of cultural and linguistic differences is the enduring basis on which Indian politics is played out and that the political center both symbolizes and actively demonstrates the unity, coherence, and sovereignty of the Indian nation-state. But while the center projects itself as protector of cultural, religious, and linguistic differences, it increasingly uses ethnic conflict to maintain its hold on power. Thus, the center increasingly ethnicizes secular regional demands as a way of striking back at those who challenge its entrenched rule. But, paradoxically, when it does so it confronts the Indian union with its gravest threat.

The role of women in Third World national liberation struggles, a role seldom examined in great detail in studies of nationalism and national movements in the Third World, is taken up by M. Bahati Kuumba and Ona Alston Dosunmu in Chapter 5. Focusing on national liberation struggles in Southern Africa, the Middle East, North Africa, and Central America and on the role of women in resistance movements in Angola, Mozambique, Namibia, South Africa, Algeria, Palestine, Nicaragua, and El Salvador, Kuumba and Alston Dosunmu find that such struggles, where questions of class, gender, and nation intersect, provide a mixed picture of progress for women but that in general, rather than causing women to submerge their own struggle, struggles for national liberation lead to improved status for women. This status, of course, may continue to improve or may deteriorate after independence is achieved: women have made limited gains in struggles led by bourgeois and petty bourgeois nationalist forces, such as in Algeria, but have achieved greater progress in movements and nations led by working-class and peasant masses relying on broad popular support, as in South Africa, Angola, and Nicaragua. The form and content of women's participation in national liberation struggles, Kuumba and Alston Dosunmu conclude, are linked to the imperatives of the struggle. In turn, the depth and breadth of female participation in the national struggle has a direct bearing on women's role in nation building after independence is achieved. Likewise, the degree to which the new government goes beyond nationalism to pursue the alleviation of class, ethnic, and gender divisions has great bearing on the subsequent status of women, and the degree to which women participate fully in the various phases of national liberation and reconstruction is an indicator of the movement's commitment to equality for all the people.

In his chapter on Puerto Rican nationalism, Juan Manuel Carrión chronicles the nationalist challenge and the colonial response during the Great Depression and the Second World War, as well as the resurgence of nationalism in the postwar period of U.S. hegemony over the island. Carrión next examines the upsurge in the struggle for independence in Puerto Rico in the

1960s and 1970s and assesses the prospects for self-determination during this period. He concludes his chapter by analyzing the Puerto Rican national movement during the 1980s and provides some important insights on the future of Puerto Rican nationalism.

Next, in Chapter 7, Martin Orr examines Irish nationalism and the struggle against British domination in Northern Ireland. He argues that this conflict is fundamentally the result of eight hundred years of British imperialism. In opposition to this attempt at domination, the Irish have mobilized in a variety of nationalist movements, and every British attempt to strengthen its rule has had the contradictory effect of eroding it. Now, mired in an urban guerrilla war that it continues to characterize as criminal terrorism, Britain is looking for a way out. It would not be surprising, Orr concludes, if these efforts continue to have contradictory results—nourishing both reactionary loyalism and militant nationalism.

In Chapter 8, on Basque nationalism, Francisco Letamendía traces the history of the Basque national movement during this century, especially since the Spanish Civil War, and its recent development as a reaction to the Francoist state, a repressive fascist state that attempted to crush the Basque national movement through its military and police apparatus. Letamendía points out that the formation of numerous national political organizations during the Franco years actually contributed to a resurgence of national consciousness, which in turn led, in the late 1950s, to the founding of a number of radical organizations that took up armed struggle against the central state. Prominent among them was ETA (Euskadi ta Askatasuna, or Basque Country and Freedom). To counter the increasingly violent situation, which had put the Basque region on the national political agenda in Spain, ETA underwent an intense internal debate as to the appropriate response to the Spanish state and, in the process, split internally into what became known as its political and military wings. Subsequent to this split in the mid-1970s, new political organizations sprang up once again and developed a unified approach through a new socialist coalition, the Patriotic Socialist Coordinating Council (KAS). Under the current situation in the mid-1990s, Letamendía believes that the armed struggle has become counterproductive; its persistence, he feels, is dividing Basque society and thereby defeating its own purpose of building a unified national movement to achieve self-determination for the Basque people.

In Chapter 9, Gilles Bourque examines the origins of Quebec nationalism and the current situation in Quebec, where the independence movement has been developing within the framework of the transformation of the capitalist economy and state in Canada during the twentieth century. Bourque points out that Canadian federalism has reproduced a multiplicity of contradictions linked on the one hand to the national question (the struggles of Acadians, Métis, Quebecois, and Ameridians) and on the other hand to the regional question (the demands made by the western provinces and the Maritimes on Central Canada—Ontario and Quebec). Even if the struggle of the Quebec national movement is the only one capable of breaking up Canada, Bourque adds, one cannot analyze the current situation as a simple conflict between two monolithic blocs, for it is the complex relationship between these national and regional conflicts that jeopardizes a compromise that would satisfy Quebec's demands. The acceleration of capitalist development after the Second World War and the establishment of the welfare state in the 1960s, Bourque argues, imposed an important reorganization of relations between the different social forces within Quebec society and thus created a new type of national movement. These dual phenomena provoked the marginalization of the Catholic Church and the traditional elites. The rise of the new middle class and of new Quebec capitalism, as well as the political coalescing of the working class, created a new, and more aggressive, type of national movement. The Quebec state, which had become resolutely interventionist, thus appeared as an instrument of national liberation, first for the new middle class, from which the state bureaucracy was primarily recruited, and then for certain members of the capitalist class, who saw in it the promotion of Quebec capitalism. After a weakening of the movement during the 1980s, Bourque concludes, one can now see a spectacular rise of the sovereigntist option. The inability of the Canadian state to satisfy even the most minimal of Quebec's demands and the failure of conservative government policies during the 1980s have recharged the movement and enlarged its grassroots base.

In Chapter 10, Levon Chorbajian argues that the national question in the former USSR, more so than in Eastern Europe, was at the cutting edge of change and led to the ultimate failure of the Gorbachev reforms by the late 1980s. Chorbajian provides an examination of Soviet nationality policy and its impact on three important regions: the Transcaucasus, the Baltics, and Central Asia. Under the centralized Soviet system, Chorbajian writes, nationalism became the vehicle for the expression not only of strictly national issues but also of a host of economic, political, and ecological concerns that took on an ethnic hue. Some of these concerns, he adds, may prove as troublesome to now-independent Commonwealth states as they were in the former Soviet Union. Without communism or a centralized state authority as a scapegoat, nationalism and ethnic conflicts in the former Soviet republics, Chorbajian concludes, will inevitably give way to growing class struggles in the years ahead.

Gerard Postiglione examines China's nationalities policy and its implications for modernization in Chapter 11. He identifies the basic dimensions of China's modernization effort as social equality, economic development, cultural autonomy, and national integration. He provides an overview of the national minority situation by focusing on population characteristics, group identification, regional variations, intergroup relations and migration, religious traditions, language, and cross-border nationalities. He also examines aspects of the Chinese constitution and the specific provisions within it for regional autonomy. Postiglione uses the cases of Tibet and Xinjiang province as a basis for discussing China's national minorities situation. Finally, he brings out various aspects of the Chinese case in order to situate China's nationalities policy and relations between its national minorities in a socialist context.

Finally, in her chapter on the former Yugoslavia, Jasminka Udovički provides a comprehensive political history of relations between the various nationalities and examines the sources of the national and ethnic conflicts that plunged Yugoslavia into civil war in the 1990s. Udovički argues that ethnic divisions in the former Yugoslavia have their roots in the history of colonization and foreign domination but that these forces of separation and conflict were coupled with and tempered by a deeply rooted sense of a common Slavic origin and language that served as a powerful force of amalgamation. The shared experience of World War II fratricide, for example, functioned on two levels: on the one hand, as a powerful agent of mistrust and fragmentation, and on the other as an agent of unification. The only possible way out of total mutual annihilation, she writes, lay in national reconciliation. Thus, the apocalypse carried within itself an undercurrent of rebirth. Conflict between the various groups was held in check under the Tito regime in the postwar period when Yugoslavia became a federation of six autonomous republics. And for nearly fifty years, the various ethnic groups lived in peace and harmony in the new federal state. Now, with the dissolution of Yugoslavia into several separate states, the various national, ethnic, and religious groups are engaging in a war for territories. Peace and national coexistence and self-determination cannot be obtained by the international community, Udovički concludes, but hinge on the readiness of the various peoples involved to support a society that commits itself to protecting the rights of all national and ethnic minorities.

Together the twelve chapters in this book provide an in-depth analysis of some of the most important national movements and struggles for national self-determination around the world. It is hoped that the analyses provided in these pages on the nature and dynamics of various forms of nationalism, ethnic conflict, and national struggles will lead interested readers to examine other such cases of struggles that movements for national liberation have waged during the course of the twentieth century.

NOTES

1. For a detailed theoretical discussion on the rise of nationalism and national movements historically and today, see James M. Blaut, *The National Question: Decolonising the Theory of Nationalism* (London: Zed Books, 1987).

2. For an analysis of the internationalization of capital and its implications in the twentieth century, see Berch Berberoglu, *The Internationalization of Capital: Imperialism and Capitalist Development on a World Scale* (New York: Praeger, 1987).

3. See Eric Hobsbawm, *The Age of Revolution: 1789–1848* (New York: World, 1962), chap. 7, and Hobsbawm, *The Age of Capital: 1848–1875* (New York: Scribner's, 1975), chap. 5.

4. For a discussion of the theory of nationalism and the various nationalist movements, see Horace B. Davis, *Toward a Marxist Theory of Nationalism* (New York: Monthly Review Press, 1978). Also see Davis's earlier study, *Nationalism and Socialism: Marxist and Labor Theories of Nationalism to 1917* (New York: Monthly Review Press, 1967).

5. See Norman Miller and Roderick Aya, eds., *National Liberation: Revolution in the Third World* (New York: Free Press, 1971); Donald C. Hodges and Robert Elias Abu Shanab, eds., *NLF: National Liberation Fronts, 1960/1970* (New York: William Morrow, 1972).

6. A number of these cases are examined at length in various essays included in this book.

7. See Albert Szymanski, *Class Structure: A Critical Perspective* (New York: Praeger, 1983), pp. 5–7, 76–84.

8. James Blaut similarly argues that national liberation struggles against imperialism at the international level are, in essence, class struggles. See Blaut, *The National Question*, pp. 176–95.

9. For an extended analysis of various theoretical positions on debates on the theory of nationalism and the national question, see Blaut, *The National Question*, esp. chap. 1.

10. Given the focus of this book on struggles for national liberation and self-determination, no attempt is made here to deal with reactionary nationalist movements, such as fascism.

11. Szymanski, *Class Structure*, p. 430.

12. Ibid. (emphasis in original).

13. Ibid. (emphasis in original).

14. See Berberoglu, *The Internationalization of Capital*, chap. 7. Also see Berch Berberoglu, *Political Sociology: A Comparative/Historical Approach* (New York: General Hall, 1990), chap. 2.

15. Ibid. See also Blaut, *The National Question*, pp. 23, 46, 123.

16. Blaut, *The National Question*, pp. 4, 46.

17. Albert Szymanski, *The Logic of Imperialism* (New York: Praeger, 1981), pp. 426–29, 537.

18. See Berch Berberoglu, "Nationalism and Ethnic Rivalry in the Early Twentieth Century," *Nature, Society, and Thought* 4, no. 3 (1991): 269–73.

◻ **I** ◻

The National Question
in the Third World

Palestinian Nationalism
and the Struggle for
National Self-Determination

The development of the Palestinian national movement can be traced at least to the end of the First World War, when the crumbling Ottoman Empire gave way to the territorial expansion of the Western imperialist powers—including France, Britain, and later the United States—into the Middle East. Palestine, the provincial territory controlled by the Ottoman state, had for centuries been home for the Palestinian people. But while successful national uprisings in the Balkans and elsewhere in the empire led to the establishment of independent nation-states, the area inhabited by the Palestinians and the surrounding regions extending to the Persian Gulf and the Arabian Peninsula came under the control of the European powers, which turned them into mandates of one or the other of the leading imperialist states of the period, Britain and France.

This occupation of Arab territories by the Western powers intensified with the creation of the state of Israel on Palestinian lands at midcentury. The Zionist oppression of the Palestinian people in Israel, their forced expulsion from their homeland to neighboring Arab states as refugees, and their harsh treatment by the Zionist state in the occupied territories of Gaza and the West Bank during the 1970s and 1980s have given rise to a strong sense of national identity and to a struggle for national independence that culminated in the popular uprising known as the Intifada.

To understand the origins and development of the Palestinian national movement and the context in which this movement developed, we need first to examine the nature and structure of the Palestinians as a people. And for this we must look briefly at the Ottoman Empire, in which the Palestinians were situated.

HISTORICAL BACKGROUND

The Ottoman Empire ruled Palestine from the sixteenth century until the final campaigns of the First World War. The empire had been the center of the world for many centuries and was directly or indirectly responsible for much that shaped today's entire Middle East region.

The Ottoman social formation foregrounded the social antagonism between city and country, between the central state apparatus and the rural direct producer. This conflict was epitomized in the household of the Ottoman ruler, the sultan. The land and other assets of the empire were the personal property of the ruler, to be distributed for the usufruct of various members of the ruling class, who were concentrated around the central state. The social relationship between this state and the direct producer in the villages of the distant provinces of the empire was one of direct authoritarian rule; the subjects had no constitutional rights, and the sultan's power was absolute. Corresponding to the generalized political domination was the exploitative economic relationship whereby the state extracted the surplus product from the masses (*raiya*). Exploitation characteristically took the form of taxation: first, the taxes on agricultural production; then, the taxes on various urban activities (commerce and handicrafts); and finally, the head taxes (*jizya*), which were levied on non-Muslim communities within the empire.[1]

By far the majority of Palestinians in the nineteenth century, perhaps over 80 percent, were peasants (*fellahin*).[2] Some cultivation was based on sharecropping, with a division of the agricultural product between peasant and the landlord of the state property (*miri*). Much was based on peasant smallholding of *miri* land. By the second half of the nineteenth century, an increasing portion of the arable land in Palestine was sown to winter wheat—a cash crop—which was rotated annually with other, subsistence, crops. Around the larger cities, olive groves flourished; orange groves were prominent on the outskirts of Jaffa. Agricultural output increased in Palestine during the late Ottoman period, largely because of an extension of the area under cultivation rather than an intensification of agricultural productivity per se. As local strife and banditry diminished following Ibrahim Pasha's departure from Damascus in 1840 and the Ottoman reassertion of authority, more and more land could be safely cultivated. Moreover, agricultural output was increasingly commodified, as cash crops replaced subsistence production.[3]

On one hand, the countryside was clearly subject to social change, at least in a quantitative sense. On the other hand, the nature of this change did not tend to be qualitative; hence the social order remained the source of a sense of solidarity and group identity in the rural areas. This identity tended to be particularistic and local, however, rather than nationalistic.

Although the majority of the population of Ottoman Palestine were peasants, the urban groups were the bearers of its civilization. Important urban centers toward the end of the nineteenth century included Jerusalem, Acre, Nablus, Gaza, Hebron, Jaffa, and Nazareth. Three of these cities—Acre, Jerusalem, and Nablus—were administrative centers for Ottoman districts (the *sanjaks*).[4] Urban social processes exhibited more change, and even qualitative change, in contrast to those in the countryside. Economic activity had been organized by guilds of artisans and shopkeepers. By the end of the nineteenth century, however, some of the industrial activity had moved outside of the framework of the handicraft guilds.

In addition, the cities were the home of the Palestinian elite (the *effendi*)—absentee landlords, religious officials, and various Ottoman state authorities—as well as, in the late nineteenth century, the intelligentsia. These literate and politically more self-conscious groups tended to be of greater concern to the central state. Ottoman economic policy sought to maintain the public finance and also to meet the needs of the urban population, at the expense of the peasants.

The success of these policies and the relative comfort of the urban groups (particularly the *effendi* and the intelligentsia) together with the Ottoman tactic of balancing the interests of the various groups, all the while stressing the unity of the empire, tended to preempt nationalist aspirations in Ottoman Palestine.

The preponderant religious group in Palestine under Ottoman rule was the Sunni Muslim. This group felt closely allied with the Ottomans in having a common religion, and it was closely allied to the central state through the co-optation of the Palestinian *effendi* into Ottoman ruling circles. Among non-Muslims (the *dhimmis*) the Greek Orthodox formed the most numerous community. Across the entire Ottoman Empire, the *millet* system had traditionally provided not only for the relative security of the various ethnic and religious minorities within the Dar es Salaam (the Islamic "Realm of Peace") but also for a measure of their political and cultural autonomy as well. The most important *millets* in Palestine were those of the several Greek Christian communities and the Jewish community (the Yishuv). Each *millet* was headed by its own religious leader. Non-Muslim persons were linked to the sultanate through the *millet*, which was responsible for gathering taxes, providing education, and resolving legal disputes within the community.

But these groups were not the juridical equal of the Muslim majority. The *dhimmi* paid the personal or head tax (the *jizya*), which was not levied on Muslims. The *dhimmi* could not testify at law against Muslims. While this systemic discrimination might well have strengthened the sense of collective identity of these minority groups, that was not necessarily conducive to the emergence of Palestinian (or even Arab) nationalism. The rise of Zionist political parties,[5] however, and armed provocations against the Arab community in Palestine during the first years of the twentieth century[6] led to greater cohesion and collective identity among the Palestinians. The Palestinian response to Zionist provocations represented a first expression of political self-consciousness.

THE PALESTINIAN NATIONAL MOVEMENT IN THE FIRST HALF OF THE TWENTIETH CENTURY

Palestinian opposition to Zionist colonization, which had emerged even before the League of Nations gave Britain mandate over Palestine, became exacerbated by British military occupation of Jerusalem and other Palestinian territories at the hand of the First World War. As the Palestinian opposition became increasingly intense, the British successfully pursued a policy of *divide et impera*, which led to the Great Palestinian Revolt, the disarming of the Palestinian people, and the decline of traditional Palestinian political culture.

With the rise of Zionism, the Arab community of Palestine did not view itself merely as a set of ethnic groups, each distinct from the Jewish colonists and from each other. Rather it began to view itself in terms of its *political* identity. Muslim and Christian Palestinians petitioned the Ottoman central state, sent delegations to the newly reconvened Ottoman Parliament, and polemicized in their newspapers. This expression of Palestinian political culture further intensified Palestinian political identity after British occupation of Jerusalem at the close of World War I.

British interests in Palestine were geopolitical—protecting the northeastern flank of the Suez Canal, which London viewed as the lifeline of the British Empire. The Ottoman general Jamal Pasha had shown the British in January 1915 that Palestine under hostile control could be the base of an attack on the canal. Those British interests were best served by a territory that was not ethnically so unified that the threat of self-determination was genuine. Those interests were also best served by a territory that did not have so much intercommunal conflict that a large British garrison was required.

British Foreign Secretary Arthur Balfour's well-known letter of November 2, 1917, to Baron Edward Rothschild, incorporating the Balfour Declaration, indicated that the British favored the establishment of a Jewish "national home" in Palestine, explicitly alongside "existing non-Jewish communities." Whatever other objectives may be imputed to the British in this declaration, it guaranteed an ethnically divided Palestine.[7]

Ethnic conflict had erupted between Zionists and Palestinians during the period of British military occupation even prior to the granting of the League of Nations Mandate. Haganah (the Defense Force) was formed in early 1920 and began training in Jerusalem. Violent ethnic clashes occurred there in April 1920. The Zionists called for increased Jewish immigration as the antidote. Palestinian political culture was already evidencing change. The newly formed Palestinian Women's Union called for an end to the Balfour Declaration and to British torture of Palestinian political prisoners.[8] Even more violent clashes, provoked by the British police against the communist movement, occurred in Jaffa on May Day in 1921. The authorities then began to realize that the ethnic conflict might get out of hand.[9] Had the British taken seriously the kind of requirements that they would soon accept as part of the League of Nations Mandate, and had the United States not passed the several Johnson Acts of the early 1920s—which severely curtailed Jewish immigration to New York in response to the spectre of bolshevism—the interests of all sides in Palestine might have been accommodated. As it was, geopolitics continued to play a role: Jewish immigration to Palestine increased in the early 1930s as the economic and political situation in Europe deteriorated. After August 1929, in response to the heightening tensions in Palestine, the Palestine Communist Party (PCP) began to pursue a policy of Arabization.

British *divide et impera* policies were not limited to manipulating intercommunal tensions. They manipulated the competition among the Palestinians *effendi* as well. As we have already observed, it was Ottoman policy to balance the interests of the various Palestinian groups against one another. British policy intensified this competition by playing off one against the other. In particular, they pitted the Husseini family against the Nashashibi family, to the ultimate benefit of neither.[10]

The Husseini family led the Majlis (the Supreme Muslim Council), secured the appointment of Haj Amin al-Husseini as the mufti of Jerusalem (the highest Muslim authority there), and had an extensive coalition of followers in the Majlesiyyoun (council supporters). As evidence of the change of Palestinian political culture, the Majlesiyyoun had its own organ of popular opinion, a newspaper called *al-Jamia al-Arabiyya* (the *Arab League*). On the other side, the Nashashibi family led the Muarada (the Opposition) and secured the election of Ragheb al-Nashashibi as mayor of Jerusalem. It too had numerous followers, organized in the Muaridoun (Opposition supporters); its newspapers was *al-Karmel*, published in Haifa. The schism within Palestinian political life had become so deep that the two groups held competing Islamic congresses in December 1931, one at the Rawdat al-Maaref School and the other at the King David Hotel, both in Jerusalem.

In 1932, dissatisfaction with the ineffectiveness of the political culture reached the point that Awni Abdul-Hadi, Hamdi al-Husayni, and others formed the Istiqlal (Independence) Party, the first purely Palestinian political party, and began to promote a policy of noncooperation with the Mandatory authorities. Indeed, by 1933, the Palestinian masses had begun to run ahead of their leadership and confront the British occupiers as well as the Zionist colonizers. A general strike was called during October of that year, and bloodshed ensued. The Muarada was so disorganized that it was unable to participate in the developments. Subsequently, some of the Muaridoun broke ranks and organized another faction, which secured the election of Hussein Fakhri al-Khalidi as mayor of Jerusalem in the 1934 elections.

The next two years saw the birth of a multitude of Palestinian political parties, including the Arab Party (of the Majlesiyyoun), the National Defense Party (of the Muaridoun), and the National Reform Party (led by Hussein Fakhri al-Khalidi). As a Palestinian working class began to emerge, the traditional political structure proved to be inadequate and new forms came into being. Under these divided conditions, the struggle against Zionism matured. Sporadic violence continued after the 1933 disturbances, culminating in the Palestinian general strike begun in April 1936 and the Great Palestinian Revolt (in 1938 and 1939). England's Peel Commission, which investigated the strike, recognized that the intercommunal tension was becoming uncontrollable and in 1937 recommended partition.

Partition would have involved population transfers on a large scale, which the British government was unwilling to sanction. Despite aggressive land-appropriation policies, the Zionists owned less than 6 percent of the land in Palestine in 1938. The Jews were concentrated in Tel Aviv and other cities and in settlements scattered about the countryside. Thus there was no possibility of fulfilling the condition of territorial contiguity that is necessary for establishing a viable nation-state, let alone the condition of a developed and extensive home market for the Zionists; their communal aspirations were unrealistic.[11] In any case, no one was able to draft a plausible partition plan. The Zionists pressed the British to enact a policy of population transfer; the British resisted.

The British arrested dozens of Palestinian leaders in late 1937, including most of the Palestinian leadership of the PCP; this triggered the Great Palestinian Revolt. Guerrilla war raged throughout 1938 and well into 1939. The PCP increasingly threw its support behind the Palestinian movement. Meanwhile, Zionist terrorism mounted. Irgun (the self-styled National Military Organization, which split from Haganah in 1935) began to bomb Palestinian civilian targets in 1938. As the Great Revolt wound down in late 1939, the Palestinians were carefully disarmed by the Mandatory authority—but the Zionists were not. Finally, the official British White Paper on Palestine of 1939 called for an end to the Mandate within ten years and the establishment of an independent state in Palestine. This would be neither a Jewish state nor an Arab state but one wherein the "essential interests of each [community] are secured."[12]

Pious official proclamations aside, there seemed to be no way to resolve the conflicting interests there. British geopolitical interests in the colonies were served by a measure of ethnic heterogeneity. Zionist interests would be served only by large-scale transfer of the Palestinian population, which would effect a radical ethnic homogenization. Perhaps because of their common European heritage, these two political cultures tended to deny the legitimacy of Palestinian interests. And the Palestinians, divided as they were (into traditionally organized family groupings, then into nascent party groupings), were unable to express their own interests effectively. But the outcome of the colonial era was to transform Palestinian political culture decisively. And with this change, political identity was transformed as well.

PALESTINIAN NATIONALISM FROM 1948 TO 1967

By midcentury the success of Zionist war plans against Palestinian civilians had led to a diaspora. In 1947, two-thirds of the people in Palestine were Palestinian Muslims and Christians, while one-third were Zionist settlers. As Palestinian political culture was reestablished within Israel, several diverging tendencies emerged. Likewise, as Palestinians in the diaspora began to mobilize, a number of trends developed, including Pan-Arabism on one hand and "pragmatic" nationalism on the other. Finally, the overarching Palestine Liberation Organization (PLO) was founded in 1964. These various tendencies, however, did not become effectively coordinated until after the June 1967 War.

As we have seen, in 1939 the British had proposed ending the Palestine Mandate within a decade. When World War II ended, the exhausted empire proceeded to "unburden" itself of all but its most vital interests.[13] The costs of keeping a garrison in Palestine were perceived as greater than any possible geopolitical benefits that could be derived by maintaining a presence there. This imperial assessment became clear to the Zionists, who continued to arm themselves and prepared to seize state power in Palestine.

Moreover, the Zionist minority was by then very well organized. Its apparatus had completely supplanted the traditional Yishuv (the Jewish *millet*). It was prepared to take any measures to enlarge its territory and to eliminate its ethnic antagonists. One of its Haganah commanders, Yigael Yadin, had presented the notorious "Plan Dalet" as early as March 1948, which proposed the mass expulsion of Palestinians from their homes and the destruction of their villages to clear the land for Zionist endeavors.[14] This plan was implemented by Haganah by early April 1948, that is to say before the British Mandate had ended. On April 9, for instance, Irgun, under the leadership of Menachem Begin, massacred 254 Palestinian men, women, and children at the "pacified" village of Deir Yassin near Jerusalem, and then stuffed the mutilated bodies down the village wells in an exercise in ritual pollution. Subsequently the Zionists publicized the atrocity and promised more; the Palestinians began to flee their homes en masse.

War broke out on May 14, 1948, one day before the date on which the British planned to end their Mandate. The Israeli Haganah had about the same number of troops as did its Arab opponents taken together, but by all accounts Haganah had superior firepower, and its efforts were better coordinated. By June 11, 1948, the first phase of the war had ended in a UN-sponsored truce. The Israeli cabinet of David Ben-Gurion agreed on June 16 to prevent the return to their homes of the hundreds of thousands of Palestinian civilians who had by then been displaced by the war.[15] The war then resumed; the Palestinians were further displaced. Indeed, according to the UN Relief and Works Agency and others, more than seven hundred thousand Palestinians were displaced as a result of the 1948 War.[16] This Palestinian diaspora (the Palestinians themselves refer to it as al-Ghourba or al-Shatat) constituted approximately 60 percent of the more than 1.3 million Muslims and Christians who had resided in historic Palestine before 1948.

The 1948 War is called al-Nakbah (the Catastrophe) by the Palestinians, an apt characterization. Their community was shattered, the people who fled the Zionist terror were consigned to refugee camps in Lebanon, Jordan, and Gaza, hundreds of Palestinian villages were obliterated—razed to the ground—and those Palestinians who were permitted to remain within Israel after 1948 were subjected to military occupation until 1965. The majority of these lived in some one hundred villages and towns in northern Israel, in the region around Nazareth, almost completely separated from the Zionist settlers.

For a decade following the 1948 War, the majority of Palestinians had to devote themselves totally to the tasks of physical survival.[17] Political culture was further transformed. For those inside Israel, there were two main tendencies—a declining one, which was associated with the traditional political culture of the elites and which gave support to the Mapai (the Labor Party); and a developing one, which was associated with Maki (the reconstituted Communist Party). The traditional tendency continued its decline, and even more rapidly than before al-Nakbah, because the elites had been thoroughly discredited by the war and their base had been largely dissolved by the proletarianization of the Palestinian masses. The progressive tendency, by contrast, sought to represent the interests of the oppressed Palestinians in Israel while avoiding the pitfalls of what it viewed as the narrow nationalism that supported Gamal Abdel Nasser's Pan-Arabism. This included an ambivalent relationship to al-Ard (the Land), a Palestinian nationalist movement that had emerged in the 1950s. Of course this nationalism had both progressive aspects (the anti-imperialism on the part of the Nasserites and the struggle for democratic rights on the part of al-Ard) and regressive aspects (the suppression of the communists and other opposition movements by the Nasserites and the romantic isolationist tendencies of al-Ard).

Among the Palestinians in the diaspora the same ambiguities manifested themselves as the political culture was reestablished. The Arab Nationalist Movement (ANM), founded by George Habash in the early 1950s, stressed a pan-Arab identity; early on, it received support from Nasser. Its political organ was *al-Hurriyyah* (*Freedom*). The ANM sought to extirpate imperialism and Zionism from the Arab world (from Morocco to the Gulf emirates) and to create in its place a united Arab state; this would solve the Palestinian problem at the same time. This movement found its greatest support among the Palestinian and wider Arab middle class, a literate class no longer submerged by the *effendi* and not beholden to any foreign power. As the movement matured, it spun off many of the "leftist" organizations of the contemporary Middle East.[18]

On the other side, Fatah, founded by Yasser Arafat in the late 1950s, stressed from the start a "pragmatic" nationalist orientation. It published a magazine titled *Filastinuna* (*Our Palestine*). The task of the moment, according to Fatah, was "the liquidation of the Zionist entity in all the occupied territory of Palestine—in its political, economic, and military forms,"[19] not the "unity" of the Arab world or any other "ideological" issue. Of course, pragmatism is itself an ideology.

In part this bifurcation reflected the fundamental problem noted earlier of the limited depth and extent of the domestic market. A solid domestic market is a precondition for a nation-state, and the Palestinians did not have one. The question was what to do about that. Some felt that the territory of

Palestine (let alone the Occupied Territories) was not large enough to allow the people to institutionalize their autonomy within a nation-state, at least within the existing antagonistic social order. For these people some form of Pan-Arabism would seem necessary to achieve Palestinian self-determination, either to enlarge the salient territory or to transcend the society which moves in its antagonisms. Others believed that the territory was large enough, but that the people were not strong enough to attain autonomy on their own. For these people the liberation movement was necessarily dependent upon resources available from the current Arab regimes (including their goodwill) and thus must acquiesce to the current nation-state system by remaining "above" or "outside" the politics of the Arab states, which would of course continue to pursue their social antagonisms.

These trends came to be subsumed within the framework of the Palestine Liberation Organization (PLO) through a process that began with the Iraqi revolution of July 1958. The Iraqi Revolutionary Command Council leader, Abdel-Karim Kassem, supported the development of an autarkic "Palestinian entity" regardless of the unity of the Arab people. Nasser convened what has come to be called the "first Arab summit" in Cairo in early 1964 to address the threat posed by the Israeli National Water Project, which would divert Jordan River water into the Negev Desert. At the same time, and not to be outflanked by Kassem, the summit called for organizing the Palestinians to achieve self-determination. The PLO was therefore founded in May 1964 in East Jerusalem, with veteran Arab League diplomat Ahmed Shuquairy as its first chairman. At it founding conference, it endorsed the Palestinian National Charter. The ANM indicated it would support the PLO if the new organization were "revolutionary." The leadership of Fatah seems initially to have been wary of the PLO's Nasserite links but maintained liaison with it.[20]

The emergence of the PLO, and the increasing presence of Fatah, occasioned the development by the ANM of the National Front for the Liberation of Palestine, which conducted its first military operation against Israel in November 1964. The first Fatah military operation was conducted by al-Asifa (the Storm) on January 1, 1965, and was directed against the Israeli National Water Project.

Thus as tensions between the Arab countries and Israel rose during the mid-sixties, the liberation movement of the Palestinians in the diaspora reflected ambiguities that would only be resolved after the 1967 war, called al-Naksah (the Setback). What was clearly a strategic setback for the liberation movement was also an occasion for deepening and unifying it.

FROM SETBACK TO RESISTANCE:
THE JUNE 1967 WAR TO THE INTIFADA

After years of careful planning, Israel attacked its Arab neighbors on June 5, 1967. As Israeli general Ezer Weisman put it, this war was "a direct continuation" of the 1948 War.[21] By nighttime, Israel had destroyed the air forces of Egypt, Jordan, and Syria. Without air cover, the Arab armies were left in an impossible situation. The war ended within a week and represented a shattering defeat for the Arab states, especially for the Nasserites. Again, as "a direct continuation" of previous Zionist strategies of territorial acquisition, the West Bank, Gaza Strip, and the Golan Heights were seized and vast numbers of Palestinians were driven from their homes.

The UN Relief and Works Agency has estimated that some four hundred thousand Palestinians were displaced as a result of the 1967 war,[22] about half of them for the second time. This number amounted to about one-third of the more than 1.1 million Palestinians who had resided within the areas of Gaza and the West Bank before the war. To put it another way, about three-fourths of all Palestinians in the world had become displaced by the cumulative effects of Zionist policies during the two decades following 1948. In addition, it is worth mentioning that some one hundred thousand Syrian civilians were also displaced from the Golan Heights after the June 1967 War. This constituted over 90 percent of the population of that territory, which was thereafter annexed by Israel.[23]

The war had a number of results. The credibility of the Pan-Arabists within the Palestinian movement dropped drastically because of the setback. This led to the founding of a new movement by the ANM, the Popular Front for the Liberation of Palestine (PFLP), in late 1967. The PFLP took a more sophisticated view of the liberation struggle: four forces opposed to Palestinian self-determination were now identified—the state of Israel, the world Zionist movement, world imperialism led by the United States, and Arab reaction. The other wing of the movement underwent a rapid transformation of another sort: the forces of Fatah conducted an important defense of the Karameh refugee camp in Jordan on March 22, 1968, and its ability to confront the Israeli Defense Force (IDF) in open combat led to greatly increased support within the camps. In addition, the earlier conception of the goal of the liberation movement—the elimination of the Zionist presence from historic Palestine—was refined in 1969 with the complementary concept of a "democratic secular state," which would replace the chauvinistic Israeli institutions.

Habash was arrested in Syria in the spring of 1968 and was incarcerated there until November of that year. During this time, the PFLP began to drift, until in late 1969 a faction of the PFLP under the leadership of the Jordanian Nayef Hawatmah seceded to form the [Popular] Democratic Front for the Liberation of Palestine (DFLP); the DFLP kept control of *al-Hurriyyah*, and the PFLP founded another paper, *al-Hadaf* (*The Target*), as its own organ.[24]

Arafat assumed the chairmanship of the PLO in 1969, and most of the Palestinian movements had entered the PLO by 1970, providing an important framework for coordination of efforts. By early 1970, the organization had become strong enough to give birth to an elaborate system of autonomous institutions in the refugee camps. This occasioned sharp conflict, especially in Jordan, where more than half of the Jordanian population was Palestinian and the Hashemite royal family was especially wary of Palestinian political expression. There was sharp debate within the PLO about strategy: the "revolutionary" wing saw further conflict with Arab regimes, especially the Hashemites, as inevitable; the "pragmatic" wing sought to remain above the politics of the Arab states. But conflict could not be avoided; the tensions led to "Black September" later in 1970, when King Hussein's forces attacked Palestinian positions in Jordan.[25] After negotiating a truce between Palestinians and the Hashemites in the internecine war, Gamal Abdel Nasser died suddenly on September 30, 1970. The PLO began to shift its institutions and activities from Jordan to Lebanon.

When the October 1973 War demonstrated that Israeli military invincibility was a myth, some Arab leaders began to believe they might negotiate with Israel from a position of strength rather than weakness. This energized the elements within the PLO that also favored negotiations. Lines quickly became drawn: in October 1974, the PFLP and several other liberation groups founded the Rejectionist Front in Baghdad, opposing such negotiations; later that month, the remaining groups came together at the seventh Arab summit at Rabat and recognized the PLO as the "sole legitimate representative of the Palestinian people." On November 13, 1974, PLO chairman Arafat delivered his famous "gun and olive branch" speech before the United Nations in New York.[26]

In Beirut, the same sharp debate within the PLO recurred in 1975, now regarding PLO strategy toward the Lebanese civil war. The "revolutionary" wing wanted to support Kamal Jumblatt and its other allies in the Lebanese National Front. The "pragmatic" wing again sought to remain outside the conflict. But again events ran ahead of the leadership. The Lebanese right-wing Phalangists besieged the Tel al-Zaatar refugee camp in early 1976. This brought in the PLO defense of its own as well as its Lebanese allies, and its fighters would remain embroiled in Lebanese politics until August 1982.

Meanwhile the desire of some Arab leaders to enter negotiations with Israel came to a conclusion of sorts. Menachem Begin became Israeli prime minister on June 21, 1977, and there was momentary doubt whether American Jewish circles would be able to support him. On October 1, 1977, after months of indecisive diplomatic wrangling, the United States and the Soviet Union issued a proposal to convene a Middle East peace conference in Geneva by that December, to include "representatives of the Palestinian people," a people who had "legitimate rights."[27]

Begin objected to the contents of the proposal. Within a week, Zionist pressure had prevailed; the United States and Israel issued a new proposal, which deleted any reference to "legitimate rights" or "representatives" of the Palestinian people; indeed, it even deleted reference to the "Palestinian people."[28] By November 9, 1977, whatever doubt Anwar Sadat may have had about Washington's continued patronage of Israel under Begin had been dispelled, and he announced he would go anywhere—even to occupied Jerusalem—to negotiate with Israel.

The outcome was predictable. A peace treaty was signed between Egypt and Israel on March 26, 1979. Relieved of the threat of a "western front," Israel applied itself even more ruthlessly to the oppression of Palestinians in the Occupied Territories. When the Palestinian popular resistance intensified into early 1982, the record of abuse became so scandalous that the Begin government almost lost a Knesset vote of "no confidence" on March 24, 1982. In an attempt to divert world attention from the mounting violence in the Occupied Territories and on the most transparent of pretexts, Begin and Defense Minister Ariel Sharon, with the complicity of U.S. Secretary of State Alexander Haig, ordered the invasion of Lebanon on June 6, 1982.[29]

After a remarkable display of courage in face of the sophisticated IDF military juggernaut and after enduring relentless aerial bombardment for days without end, PLO fighters with their weapons in hand evacuated Beirut under UN auspices. Chairman Arafat was among the last to leave, on August 30, 1982. Two weeks later, despite United States security guarantees, thousands of Palestinian civilians were massacred by Phalangist irregulars, whose attack on the Sabra and Shatila refugee camps was coordinated by the IDF.[30]

Overall, the Israeli invasion of Lebanon served to underscore the lesson of the October 1973 War. Israeli military invincibility was debunked again, this time in a "people's war." The IDF continued to be battered by mobilized Lebanese patriots even after Israel took thousands of "hostages"; it finally was obliged to pull its troops back to the current "security zone" north of the Israeli border. The resistance of the Lebanese people provided a beacon for the Palestinians in the Occupied Territories in their own search for liberation. The dialectics of the process are straightforward: the Palestinian struggles in the Occupied Territories during the early 1980s led to the attack on Beirut; the Lebanese struggles against the Israelis in the mid-1980s were reflected back into the Occupied Territories, leading to the Intifada at the end of the decade. In the meantime, the solemn United States security guarantees were proven untrustworthy by the blood of Palestinian women, children, and old men, all dead in the camps around Beirut.

During the twenty years that followed 1967, the Israeli occupation of the West Bank and Gaza sought to subjugate the Palestinians through the official violence of the military and paramilitary apparatus and through the so-called structural violence of political, economic, legal, and social institutions. Israel sought to recoup the costs of occupation by taxing its victims. The occupied people responded by deepening and maturing its nationalist movement. Finally, in December 1987, the Occupied Territories exploded in the uprising known as the Intifada (the uprising against, or the "overturning" of, the Israeli occupation). It is to that important event that we must now turn.

THE INTIFADA AND THE PROSPECTS FOR PALESTINIAN NATIONAL SELF-DETERMINATION

The protests that marked the beginning of the Intifada broke out in the Jabalia refugee camp in Gaza following an automobile collision on December 9, 1987, in which four Gazans were killed by an Israeli vehicle.[31] On that first day, Israeli authorities shot and killed a number of Palestinians, including an infant, Fatmeh Alqidri of Gaza City. The protests spread to Nablus on the West Bank the next day, where the Israeli authorities shot and killed more Palestinians, including eighteen-year-old Ibrahim Ekeik. Protests broke out in East Jerusalem on December 13, and by the end of the first week, a general strike had paralyzed all the Occupied Territories.[32] This was the beginning of the Intifada.

There are certain analogies between the Intifada and the Great Palestinian Revolt, but the differences seem to be more important since the Palestinian political culture was just emerging in the 1930s while in the 1980s it had matured. Let us consider some of those crucial particularities.

Knowledge of several demographic factors is necessary for understanding the Intifada. Gaza is one of the most densely populated areas on earth. About 60 percent of the approximately 650,000 Palestinians who resided in Gaza in 1987 were under fifteen years of age. This population was expected to more than double by the year 2000.[33] On the other hand, there were very few Zionist settlers in Gaza; yet they occupied one-third of the land and used one-third of the water. Finally, of the approximately 100,000 Palestinians in the Gaza labor force in 1987, about half worked as day laborers in Israel. The labor force was highly proletarianized as well as brutally oppressed. Truly, Gaza was, as Danny Rubinstein of the Israeli newspaper *Haaretz* once told me, "the Soweto of Tel Aviv."

Even though the two Occupied Territories are separated by Israel, the events of Gaza are almost instantly the news of the West Bank and vice versa. There is no way that the two regions can be isolated from each other. Consequently, the Intifada spread instantly from Gaza to the West Bank and even inside the so-called Green Line (the boundaries of Israel in 1948) itself.

The Palestinian people under occupation, like their counterparts throughout the Middle East, are among the most highly educated people in the region. In light of the limited occupational opportunities available to them in the ethnically chauvinistic labor market of Israeli society, the Palestinians in Gaza as well as the West Bank might even be considered overeducated. Often a Palestinian worker will be more educated than his or her Israeli boss. Israeli occupation policies have been designed to ensure that a generation of young Palestinians will be less educated.[34] The escape valve for these overeducated Palestinians, especially the young men, has traditionally been emigration to the Gulf area for jobs. With the downturn of world oil prices in the early 1980s, however, this alternative began to close off. By 1987, the emigration rate had fallen to one-third its level in the early 1980s. The result was an increasing frustration of personal, let alone the national, aspirations among the Palestinian people under occupation, especially the youth.[35]

Several political factors must also be considered. The violence perpetrated by Israeli settlers against Palestinians had markedly escalated prior to the Intifada. Since the settlers were heavily armed, this violence can only be described as terroristic. The escalating level of violent incidents made the unarmed Palestinian people increasingly desperate. In addition, the spring 1987 PLO meeting in Algeria brought a notable unity to the ranks and orientation of the liberation movement, one with a distinctly progressive direction. This raised the morale of all Palestinians, including of course those living under Israeli military occupation. Finally, there was the fall 1987 Arab summit held in Amman, Jordan, within sight of the West Bank. That meeting virtually ignored the plight of the Palestinian people under occupation, thereby strengthening their conviction that they must act on their own behalf.

In response to all these considerations—the increasingly severe population pressures, the frustrations of unfulfilled lives, and the growing militance of Palestinian national consciousness—there was a rise in the number of Palestinian retaliations against Zionist settlers in the Occupied Territories. It has been estimated that there was a tenfold increase in violent incidents during the 1980s, all before the beginning of the Intifada.[36] It was becoming increasingly clear to the Israelis that the Occupied Territories were already—or would very soon become—ungovernable, even by the IDF military authorities.

Several aspects of Intifada policy should be stressed. Most generally, the Intifada represents the coming to full maturity of Palestinian political culture. The political mobilization of the Palestinian diaspora in the 1960s was reflected back into the Occupied Territories after 1967, giving rise to the resistance, which led in turn to the Israeli military debacle in Lebanon after 1982—all of which came together and found its dialectical expression in the Intifada.

More specifically, "popular committees" emerged as a form of Palestinian opposition to Israeli occupation measures.[37] For example, the FACTS Information Committee, based in East Jerusalem, was one of a network of popular committees that developed as an aspect of Palestinian resistance and nation-building efforts.[38] FACTS began publishing in January 1988, in order to spread the local Palestinian understanding of the Intifada and to provide a Palestinian voice to the English-speaking world. It has published *Diaries* from a number of Palestinian villages, including al-Yamoun, Arroura, Idna, Kufr Rai, and Yatta, as well as from the Jenin refugee camp. These give day-by-day accounts of life under Israeli occupation from the viewpoint of the oppressed. FACTS has also translated and reprinted many of the *Communiqués* of the Unified National Leadership (UNL) of the Intifada, beginning with the first, which was issued in Gaza nine days after the beginning of the Intifada.

By July 1, 1988, the Israeli Central Command declared all these popular committees to be illegal. On August 18, Defense Minister Yitzhak Rabin reiterated that they were "illegal organizations" and were the "moving force behind the uprising" and an "alternative to the military government."[39] Rabin sought to justify the deportation of Palestinians—in contravention of the fourth Geneva Convention of international law—by claiming that the deportees were "committee activists."

The Intifada also pursued policies of nation-building—that is, of establishing an independent government and independent socioeconomic structures in the West Bank and Gaza Strip. In pursuit of this policy, Palestinians resigned from the local police forces and from the civil administration, and

Palestinian shopkeepers attempted to set their own hours and prices. The goal of disengagement was to demark clearly the boundaries between Palestinian society and Israeli authority.

This had several consequences for Palestinian political culture. After refusing to deal with the PLO for decades, the United States finally entered into low-level public negotiations with the PLO in Tunis in December 1988. These negotiations were terminated on a pretext by the State Department just before the outbreak of the Gulf crisis in 1990.

Then, after much posturing during the Gulf crisis about the inadmissability of acquiring territory by force, the United States pressured its Israeli client to enter peace negotiations in late 1991, first in Madrid and then in Washington. The new relation between Palestinians of the diaspora and the Occupied Territories was symbolized by the diplomatic role Professor Hanan Ashrawi of Bir Zeit University (still closed by Israeli authorities) played in those negotiations. But at the same time, Islamic forces in the Occupied Territories, organized as Hamas,[40] as well as the Rejectionist Front within the PLO had the potential for drastically radicalizing the Intifada if the diplomatic effort were to stagnate.

Over the course of the twentieth century, Palestinian aspirations for national self-determination developed to the point that they came to represent a coherent and realistic strategy and tactics for attaining Palestinian objectives. In strategic terms, the shift from seeking the overthrow of Zionism, to creating a democratic secular successor to the Zionist state, to creating a state that would be geographically contiguous to Israel represent stages in a maturing understanding of what the objective of self-determination entails at different historical moments. Likewise, in tactical terms, the rise of armed resistance, the development of diplomatic alternatives to armed resistance, and the emergence of systematically organized and broadly based forms of civil disobedience, along with institution building even under military occupation, represent an enhanced repertoire of responses for the Palestinian community in the face of continued oppression. It appears that the Palestinians have throughout all this retained the integrity of their community;[41] hence, the likelihood of successful nation building in the longer term—given the end of occupation—seems high. By contrast, their direct oppressor, Israel, seems to have failed in its nation-building efforts. The future of the Zionist project, sustained today by little more than manufactured fear in the hearts of the Israeli citizenry, is bleak. In the meantime, the short-term prospect for the Palestinians is not bright either.[42] So long as their indirect oppressor, the United States, is unchecked in its hegemony, in the "new world order," the likelihood of Palestinians exercising their internationally recognized right of national self-determination is slim. But history is the graveyard of empires and will continue to be. It took two hundred years for the last crusader to be driven out of Palestine. Palestine will at last be free.

NOTES

Acknowledgments: This essay has benefited from the criticisms and comments of many colleagues, including Naseer Aruri, Anna Bellisari, James Dickinson, Samih Farsoun, Tuhfeh Habash, and Dennis Rome. The author alone is responsible for the interpretation and for any errors remaining.

1. On the Ottomans, see S. J. Shaw and E. K. Shaw, *History of the Ottoman Empire and Modern Turkey* (Cambridge: Cambridge University Press, 1977); see also Beshara Doumani, "Rediscovering Ottoman Palestine," *Journal of Palestine Studies* 21, no. 2 (Winter 1992): 5–28.

2. Justin McCarthy, *The Population of Palestine* (New York: Columbia University Press, 1990), pp. 10, 15, indicates a total population of about 550,000 and an urban population of about 110,000 for 1896.

3. See Roger Owen, *The Middle East in the World Economy* (London: Methuen, 1981), and the several studies in Roger Owen, ed., *Studies in the Economic and Social History of Palestine in the Nineteenth and Twentieth Centuries* (London: Macmillan, 1982). See also Nahla Zubi, "The Development of Capitalism in Palestine," *Journal of Palestine Studies* 13, no. 4 (1984): 88–109.

4. McCarthy, *The Population of Palestine*, p. 15.

5. The major Zionist political parties in Palestine during this period were HaPoel Hatzair (the Young Worker Party), a predecessor to Mapai (the Labor Party), and Poale Zion (the Workers of Zion Party), founded in 1905. Poale Zion had a socialist left wing led by Nahum Nir, a nationalist right wing led by David Ben Gurion and Itzhak Ben-Zvi, and a romantic-populist tendency led by Israel Shochat. As the right wing came to be dominant, the party went on to become Achdut HaAvoda (the United Labor Party) in 1919. A left-wing faction espousing an increasingly anti-Zionist line split off at this time and began organizing among Palestinian workers and subsequently went on to become the Palestine Communist Party (PCP). See Joel Beinin, "Communism in Palestine," *MERIP Reports*, no. 55 (March 1977); Musa Budeiri, *The Palestinian Communist Party* (London: Ithaca Press, 1979).

6. As Ben Gurion's right wing of Poale Zion became increasingly dominant, Ben-Zvi and the leader of another faction, Shochat, both former members of Jewish self-defense groups in Czarist Russia, formed vigilante gangs: Bar-Giora in 1907 and Hashomer in 1909. Under the pretext of self-defense, these armed gangs provided Jewish guards for the Zionist settlements. Most important, however, "the main object of the [gangs'] activity was the dynamic of conquest," according to Shochat, as cited in Gershon Shafir, *Land, Labor and the Origins of the Israeli-Palestinian Conflict* (Cambridge: Cambridge University Press, 1989), p. 138. These vigilante bands also gave the other factions greater leverage within Poale Zion. Hashomer was finally absorbed into the Haganah (the defense force) after 1920, becoming an instrument of land appropriation up to the present day. See Neville Mandel, *The Arabs and Zionism before World War I* (Berkeley: University of California Press, 1976); Rashid Khalidi, "Palestinian Peasant Resistance to Zionism before World War I," in Edward Said and Christopher Hitchens, eds., *Blaming the Victims* (London: Verso, 1988), chap. 10.

7. By the time this declaration was published, General Edmund Allenby had begun the British campaign to capture Jerusalem. In fact, the British occupied Jerusalem on December 11, 1917. See W. Thomas Mallison and S. V. Mallison, *The Palestine Problem in International Law* (New York: Longman, 1986), chap. 1. For recent discussion of British intentions, see Mark Levene, "The Balfour Declaration," *English Historical Review* 107 (January

1992): 54–77, and Jehuda Reinharz, "The Balfour Declaration and Its Maker," *Journal of Modern History* 64, no. 3 (September 1992): 455–99.

8. Julia Rahib Petry, "The Palestinian Woman: A History of Struggle," *University of Dayton Review* 21, no. 2 (1991): 37.

9. Ann Mosely Lesch, *Arab Politics in Palestine* (Ithaca: Cornell University Press, 1979), chap. 9; W. F. Abboushi, *The Unmaking of Palestine* (Cambridge: Middle East and North African Studies Press, 1988).

10. See M. S. Hassassian, *Palestine: Factionalism in the National Movement* (East Jerusalem: PASSIA, 1990); also Salim Tamari, "Factionalism and Class Formation in Recent Palestinian History," in Roger Owen, ed., *Studies in the Economic and Social History of Palestine*, chap. 3. See also Adnan Abu-Ghazaleh, "Arab Cultural Nationalism in Palestine during the British Mandate," *Journal of Palestine Studies* 1, no. 3 (1972), esp. pp. 55–56.

11. The Zionists' proposal to the 1919 Paris Peace Conference clearly recognized that *all* the territory of an Eretz Yisrael was "essential for the necessary economic foundation of the country" of Israel, and "in the interests of economical administration . . . the geo-political area . . . should be as large as possible so that it may eventually contain a large and thriving population which could easily bear the burdens of modern civilized government." See Walter Rothschild et al., "Statement of the Zionist Organization Regarding Palestine" (London, February 13, 1919), now available in Ben Halpern, *The Idea of the Jewish State* (Cambridge: Harvard University Press, 1961), pp. 303–4. In these terms, Zionism can be characterized as *reactionary*: "It presents the nationality with a goal of collective action that cannot articulate with the full potential of the nationality itself." See Gordon Welty, "Progressive versus Reactive Nationalism," in Hani Faris, ed., *Arab Nationalism and the Future of the Arab World* (Belmont, Mass.: Association of Arab-American University Graduates, 1987), p. 121. For background on Zionist aspirations, see Georges Corm, "Thoughts on the Roots of the Arab-Israeli Conflict," *Journal of Palestine Studies* 21, no. 3 (Spring 1992): 71–79.

12. See *Palestine: Statement of Policy* (London: Her Majesty's Stationery Office, May 1939), pp. 4–6. See also *Parliamentary Debates* (House of Commons), vol. 347 (May 22, 1939), column 1951.

13. The British still sought to retain control of the Suez Canal, Kuwait, Cyprus, etc. See Ritchie Ovendale, *Britain, the United States, and the End of the Palestine Mandate* (Woodbridge: Boydell and Brewer, 1989), esp. chap. 7. See also Matthew Coulter, "The Joint Anglo-American Statement on Palestine, 1943," *Historian* 54, no. 3 (Spring 1992): 465–76.

14. See Walid Khalidi, "Plan Dalet," *Journal of Palestine Studies* 18, no. 1 (1988): 4–70; Benny Morris, *The Birth of the Palestinian Refugee Problem* (Cambridge: Cambridge University Press, 1987), pp. 62–63; and Nur Masalha, *Expulsion of the Palestinians* (Washington, D.C.: Institute for Palestine Studies, 1992).

15. Morris, *Birth of the Palestinian Refugee Problem*, p. 141.

16. See Janet Abu-Lughod, "The Demographic Transformation of Palestine," in Ibrahim Abu-Lughod, ed., *The Transformation of Palestine* (Evanston, Ill.: Northwestern University Press, 1971), p. 161.

17. Sabri Jiryis, *Arabs in Israel* (Beirut: Institute for Palestinian Studies, 1968); Ian Lustick, *Arabs in the Jewish State* (Austin: University of Texas Press, 1980).

18. Tareq Y. Ismael, *The Arab Left* (Syracuse: Syracuse University Press, 1976), chap. 4.

19. Sameer Y. Abraham, "The Development and Transformation of the Palestine National Movement," in Naseer H. Aruri, ed., *Occupation: Israel over Palestine* (Belmont, Mass.: Association of Arab-American University Graduates, 1983), p. 396.

20. Helena Cobban, *The Palestinian Liberation Organization* (Cambridge: Cambridge University Press, 1984), pp. 28–32.

21. Cited in John Quigley, *Palestine and Israel* (Durham, N.C.: Duke University Press, 1990), pp. 164–65. On the relative absence of Arab preparation for this war, see Richard

Parker, "The June 1967 War: Some Mysteries Explored," *Middle East Journal* 46, no. 2 (Spring 1992): 177–97.

22. Ibrahim al-Abid, *Israel and Human Rights* (Beirut: Palestinian Liberation Organization Research Center, 1969), pp. 95–96. See also Abu-Lughod, "The Demographic Transformation of Palestine," p. 163.

23. Donald Neff, *Warriors for Jerusalem* ((New York: Simon and Schuster, 1984), p. 295. See also Israel Shahak, "Memory of 1967 'Ethnic Cleansing' Fuels Ideology of Golan Settlers," *Washington Report on Middle East Affairs* 10, no. 7 (November 1992).

24. See Riad el-Rayyes and Dunia Nahas, *Guerrillas for Palestine* (New York: St. Martin's Press, 1976), pp. 36–49. Also see Yezid Sayigh, "Turning Defeat into Opportunity," *Middle East Journal* 46, no. 2 (Spring 1992): 244–65.

25. See John Cooley, *Green March, Black September* (London: Frank Cass, 1973), pp. 109–22.

26. See David Hirst, *The Gun and the Olive Branch* ((New York: Harcourt, Brace, Jovanovich, 1977), chap. 9.

27. *New York Times*, October 1, 1977, p. 1.

28. *New York Times*, October 14, 1977, p. 9.

29. For background, see Samih Farsoun, "Israel's Goal of Destroying the PLO Is Not Achievable," *Journal of Palestine Studies* 11, no. 4 (1982): 100–106. On Haig's relation to Sharon, see Zeev Schiff and Ehud Yaari, *Israel's Lebanon War* (New York: Simon and Schuster, 1984), pp. 67–77; also Claudia Wright, "The Turn of the Screw," *Journal of Palestine Studies* 11, no. 4 (1982): 5.

30. See *The Beirut Massacre* (New York: Claremont Research, 1984); Sean McBride, *Israel in Lebanon* (London: Ithaca Press, 1988). See also Jean Genet, "Four Hours in Shatila," *Journal of Palestine Studies* 12, no. 2 (1983): 3–22.

31. *New York Times*, December 10, 1987, p. 10.

32. Jerusalem Media and Communication Centre, *The Intifada: An Overview* (East Jerusalem: JMCC, 1989), p. 4. Lest one think that the killing of Palestinian children by Israeli authorities has diminished in recent years, the JMCC has reported that "the policy of killing children is clearly on the increase" since Rabin took office as Israeli prime minister in July 1992. See JMCC, "Child Killings on Increase," Press Release 26 (January 1993). Amnesty International provided corroborative testimony to this effect in its presentation to the UN Commission on Human Rights, 49th Session, Agenda Item 4 (February 2, 1993). For a more general review of human rights issues, see *The Israeli Army and the Intifada* (New York: Human Rights Watch, 1990); Al-Haq, *Punishing a Nation* (Boston: South End Press, 1990); and Roni Talmor, *The Use of Firearms by the Security Forces in the Occupied Territories* (Jerusalem: Btselem, 1990).

33. See Don Peretz, *Intifada* (Boulder, Colo.: Westview Press, 1990), chap. 1.

34. Jerusalem Media and Communication Centre, *Palestinian Education: A Threat to Israel's Security?* (Belmont, Mass.: Association of Arab-American University Graduates, 1989), pp. 7–8. Some of the consequences of these policies during the Intifada are recounted in Herbert Watzman, "Long Shuttered by Israel, Palestinian Universities Face Financial Crisis and Unprepared Students," *Chronicle of Higher Education* 38, no. 29 (March 25, 1992): A-35.

35. Thomas Ricks, "Palestinian Students Face the Future," *Commonweal* 113, no. 21 (1986): 654–58. See also Clyde Haberman, "Constants of a Youth's Life in Gaza," *New York Times*, February 7, 1993, 9.

36. John Bierman and P. Reynolds, "Bitterness in Bethlehem," *Maclean's* 100, no. 1 (January 5, 1987): 10–12.

37. Helena Cobban, "The PLO and the Intifada," *Middle East Journal* 44, no. 2 (1990): 207–33. See also the interviews with Daoud Kuttab and especially Ibrahim Dakkak in Eric Alterman, "Report from the Occupied Territories," *World Policy Journal* 5, no. 3 (1988): 519–41. Several kinds of popular committees have been treated in detail in Joost Hiltermann,

Behind the Intifada (Princeton, N.J.: Princeton University Press, 1991) and Elise Young, *Keepers of the History* (New York: Teachers College Press, 1992).

38. See Samir Abed-Rabbo and Doris Safie, eds., *The Palestinian Uprising* (Belmont, Mass.: Association of Arab-American University Graduates, 1990).

39. *New York Times*, August 19, 1988, p. 3. All this could be taken as a foreshadowing of Rabin's deportation of more than four hundred Palestinians to southern Lebanon in mid-December 1992. That episode was condemned by UN Security Council Resolution 799. As Avi Raz pointed out in late January 1993, the Israeli government not only had made no charges against the Palestinians but could not even provide a list of those actually deported. See Avi Raz, "Who was Actually Deported?" *Maariv*, January 29, 1993, p. 7. Alexander Cockburn commented, "if not for the arrogance of his disdain for international law and for elementary human rights, there would be something comic about Israeli Premier Yitzhak Rabin's antics in the Hamas affair." See his "With Less at Stake, We Could Laugh at Rabin," *Los Angeles Times*, February 7, 1993, p. M-5.

40. On the background of the Islamic Resistance Movement (Hamas), an offshoot of the Muslim Brotherhood, see Pinchas Inbari, "Hamas: Beyond Stereotypes," *The Other Israel*, no. 55 (January 1993). Regarding Israel's attempt to "decapitate" Hamas through the deportation of Palestinians, see David Hoffman, "Hamas's Resilience Surprises Israel," *Washington Post*, February 3, 1993, p. 16.

41. See Staughton Lynd et al., *Homeland* (New York: Olive Branch Press, 1993).

42. See Don Peretz, "The Palestinians since the Gulf War," *Current History* 92 (January 1993): 32–36.

The Kurdish National Movement
and the Struggle
for National Autonomy

Kurdistan is located in an area covering northwestern Iran, northeastern Iraq, southeastern Turkey, and northeastern Syria.[1] Although a precise geographical description of the region cannot be made under present political conditions, estimates do exist. According to Abdul Rahman Ghassemlou, for example, the region of Kurdish settlement covers 409,650 square kilometers, of which 194,400 are in Turkey, 124,950 in Iran, 72,000 in Iraq, and 18,300 in Syria.[2] Similarly, since official data is either unavailable or distorted, we must rely on estimates regarding the number of Kurds. Ferdinand Hennebichler, for example, places their number in Kurdistan at approximately twenty-two million, with about half or eleven million living in Turkey (24 percent of the total Turkish population), six million in Iran (16 percent of the total Iranian population), four million in Iraq (28 percent of the total Iraqi population), about one million in Syria (9 percent of the total Syrian population), and an undetermined number of Kurds, most of them members of the Jezidi sect, in the countries of the former Soviet Union.[3] Another million or so Kurds are estimated to live dispersed throughout the world: approximately one hundred thousand in Lebanon; about two hundred thousand in other Arab states; and more than half a million in various European countries, the majority of whom have settled in Germany and the Benelux countries as labor migrants from Turkey.

The Kurdish language enjoyed a brief blossoming in the sixteenth and seventeenth centuries but was rarely used as a written language until the nineteenth century, when, with the emergence of Kurdish nationalism, the language came into common use in written form.[4] The Persian-Arabic alphabet was used by all literate Kurds until the end of the First World War. Then, in the 1920s, the Bedirkhan brothers introduced the Latin alphabet, which became standard in Turkish and Syrian Kurdistan. In Iranian and Iraqi Kurdistan the Arabic alphabet was adapted to the peculiarities of the Kurdish language. In the former Soviet Union the Kurdish language was written in Cyrillic letters. The variety of alphabets and the lack of uniform Kurdish language has made intellectual communication among Kurds difficult.[5]

The largest number of Kurds belong to the Shafiit school of Sunni Islamic law. In this respect they are different from their neighbors: the Turks as well as the Arabs follow the Hanafite school of Sunni religious law; the Persians and Azerbaijanis are Shiites. Not all Kurds are Sunnis, however. In Iran and Iraq some belong to the Shiite sect. In Turkey, a considerable number are followers of the Alevi. The only religion whose followers are exclusively Kurds is the Jezidi, which includes various elements of old Iranian religions in its religious beliefs and rituals and has no affinity with Islam. Consequently, the Jezidis have been persecuted and decimated by their Kurdish Muslim neighbors as well as by the Ottoman state.

Before the founding of Israel, more than thirty thousand Jews lived in Kurdistan, primarily in northern Iraq. Christian groups were also distributed throughout all parts of the region, but politically motivated deportation and social conflicts increasingly decimated their numbers and many Christians emigrated to the urban centers of their respective states or went overseas. At present small Christian groups are settled in Iranian, Iraqi, and Turkish Kurdistan, although in the latter armed conflict between the militant Workers Party of Kurdistan (PKK) and the Turkish government has led some Christians to emigrate. In Iraqi Kurdistan Christians played an active role in the changes taking place after the establishment of the safe haven in 1991. They were represented in the regional Kurdish parliament and in the autonomous Kurdish government. The number of Christians in Kurdistan amounts to about 4 percent of the population. In contrast, the one-time Jewish inhabitants of Kurdistan have emigrated to Israel. There they constitute a separate group that keeps alive the cultural traditions of their native land.

The picture of the wild, warlike, free Kurds promulgated by European and American travelers, traders, and missionaries never corresponded with reality but rather was a part of the phenomenon of "Orientalism," as it was critically described by Edward Said.[6] In actuality, until the twentieth century Kurdistan was a stronghold of classic Islamic education maintained by the ubiquitous religious orders (*tariqa*). In all heavily Kurdish regions, the religious schools, the so-called *hujra*, accommodated hundreds of students. But the establishment of the new Middle Eastern states and the accompanying political and socioeconomic changes brought about the decline of these schools. The central governments either forbade the Kurdish language (as in Turkey, Iran, and Syria) or permitted its use in the schools under various restrictions. In fact, education was so neglected in all parts of Kurdistan that, in all four Middle Eastern states that rule a part of Kurdistan, the Kurdish region has the lowest level of education.

Higher education was similarly neglected. Only five years after the first Kurdish university was founded in the city of Sulaimaniya in Iraqi Kurdistan, the university was moved to the city of Arbil and almost completely Arabized. Likewise, the only Kurdish language academy, which was established in Iraq in 1970, was disbanded after the collapse of the Kurdish uprising in 1975. Despite the adverse political conditions in the 1970s and 1980s, however, a considerable number of Kurdish books, magazines, and newspapers were published in Kurdistan and other regions populated by the Kurds.[7]

The social structure of Kurdistan was affected in important ways after its partition by the European powers following the collapse of the Ottoman Empire at the end of the First World War. Kurdish society was based on agriculture. The prevalence of large-scale landholdings, together with progressive retribalization, led to the impoverishment of small farmers, who were forced to migrate to the Kurdish towns. In the peripheral areas, the tribes remained more or less intact. However, tribe members constitute only a small percentage of the Kurdish population, 40 percent of whom reside in the Kurdish cities.

THE ORIGINS AND DEVELOPMENT
OF THE KURDISH NATIONAL MOVEMENT

After the Ottomans conquered Kurdistan in the sixteenth century, they set up a vassal system throughout the Kurdish territories. This system remained in force later, albeit modified by changing historical circumstances.[8] The tribal *aghas* (landlords) competed with each other for power and influence; a conflict by one with the central state was seen by his rivals as an opportunity for weakening him. These traditional rivalries determined later political alignments in both Iraqi and Turkish Kurdistan.

Despite adverse conditions under colonial rule, the Kurds in Iraqi Kurdistan achieved a high degree of ethnic cohesion under the Baban Emirate (seventeenth to nineteenth centuries) and the Rawanduz Emirate (eighteenth and nineteenth centuries). In Turkish Kurdistan, the several semiautonomous emirates that ruled up to the mid-nineteenth century never succeeded—even briefly—in extending their influence over the whole of the area settled by the Kurds because of the geographic proximity of the Ottoman central government. The transtribal network of orthodox Sunni religious orders (*tariqa*) that expanded throughout Kurdistan in the nineteenth century, above all the Naqshbandiyya and the Qadiriyya, promoted ethnic cohesion, but they also promoted discrimination and the exclusion of heterodox groups, above all the Alevis and Jezidis.

Thus, historical conditions favoring ethnic cohesion among the Kurdish people were present only in rudimentary form in Kurdistan before the creation of the modern Middle Eastern states. In its early stages, at the end of the nineteenth century, the Kurdish national movement was promulgated solely by the Kurdish intelligentsia, who were a by-product of the Tanzimat reforms and came from the class of tribal chieftains.[9] Targeting the sheikhs and aghas in Kurdistan and the despotic and corrupt Ottoman central state to which the *aghas* owed their allegiance, the Kurdish intellectuals propagated their nationalist views through such organs as the journal *Kurdistan* and the political organization Kurdistan Taali ve Terakki Cemiyeti (Society for the Advancement and Progress of Kurdistan). After the Young Turk revolution in 1908, the first Kurdish parties were political associations of the Kurdish intelligentsia. Sheikh Abdul-Salam Barzani, the father of the legendary Kurdish leader Mulla Mustafa Barzani, in 1912 petitioned for a kind of national autonomy for the Kurds, pushing the Kurdish question further than the Kurdish intellectuals in Istanbul.[10] For traditional leaders like Barzani national autonomy meant maintaining their independence visà-vis the central state.

With the collapse of the Ottoman Empire in the early twentieth century, Kurdistan came under the control of the major European powers, in particular Britain and France, who acquired various territories of the empire at the conclusion of the First World War. The situation after the Ottoman capitulation was anything but favorable for the Kurds, as the main portion of Kurdistan remained under Turkish control. Kurdistan in Iran had already been under the rule of the Persians since 1639, and South Kurdistan, which was identical with the former Ottoman province of Mosul, came under British rule. Turkish Kurdistan and South Kurdistan became the scene of the failed attempts of the Kurds to achieve independence.

In 1918 in South Kurdistan, the head of the Order of Quadiriya Dynasty in Kurdistan, Sheikh Mahmud Barzanji, declared himself *hukmdar* (ruler) of Kurdistan. Initially the British administration in Mesopotamia tolerated the attempts of the Kurdish leaders to gain independence; it had not yet decided what was to become of Mesopotamia and South Kurdistan. But in 1919 the British deprived the *hukmdar* of his power, fearing that Sheikh Mahmud would present them with a fait accompli before they were able to decide the fate of the occupied region.

In January 1920, within the framework of the Treaty of Sèvres, the victors of the First World War decided that an autonomous Kurdish state would be established in the region controlled by Turkey. South Kurdistan would later be included in this Kurdish state if the Kurds decided on independence a year after the establishment of the self-governing state.[11] At the 1921 Cairo Conference of the British Colonial Ministry, the prevailing position was that South Kurdistan should be connected to the new Mesopotamian state of Iraq. In 1922, within the framework of meetings in Lausanne, the British government negotiated with Kemalist Turkey over the membership of the Mosul province. Sèvres had already become history. The British were of the opinion that for economic and strategic reasons South Kurdistan was indispensable for the new state of Iraq.[12] For these reasons, all Kurdish initiatives toward independence were forcibly suppressed. Although the incorporation of the Kurdish province of Mosul into the new state was pushed through against the wishes of its population, the British Mandatory power nonetheless succeeded in the mid-1920s in integrating a considerable number of the Kurdish tribal *aghas*, and even the modern Kurdish elite, into the new state's institutions.

In Turkish Kurdistan, a broad-based resistance movement formed after it became apparent to the Kurds that the new Kemalist state was a Turkish state that would not permit ethnic pluralism. Although the concept of Kurdish opposition spread initially among the former officers and members of the intelligentsia, it relied on the support of traditional Kurdish society. The abolition of the caliphate by Mustafa Kemal was in fact a favor to the Kurdish nationalists, who were led by former officers Khalid Beg Cebran and Yusaf Ziya Beg, descendants of the Mir Dynasty of Bitlis. This made it possible for them to win the sympathy of the religious sheikhs. Since the decline in influence of the emirate in the nineteenth century, the religious sheikhs in Kurdistan had become the bearers of social power. For this reason it was no coincidence that in South Kurdistan Sheikh Mahmud and in Turkish Kurdistan Sheik Said became leaders of the Kurds.

After the failed revolts in Turkey, a new movement was formed under the secular nationalist Khoybun (Independence) Party, which between 1928 and 1930 waged resistance against the Turkish central government.[13] In 1937, in the region of Dersim, there were further disturbances, which led to large-scale deportations. The Kremalist state's rigorous assimilation policy and the failure of the armed uprisings in the 1920s and 1930s resulted in the complete paralysis of the Kurdish national movement in Turkey for more than three decades. It was not until the 1960s that the Kurdish parties were able to reestablish themselves in Turkish Kurdistan.

Because of the completely different developments in Kurdish society in Turkey, the Democratic Party of Kurdistan (DPK) in Turkey, founded in 1965 along the lines of the older DPK in Iraq, never had a realistic chance of performing a role similar to its Iraqi counterpart, which developed into a mass party soon after its founding in 1946.[14] In its competition with the other left-wing Kurdish parties, the DPK-Turkey espoused Marxism-Leninism and demanded independence (instead of, as previously, national autonomy) for Kurdistan.[15] It recruited its members from the rural areas in eastern Turkish Kurdistan. Its alliance with the tribes was maintained despite its ideological shift. It was thus largely a peasant party with scarcely any members in the urban centers.[16]

The attitude of the left-wing Turkish parties to the Kurdish question has influenced the specific features of the Kurdish national movement in Turkey. By and large, the Communist Party of Turkey (Türkiye Komünist Partisi, TKP) concurred with Kemalist doctrine with respect to the Kurdish question. The demand for a solution to the Kurdish question was not made part of its program until the 1970s. Thus, unlike the Iraqi Communist Party, the TKP was unable to exert an integrative influence on the Kurdish labor movement. This is also true, though to a lesser extent, for the legal Workers Party of Turkey (Türkiye İşçi Partisi, TIP), founded in the mid-1960s. It was only in 1970, at its Fourth Party Congress, that the TIP incorporated the demand for a solution to the Kurdish question into its program.[17]

The most important group to emerge from the TIP is the Socialist Party of Kurdistan-Turkey (Partiya Sosialisti Kurdistana Turkiye, PSKT). The party was formed out of the circle of intellectuals around Kemal Burkay, a former leader of TIP who in 1975 began publishing the journal *Özgürlük Yolu* (*Liberation Path*). Martin van Bruinessen characterized the group as a "typical urban organization of workers and intellectuals, numerically weak, but with some influence in the unions and in the teachers' association."[18]

The TIP's assertion that the "national democratic revolution" was already a reality in Turkey and that the mass party of the working class must achieve socialism by parliamentary means was disputed by the student Federation of the Revolutionary Youth of Turkey (Türkiye Devrimci Gençlik Federasyonu-Dev Genç), founded in 1969, which had previously been close to the TIP. Even before the 1971 coup, several left-wing groups were established with the aim of overthrowing the state and achieving socialism by means of a guerrilla war.

The Workers Party of Kurdistan (Partiya Karkeren Kurdistan, PKK), founded by Abdullah Öcalan in 1978, was the political forum of the marginalized classes.[19] Contrary to the positions of the TKP and the TIP, Mahir Cayan, the leader of the People's Liberation Party of Turkey, was of the opinion that Turkey was "a semi-colonial country with a dependent capitalism," that the economic system was in a permanent crisis, and that the proletarian party had the task of shattering the artificial stability by armed struggle and enabling a revolutionary situation to be created.[20]

The PKK's militant ideology and activities in the first two years after it was founded resulted in its rigorous persecution under the military regime. Most members of the PKK's Central Committee were not able to escape from Turkey after the coup in 1980. The arrest of part of the leadership was a heavy blow to the party. It was not until the mid-1980s that the PKK was again able to become active throughout Turkish Kurdistan.

In Iranian Kurdistan, in the Kurdish city of Mahabad, a small group of nationalists emerged in the early 1940s under the name Resurrection of Kurdistan (Jianawi Kurdistan, JK). Since Mahabad was located in the neutral zone between the area occupied by the Soviet Union and that by Great Britain, the Kurdish nationalists could rapidly extend their influence without any foreign interference.[21] In 1944 the first contacts were made with the Soviet occupying army, and in 1945 the religious dignitary Zazi Muhammad became leader of the JK, which subsequently changed its name to the Democratic Party of Kurdistan (DPK) in Iran. In the same year, Kurdish rebels from Iraq under the leadership of Mulla Mustafa Barzani found refuge in Iranian Kurdistan. In 1946, following negotiations with the leaders of the Soviet Republic of Azerbaijan in Baku, the Kurds came to the conclusion that they should proclaim an autonomous republic in Mahabad. However, the Republic of Mahabad, established in January 1947, was immediately crushed by invading Iranian troops. After the collapse of the republic, the DPK shrank to a small cadre of leaders and supporters. It was not until after the Iranian revolution in 1979 that the party could again begin to develop its influence among the Kurds in Iran.

In Iraqi Kurdistan, the Kurdish national movement came into being at the end of the 1930s and took shape in the form of the Iraqi-Kurdish party Hiwa (Hope), founded in 1939. Later, in the mid-1940s, the Democratic Party of Kurdistan-Iraq (DPK) emerged as a major political force with a widespread grassroots base. The DPK, which was a movement of urban Kurds, tried to form a national front under its own leadership, defining itself as a people's party representing all social classes. The ideological and political discussions with the Kurdistan section of the Communist Party of Iraq (CPI) at the beginning of the 1950s probably led, among other things, to the inclusion of socialist positions in the DPK's political program. The

Kurdish parties saw no contradiction between the adoption of socialist positions on one hand and the front style of organization (which did not even exclude the *aghas*) on the other.

The DPK-Iraq and the parties that were established in its image experienced great political and ideological changes in the two decades after their founding. While in its 1950 program the party still stated its long-term aim as the "establishment of a Kurdish People's Republic through the struggle in all parts of Kurdistan," the DPK had revised this objective to "national autonomy" by the time the "Kurdish war" began in Iraqi Kurdistan in 1961. A decade before the guerrilla war broke out, the DPK had come to realize that the prevailing regional structure would not permit a Kurdish state to be established. It thus shifted from a position advocating the "forced incorporation" of Kurds into a heterogeneous Iraqi society to one advocating a form of regional autonomy that would permit Arabs and Kurds to live together voluntarily. The Iraqi Communist Party was not alone therefore in supporting the slogan "democracy for Iraq and autonomy for Kurdistan." This position favoring autonomy also received general approval from other left-wing and liberal parties in Iraq, particularly after the fall of the monarchy in 1958, but it was rejected by the Arab nationalist parties.

The new Iraqi government made concessions to the Kurds. Among other things, the provisional constitution acknowledged Arabs and Kurds to be partners in Iraq. Soon, however, conflicts arose between the DPK, which in 1960 had become a legal party, and the government of Abdel-Karim Qasim. The Kurds demanded free parliamentary elections and self-administration for Kurdistan, demands Qasim was not prepared to meet. The result was, of course, the war that broke out in 1961 and has continued to this day, interrupted only by periods of cease-fire and negotiations.[22] As regional and international powers were increasingly drawn into this conflict, the Kurdish question gained significance beyond the borders of Iraq.

In March 1970 the Iraqi Baath government, which had come to power two years earlier, was forced to conclude an agreement with the Kurds under the leadership of Mulla Mustafa Barzani, who became the undisputed leader of the Iraqi Kurds after his return from exile in the Soviet Union in 1958. A year later, however, the agreement became the object of a conflict between the Baath government and the Kurds. The demarcation of the territory of the autonomous region and the role of the Kurds in the central government, which the Baath Party considered its exclusive domain, could not be resolved through compromise.[23]

In 1972, the Iraqi government consolidated its international position through a treaty of friendship with the Soviet Union. A large increase in income from the sale of oil further strengthened the government's position.

The Kurds attempted to improve their own position through an alliance with Iran and through a secret agreement with the United States. And again, at the outbreak of the Kurdish War in 1974, when the government interrupted negotiations and attempted to assert its concept of autonomy, the Kurds were dependent upon external support. In the escalation of the war, Iraq attempted to avoid a direct confrontation with Iran so as not to threaten negotiations with the regime of the Shah. In March 1975 Iraq and Iran signed the so-called Treaty of Algiers, and Kurdish resistance collapsed a few weeks after Barzani decided to end the war.

RECENT DEVELOPMENTS IN THE KURDISH NATIONAL MOVEMENT

Beginning in the late 1970s four events led to fundamental changes in the Kurdish national movement across Kurdistan: the collapse of the movement in Iraq; the Iranian Revolution of 1979; the military coup in Turkey in 1980; and the Iran-Iraq war, which raged on for nearly a decade.

In Iraqi Kurdistan, the collapse of the Kurdish national movement had a number of consequences. First, it meant the end of the monopoly that the DPK had attempted to claim since its foundation in 1946. A few months after the collapse, the Patriotic Union of Kurdistan (PUK) was established by intellectuals associated with Jalal Talabani, a former member of the polit-buro of DPK-Iraq and one of the Peshmerga commanders. Talabani had always stood at a distance from the leader of the DPK, Mulla Mustafa Barzani.[24] Soon the PUK came into confrontation with the reorganized DPK, as it held the conservative leadership of the DPK under Barzani responsible for the failures of the Kurds. Moreover, it criticized DPK's links to Iran, the United States, and Israel, arguing that these linkages compromised the independence of the Kurds and made them tools of the West. From an organizational standpoint, the PUK was a coalition of Kurdish democrats, socialists, and Marxists who were able to present a united front within the PUK.[25]

In 1976, both the DPK and the PUK commenced guerrilla operations against the Iraqi government. Their differences, however, led in 1978 to a major clash that paralyzed both movements. In Iraqi Kurdistan the government retaliated with a methodical depopulation and destruction of Kurdish villages. Kurdish farmers were interned in guarded settlements in order to isolate the guerrillas. By the end of the decade, however, the situation improved for the Iraqi Kurdish opposition when the Iraqi Communist Party left the government, after arguments with the Baath Party over foreign policy and the Kurdish question, and joined the opposition.

The Iranian Revolution of 1979 was far more important in influencing the course of the Kurdish national movement. In effect, it nullified the Treaty of Algiers, signed in 1975, which had prohibited the movement of arms across the borders of Iran and Iraq. Positive developments for the Iraqi Kurds following the Iranian Revolution, however, were overshadowed by the ensuing struggles between the DPK-Iran and the new Islamic regime over autonomy for the Kurds in Iranian Kurdistan.[26] Soon the political organizations of Iraqi Kurdistan became involved in the conflicts between the Iranian Kurds and the central government.

Since 1980, and especially after the Iranian government increased its support for the DPK Iraq, there emerged new power relations among the guerrilla groups of Iraqi Kurdistan. The DPK succeeded in gaining the support of the Iraqi Communist Party and of the Socialist Party of Kurdistan (SPK), especially since the PUK hardly granted these parties any spheres of influence in the territories it controlled since 1976 (the so-called liberated areas), fearing their political and ideological competition. In 1983 the PUK even attempted to expel the SPK from the liberated area in reaction to its alliance with the DPK-Iraq. This led to a formation of an alliance under the leadership of the DPK-Iraq against the PUK on the one hand and to a complete Iranian blockade against the PUK on the other.

The DPK-Iraq supported the so-called Pasdaran (Iranian Revolutionary Guards) and the troops in their offensive against the DPK-Iran, while the PUK lent its services to the DPK-Iran, which had run into difficulties. The conflict between the DPK-Iraq and the PUK also interfered with the attempts of the Iraqi opposition to overthrow the regime of Saddam Hussein after the outbreak of the Iran-Iraq War. Following the alliance of the DPK and the CPI in Iraq at the beginning of the 1980s, the PUK became steadily more isolated.

While the DPK-Iraq was based in Iran, the PUK operated out of the so-called liberated areas of Iraqi Kurdistan and feared it would find itself in the crossfire between the two fronts when the Iran-Iraq War spread. In view of this threat it commenced negotiations with the Iraqi government at the end of 1983, talks that broke down only a year later. Subsequently, the PUK established links with the Iranian government. It was in fact in the interests of the Iranian government, which had largely decimated the DPK-Iran, to see that the Iraqi Kurds merge into a single organization.

In 1986 the DPK-Iraq and the PUK terminated their lengthy fratricidal war. At the end of 1987 the various guerrilla groups of Iraqi Kurdistan began to negotiate over the establishment of a Kurdish front. In 1988, shortly after chemical weapons were used in an attack on the Kurdish city of Halabja, the Kurdistan Front was founded as an umbrella organization for all political parties of Iraqi Kurdistan. The armistice in the Iran-Iraq

War in August 1988 and the subsequent large-scale offensive of the Iraqi army—the so-called Anfal offensive—was a hard blow to the guerrillas, who had to put a virtual halt to their armed operations until the Iraqi invasion of Kuwait in August 1990. Between the time of the armistice in the Iran-Iraq War and the invasion of Kuwait, the Iraqi government destroyed practically all Kurdish villages and built guarded internment camps. Midsized cities like Qala Diza and Halabja were completely destroyed.

Following the 1990 Iraqi occupation of Kuwait, guerrillas again attempted to gain a foothold in Iraqi Kurdistan. Initially the leadership of the Kurdistan Front appeared cautious about a possible Kurdish collaboration with the anti-Saddam coalition. Nevertheless, the leadership of the Front (above all PUK leader Jalal Talabani) joined in exploratory talks about the possibility of support from the United States and other Western powers. The Kurds then made efforts to persuade Iraqi opposition groups abroad to establish a common program. In Damascus, the Iraqi opposition agreed to a platform that was later confirmed at the opposition conference in Beirut in March 1991. The essential points of this platform were the building of an interim government after the overthrow of Saddam Hussein and the holding of free elections.[27]

The initial spontaneous uprising in Iraq, at first in the Shiite South and then in Kurdistan, surprised the Iraqi opposition assembled in Beirut. The swift response of troops loyal to Saddam Hussein and the absence of hoped-for support from the anti-Saddam coalition led within a few days to the collapse of the resistance and to a massive exodus of refugees from Iraqi Kurdistan. Belated intervention by the Western nations in Iraqi Kurdistan, a result of pressure from global public opinion, occurred when the Kurds had already entered into negotiations with the Iraqi government. However, the negotiations failed on two important points: democratization of the Iraqi political system and the provision for an autonomous Kurdish region. The competition between the leadership of the DPK-Iraq and the PUK impeded the formation of a definitive Kurdish position. In response to the Iraqi government's threat to renew military operations against the Kurds, free elections were planned for the purpose of determining the decision-making authority in Iraqi Kurdistan. The elections had both a political and strategic meaning for the Kurds. First, the vacuum that had arisen following the withdrawal of the Iraqi administration was to be filled by an elected body. Second, the power of the political parties would be legitimized both internally and externally. Furthermore, elections would make clear which party represented the majority of the population.

In Turkey, the military coup in 1980 led to a temporary paralysis of leftist parties and organizations in Turkish Kurdistan. Kurdish organizations were particularly exposed to massive persecution by the military government. They were able to rebuild their strength only in exile in Syria and Lebanon, as well as in Europe. However, the political differences between the major Kurdish groups—the DPK, the PKK, the PSKT, and others—prevented their collaboration abroad. While the Socialist Party, supported by organizations such as Komkar (an association that was active among Kurdish migrant laborers in Germany), opted for a political strategy and continued its activities through political organizing, the PKK opted for armed struggle and launched a guerrilla war from its headquarters in Lebanon, where it had contacts with Palestinian guerrilla groups.

The political education of PKK's most important leaders took place in Turkish towns. Later, they were almost exclusively active in the larger Kurdish towns and among the marginalized Kurdish migrant workers in West Anatolia. Poverty is widespread in Kurdistan, and some of PKK's actions are an expression of the enormous social tensions created by the system. PKK's attacks on the village guards (armed Kurdish peasants recruited by the Turkish government) and their families, for example, can only be understood in this light. Those carrying out the attacks do not appear to see the village guards and their families as paupers who for a pittance have taken up arms for the "wrong side" but as collaborators of the Turkish state who are trying to prevent social and national liberation. In PKK's view, only revolutionary violence can mobilize and liberate. Parallel to this, ethnic cohesion is to be accelerated and the Turkish state's "bridgeheads" in Kurdish society (which the tribal chieftains are considered to be) should be destroyed. The PKK analysis saw no room for the reformist Kurdish parties that were ready to compromise; this precluded a national front of independent organizations.

The PKK's successes through guerrilla war have affected the members of the Kurdish elite, who are considered collaborators because of their work in the Turkish parties and in the Turkish parliament. The support of Kurdish parliamentarians in the Social Democratic Populist Party (Sosyaldemokrat Halkçi Partisi, SHP) for a solution to the Kurdish question led to their expulsion from the party, whereupon they founded the People's Labor Party (Halkin Emek Partisi, HEP).[28] Since 1988, the SHP's Kurdish members of parliament, Ibrahim Aksoy and Mehmet Ali Eren, have actively supported the recognition of Kurdish national rights in Turkey, and after their expulsion from the SHP they were instrumental in setting up the HEP. By 1991 the HEP had become an important force in Turkish Kurdistan.[29]

Administrative and political measures taken by the Turkish government since 1984 make it clear that the guerrilla war is also having a strong impact on its policy in Kurdistan. In addition to forming the village guards and reinforcing the army units in the Kurdish provinces, the Turkish government centralized the regional administration in 1987 by forming a "super province."[30] The continuation of a state of emergency gives the "super governor" extensive powers, as all the army and police units in the Kurdish provinces are under his command.

The Turkish government's attempts to oppose Kurdish separatism are not confined within its own borders. On the basis of a security agreement with Iraq, which was renewed annually until 1990, Turkey crossed over to destroy Kurdish guerrilla bases in Iraqi Kurdistan beginning in 1983.

After the Kuwait crisis in the Turkish government attempted to adapt its policy on Turkish Kurdistan to the new regional structures and to establish contact with all protagonists regarding official links with the leaders of the PUK and the DPK. Both parties were permitted to open regional offices in Ankara. Nevertheless, Turkey maintains better relations with the DPK, which shares its interest in weakening the PKK. The DPK-Iraq fears that the radical PKK will extend its influence to the northern part of Iraqi Kurdistan. The DPK considers this region to be its exclusive sphere of influence.

The government's policy toward the Kurds in Turkey showed no significant changes. No further steps were taken following the government's lifting of the ban on the Kurdish language in 1991, and Turkish president Turgut Özal announced in an interview that no other concessions would be made. While the new governing coalition acknowledged the multiethnic structure of Turkey when it came to power in the early 1990s, there have been no further steps to improve the situation in Turkish Kurdistan. The hesitant policy of the coalition and subsequent violent events like the uprising of the Kurdish population in March 1992 have since driven the Kurdish people into the arms of the PKK, an outcome the government had desperately tried to avoid.

Since the Persian Gulf War of 1991, the Kurdish question has been linked more closely than ever before to international and regional politics—above all to the unstable and transitory constellation of regional power relations—that emerged after the war. The Kurdish question in Iraq also determines the position of the Kurds in other states with a partly Kurdish population. The involvement of the Western powers following the establishment of safe havens in Iraqi Kurdistan in 1992, and the stationing of military aircraft in Incerlik, Turkey, to monitor the safe havens, has internationalized the Kurdish question. For reasons of security and regional politics, Turkey had to agree to the stationing of Western troops within its territory, and it had to agree to establish semi-diplomatic relations with the Iraqi Kurds, who have had representation in Ankara since 1991. Turkey must, nevertheless, fear threats to its security from Iraqi Kurdistan, especially since the election of the Kurdish parliament and the formation of a federative Kurdish government in Iraq in 1992.

The conference of foreign ministers from Iran, Syria, and Turkey, which was held in Ankara in October 1992, dealt with one main topic, namely, the situation in Iraqi Kurdistan. The conference of the foreign ministers of these countries in Damascus in February 1993 and in Tehran in May 1993 dealt with the same topic. Apparently the discussions were an attempt to find a way to control the Kurdish question. It would appear that none of these three states is to play the "Kurdish card" against the others and that the Kurds are not to exceed their role as junior actors in regional politics. In this context, the regional powers' distrust of each other is understandable, as each of these powers maintains active relations with one or more Kurdish groups.

The clash of interests between the Kurds and the regional powers brought renewed armed conflict among the Kurds themselves, as well as direct and indirect intervention by these powers. The background to these conflicts, which occurred in autumn 1992, was the refusal by the PKK leader Öcalan to meet the demand by the Iraqi Kurdish leaders Talabani and Barzani to cease operations against Turkey. Turkey held the Iraqi Kurds responsible for these operations because the PKK units were located in Iraqi Kurdistan, and at various meetings with the two leaders the government intimated that it would have to reconsider the stationing of Western troops in Turkey and could cut off the supply routes to Iraqi Kurdistan.[31]

The tense situation between the PKK and the Iraqi Kurdish parties escalated in autumn 1992 when the Peshmerga units (an alliance of the DPK and PUK guerrilla) of the Kurdistan Front in Iraqi Kurdistan attempted to drive the PKK units out of Iraqi Kurdistan by force. The simultaneous intervention by the Turkish army against the PKK reduced the combat strength of the PKK, which entered into negotiations with the Kurdistan Front and declared its readiness to cease operations against Turkey from Iraqi Kurdistan.

It is also interesting to note the role of Iran, which permitted the PKK units stationed in Iran to intervene in the military action and even provided logistical support for PKK's combat units. By doing so the Iranians were pursuing more than one aim.

Iran's hostility to the idea of increased autonomy for Iraqi Kurdistan was initially expressed in press attacks against leaders of the Kurdistan Front and then escalated to include direct attacks on and acts of sabotage against federative institutions and Kurdish politicians in Iraqi Kurdistan.

Second, the presence of DPK's Peshmerga has always been a point of controversy in the talks with the leaders of the PUK and the DPK. Iran's demands ranged from the disarmament of the Peshmerga of the DKP Iran to their extradition to Iran.

Third, the Iranians disapproved of the pluralistic political structure in Iraqi Kurdistan, above all because the democratic order in Iraqi Kurdistan could serve as a model for the whole of Iraq. In general, the Iranians made it clear that they would tolerate only an "Islamic order" in Iraq. But because this option is increasingly seen as unrealistic in view of Iraq's ethnic and religious structure, the Iranians prefer Saddam Hussein's regime to a democratic and pluralistic one.[32]

The November 1992 accord between the PKK and the Kurdistan Front ushered in a process of rapprochement between the two movements. PUK leader Jalal Talabani in particular played a central part in the negotiations with the PKK and its leader Öcalan. In the negotiations with Öcalan, Talabani's aims were to persuade the PKK on one hand to renounce its claim to be the sole representative of Kurdish nationalism and on the other to signal its readiness for political negotiations with the Turkish government by means of a cease-fire in the guerrilla war. Faced with changes worldwide and in the region, Öcalan was forced to acknowledge political reality. His talks in early 1993 with Kemal Burkay's Socialist Party of Kurdistan[33] and with other, smaller Kurdish parties ended with the establishment of the "Coordination Committee," which—in addition to Öcalan and Burkay—included representatives of the other groupings.[34] The legal Kurdish party HEP probably played a part in changing the PKK's position. Öcalan's appearance with Burkay, Talabani, and the leaders of other parties from Turkish Kurdistan at a press conference in the Bega's region, which is under Syrian control, symbolized the extent of change in the PKK.

Talabani's efforts, subsequent to Öcalan's declaration of a cease-fire, to induce the then prime minister and later president Suleyman Demirel to take positive and decisive steps in the Kurdish question were bound to fail because of resistance by the Turkish military. It proved impossible to save the situation despite the declaration of an unlimited cease-fire. The Turkish government seemed to be sticking to its uncompromising position toward the Kurds. Even after the cease-fire had come into effect, the constitutional court was busy preparing to ban the HEP on charges of separatism and on account of its contacts with the PKK.[35] Although the fighting that flared up at the end of May 1993 between the PKK and the Turkish army ended hopes for a positive and peaceful settlement to the Kurdish question, the situation in the aftermath of the cease-fire clearly benefited the PKK, which for the first time had found a way to live with the other Kurdish parties. More important still is the fact that all the Kurdish parties of Turkish Kurdistan have acknowledged the leading role of the PKK. While the party has been slow to react to the changing political realities, and although its transformation from a Marxist-Leninist group engaged in armed struggle to a "people's party" along the lines of the DPK in Iran and Iraq is not yet complete, it is well on the way. Given the rising popularity of the PKK among the Kurdish masses throughout Turkish Kurdistan, Turkey cannot for long avoid negotiating with the PKK, whether the party calls itself the HEP, the DEP, or anything else.

THE STRUGGLE OVER LEADERSHIP OF THE NATIONAL MOVEMENT IN KURDISTAN

The claim to pan-Kurdish leadership was first raised by the DPK-Iraq. The DPK and its leader, Mulla Mustafa Barzani, had led the guerrilla movement in Iraqi Kurdistan beginning in 1961, and it held that multicentralism weakened the Kurdish national movement. For this reason, the guerrilla movement, a splinter group of the DPK-Iran from 1967 to 1968, was offered no support. The DPK-Iraq and Barzani opposed all groups that called for armed resistance in Turkish Kurdistan for the same reason. After the defeat in 1975, neither the DPK-Iraq nor the newly established PUK had the capability of pursuing a pan-Kurdish policy. Both parties, however, had connections to many Kurdish organizations in all parts of Kurdistan. This led the PKK to view both parties as competitors in the struggle for pan-Kurdish leadership. This was only logical in that the PKK had never considered itself a movement solely of Turkish Kurdistan. In order to emphasize its claim to pan-Kurdish leadership, the PKK first had to prove to the other organizations and parties that it was the leading power in Turkish Kurdistan.

In the summer of 1984, the PKK formed the Armed Forces for the Liberation of Kurdistan (Hezen Rizgariya Kurdistan, HRK). According to an agreement with the DPK-Iraq, the HRK was allowed to conduct guerrilla attacks against Turkish military bases in Turkish Kurdistan from areas in Iraqi Kurdistan controlled by the DPK. In 1985, the PKK tried to justify its claim to be the sole representative of the Kurdish people by founding the National Liberation Front of Kurdistan (Eniya Rizgariya Netewa Kurdistan, ERNK) and calling on all forces supporting independence for Kurdistan and the HRK's armed struggle to cooperate with the PKK in the National Front.

PKK's alliance with the DPK-Iraq ended in 1985, probably because the DPK did not want to give the Turkish government cause for cross-border operations. Despite armed clashes with the Iraqi Kurds, the PKK succeeded in keeping its bases in Iraqi Kurdistan even after the cease-fire in the Iran-

Iraq War.[36] However, notwithstanding its self-criticism (in connection with its policy before the 1980 coup), the PKK's cooperation with the Turkish and Kurdish organizations in Turkish Kurdistan did not result in any appreciable progress. The United Resistance Front against Fascism (Faşizme Karşi Birleşik Direniş Cephesi), founded in 1982 together with several radical left-wing Turkish organizations, was dissolved a year later in view of the groups' differing assessments of the guerrilla movement's chances of success in Turkey and because of the PKK's dominance.[37] The Kurdish organizations refused to cooperate with the PKK because of political and ideological differences.[38]

The marked expansion of guerrilla operations throughout Turkish Kurdistan in 1988 enabled the PKK to overcome its political isolation. It became increasingly popular in the rural areas and in the towns as well. Although mass demonstrations for the PKK in the towns of Cizre and Nusaybin in the spring of 1990—conceived by the PKK as a "Kurdish intifada"—were put down, they did show that the PKK had built up a broad-based political organization parallel to its guerrilla activities.[39]

Unlike the Kurdish parties in Iran and Iraq, the PKK contends that Kurdistan is "a classical colony," that it was colonized by Iran, Iraq, Turkey, and Syria in this century.[40] Moreover, the PKK works on the assumption that the Kurdish "feudal class" is collaborating closely with the "colonial capitalists" and has developed into a "comprador burgeoisie" in the framework of capitalist development and has abandoned its national identity.

The Kurdish parties of Turkish Kurdistan agree that the region is a "colony" of the Turkish state. Nor is there any great disagreement about the possibilities for resolving the Kurdish question. Neither the PSKT, to name but one of the PKK's Kurdish opponents, nor the PKK itself precludes a federation as the solution to the Kurdish question. However, the PKK's use of force after it was established in 1978 and the timing of its 1984 guerrilla war are both controversial. The PKK had been working on the assumption that a peaceful struggle for national rights was impossible within the framework of the "colonial structures" and the Turkish state's denial of the very existence of the Kurdish people. Thus, PKK's attacks have been leveled against both the Turkish "colonial power" and the "traditional structures" of Kurdish society, as well as against all other Kurdish and Turkish political groups that it opposes.[41]

In the circumstances prevailing today, the PKK considers violence to be the only form of resistance possible against the repressive actions of the Turkish state and the violence perpetrated by its local Kurdish agents, the *aghas* and the sheikhs. The clientele system, which in Turkey functions as a transmission belt between the Kurdish elite and the state, ensures the elite extensive economic and political power. Both in the economically more developed areas of the Kurdish region and in its underdeveloped eastern parts, the *aghas* either maintain private troops or—as in the regions with stable tribal structures—rely on tribal solidarity. Thus, through its attempts to break the power of the Kurdish *aghas*, the PKK has fought to neutralize the "pillars" of the central state while at the same time waging a guerrilla war against it.[42]

The PKK's claim to be the sole legitimate representative of the Kurdish national movement, however, has been an insurmountable obstacle in its relations with other Kurdish groups since its founding in 1978. The PKK is not restricted to Turkish Kurdistan but encompasses the whole of Kurdistan, and its claim to represent the movement is based on its rejection of all other manifestations of the Kurdish national movement, advancing its own typology of the Kurdish question.

The PKK considers all Kurdish armed rebellions since the end of the First World War as manifestations of "archaic nationalism." The essential characteristics of such ideology are the influence of tribal leadership and the demand for "national autonomy." This type of nationalism, the PKK argues, is an expression of the "ideology of the Kurdish feudal and tribal leaders, who want to guard their economic and political strength against the developing colonial capitalism and on this basis become the bourgeoisie."[43]

Reformist "petit-bourgeois nationalism" is another variant of Kurdish nationalism that the PKK rejects. The petit-bourgeois class has produced this type of nationalism, the PKK argues, because of the absence of a national bourgeoisie in Kurdistan.[44] The PKK considers the Kurdish petit bourgeoisie to be dependent on the "capitalism of the colonial state" and on the ruling Kurdish "feudal comprador class,"[45] as well as being reformist and favoring autonomy. The PKK, on the other hand, represents a revolutionary change in Kurdish society and the independence of Kurdistan.

The question is seldom asked why the PKK, founded by a radical left-wing group in 1978, became Turkish Kurdistan's strongest party and, after the start of the guerrilla war in 1984—and especially since the late 1980s—the only group that was able to mobilize the masses. How did the PKK succeed in wresting the leadership in Turkish Kurdistan from the other groups and holding its own against them?

The PKK differed from all the other organizations in one important respect, which it consistently put into practice from the very beginning: its unflinching use of force against the violence of traditional Kurdish society, against its down dissidents, against its political opponents, and against the power of the Turkish state. It is indeed a remarkable development that the

PKK, as a secular and socialist party, has been able to extend its influence beyond the particularism of Kurdish society and mobilize an extremely passive population that has put up with oppression for centuries. It is, however, extremely difficult to come up with plausible reasons for its violence against its dissidents and political opponents. It seems that the PKK was aware that it would be accused of "terrorism" for its actions but took the risk so as to gain the upper hand in Kurdistan. It rightly expected nothing else from the Turkish state, whose main doctrine—the nonexistence of the Kurdish people—is questioned every day by the PKK's actions.

It would seem that PKK's violence, used as a disciplinary measure and as an instrument of mobilization, is tolerated by the Kurdish population.[46] Ömer Erzeren is correct when he states that it was not PKK's "Marxist-Leninist" ideology that made it the strongest Kurdish group but its actions, by means of which it has achieved one of its declared aims—namely, putting an end to the passivity of the population.

Although violence has continued to be an important sanction against collaboration with the Turkish state by Kurdish groups or individuals, it is no longer used against the Kurdish elite—the "feudal landowners" and the urban "comprador bourgeoisie,"—which the PKK had characterized as "the objective enemies of the revolution" in Kurdish society.[47] Although, unlike the DPK after the outbreak of the Kurdish war in 1961, the PKK saw no reason to modify its program to make it acceptable to all the social classes who supported the guerrilla movement, it has since the mass demonstrations in March 1992 in East Anatolia come to see itself as a "national movement." The extent of the protest movement and the population's readiness to support the guerrilla movement openly have evidently surprised not only the Turkish state but the PKK as well, and in part they have made violence redundant as a disciplinary measure and as an instrument for mobilization.

The Turkish state's reaction to the PKK, especially after the mass demonstrations in the spring of 1990, has been contradictory. The army, as the guardian of the Kemalist legacy, continues to push for a military solution to the Kurdish question, which (following the Iraqi example) would also permit the use of chemical weapons against the guerrillas.[48] Turkey has carried out deportations of the population from the border areas—as Iraq has done as well—for some years now. And despite Turkish president Turgut Özal's new Kurdish policy, including steps such as lifting the ban on the Kurdish language, which is designed to increase Turkey's chances of admission into the European Community, the gap between Kurdish demands for an independent state and Özal's policy remains wide indeed.

At the beginning, the Kurdish parties of Iraqi Kurdistan attempted to

attain a modus vivendi with the PKK by joining forces and working together. In the 1980s the PUK as well as the DPK attempted to establish
closer relations with the PKK. However, the repeated efforts of the Iraqi
Kurdish parties failed because of the PKK's claims to sole representation.
At the end of the 1980s, the PKK began both to establish direct party organizations in other parts of Kurdistan (e.g., in the Kurdish region of Syria)
and to found parties with which it was ideologically and politically in agreement, such as the Party for an Independent Kurdistan (Partiya Azadiya Kurdistan, PAK), which it established in Iraqi Kurdistan. Still, despite such
recent renewed efforts for unity, the future course of the Kurdish national
movement remains uncertain, and the prospects for a free and independent
Kurdistan remain an ever more distant goal of the Kurdish people throughout Kurdistan.

CONCLUSION

Soon it will be a century since the pioneers of Kurdish nationalism attracted
attention, first in the form of a literary movement and subsequently as a
political movement. The Kurds, of all the peoples once belonging to the
Ottoman Empire, have not only remained a people without a state but have
been divided and persecuted.

There is no doubt that the Kurdish elite in the period before the First
World War, and during the war itself, were incapable of setting definite
objectives and attempting to mobilize the Kurdish people. During this phase
Kurdish nationalists also did not realize that the collapse of the Ottoman
Empire was imminent. It was not until after the First World War, when a
variety of plans had already been put forth for the partition of the region,
that the nationalists brought up their demands for a sovereign Kurdistan.
This demand, however, was scarcely an issue the Kurdish population supported at the time. In particular, during the war of liberation in Turkish
Kurdistan, the Kemalist movement attempted to win over support of the
Kurds through the use of religious symbols. The ''danger'' that the planned
Armenian state might also expand to include districts with an ethnically
mixed population persuaded the Kurdish *aghas* of the region to form an
alliance with Kemalism.

Only after it became clear that the state that succeeded the Ottoman
Empire was a Turkish national state, and that Kemal Atatürk was in the
process of establishing a secular state, were the Kurdish nationalists able to
hope for broader support. The revolts of Sheikh Said in 1925 and of the
Khoybun Party between 1928 and 1930 were quite clearly efforts toward

attaining independence. This was also the case with Sheikh Mahmud Berzenzi in Iraqi Kurdistan.

The goal of the Kurdish national movement, which during and following the Second World War assumed socialist and Marxist content, remained sovereignty, even when its short-term and long-term objectives are distinguished. In line with this, the DPK-Iraq incorporated the building of a democratic republic of Iraq into its party program of 1946. Within the framework of this republic an ''autonomous republic of Kurdistan'' was to be established, and the liberation and unification of all Kurdistan remained a distant goal.[49]

After the Iraqi coup of 1958 the DPK-Iraq made further concessions insofar as it did not mention the components of its party program. Until 1975 this course remained constant. After the defeat of 1975, all parties of Iraqi Kurdistan, as well as of Turkish Kurdistan, included the right of self-determination as a component of their programs. The meaning of this right, however, was not defined. In Iraqi Kurdistan the Kurdish parties reacted to the propaganda of the Iraqi government (according to which the Kurds were already granted autonomy'' through the Act of Autonomy of 1974) by demanding an ''authentic autonomy,'' that is, the extension of autonomy over the entire Kurdish region in Iraq and participation in the central government. The reason for the hesitation of the Kurds in demanding a confederative Iraqi republic is the fact that the Arab opposition parties in Iraq (which are allies of the Kurds) rejected the idea of a confederation.

In Iranian Kurdistan the DPK-Iran never went beyond the demand for autonomy. Until his death in 1989, Abdul Rahman Ghassemlou avoided any pan-Kurdish action that could not have been interpreted as separatist activity. While most of the political parties of Iraqi Kurdistan want to transform the coexistence with the Arabs that was forced upon them by the British into a voluntary relationship, they define Turkish rule over the Kurds as a colonial relationship that must be terminated. Although none of these parties has set autonomy as goal, a confederation is, at the most, discussed by some parties as a compromise. Of all the political parties in Kurdistan, the PKK strives most unequivocally for an independent state, yet it has indicated that it is willing to accept any solution chosen in a free referendum.

Along with changes in the goals of the Kurdish national movement in the past hundred years, the social base of the movement has spread. Today it is not merely a small class of intellectuals who support the national movement but the broad masses of Kurds in the countryside and in the urban centers, where migration has multiplied the Kurdish population. In the absence of economic development programs by the governments in the region to improve the conditions of both rural and urban dwellers, such migration has resulted in the impoverishment of the masses in the cities and has at the same time led to the development of substantial support for the Kurdish national movement among a growing segment of the marginalized urban Kurdish population.

There is little regional acceptance of the solutions to the Kurdish question as conceived by the Kurds. Their success in becoming participants in regional and international politics has been modest. The various economic and political conflicts in the region will inevitably ensure that the Kurdish question remains an active instrument of regional policy. After the dissolution of the Soviet Union and the disintegration of Yugoslavia, the Kurds themselves will probably hardly consider autonomy as the fulfillment of their goals. In view of the refusal of the regional powers to grant autonomy, and considering the vacillation of the traditional Kurdish parties, the militant organizations who plead for an independent Kurdish state, will gain the upper hand in the Kurdish struggle for national self-determination.

NOTES

1. Abdul Rahman Ghassemlou, *Kurdistan and the Kurds* (London: Collets Holdings, 1965), p. 14; Erhard Franz, *Kurden und Kurdentum* (Hamburg: Deutsches Orient-Institut, 1986), pp. 12–13.

2. Ghassemlou, *Kurdistan and the Kurds*, p. 23.

3. Ferdinand Hennebichler, *Die für die Freiheit Sterben* (Those who die for freedom) (Vienna: Verlag der Österreichischen Staatsdruckerei, 1988). It should also be noted here that in 1964 the Syrian Baath government withdrew Syrian citizenship from about 150,000 Kurds for political reasons. See Mustafa Nazdar, ''The Kurds in Syria,'' in Gérard Chaliand, ed., *People without a Country: The Kurds and Kurdistan* (London: Zed Press, 1980), p. 217.

4. The Kurdish language belongs to the northern branch of the western Iranian language group. It is spoken in various dialects that can be divided into three main categories: (1) Kurmanji (the western Kurdish dialect spoken by more than half of the Kurds, primarily in Turkish Kurdistan); (2) Eastern Kurdish (the Sorani and Silemani dialects spoken in Iraqi Kurdistan and the Mukri and Sinayi dialects spoken in Iranian Kurdistan); and (3) the Gorani dialect, which is spoken by a small minority in Iranian and Iraqi Kurdistan, and the Zaza dialect, which is related to the Gorani dialect and is spread throughout western areas of Turkish Kurdistan.

5. See Jamal Nebez, ''Die Schriftsprache der Kurden'' (Written language of the Kurds), in H. S. Nyberg, ed., *Hommages et opera minora* (Leiden: Brill, 1975), pp. 97–122.

6. See Edward Said, *Orientalism* (London: Routledge and Kegan Paul, 1978).

7. See *Kurden im Exil* (Kurds in exile), vols. 1–2, published in 1991 by the Berliner Institut für Vergleichende Sozialforschung (Berlin Institute of Comparative Social Research).

8. Martin van Bruinessen, *Agha, Scheich und Staat: Politik und Gesellschaft Kurdistans* (Agha, shaikh, and state: On the social and political organization of Kurdistan) (Berlin: Parabolis, 1989), p. 172.

9. The Tanzimat reforms of the Ottoman Empire were introduced in 1839 by Sultan Mahmoud. Their main objective was the consolidation of central power and the elimination of all forms of autonomy (regional, religious, ethnic) as well as the establishment of a modern

school system. The first generation of Kurdish intelligentsia were graduates of a school that was founded concomitantly with these reforms to educate the sons of the Kurdish aghas in Istanbul. See S. J. Shaw and E. K. Shaw, *History of the Ottoman Empire and Modern Turkey*, 2 vols. (Cambridge: Cambridge University Press, 1977), 2:1–54.

10. Robert Olson, *The Emergence of Kurdish Nationalism and the Sheikh Said Rebellion, 1880–1925* (Austin: University of Texas Press, 1989), p. 17.

11. Kendal, "The Kurds under the Ottoman Empire," in Chaliand, *People without a Country*, pp. 41–42.

12. United Kingdom, *Lausanne Conference on Near East Affairs 1922–23. Records of Proceedings and Draft Terms of Peace* (London, 1923), p. 400.

13. See Kendal, "Kurdistan in Turkey," in Chaliand, *People without a Country*, pp. 64–65.

14. The Turkish DPK leader, Faik Bucak, a former member of the Turkish parliament, was murdered in mysterious circumstances in 1967. Sait Elci, the leader of the party's moderate wing, and Sivan, that of its left wing, died in internal party quarrels in their place of refuge in Iraqi Kurdistan. See Michael Gunter, *The Kurds in Turkey* (Boulder, Colo.: Westview Press, 1990), p. 16.

15. Lothar Heinrich, *Die Kurdische Nationalbewegung in der Türkei* (The Kurdish nationalist movement in Turkey) (Hamburg: Deutsches Orient-Institut, 1989), p. 19. In 1977, the DPK-Turkey was renamed the National Liberators of Kurdistan (Kürdistan Ulusal Kurtulusculari, KUK).

16. The Revolutionary-Democratic Cultural Clubs (Devrimci Demokratik Kültür Dernekleri, DDKD), which had become active under the Kurdish intelligentsia in the 1970s, were an offshoot of the KDPT. However, they remained insignificant even after they had been transformed in 1983 into the Avant-Garde Workers' Party of Kurdistan (Partiya Pesenga Karkeren Kurdistan, PPKK). The Maoist Kave (Kawa) group split off from the DDKD in 1975. After the 1980 military coup it split into several factions, which reunited in 1988 as the Union of the Proletariat of Kurdistan (Yekitiya Proletariya Kurdistan, YPK).

17. Ismet Sheriff Vanly, *Die Nationale Frage Türkisch-Kurdistan* (The national question in Turkish Kurdistan) (Frankfurt am Main: Komkar, 1980), pp. 84–85.

18. Martin van Bruinessen, "The Kurds in Turkey," *Middle East Report*, no. 121 (1984): 10.

19. Abdullah Öcalan was reputedly close to the Revolutionary University Club of Ankara (Ankara Devrimci Yüksek Öğrenim Derneği, ADYÖD) while a student of political science at Ankara University in 1974. Mahir Cayan, the leader of the People's Liberation Party of Turkey—Front (Türkiye Halk Kurtuluş Partisi—Cephe), who was killed in an armed clash with the Turkish army in 1974, had a strong influence on Öcalan's political thinking and on the ethnically mixed circle of students around him.

20. Gunter, *The Kurds in Turkey*, pp. 17–21.

21. Regarding the Republic of Mahabad, refer to the standard work by William Eagleton, *The Kurdish Republic of 1946* (London: Oxford University Press, 1963).

22. For the history of the Kurdish uprising in Iraq, see Ismet Sheriff Vanly, "Kurdistan in Iraq," in Chaliand, *People without a Country*, pp. 153–210.

23. Ibid., pp. 170–73.

24. During the years 1966 –70 Jalal Talabani led a leftist dissident group against the DPK. At the end of 1970 this group disbanded. For a biography of Talabani, see Ferhad Ibrahim, "Die Patriotische Union Kurdistans und ihr Führer Jalal Talabani" (The Patriotic Union of Kurdistan and its leader Jalal Talabani) in Bahman Nirumand, ed., *Die Kurdische Tragödie* (The Kurdish tragedy) (Reinbek: Rowohlt, 1991), pp. 97–110.

25. The democrats organized in a suborganization, the Line of Readiness, the socialists in the Socialist Movement, and the Marxists in the League of Workers in Kurdistan.

26. The DPK-Iran, like the DPK-Iraq and other Kurdish parties, was dependent upon the charismatic personality of its leaders. This made it possible for the Iranian government to

strike such a devastating blow to the party after the assassination of its leader, Abdul Rahman Ghassemlou, in 1989.

27. Ferhad Ibrahim, "Der Golfkrieg und die Kurdische Widerstandsbewegung: Opfer der Realpolitik" (The Gulf War and the Kurdish resistance movement: Victims of Realpolitik), in Georg Stein, ed., *Nachgedanken zum Golfkrieg* (Reflections on the Gulf War) (Heidelberg: Palmyra, 1991), p. 141.

28. On this point, see Gunter, *The Kurds in Turkey*, pp. 50–51.

29. The PKK is, however, still far from developing a relationship to the HEP similar to that between the IRA and the legal Sinn Fein in Northern Ireland. The mysterious kidnapping and murder of HEP's chairman, Vedat Aydin, caused mass demonstrations in the larger towns of Eastern Anatolia in early July 1991. The demonstrators proclaimed their support for both the HEP and the PKK. On Aydin's murder, see the report in *Milliyet* (Istanbul) (July 13, 1991).

30. The "super province" covers most of the Kurdish provinces and is administered by a "super governor" who resides in the largest Kurdish city in Turkey, Diyarbakir. He governs through martial law, which has been imposed on the Kurdish territories since 1980.

31. Interview with the leader of the Patriotic Union of Kurdistan, Jalal Talabani (Berlin, Germany, September 18, 1992).

32. Interview with Muuaffaq al-Rubaii, a member of the leadership of the Iraqi Shiite Hizb al-Daua (London, England, April 24, 1993).

33. The Kurdish Alawite lawyer Kemal Burkay (who has been living in exile in Sweden since 1980) and his party, the Socialist Party of Kurdistan, were among Öcalan's severest critics.

34. It includes the Partiya Domokrata Kurdistan—Hevgirtin (Democratic Party of Kurdistan—Union) led by Hemres Reso. The party was founded in 1992 as a union of various liberal and leftist groupings. It is primarily active among Kurdish migrant laborers and intellectuals in exile in Europe.

35. In April and May 1993 the leaders of HEP were preparing to set up a new party, the Demokrasi Partisi (DEP), to replace the banned HEP. Its cofounders include the parliamentarians Ahmad Turk and M. Emin Sever, as well as former parliamentarian Ibrahim Aksoy. In 1993 six Kurdish members of parliament were accused of separatist acts and arrested. They were sentenced to prison in December 1994. After the DKP was banned because of alleged connections to the PKK, the party had to change its name to Halkin Demokrasi Partisi (HADEP) to attain legal status.

36. The Iraqi government tolerated PKK's presence in Iraqi Kurdistan after the ceasefire in the Iran-Iraq war because it hoped this would prevent renewed infiltration by Iraqi Kurds into the area.

37. The most significant Turkish organization in the Front was the Revolutionary Path (Devrimci Yol).

38. In 1988 the PKK's opponents set up the umbrella organization Tevger (Movement), which is active mainly in Europe.

39. According to the Turkish sociologist Ismail Beşikçi, the PKK's guerrilla war and its political work have resulted in a high degree of politicization among the Kurds. The most important effect of the guerrilla movement, he argues, has been to change the Kurdish population's mental and spiritual attitude. He sees a sign of this psychological change in the revival of the phenomenon of martyrdom (*sahadet*): The nation lays claim to the corpses of the guerrillas killed in action, and "funeral ceremonies" that last for weeks have a politically mobilizing effect on the population. See Ismail Beşikçi, *Devletlerarasi sömürge Kürdistan* (Kurdistan: Colony of several states) (Istanbul: Alan Yayincilik, 1990), pp. 52–54. Beşikçi, a leading Turkish Kurdologist, has during the past two decades published a series of important ethnological and sociological studies about Turkish Kurdistan. He has spent more than ten years in prison on account of his scientific interest in the Kurds.

40. Workers Party of Kurdistan (Partiya Karkeren Kurdistan, PKK), *Program* (Cologne: Serxwebun, 1984), p. 32.

41. While the very existence of other Kurdish groups refutes PKK's claim to be the sole representative of the Kurdish people, the left-wing Turkish groups question its assessment of Kurdistan as "classical colony" and in so doing repudiate its main theoretical position.

42. Abdullah Öcalan, "al-Dhikra al-saniwiyya li al-tasis," (Anniversary of the foundation) *Denge Kurdistan*, no. 4–5 (1986): 8–9.

43. *Kurdistan Report*, no. 17 (September 1986): 48.

44. Ibid.

45. Ibid.

46. On this question, see Ömer Erzeren, "Von der Guerrilla zu Intifada?" (From guerrilla to Intifada?) in Nirumand, *Die Kurdische Tragödie*, p. 158.

47. PKK, *Program*, pp. 34–35.

48. See, for example, Erzeren, "Von der Guerrilla zu Intifada?" p. 160, who quotes the former brigade commander in Hakkari province, General Altay Tokat.

49. Ferhad Ibrahim, *Die Kurdische Nationalbewegung im Iraq* (The Kurdish national movement in Iraq) (Berlin: Schwarz, 1983), p. 410.

MARTIN J. MURRAY

Apartheid and
the National Question
in South Africa

In both theory and practice, the national question has long been a source of controversy and disagreement within the liberation movement in South Africa. Despite widespread agreement that South Africa's ruling class has cynically promoted tribalism and racialism, as well as fraudulent types of nationalism, in order to divide the oppressed and exploited majority, there is no consensus over how to define the nation, national identity, and nationalism. These disputes over the national question cannot be seen as merely academic hairsplitting. With the collapse of white minority rule and installation of a democratically elected government under the leadership of the African National Congress (ANC), the problem of unraveling the national question has become more important than ever. The ways in which the nation, national oppression, and nationalism are understood provide key building blocks in the formulation of political strategies to confront the legacy of white domination.

APPROACHES TO THE NATIONAL QUESTION IN SOUTH AFRICA

The national question cannot be conceived apart from its peculiar historical context, or put in another way, it cannot be reduced to a single general definition appropriate for all times and places.[1] Ethnicity, race, and nation are neither natural nor immutable social categories. The boundaries of ethnic, racial, and national identities are fluid and have continually shifted in response to political, social, and economic circumstances.[2] Equally important, nation building and the forging of a distinctive "national identity" are not the exclusive preserve of a single class or bloc of class forces.

In South African historiography, one area where liberal and radical scholarship tend to converge and overlap is in characterizing much of twentieth-century South African history as a struggle between an exclusive form of white Afrikaner nationalism, with its explicit objective the capture of the organs of state power by the white Afrikaner nation, and an emergent pan–South African black nationalism, which has sought the extension of full citizenship rights to all those who inhabit South Africa regardless of racial or ethnic origin. As Charles Bloomberg has eloquently shown, Afrikaner nationalism drew its inspiration from a distinctive Christian-nationalist creed proclaiming Afrikaners to be a chosen people on a sacred mission. The idea of territorial separation, or apartheid, was not the invention of H. F. Verwoerd but instead had its roots in the exclusivist ideology of Christian nationalism.[3] Others have shown that apartheid did not emerge de novo but developed organically out of segregationist and white supremacist ideologies that preceded it.[4] In contrast, black nationalism, with its strong Africanist underpinnings, represented the ideological response of oppressed people to centuries of subjugation in the land of their birth.[5]

While it is certainly possible to do so, the aim of this chapter is not to challenge this characterization of twentieth-century South African history as a conflict of rival nationalisms, or to survey the historical origins of the lively debates over the national question. Instead, the purpose here is to concentrate on the divergent conceptions of nation, nationality, and race that developed in response to the National Party's efforts to implement its apartheid program during the 1950s and 1960s. It is hoped that this narrower focus can help illuminate the terrain of ideological struggle as it has shifted and changed over the past four decades.

THE NATIONAL PARTY AND AFRIKANER NATIONALISM

Among many things, the 1948 electoral victory of the National Party symbolized the triumph of Afrikaner nationalism.[6] When the Afrikaner state managers began implementing apartheid (or "separate development") policies, they were merely following in the footsteps of their English-speaking predecessors, who had devised informal mechanisms for dividing and ruling the indigenous peoples of southern Africa.[7] The Afrikaner intellectuals who designed apartheid conceived of South Africa not as a unitary political entity composed of a single people but as a "multinational" state comprising between ten and twelve "nations," each of which was entitled to the "right

of self-determination'' including eventual ''national independence.''
Whether in its *verkrampte* (narrow-minded) or in its *verligte* (enlightened)
versions, this view of the nation depended upon a rigid and frozen notion
of ethnicity by which individuals were defined exclusively in sociocultural
terms.[8] The National Party used this conception of the nation ideologically
to justify the Bantustan strategy of establishing fraudulent homelands, or
''mini-states,'' with local clients in power.[9] The apartheid planners rationalized the territorial division of South Africa along these putatively national
lines. Afrikaner intellectuals went to great pains to present the ten homelands as natural entities rooted in notions of primordial origin, divine mission, spiritual unity, shared culture, common language, and, especially,
racial homogeneity.[10]

In essence, this ''multinational'' perspective functioned as little more
than an ideological mask justifying the rigid implementation of apartheid
policies. Among the oppressed classes, only the most reactionary ''tribal
chiefs,'' aspiring entrepreneurs, and high-ranking civil servants in the
homelands actively adhered to this point of view. Yet apartheid policies did
have significant ideological effects. Even today, atrophied and truncated
variations of this ''multinational'' perspective still resonate under the guise
of ''tribalism'' and ''tribal'' identity as Bantustan leaders and local warlords often manipulate a shared language and common heritage to evoke
images of the Zulu nation, the Xhosa nation, and so on.

THE POLITICAL RESPONSE TO EARLY APARTHEID

From the 1950s through the 1970s, the political response within the liberation movement to the National Party's apartheid strategy largely coalesced
around what Neville Alexander has called the ''four nations'' thesis.[11]
While it is possible to identify different variants to this approach, the roots
of the four-nations paradigm can be traced to classical liberal thinking regarding race relations. According to this view, South Africa is made up of
four different groups of people: (1) the indigenous Bantu-speaking African
peoples, themselves fissured into various ''tribal'' groupings; (2) the so-
called Coloured people, or those sometimes referred to as ''mixed-race'';
(3) the so-called Asian people, largely those who can trace their geographical origins to the Indian subcontinent; and (4) the Europeans, or those who
originally migrated to South Africa as settlers and who mainly trace their
geographical origins to the British Isles, Holland, Germany, and France.

As should be obvious, these alleged racial distinctions are artificial and
embarrassingly crude. In the 1950s, the National Party took these distinctions as a point of departure and, via the Population Registration Act, classi-

fied everyone into one or another rigidly defined group or subgroup. In the classical liberal paradigm, these four groups were separate "races," and "nation building" was conceived as uniting these distinct entities in "multiracial" harmony.[12]

For more than forty years, a succession of apartheid regimes have operated within a rigidly demarcated racial paradigm that has ingrained racial consciousness into the fabric of South African daily life. The practice of population registration, job reservation, separate amenities, residential segregation, and so on, has tended to entrench racial divisions. Hence, for all sorts of socioeconomic reasons, the idea that South Africa comprises four "races" has deep roots in all sectors and social classes.[13]

Elements of the liberation movement, like the Unity Movement, did not accept these racial distinctions. But, beginning in the 1950s, the Congress Alliance, with the ANC as the leading partner, evoked this image of "four nations," most vividly in its symbol of the four-spoke wheel, intended to express the unity in diversity of four separate "racial" groups. Equally important, the Congress Alliance in its daily administrative and bureaucratic operations was also divided along these lines. At the top, individuals from different racial groups came together in single bodies like the National Consultative Committee yet ordinary supporters operated within separate organizations: the ANC, the Coloured Persons' Congress, the Congress of Democrats, and the Indian Congress. In response to criticism that the arrangement represented voluntary segregation within the liberation movement, Joe Slovo, a leading member of the South African Communist Party (SACP) also influential within the Congress Alliance, defended it by reference to the "group consciousness" of the mass movement. Slovo contended that while he had no principled objection to the idea of creating a single nonracial organization in the struggle against white minority rule, this idea would have appealed in the 1950s only to "the ideologically advanced" and not to "the masses."[14]

"COLONIALISM OF A SPECIAL TYPE"

The view that racial oppression is best understood when it is considered as an instance of colonial domination has wide currency within the South African liberation movement. Because socioeconomic realities in South Africa differ in some significant respects from a classical colonial situation, advocates of this "colonialist" formulation prefer terms like "colonialism of a special type" or "internal colonialism" to describe the peculiarities of the South African situation. This perspective originated with the SACP in the 1950s and remains, with some variation, perhaps the main doctrinal tenet of the SACP's ongoing political program. This idea of "colonialism of a special type" not only establishes the foundation for the SACP's long-time political alliance with the ANC but also defines its immediate political tasks in the current conjuncture.

With the publication in 1976 of Slovo's "South Africa. No Middle Road," the idea of "colonialism of a special type" gained wider popular recognition. In this perspective, because of the specificity of colonial oppression whereby Europeans rule over the remainder, South Africa must first traverse a distinct "national democratic" stage before the transition to socialism can occur. In practical political terms, this analysis means two things: first, the immediate task of the liberation movement is to build broad, multiclass, nonracial alliances with the aim of dismantling all laws, institutions, and structures that maintain racial discrimination; second, the issue of socialism, or ideas about social blueprints for the future, should not be pushed too strongly because socialist agitation might undermine the basis for the broadest possible unity in the struggle for national liberation.

In the 1960s, both the SACP and the ANC adopted as official doctrine this viewpoint characterizing the liberation struggle as an anticolonial movement directed against a "colonialism of a special type." This position was strongly influenced by the wave of anticolonial, nationalist struggles sweeping the African continent. In the conventional wisdom of the time, "national liberation" stood for democratic rights, including the right of the colonized nation as a whole to achieve independence from foreign colonial rule and to gain national self-determination. In the South African case, by contrast, British colonial domination faded with the 1910 Act of Union and, subsequently, the granting of dominion status by the Statutes of Westminister in 1934. In the conception of the SACP, this theory of "colonialism of a special type" suggested that "it is analytically correct" to "talk of 'two South Africas' defined, *at a certain level*, in national rather than class terms." The SACP also proclaimed:

> On one level, that of "white South Africa," there are all the features of an advanced capitalist state in its final stage of imperialism. . . . But on another level, that of "non-white South Africa," there are all the features of a colony. The indigenous population is subjected to extreme national oppression, poverty and exploitation, lack of all democratic rights and political domination by a group which does everything it can to emphasise and perpetuate its alien "European" character. . . . Non-white South Africa is the colony of white South Africa itself.[15]

For both the ANC and the SACP, the idea of "colonialism of a special type"—even its contemporary variants—functioned as the linchpin of their strategy of defining the immediate goals of political struggle as "national liberation." At the third Consultative Conference, held in 1969 at Morogoro, Tanzania, the ANC adopted a document entitled "Strategy and Tactics of the African National Congress." This document outlined the organization's position on nationalism and national liberation quite clearly:

> The national character of the struggle must therefore dominate our approach. But it is a national struggle which is taking place in a different era and in a different context from those which characterized the early struggles against colonialism. . . . Our nationalism must not be confused with chauvinism or narrow nationalism of a previous epoch. It must not be confused with the classical drive by an elitist group among the oppressed people to gain ascendancy so that they can replace the oppressor in the exploitation of the mass.[16]

The ANC clearly distinguished its conception of nationalism from the types of African nationalism that emerged in the 1960s when neocolonialism displaced colonial rule. "Strategy and Tactics" continued:

> The main content of the present stage of the South African revolution is the national liberation of the largest and most oppressed group—the African people. This strategic aim must govern every aspect of the conduct of our struggle, whether it be the formulation of policy or the creation of structures. Amongst other things, it demands in the first place the maximum mobilization of the African people as a dispossessed and racially oppressed nation.[17]

This document also stressed that "the African, although subject to the most intense racial oppression and exploitation, is not the only oppressed national group in South Africa. The two million strong Coloured community and the three-quarter million Indians suffer varying forms of national humiliation, discrimination and oppression. They are part of the non-White base."[18]

In describing the "revolutionary cause," the ANC spoke of "a speedy progression from formal liberation to genuine and lasting emancipation."[19] While the ANC stopped short of referring to this stage of "genuine and lasting emancipation" as the socialist revolution, the SACP was more explicit. The SACP has always regarded the ANC as the principal vehicle for bringing about national liberation (or "the national democratic stage") in South Africa. For the SACP, the ANC's Freedom Charter, adopted in 1955, was not a blueprint for socialism but rather "a common programme for a free, democratic South Africa agreed on by socialists and non-socialists," to which it pledged its unqualified support. In the late 1970s, the SACP argued that the achievement of the aims of the Freedom Charter would establish "the indispensible basis for the advance of our country along non-capitalist lines to a socialist and communist future."[20] It also called for "a national democratic revolution which will overthrow the colonialist state of white supremacy and establish an independent state of national democracy in South Africa."[21]

THE SOWETO UPRISING AND BLACK CONSCIOUSNESS

During the 1950s, mass popular protests against the implementation of apartheid rule energized the liberation movement.[22] The 1960 Sharpeville massacre, in which at least sixty-nine unarmed peaceful protesters were killed at an antipass rally, signaled the extent to which the state security apparatus was prepared to go to crush the popular movement. The various sections of the liberation movement turned to what at the time was called "armed struggle" but which in reality amounted to little more than a clandestine sabotage campaign directed against symbols of apartheid rule. The apartheid regime intensified its repression, effectively jailing, killing, or driving into exile the underground liberation movement within a space of three years. By separating the leadership of the liberation movement from its mass following, the security apparatus was able to buy time. This period from the early 1960s to the mid-1970s represented the heyday of apartheid rule.[23]

Yet as the ANC, the newly formed Pan Africanist Congress (PAC) and other sections of the liberation movement were crushed as above-ground popular organizations, the underlying seething tensions were generating alternative responses of the oppressed people. In 1969, black college students broke away from the white liberal National Union of South African Students (NUSAS) to form the South African Students' Organization (SASO) as a separate, exclusively black political organization. This emergent black student movement was strongly influenced by the civil rights and black liberation struggles in the United States. Under the leadership of Steve Biko and a host of others, SASO distanced itself from liberalism. In 1970, SASO issued a strongly worded ideological attack on what it regarded as white paternalism. Declaring that "the emancipation of black people in this country depends entirely on the role black people themselves are prepared to play," SASO argued:

We are concerned with that curious bunch of nonconformists . . . that bunch of do-gooders that goes under all sorts of names—liberals, leftists, etc. These are the people who argue that they are not responsible for white racism. . . . These are the people who claim that they too feel the oppression just as acutely as the blacks and therefore should be jointly involved in the black man's struggle. . . . In short, these are the people who say that they have black souls wrapped up in white skins.[24]

Besides warning against the dangers of liberal interference in defining the struggle of black people, SASO also embraced the ideology of black consciousness. In July 1971, the SASO Manifesto declared that black consciousness was "an attitude of mind, a way of life" in which black people saw themselves as "self-defined and not as defined by others." It required, above all, "group cohesion and solidarity" so that black people could be made aware of their collective economic and political power."[25]

Black-consciousness organizations spread rapidly during the 1970s. The banning of the ANC, the PAC, and their allied organizations had left a political vacuum that groups like SASO, Black People's Convention (a nonstudent group espousing black consciousness), and, eventually, the Azanian People's Organization (AZAPO) filled. SASO, in particular, aggressively promoted a positive self-image among the oppressed people and adopted self-reliance as a principle. Black-consciousness ideology broke firmly with the liberal prescription that multiracial integration served as both the means and the end to South Africa's internal problems. The objectives of the Black People's Convention included liberation from psychological and physical oppression and the implementation of "black communalism" through economic cooperatives, literacy campaigns, health projects, cultural activity, and a general workers' union, the Black Allied Workers' Union (BAWU).[26]

By 1972, black high school students had formed all sorts of youth organizations across the country. In January and February 1973, a wave of spontaneous strikes by black workers erupted in Durban and other urban areas of Natal. These strikes demonstrated the capacity of black workers to gain economic concessions through militant action. In 1973, and again in 1974, state security forces attempted to suppress SASO and its allied organizations by means of bans and detentions.[27] The outbreak of Soweto rebellion in June 1976 altered the political landscape in South Africa.[28] The sheer endurance of township students and youth in confronting the South African police and army animated the liberation struggle and transformed black consciousness into the dominant ideological current virtually overnight. By the early 1980s, the ANC was able to establish itself, once again, as the dominant political force within the liberation movement. Yet black-consciousness ideology reshaped the way in which political organizations understood the way forward to liberation.[29]

The black-consciousness movement rejected the division of the South African populace into racial groupings as an apartheid tactic of "divide and rule," and it made a concerted effort to cleanse the liberation movement of the words *non-European, nonwhite, Indian,* and *Coloured.*[30] In substituting the language of black unity, the black-consciousness movement divided South Africa into two camps, the oppressed and the oppressors. Proponents of black consciousness have sometimes conflated "race" and "class," adopting in certain instances an argument that all whites are capitalists and all blacks are workers. This stark division into two separate spheres is the substance of what Neville Alexander calls the "two-nations" thesis.[31]

THE PAC AND THE "TWO-NATIONS" THESIS

Long-simmering disagreements over "multiracialism" and "Africanism" led to the bitter split in the ANC in 1959 in which some dissenters left to form the PAC. These "Africanists," as they referred to themselves, had strongly resisted the prominence of whites in the Congress Alliance and had opposed the 1955 Freedom Charter with its clauses guaranteeing the rights and status of all national groups. The PAC's first president, Robert Sobukwe, called upon sympathetic whites to adjust their outlook in such a fashion that the slogan "Africa for the Africans" could "apply to them even though they were white."[32] The Africanists established this principle as their litmus test, defining as African everyone who owed his or her loyalty to Africa. Sobukwe outlined this viewpoint at the PAC's inaugural convention:

> To us the term "multiracialism" implies that there are such basic insuperable differences between the various national groups here that the best course is to keep them permanently distinctive in a kind of democratic *apartheid.* That to us is racialism multiplied, which probably is what the term truly connotes.
>
> We aim, politically, at government of the Africans by the Africans for the Africans, with everybody who owes his only loyalty to Africa and who is prepared to accept the democratic rule of an African majority being regarded as an African. We guarantee no minority rights, because we think in terms of individuals, not groups.[33]

The flip side of this principle was the belief that white South Africans, because of the material benefits they had accrued as a consequence of the system of white supremacy, were at present unable to owe their primary allegiance to Africa. Groups in privileged positions, as the PAC stressed, never relinquished their status voluntarily. As a result, the strident African nationalism of the PAC, captured in the popular slogan, "Africa for the Africans," has often been regarded as "anti-white."[34]

The PAC defined South Africa along classical colonial lines. European settlers had stolen the land from its original inhabitants, and the essence of the national liberation struggle was the restoration of the land and wealth to their rightful owners, the African people. By thus stressing the divisions between colonizers and colonized the Africanist ideology advocated a variant of the "two-nations" thesis: the aim of liberation was for the African nation to throw off the yoke of the colonizers and reestablish the rightful owners on the land. Thus, African nationalism contains a "backward-looking" element demanding redress of past grievances.

With the resurgence of the PAC in the late 1980s and the emergence of a younger internal leadership cadre schooled in the popular struggles of the post-Soweto generation, the slogan "Africa for the Africans" assumed a new meaning. Africans came to be defined not by skin color or racial grouping but by ideological commitment and loyalty.[35]

Despite the differences of their approaches, both the black-consciousness movement and the PAC relied upon a loosely defined colonialist analogy (oppressed and oppressors, settlers and Africans) in order to understand the specific nature of racial domination in South Africa. The problem with this perspective, "and with any other many-nations thesis in the South African context," Alexander suggests, "is that it holds within it the twin dangers of anti-white black chauvinism and ethnic separatism."[36]

"ONE AZANIA, ONE NATION"

The concept of "colonialism of a special type" remains the official doctrine of the ANC-SACP alliance, and it enjoys widespread popular support today.[37] This idea refers to "a form of colonialism where the colonial community occupies the same territory as the colonized people."[38] Wolpe puts it this way: "It is the racial structure which guarantees the dominance of all white class fractions and the corresponding subordination of all black class fractions. . . . It is race which unifies each of the blocks across class lines and it is the dominance of the alliance of white classes which signifies colonialism of a special type."[39]

Even if one accepts the ANC/SACP argument that the struggle for majority rule *takes precedence* over the struggle against capitalist exploitation, the question still remains: What is the political form in which the democratic struggle is waged?[40] It is an undeniable fact that black people in South Africa have been subjected to racial oppression. But racial oppression has led historically to a variety of political responses among the oppressed:

different and sometimes rival expressions of African nationalism, alternative forms of black nationalism, as well as many diverse currents of socialism and even liberalism. The simple deduction of nationalism from the struggle against racial oppression glosses over the variety of different political responses that have emerged with varying degrees of resonance. Yet this view that nationalism is naturally the response of those who suffer from racial oppression is so embedded in the prevailing literature that it has become the conventional wisdom.[41]

Critics have challenged the "colonialism of a special type" thesis, arguing that it provides the conceptual foundation for the analytic separation between distinct "stages" in the revolutionary process and thereby admits the possibility that the liberation movement could be hijacked by aspiring bourgeois opportunists who, because they held or shared state power, would be enabled to soft-pedal the genuine interests of the black working class.[42] Alexander has been one of the most cogent critics of both the "four-nations" and "two-nations" perspectives as well as the theory of "colonialism of a special type."[43] His main argument has been that the ideology of nationalism in these forms is in fact a pseudonationalism, concealing a form of "color-caste" consciousness. His own intellectual effort has been directed toward defining a true nationalism purged of all racialist taints. Under the slogan of "One Azania, One Nation," he has argued that in the South African context genuine nationalism should be seen not in terms of separate racial or ethnic groups coming together but rather in terms of abolishing these distinctions altogether.[44] For Alexander, the principal political task of unification is one of "nation-building," that is, "the national question in South Africa consists in the tasks of unifying the nation and extending equal rights to all who constitute it."[45] He spells out this position more explicitly:

> Only the black working class can take the task of completing the democratisation of the country on its shoulders. It alone can unite the oppressed and exploited classes. It has become the leading class in the building of the nation. It has to redefine the nation and abolish the reactionary definitions of the bourgeoisie and of the reactionary petty bourgeoisie. The nation has to be structured by and in the interests of the black working class. But it can only do so by changing the entire system. A non-racial capitalism is impossible in South Africa. The class struggle against racial oppression becomes one struggle under the general command of the black working class and its organizations. Class, colour and nation converge in the national liberation movement.[46]

If nationalism is, as Tom Nairn suggests, "Janus-faced,"[47] looking to the past as well as the future, Alexander has sought to define nationalism in

South Africa as unequivocally future oriented, looking to the construction of a new nation rather than to the restoration of what he sees as the largely imaginary rights of the primordial "nations" of South Africa.[48] Alexander offers a definition of nationalism that radically breaks from all racial categories that suggest hermetically sealed inherent differences.

Alec Erwin, a leading trade union organizer closely associated with the Congress of South African Trade Unions (COSATU), takes a similar view. Purely defensive nationalism, he suggests, looks to the past for justification and even inspiration. The importance of "nation-building," he argues, "is that the nation is being constructed with reference to the future rather than the past—the past being a source of division rather than unity. Attempts to build a nation give rise to a modernising tendency . . . a stress on education, change, and adaptation."[49]

Though initially treated with hostility by the ANC and SACP, Alexander's conception seems to be increasingly embraced by the mainstream of the liberation movement.[50] By the 1980s, the Congress movement had jettisoned the conception of multiracialism, replacing it with "nonracialism." In practice, however, old ways of forging alliances lingered: popular organizations like the United Democratic Front (UDF) clearly espoused the nonracialist viewpoint of the Congress movement yet continued to bring together affiliates that were defined on a racial basis. With the unbanning of the ANC, however, membership has been thrown open to all persons on a strictly nonracial basis.

CONCLUSION

Over the course of the apartheid years, the national question has been subjected to considerable scrutiny and refinement within the liberation movement. At each critical stage in the liberation struggle—the defiance campaign of the 1950s, the launching of armed struggle in the early 1960s, the rise of black consciousness and the Soweto rebellion of the 1970s, the outbreak of township rebellions in the 1980s, the negotiations over a new constitution, and, finally, democratic elections that installed South Africa's first nonracial government, led by the ANC and Nelson Mandela—the liberation movement has been forced to come to grips with new ideological currents engendered in popular struggle. At each juncture the liberation movement has incorporated these new ideas into its understanding of the way forward. What needs to be stressed is that popular consciousness is not simply a given but is historically constructed through dialogue, debate, and multiform experiences of struggle. The national question thus cannot be treated as inscribed in stone; rather, it is a perspective intregally connected to the limits and possibilities of the liberation struggle.

The language of the 1950s—multiracialism and the associated concept of four separate national groups—has largely faded, and the idea that the liberation struggle can be carried forward by four separate organizations has passed out of existence. The Congress movement today proclaims its commitment to the principle of nonracialism, and this principle is embodied in the fact that the ANC has thrown open its doors to all South Africans who espouse its political point of view. Black-consciousness ideology, once looked upon with a degree of suspicion by the exile leadership of the Congress movement, has made a permanent contribution to liberation politics in South Africa. It continues to stress the principle of exclusive black leadership of the liberation struggle, both within the trade union movement and within popular organizations. AZAPO's insistence that black unity is more important than forging alliances with white liberal groups, like business leaders and student groups, epitomizes this perspective. Similarly, the PAC, under younger leadership schooled in the struggles of the 1960s, has stressed color blindness in its vision of Africa for the Africans, despite the identification by many rank-and-file members of whites with oppressors. The growing strength of socialist ideology within the black trade union movement has brought an awareness of the necessity of understanding the relationship between class exploitation and national oppression, and, in particular, of stressing the class content of national struggles.

Postapartheid South Africa does not mean nonracial South Africa. With the collapse of the main pillars of apartheid, South Africa's rulers are now faced with the challenge of redefining the nation in accordance with their vision of "group rights" and the inviolability of private property. In contrast, the liberation movement is faced with the challenge of looking beyond the scrapping of South Africa's peculiar race laws in order to construct a nation where the free play of market forces does not become a mechanism ensuring white property and privilege and thereby reproducing the old racial order under a new guise. Hence, the struggle over the national question remains a principal task of the liberation movement in the years ahead.[51]

NOTES

Acknowledgments: I would like to thank Neville Alexander and Berch Berberoglu for helpful comments on this essay. They, of course, are not responsible for my interpretation of the issues explored here.

1. Neville Alexander, "An Approach to the National Question in South Africa," *Azania Worker* 2, no. 2 (1985): 3–4.

2. See Shula Marks and Stanley Trapido, "The Politics of Race, Class, and National-

ism," in Marks and Trapido, eds., *The Politics of Race, Class, and Nationalism in Twentieth Century South Africa* (London and New York: Longman, 1987), pp. 61–62.

3. See Charles Bloomberg, *Christian-Nationalism and the Rise of the Afrikaner Broerderbon in South Africa, 1918–1948* (Bloomington and Indianapolis: Indiana University Press, 1989).

4. Saul Dubow, *Racial Segregation and the Origins of Apartheid in South Africa, 1919–1936* (New York: St. Martin's Press, 1989); Dan O'Meara, *Volkskapitalisme: Class, Capital, and Ideology in the Development of Afrikaner Nationalism, 1934–1948* (Cambridge: Cambridge University Press, 1983); and Saul Dubow, "Race, Civilisation, and Culture: The Elaboration of Segregationist Discourse in the Inter-War Years," in Marks and Trapido, *The Politics of Race, Class, and Nationalism*, pp. 71–94.

5. Peter Walshe, *The Rise of African Nationalism in South Africa: The African National Congress, 1912–1952* (Berkeley and Los Angeles: University of California Press, 1970); Colin Bundy, "Land and Liberation: Popular Rural Protest and the National Liberation Movements in South Africa, 1920–1960," in Marks and Trapido, *The Politics of Race, Class, and Nationalism*, pp. 254–85.

6. See Isabel Hofmeyr, "Building a Nation from Words: Afrikaans Language, Literature and Ethnic Identity, 1902–1924," in Marks and Trapido, *The Politics of Race, Class, and Nationalism*, pp. 95–123.

7. See John Cell, *Segregation: The Highest Stage of White Supremacy: The Origins of Segregation in South Africa and the American South* (Cambridge: Cambridge University Press, 1982).

8. Neville Alexander, "Approaches to the National Question in South Africa," *Transformation* 1 (1986): 75–76.

9. See Frank Molteno, "The Historical Significance of the Bantustan Strategy," *Social Dynamics* (Cape Town) 3, no. 2 (1977): 15–33.

10. Robert Fine, "The Antinomies of Nationalism and Democracy in the South African Liberation Struggle," *Review of African Political Economy*, no. 45/46 (1989): 100.

11. Alexander, "Approaches to the National Question," 76–78.

12. For a description of liberalism, see Leo Marquard, *Liberalism in South Africa* (Johannesburg: South African Institute of Race Relations, 1965).

13. For how these terms were used in defining the liberation struggle, see Nelson Mandela, *No Easy Walk to Freedom: Articles, Speeches, and Trial Addresses of Nelson Mandela* (London: Heinemann, 1965).

14. Joe Slovo, "South Africa: No Middle Road," in Basil Davison, Joe Slovo, and Anthony Wilkinson, *Southern Africa: The New Politics of Revolution* (London: Penguin Books, 1976), pp. 171–75.

15. *The South African Communist* (First Quarter, 1963): 24–70, cited in Joe Slovo, "South Africa: No Middle Road," pp. 132–33.

16. "Strategy and Tactics of the African National Congress," adopted by the Third Consultative Conference of the African National Congress, April 1969, Morogoro, Tanzania. Reprinted as ANC, "Strategy and Tactics of the South African Revolution," *Forward to Freedom* (London: Sechaba Publications, 1969): 1–2.

17. Ibid, pp. 8–9.

18. Ibid, pp. 9–10.

19. Ibid, pp. 10–11.

20. Joe Slovo, "South Africa: No Middle Road," pp. 144–45.

21. Ibid, pp. 145–46.

22. See Tom Lodge, *Black Politics in South Africa since 1945* (Johannesburg: Ravan Press, 1983), pp. 33–66. For a classical liberal treatment of the ANC and the 1950s popular protests, see Edward Feit, *South Africa: The Dynamics of the African National Congress* (London: Oxford University Press, 1962).

23. See Lodge, *Black Politics*, pp. 201–60.

24. *SASO Newsletter* (August 1970), cited in Gail Gerhart, "The South African Students' Organization, 1968–1975" (paper presented at the Annual Conference of the African Studies Association, San Francisco, 1975).

25. *SASO Policy Manifesto*, cited in Gail Gerhart, *Black Power in South Africa: The Evolution of an Ideology* (Berkeley and Los Angeles: University of California Press, 1978).

26. Lodge, *Black Politics*, pp. 322–24.

27. See Gerhart, *Black Power*, pp. 295–99.

28. John Kane-Berman, *Soweto: Black Revolt, White Reaction* (Johannesburg: Ravan Press, 1978); Baruch Hirson, *Year of Fire, Yeah of Ash* (London: Zed Press, 1979).

29. Lodge, *Black Politics*, pp. 328–39.

30. For a white liberal view of black-consciousness ideology, see Donald Woods, *Asking for Trouble: The Autobiography of a Banned Journalist* (New York: Atheneum, 1981).

31. Alexander, "Approaches to the National Question," pp. 80–82.

32. Robert Sobukwe quoted in Lodge, *Black Politics*, p. 84.

33. Robert Sobukwe's opening address to the PAC's inaugural convention, in Thomas Karis, Gail Gerhart, and Gwendlyn Carter, eds., *From Protest to Challenge: Documentary History of African Politics in South Africa, 1882–1964*, vol. 3 (Stanford: Hoover Institution Press, 1973), pp. 510–16.

34. Gerhart, *Black Power*, pp. 173–211.

35. "We are non-racial, so we do not refer to people in terms of colour. To refer to people in terms of the alleged features of his person or group is violently repulsive and mythical nonsense. There is only one race, the human race.... An African is defined as someone who is indigenous or who pays his only allegiance to Africa and its people and its development and accepts straightforward democratic practices. It is up to each individual to say whether he is an African." Benny Alexander, "Afrikanism Stakes Its Claim," *Work in Progress*, no. 64 (1989): 31.

36. Alexander, "Approaches to the National Question," p. 83.

37. Robert Fine, "The Antinomies of Nationalism and Democracy," 102.

38. Maria van Diepen, "Introduction," in Maria van Diepen, ed., *The National Question in South Africa* (London: Zed, 1988), p. 4.

39. Harold Wolpe, "Race and Class in the National Struggle in South Africa," in van Diepen, *The National Question in South Africa*, p. 62.

40. For another official ANC/SACP view on "colonialism of a special type," see Comrade Mzala, "Revolutionary Theory on the National Question in South Africa," in van Diepen, *The National Question in South Africa*, pp. 30–55.

41. Fine, "The Antinomies of Nationalism and Democracy," 98.

42. A writer using the pseudonym "Dialego" described the political implications of the "colonialism of a special type" thesis: "Democracy is the essential precondition for socialist advance and the national question is indissolubly linked to this democratic stage. The question of working class emancipation as such cannot be posed until workers have a nation in which they can be emancipated: the oppressed black people of South Africa cannot begin to raise the question of a specifically proletarian character until the question of citizenship and nationhood has been settled. As Kodane emphasized in his celebrated Cradock letter, 'the majority of the African working population are more national conscious than class conscious,' and this will necessarily remain so until the Freedom Charter becomes a reality. Socialist consciousness only arises through national democratic struggle. Only when formal and legalized race discrimination is removed will the precise mechanism of class discrimination stand revealed." *The African Communist*, no. 111 (Fourth Quarter, 1987): 23–24.

43. See also Bill Freund, "Some Unasked Questions on Politics: South African Slogans and Debates," *Transformation* 1 (1986): 118–29.

44. See No Sizwe [Neville Alexander], *One Azania, One Nation: The National Question in South Africa* (London: Zed Books, 1977).

45. Alexander, "An Approach to the National Question," 7.

46. Neville Alexander, "Nation and Ethnicity," *Sow the Wind* (Johannesburg: Skotaville Press, 1985), pp. 53–54.

47. Tom Nairn, "The Modern Janus," *New Left Review*, no. 94 (1975): 3–29.

48. Fine, "The Antinomies of Nationalism and Democracy," 102–3.

49. Alec Erwin, "The Question of Unity in Struggle," *South African Labour Bulletin* 11, no. 1 (1985): 53.

50. Fine, "The Antinomies of Nationalism and Democracy," 104.

51. See Martin J. Murray, *The Revolution Deferred: The Painful Birth of Post-Apartheid South Africa* (London and New York: Verso, 1994).

Ethnicity, Religion, and National Politics in India

Even though four decades have passed since India became independent, doubts remain in the minds of many regarding its future as a viable nation-state. Every now and again commentaries on the Indian political situation fill with speculation about how long Indian unity will hold.[1] These speculations are inspired by Western notions of the nation-state where ideally language, religion, and political sovereignty have coterminous boundaries. Notwithstanding the fact that such notions disregard the historical processes by which some nationalities were subsumed by more powerful nationalities in the making of modern Western nation-states, the belief that language and religion, in their pristine form, are the twin ballasts of national identity is almost universal.

India deliberately rejected this understanding of the nation-state. From the early decades of the twentieth century, when the independence movement began to take shape in the subcontinent, it was clear to Indian nationalists that liberation from colonial domination must necessarily be all-Indian in character. Factions that did not share this viewpoint were assiduously encouraged by the British rulers. One of these was the Muslim League, which argued that only religion could be the basis of an enduring nation-state. Hindu nationalist organizations with the same conviction indirectly helped the British administrators to rationalize their decision to undermine the secular nationalist parties, such as the Indian National Congress, which since 1920 had been the dominant representative of the nationalist urge in the subcontinent. In order to subvert this impulse, colonial policy played upon the xenophobic sentiments of Hindu and Muslim organizations.[2]

In this chapter I argue that the acceptance of cultural and linguistic differences is no superficial acquiescence but is the enduring basis on which Indian politics is played out. In the following pages I test this proposition against historical instances where cultural passions of one form or another have loomed large on India's political stage since independence. The terrain on which this argument is tested is certainly not a hospitable one at first sight, but it is in the context of such inhospitable circumstances that one comes to appreciate the claims to endurance of the Indian nation-state. During all of these episodes, the political center, which both symbolizes and actively demonstrates the unity, coherence, and political sovereignty of the Indian nation-state, was never questioned or inauthenticated.[3] It is hoped that this exercise will provide a clearer perspective on the question of cultural differences with respect to the Indian nation-state. Perhaps as a consequence the Eurocentrism behind the Western formulation of the nation-state will also become readily apparent.

NATION-STATES AS ORIGINAL COMBINATIONS

It may be useful to begin by recalling some of the peculiarities that characterize India and that make the Indian experience as a modern nation-state not only different from the Western model but also different from the experiences of other newly liberated nation-states throughout the world.

It is not as if the Indian subcontinent was unified for the first time under British imperial rule. The boundaries of the Mauryan Empire, which flourished from the fifth century B.C. to the first century B.C., were also confined largely to the limits of the subcontinent. This was true as well of the Gupta Empire, which came five centuries later, and of the more recent medieval Mogul Empire, especially during the sixteenth and seventeenth centuries. It is interesting that none of these empires spread into areas that are today's Iran, Russia, and China. Even China, whose cultural homogeneity is certainly greater than India's, was a segment of the larger empire of the Mongols during the period of the Yuan Empire in the thirteenth century. Are the high mountains in the north and the great waters in the south responsible for India's uniqueness? Or should the responsibility be placed at the door of the caste system whose peculiarity characterizes Indian society and culture? Does one also have to consider the fact that educational and religious centers all over the subcontinent were esteemed and revered by different regional and linguistic groups throughout India? The fact is that India existed as a cultural and social entity, in spite of its diversity, even before it became a modern political entity.[4]

The division of India between British India and the princely states did not, however, hold back in any appreciable manner the unified formation of the Indian-nation state. The various presidencies of Bombay, Calcutta, and Madras had their own institutions of higher learning, and yet each of these presidencies threw up the most ardent nationalist leaders. One might also note in this connection that the internal administrative boundaries of colonial rule in India were not respected in the formation of provinces after India became independent. If nation-states are imagined communities, then the only way to do justice to this conceptualization is not to impose formats borrowed from Western experiences, within which such imaginings must necessarily take place. Nor should one be tempted to consider the histories of postcolonial countries as limited to the colonial experience alone. The Indian case should make at least this much clear.

LINGUISTIC, NATIVIST, AND REGIONAL POLITICS

There have been three great occasions in India's short postindependence history that threatened to negate the optimists' projections. The first erupted shortly after independence, when the demand for unilingual states (or provinces) arose in large areas of the subcontinent. The second followed soon after natives of these unilingual states demanded that economic opportunities in their states be reserved preponderantly for them. The third great occasion is the contemporary demand for greater autonomy for the states in economic matters. Superficially viewed these three disputes can be seen as manifestations of an original and unquenchable sentiment that the structure of the Indian nation-state cannot contain. The political center is viewed as coercive for it exerts various kinds of pressure to unite culturally distinct groups ranged in various degrees of opposition. According to this line of reasoning, the linguistic, the nativistic, and the more contemporary regional movements are all expressions of an original and restless cultural disaffection among the different "nationalities" forced to cohabit in the Indian nation-state.

It would be more revealing, however, if one were to examine these three movements in terms of their central demands, their constraints, and the nexuses they activate. While such an exercise is rarely, if ever, undertaken, it would qualify the superficial similarities between them. These ostensible similarities appear to argue for conceptualizing the three different movements as one, such that the last is visualized as a fuller efflorescence of the first.[5] In my opinion this does an injustice to the realities of the situation.

Although I discuss these three kinds of political mobilizations sequentially, they have not occurred in wholly separate temporal phases. Indeed, on many occasions they are temporally superimposed. This, however, ought not to invalidate the fact that nativist and regional movements are powered by distinct and separate motivations.

In the case of linguistic movements (i.e., those movements demanding a unilingual state), it was their insistence upon a primordial identity based on language that bound the partisans into a coherent political group and signified them as "natives." Doubtlessly, certain economic issues accompanied the linguistic demands, but the right of natives to govern their state or province of origin, in their own tongue, was the all-important concern. The Samayukta Maharashtra Samiti and the Maha Gujarat movements of the 1960s, which campaigned respectively for the unilingual provinces of Maharashtra and Gujarat, are instances of such mobilizations.

The demand for unilingual states had more or less subsided by the late 1960s. Its last great mobilization was the campaign for the formation of the unilingual state of Punjab. Once that was acceded to in 1969, political campaigns of this kind slowly lost their appeal. But soon after the most significant demands for states defined by language had been met on a national scale, India witnessed the emergence of "nativistic" movements.

The protagonists of these movements claimed that linguistic autonomy was not enough; it had to be supplemented by tangible economic opportunities. For example, the Shiv Sena, active in Bombay during the 1960s and 1970s, demanded that at least 80 percent of the jobs and economic opportunities in Bombay be reserved for the Marathi-speaking people of Maharashtra. Nativistic activists argued that Bombay was after all the provincial capital of Maharashtra and that its language and culture should be predominantly Maharashtrian.

In the case of regional movements, language and nativism per se were not central issues. Their demands were primarily economic and were specific to the region, and the fact that the region also happened to be largely populated by members of a single linguistic group did not substantially alter their character.

It is important to establish the separate identities of nativist, linguistic, and regional mobilizations because the experiences of the three are markedly different.[6] These differences are also accentuated to a significant extent by the way in which the Congress Party and other national parties have interacted with each movement. It is only by concentrating on this web of interaction that the distinctions between the three kinds of movements can be clearly drawn. Moreover, if it is to be shown that such political impulses are not inimical to the political unity of India (or to the notion of a political center), then it is just these types of objective factors that need to be focused on inasmuch as they reflect not only the constraints on subnational movements and their respective organizations but also the conditions of their origin.

Finally, this chapter has been prompted by a somewhat paradoxical observation. As these movements progress from primordial to secular economic demands, the federal government seems to become progressively more maladroit. In other words, the central government seems more at home and comfortable with ethnic-based movements than with those focused upon secular economic demands. The pages that follow will try to substantiate this formulation.

INDEPENDENCE AND THE HINDU-MUSLIM DIVIDE

Independent India inherited a great many things from its colonial past. Among them was the fear, a persistent undertow, that the cultural diversity of the subcontinent would soon bring about the fragmentation of the Indian state. The immediate partition of the subcontinent into India and Pakistan appeared to validate these apprehensions. A moment's reflection will tell us, however, that the partition was not a necessary or logical outcome of the Indian national movement.

The stated objective of the participants in the national movement, including the Communists, was not the division of India between Hindus and Muslims but political independence from the British in the subcontinent. As a matter of fact every time the Hindu-Muslim divide surfaced politically, it constituted a setback for the national movement and weakened its bargaining power. The demand for division on purely religious grounds was not the logical culmination of the national movement but grew on its fringe, preying on its inconsistencies.[7] The personal proclivities of some leading nationalists and the symbols that they often and quite spontaneously adopted were utilized to rationalize the demands for Pakistan as these symbols and proclivities did not explicitly disavow the possibility of communalist interpretations.[8] In some other cases Hindus in leadership positions in the Congress Party quite clearly expressed chauvinist sentiments. These leaders gave the nationalist program a Hindu character[9] that was justifiably resented by large numbers of Muslims in India. This strain continues even in contemporary India, but it would be an exaggeration to say that it is a dominant theme in Indian politics today.

Religion-based politics, whether Sikh, Hindu, or Muslim, has a limited future in India. Even Hindu politics is constrained by the fact that nationally nearly 40 percent of the population will never identify with the Hindu cause.[10] This includes the minorities and the scheduled or so-called untouchable castes and tribes. Therefore the impact of such politics will also be local and will depend on local population characteristics. By the same token scheduled caste and tribe political mobilizations must necessarily be supralocal in character as these groups are locally overwhelmed. In terms of their consequences to the Indian union, such religious mobilizations pose little threat to the integrity of the nation-state; they threaten humanity more.

Partition could have been an ideal opportunity for the Hindu nationalists to make India a Hindu state.[11] This, however, would only have been possible if separatist forces detrimental to the unity of India had not been politically overwhelmed during the years of the nationalist movement. This too is an aspect of India's "original" combination.

During this period of national struggle there were two distinct movements: One brought about the partition of India and the other political independence from the British. The former never participated in the mass upheavals of the latter but was content instead to remain angularly positioned, elbowing and tugging at the seams of the latter movement, willing it to fall apart. The Muslim League did not demand a Pakistan free from British domination but from what it saw as Hindu domination. It was because India got independence that the Muslim League got its Pakistan.

But after independence, and after the partition, the center and its "men of straw," as the British officials often dubbed the Indian nationalists, did not come crashing down. Slowly, almost unbelievably, the central government consolidated itself. Cultural diversities remained, regional inequalities persisted and some were heightened, and yet a separatist impulse could not work itself to the fore. Cultural disparities and regional inequalities continued to spur discontent, as they had in British India, and now the mobilizations on their behalf were better organized. But at all these flash points the existence of the central government, as we shall soon see, was never seriously threatened.

To demonstrate this let us look more closely at the interactions between the central government, the national parties, and the different subregional organizations, beginning first with the linguistic movements.

LINGUISTIC MOVEMENTS

In the mid-1950s the demand for unilingual states enveloped the whole country, necessitating the formation of the States Reorganization Commission to draw the boundaries between the different provinces of the country. All national parties, as well as local branches of Congress, participated in these movements, sometimes taking positions contrary to those of the national Congress Party leadership, which did not want any more upheavals so soon after independence. While it is true that the majority of participants were explicitly parochial and even primordial in their outlook, the leaders of the movement were not portrayed simply as regional heroes but as nationalists who had the interests of the nation uppermost. They were thorough patriots and it was their patriotic duty to India to demand unilingual states.[12]

The demand for unilingual states was not seen either by its partisans or by the national Congress Party leadership as anti-India or antinational. This is because the Congress in the 1920s had explicitly proclaimed, as part of its charter, that once independence was won India would be administratively demarcated on linguistic lines. It was felt that provincial boundaries thus delineated would encourage greater participation at the lower levels and help to root democracy deep in Indian soil. This is why national parties had little ideological reluctance to enter the agitation for linguistic states.

The other reason why national parties could participate wholly in these linguistic movements was that states could be linguistically demarcated without damaging the language rights of any other major linguistic community. The Congress-run federal government, however, did not initiate this demand; the party had just come to power, and political stability was its major concern. But once the issue arose, all national parties, including local chapters of the Congress, came together to form movements, like the Samayukta Maharashtra Samiti, while retaining their separate organizations. The national Congress Party leadership was not intrinsically opposed to the demand for unilingual states, but by virtue of being in control of the central government they had to arbitrate the somewhat exaggerated claims of each linguistic community and at the same time consider (or appear to consider) the interests of those like the Gujaratis in Bombay.[13]

Since pressure for a unilingual system originated with the national parties, the various linguistic movements reinforced each other and perforce became caught up in national politics. The national Congress Party leaders did not oppose the formation of linguistic states, and in fact the party had announced such a plan long before independence came to India. What caused them difficulty was not the principle behind the demands but how best to accede to them without sacrificing its political bases, or potential bases, in various geographic areas and among different linguistic communities.

By 1960 the demand for the formation of unilingual states in India had been satisfied, and the various national parties that had joined together in coalitions, like the Samayukta Maharashtra Samiti, withdrew from such alliances and returned to business as usual. On the occasions when efforts were made to revive these coalitions, the response was near indifference, both nationally and, what was worse, subnationally.

The linguistic movements proved that they were not antagonistic to the notion of a strong union and were, if anything, hostile to their neighboring states, not because they opposed the formation of linguistic states elsewhere but because of rival territorial claims. The ruling Congress Party was also not opposed to such demands, although it did not directly participate in their genesis. It seemed to equivocate because it had to arbitrate, and rise above, the demands of each linguistic community. Its major problem was to handle territorial claims involving disputes along the proposed borders separating contiguous linguistic states, or involving major cities like Bombay or Chandigarh, which rival linguistic groups claimed. But at no stage was the political unity of India ever questioned, nor, as I have tried to demonstrate, were the organizations that supported the linguistic movements even remotely separatist or antifederationist in character.

NATIVIST MOVEMENTS

Before the 1960s were over, and well after linguistic divisions had been accepted as a basis for the formation of states in the Indian union, another movement began. The "sons of the soil," as the partisans of the nativist movement called themselves, began to demand that they be given the major if not the sole right to work the land of their linguistic states and to reap the economic benefits of their labors without interference from people belonging to other linguistic communities. While their demand was economic, it was mediated through specific linguistic identities. The national parties could not take advantage of this groundswell, and organizations that were explicitly local and nativistic in their nomenclature and orientation emerged. They began haltingly and unambitiously; but before many could look back to redefine their positions, they were swept up in a staggering wave of popular sympathy.[14]

The Shiv Sena of the 1960s and 1970s and the Assam campaign, which culminated in 1985, may be considered examples of this movement. In both cases enemies were seen as within, as aliens who by careful manipulation denied the indigenous population the economic benefits offered by their native state. Their economic demands thus entailed a vital linguistic element, and it was through discrimination on linguistic grounds that these demands were sought to be resolved. The development of Assam or the development of Bombay, of course, figured in the many pronouncements made by the two movements but never formed the basic core of their demands. The principal enemies of such movements were not other states; rather, it was the linguistic groups from these other states who were seen as threats by the natives. If the states from which these aliens came were criticized, it was because of presumed policies that sought to encourage the exploitation of the aggrieved state or region through their "agents." Only some states were singled out as particularly offensive, and never was the whole country held responsible. In fact, nativist movements acknowledged that it was only through the machinery of the federal government that their grievances could be redressed. If these movements were critical of the national government, it was because of its irresolute attitude toward those whom they considered to be aliens. In other words, if the government became the enemy at all, it was not a generic one and the hostility shown toward it was reactive.

The Congress and other national parties, with the exception of the Communists, were not averse to arriving at agreements with the nativist forces. This was of course difficult in the first stages of these movements, when other linguistic groups in the country were chosen as targets. This meant no national party could align with the movements without risking its political bases elsewhere in the country. Gradually the Shiv Sena in Bombay shifted its attention away from the South Indians and concentrated instead on the Communists. By 1968 the Communists had become their principal target, for, they argued, while a South Indian was still an Indian, a Communist owed allegiance to Russia and China.[15] By 1980 the Assam movement too moved away from being anti-Bengali to becoming hostile to Muslim immigrants from Bangladesh. Once the principal enemy was defined as "extraterritorial," the national parties found their voice. But more interesting is the fact that these nativist movements (that later established themselves as political parties) were compelled by various political realities to change their targets and enter the political mainstream.

National parties and national politics surely had a role to play in altering the principal focus of these nativist movements. However, the major beneficiaries were the nativist forces who won the measure of national legitimacy that was essential for their continued survival. This newly acquired legitimacy also sheltered them from a full-scale attack by the government's coercive apparatuses, a fate reserved for oppositionist elements that could be successfully portrayed as antinational by the ruling party. Additionally, it was now legitimate for the national parties, including the Congress, to negotiate openly with the Shiv Sena or with the All Assam Students' Union (ASSU). The right-wing Bharatiya Janata Party supported the major demands of the ASSU, and all noncommunist parties nationwide, including the Congress, have from time to time made accommodations with the Shiv Sena in Bombay. The nativist forces too complied. The Shiv Sena stepped up its anticommunist activities, which included assassinations and strike breaking, and the Assam movement leapfrogged from one peak of anti-

Bangladeshi violence to another, until it captured provincial power in Assam in 1985.

REGIONAL MOVEMENTS

Unlike the nativist movements and their somewhat shaky efforts to become political parties, the regional movements gave rise to stable party formations. The Akali Dal, the Dravida Munnetra Kazhagam (DMK), and the Telugu Desam parties are convincing examples of this.

Over time the federal government learned to react to them as it would to any opposition group, but in their initial stages it viewed the emergence of regional parties with great alarm, not only because they were stable political contenders but also because the growth of such parties, and their subsequent viability, depended upon their single-minded hostility toward the national government. Unlike the other movements, the regional movements were thus against the central government first and foremost. Consequently, the development of regional party formations meant the attenuation of political support for the party in power. The federal government's response to such regional parties is not equivocal, as it sees such parties as clear political rivals.

The opposition parties that are national in character may react to the emergence of regional parties variously. Usually, however, they seek some kind of political understanding with the regional organizations, hoping thereby to share their mass support and weaken the party in power, which they believe is the main obstacle to their own assumption of power at the national level. This support also aids the regional party by enhancing its credibility, a very significant factor in its fledgling years.

Unlike the case of the nativist parties, when the opposition parties support such regional organizations they do not necessarily endanger their bases in other states. An important feature of regional parties is that they have no essential quarrel with other states; their dispute is only with the central government. If they do attack any one state in particular, it is usually over a peripheral issue, and then too the center is seen as the provocateur inciting that province to take a hostile stand.

The appeal of these regional movements is limited to the boundaries of particular states or provinces. The Akali Dal, the Telegu Desam, and the Dravida Munnetra Kazhagam are respectively limited to Punjab, Andhra Pradesh, and Tamil Nadu. By virtue of circumscribing their areas of influence in this fashion, these parties can never hope to capture national power on their own. This, however, does not deter them from playing politics at the national level by aligning with other regional and national parties. This is true of all the known regional parties in India today.

It needs also to be acknowledged that none of these regional parties has ever publicly or actively disowned a particular sector of the population of their state or province and classified it as "alien." The Akali Dal, in spite of being a Sikh-based party, is compelled to consider the non-Sikh Punjabis as full-fledged Punjabis, no matter what the private opinions of some Sikh leaders may be. The Assam Ganatantrik Parishad (heir to the ASSU movement) is compelled to consider the Bodo tribals as one with the nontribal Assamese today, though the Bodos do not quite accept this designation. As a matter of fact the nativist ASSU movement in Assam assumed regional power as the Assam Gana Parishad Party once it accepted that persons of Bangladeshi origin who had settled in Assam since 1971 were full-fledged Assamese.

The point is that, in spite of their ethnic labels and provincial sway, these regional parties have no ethnic enemies. Therefore, their strivings for power must necessarily be expressed in economic demands that address the needs of their particular region. The question that naturally arises here is the following: Given the economic nature of their demands, why is it the regional and not the national parties who are more successful in mobilizing local sentiment on these demands? Tentatively, we might answer in the following way.

The primary and most important aim of the national parties is to gain control of the federal government. They thus find it difficult to identify themselves exclusively with the demands of a particular state. As long as the demands from several states coincide or overlap, there is no major obstacle. But when the people of a state demand special consideration from the national government, the national parties find themselves unable to sponsor such demands. If they could, regional politics in the form of regional parties would probably not have become so dominant in the first place.

The ruling party and the regional parties are inherently hostile to each other, and the national opposition parties at best can play only a peripheral supportive and oppositional role. But does this mean that with the emergence of regional parties the Indian union is likely to collapse? Or, to put it more sharply, will regional movements jeopardize the future of India as a political union?

In this context one has to recognize two additional characteristics of the relationship between the regional parties and the national government. First, the one supreme fact that may rob a regional party of its significance is the absence of a central government. Parties are regional when they are opposed to the party in power. Moreover, they get additional justification when the party controlling the national government is strong and cannot easily be dislodged. If the center is itself unstable, much of the motivation behind regional parties is lost. Therefore, the fate of regional parties is to a considerable extent determined by the character of the center and is not independent of it; nor are these parties autonomously propelled. Alternatively, if the center is made up of a coalition of regional parties, then the regional parties become national parties in an important sense. This in fact has happened at various times with the DMK and Akali Dal. One must therefore consider these facts before one can say with confidence that the center will not hold if the current spate of regional parties continues to be active or that regional parties by their very existence threaten the survival of India as a political union with a center.

It is worth noting in this context that, in spite of the recurrence of centrifugal forces that appear hostile to the Indian union as a political entity, there has not been to date any major movement or political party in the subcontinent that has had the destruction of the center as its stated goal. Nor, it may be added, is any one of them logically positioned to bring about this eventuality. Why India has never thrown up a viable separatist political culture is an issue well worth investigating, and probably answers are not difficult to find. However, this chapter is primarily concerned with whether the movements and parties that have been assumed to attack the political unity of India did in fact do so. The division of such organizations into regional, nativist, and linguistic groupings has helped in analyzing how the center, the opposition parties, and the subnational organizations and parties have actually interacted. At no stage do we find the extirpation of the center to offer any particular advantage to any of these bodies; rather, its destruction likely to be particularly disadvantageous for them.

Furthermore, it is not cultural diversity so much as economic disparity that is a potent source of subnational political formations in India today. Neither linguistic nor nativist movements can approximate the enduring structure of regional parties. The fact that even regional parties have not led to the splintering of India's political union, as I have tried to argue, is true at one level. But at another level it could be said that the most potent variety of subnational politics in India is fed not so much by cultural diversities, or by unquenchable primordialism, as it is by regional economic inequalities.

ETHNICIZATION IN REVERSE: THE CASE OF PUNJAB

In the previous pages we found that the modern Indian nation-state has had no major problems in handling issues of cultural diversity such as it has had with economic and secular regional issues. As the structure of the Indian union is severely tested by economic and secular regional demands, the central government tries to portray these issues as ethnic and cultural ones. The case of Punjab points to this conclusion.

Nowhere in the much-disputed Akali Dal resolution (the so-called Anandpur Sahib Resolution of 1978)[16] did the Akali Dal Party demand the dissolution of India. More than nine-tenths of the document is concerned with secular and economic issues. But Mrs. Gandhi and the Indian government successfully portrayed the resolution as antinational, as both ethnic and secessionist in essence, and this characterization roused the "one nation" sentiment of the whole country against it. This was possible primarily because the Akali Dal is largely a party of Sikhs and thus a Sikh-Hindu schism could be activated on a national scale.

A glance at the Punjab situation would be revealing in this connection. While it does not exemplify a host of other tactics that the Congress Party has used to combat regional parties, Punjab nevertheless suggests how ethnicity may be used by the party in power to gain leverage against secular regional opposition. From 1980 onwards the Akali Dal has agitated on three principal issues. The first is that Chandigarh should be the capital of the state of Punjab alone.[17] (Today Chandigarh is in the anomalous position of being the capital both of Punjab and of the contiguous state of Haryana.) The second is for a greater share in the river waters that flow through Punjab. Finally, it wants the borders of Punjab redrawn to include Punjabi-speaking areas that are now excluded. Of the three issues, the first (i.e., the demand for Chandigarh) was the most transparently just: Mrs. Gandhi had herself declared in 1970 that Chandigarh would be the capital of Punjab and that it was built with that purpose in mind. On river waters and on territorial claims the Akali Dal demanded that the questions be referred to the Supreme Court and to the Territorial Commission respectively, and they agreed to accept the verdict of these bodies. The demands, such as they were, were expressed in such seemingly noncontrovertible terms that the government's dithering over them increased the credibility of the Akali Dal among the Sikhs and gave birth to the belief among this community that the Congress-ruled government was anti-Sikh. This belief was accentuated by the support given to the Congress by the Punjabi Hindus, who resented the Sikh domination of Punjabi politics. It should also be noted that the Hindus in Punjab are primarily settled in urban areas and are not much interested in the dispute over river waters anyway. Historically too, the Hindus in Punjab, through the Arya Samaj movement, kept up a near-rabid Hindu revivalist posture against the Sikhs, and many even went to the extent of claiming Hindi and not Punjabi as their mother tongue.

On Chandigarh, river waters, and territorial claims, the Akali Dal also faced opposition from the states of Haryana and Rajasthan. Both states depend upon Punjab rivers for irrigation. The fact that Akali Dal never said that it would terminate the flow of water outside Punjab, but merely that the terms of agreement should be referred to the Supreme Court, never received much publicity. Moreover, Haryana also began to claim Chandigarh for itself, and politicians from Haryana feared that they would lose credibility in their own state if they did not oppose the Akali Dal demands in toto.

The Akali Dal's position on the sanctity of the Indian nation-state was clarified in the Anandpur Sahib Resolution. The first point contained therein is a reaffirmation of the Indian union. More than nine-tenths of the resolution, as I have said, are devoted to economic, federal, and territorial matters. A small section talks of how the Akali Dal should keep Sikh tradition alive and combat atheism. The Akali Dal is after all a communal organization and must therefore speak about Sikh traditions. But the space devoted to this issue does not in any case exceed one-tenth of the full text of the resolution.

The national Congress Party leadership, however, chose not to address the major demands of the resolution but emphasized instead the argument that the Anandpur Sahib Resolution was secessionist in character. This falsehood was proclaimed widely, including by the late Indira Gandhi. The mass media were pressed into service for this cause, and everyone but the Sikhs became convinced of the secessionist character of the Akali Dal initiative. The government also publicized spurious versions of the resolution that did not bear the imprimatur of the Akali Dal leadership. In this manner a secular and regional movement was "ethnicized" by the national government—another version, perhaps, of the empire striking back. The June 1984 Army operation in the holiest of Sikh shrines, the Golden Temple in Amritsar, and then the senseless assassination of Mrs. Gandhi by two Sikhs, consolidated this process of ethnicization.[18] Rajiv Gandhi used the rift to great advantage in corraling an unprecedented number of votes for the Congress in the 1984 national elections, arguing that the country must unite in opposing Sikh secessionism. The success of the Congress left established opposition parties like the Bharatiya Janata Party (BJP) in a shambles. Large numbers of voters who had in previous years supported the BJP deserted it for Rajiv's Congress, feeling that under his leadership India would remain united. This once again demonstrates how regional parties get sidelined if the people perceive the center as being threatened.

It should not be forgotten that during this phase of Akali agitation in Punjab the central government was quite responsive to many of the ethnic aspects of the Akali demands but never to their secular and economic aspects. It willingly conceded to a transmitter being set up in the Golden

Temple for relaying the holy scriptures; and it also was more than willing to concede to a separate Sikh Code Bill to govern matters relating to marriage and inheritance, just as the Muslims in India have a separate Code Bill. But the Akali Dal's secular, economic, and political demands were studiously avoided and actively ethnicized. The issue of the Code Bill was, however, never fully discussed inasmuch as all attention was concentrated on the question of secession. The government claimed that the Akalis were separatists, and the Akalis responded by denying the charge and adding that the federal government was becoming increasingly Hindu.

Surprisingly, after Rajiv Gandhi came to power, an agreement between the national government and the Akali Dal was reached in August 1985. While preparing for this agreement, Rajiv Gandhi publicly declared that the Anandpur Sahib Resolution was not a secessionist document, certainly a dramatic turnaround.[19]

The crucial issue that won over the Sikh masses related to the handing over of Chandigarh to Punjab on January 26, 1986. But the government reneged on its promise. Moderates in the Akali Dal who came to power on the strength of the accord were disgraced, and the Punjab tangle was ethnicized with renewed vigor.[20] During all these years the government has not dealt with established moderate Sikh leaders in attempting to negotiate a lasting solution in Punjab, but has instead, on more than one occasion, sponsored a known Sikh religious militant and criminal, Jasbir Singh Rode, as chief of the sacred Sikh shrine, the Golden Temple.[21] In this process of reverse ethnicization, not only is the Akali Dal portrayed by the Congress as fomenting secession from the Indian union but the other regional parties are also accused of abetting this process.

Casting political disputes that are not necessarily sectarian as minority or ethnic issues is a tool the government has increasingly resorted to. It is sometimes argued that if the government in power headed the economic demands issuing from different regions it would jeopardize the class coalition on which it survives. This makes it tempting to distort regional demands instead and to castigate regional groups for allegedly promoting the break-up of India. The fact that this strategy is seen as a feasible option, and one that has repeatedly worked in the past, is an indication that nation-state imaginings have left a much deeper impression on Indian politics than most commentators and scholars acknowledge. Concurrently, one must also note that, in spite of the national government's striking back ethnically, it must continually portray itself as the protector of cultural differences. This paradox is firmly embedded in Indian national politics and will constrain all aspirants to central power today and in the future. This is why no one can confidently conclude that the Indian variant of the nation-state has exhausted its potentiality.

We should not, however, ignore the grave dangers inherent in the national government's ethnic strategy. In this process of reverse ethnicization, the community that has been stigmatized may eventually become a reluctant partner in the Indian nation-state. Fortunately, even today the Sikh majority in Punjab show no inclination toward secession even though they feel very strongly about the way they have been suddenly marginalized. Over time, this resentment may strengthen and evolve into a separatist sentiment, but the Indian union is not likely to dissolve as a result, for the central government, as I noted earlier, must also portray itself as a protector of differences. Yet ethnicization in reverse introduces social dynamics whereby differences are not celebrated or amicably reconciled but instead are forcibly held in line. It must be remembered that such tensions are not inevitable accompaniments to the cultural differences that make up the Indian union but arise because the ruling party actively promotes an ethnicization of specific secular options in politics to stay in power.

CONCLUSION

It is hoped that this study, by separating linguistic, nativist, and regional politics in terms of their principles, agencies, motivations, and interactions, demonstrates that cultural differences in India pose no threat to the Indian union, nor do they exist in their pristine "irreconcilable" form when they are politically manifested. The three kinds of political movements are separate and distinct. In each case, the national government, the opposition parties, and the subnational or local political formations interact differently, activating different ideologies. Nor do we find that the nation-state, or the center, is ever threatened by the three forms of political mobilization and activism. Paradoxically, it is when the center plays the ethnic card in response to secular regional demands that the Indian union faces its gravest threat. Thus it is not cultural differences per se, but defects in statecraft that strain the Indian nation-state.

This chapter begins with the observation that each nation-state is constructed differently. Unique and original features are contained in the sentiments and structures of nation-states, but, as all of them are "constructed," a certain self-consciousness must accompany all imaginings of a nation-state, Indian or Western. This chapter argues, through an examination of linguistic, nativist, and regional movements, that for any mobilization to function in the political mainstream of India it must conform to the self-conscious sentiments underpinning the Indian nation-state. This argument runs parallel to the empirical and substantive demonstration that cultural differences have never actually threatened the viability of the Indian union.

POSTSCRIPT

In late 1992 the government began cracking down on Sikh militants in a concerted fashion, and today, as a consequence, there is no militancy worth its name in Punjab, nor are the Sikhs grieving about it. In fact there is relief among the Sikhs that the conflict has subsided, even though the issues are still unresolved. This outcome is contrary to the prediction of commentators who argued that Sikh culture and religion would push relentlessly for a separate state. The militants were admired at a distance by ordinary Sikhs, much as most people admire Robin Hood and daredevils. But this public sympathy did not generate in Punjab a mass movement for secession from India. Moreover, as the militants began to lose battles with the government, their charisma diminished. The interesting issue is why this crackdown was not initiated earlier. If the militants, or terrorists, could be defeated militarily in a few months, why was action not taken against them earlier? Nothing had really changed. It is true that some militants were disgracing themselves by looting and extortion, but this had always been the case. And yet in the past ordinary Sikhs had sympathized with the ideas of the militants without being militants themselves. Obviously the delay by the government was to teach a few political lessons, no matter how many lives were sacrificed needlessly in the process. Today politics in Punjab is suspect, and especially suspect are the various factions of the Akali Dal. If this was the government's intention, then it has eminently succeeded. Even so, it needs to be said that the chimera of Sikh secessionism was exaggerated by the government and by those who fell victim to their own prejudices.

NOTES

1. See Jyotirindra Das Gupta, *Language Conflict and National Development: Group Politics and National Language Policy* (Bombay: Oxford University Press, 1970), pp. 9–19.
2. Daniel Thorner, *The Shaping of Modern India* (New Delhi: Allied Publishers, 1980), pp. 85, 88.
3. I have kept movements in Mizoram and Nagaland in northeast India outside the scope of discussion in this chapter. In many ways these areas in the northeast have been forcibly subjugated into the Indian union. This however is not true for the rest of the country with which this essay is concerned.
4. Jawaharlal Nehru, *The Discovery of India* (Garden City, N.Y.: Anchor, 1960), pp. 27–32.
5. See D. L. Sheth, "State, Nations and Ethnicity: Experiences of Third World Countries," *Economic and Political Weekly* (Bombay) 24 (1989): 624–25.

6. Myron Weiner, *Sons of the Soil: Migration and Ethnic Conflict in India* (Delhi: Oxford University Press, 1978).

7. See Thorner, *The Shaping of Modern India*, pp. 85, 88.

8. Ibid., p. 63.

9. Walter Anderson and Shridhar Damle, *The Brotherhood in Saffron: The Rashtriya Swayamsevak Sangh and Hindu Revivalism* (New Delhi: Vistaar Publishers, 1987), pp. 28–29.

10. See S. S. Gill, "Casting Aspersions on Caste," *Indian Express* (Bombay), July 2, 1989.

11. Rajni Kothari, "Nation Building and Political Development," in S. C. Dube, ed., *India since Independence: Social Report on India* (Delhi: Vikas, 1977), p. 514.

12. Baldev Raj Nayar, *Minority Politics in Punjab* (Princeton, N.J.: Princeton University Press, 1966), p. 33.

13. See Dipankar Gupta, *Nativism in a Metropolis: The Shiv Sena in Bombay* (Delhi: Manohar Publishers, 1982), pp. 44–45.

14. Ibid., pp. 72–74.

15. Ibid., p. 190.

16. The Anandpur Sahib Resolution was formally ratified in 1978 by the Akali Dal. In 1978 Akali Dal was in power in Punjab and was supportive of the national government headed by the Janata Party. This resolution has since 1980 provided the basis for the Akali Dal's opposition to and continued agitation against the Congress. The Congress claimed that this was a secessionist document, and the Akali Dal went to great lengths to deny it.

17. Chandigarh was built as the capital of Punjab. But after 1969, when Punjab was broken up into three unilingual provinces (Punjab, Haryana, and Himachal Pradesh), Chandigarh continued as the capital of both Punjab and Haryana. This anomalous situation continues to this day.

18. See Dipankar Gupta, "The Communalizing of Punjab, 1980–85," *Economic and Political Weekly* 20 (1985).

19. Later, when the Akali Dal leader Sant Harchand Singh Longowal was assassinated, Rajiv Gandhi declared that Longowal was a nationalist who had been martyred for the cause of Indian unity. In 1988 the government issued postage stamps in memory of Longowal. In 1988 the Punjab governor's office in Chandigarh had two large portraits of equal size hanging on the wall—one of Rajiv Gandhi and the other of Longowal.

20. See Dipankar Gupta et al., "Punjab: Communalized beyond Politics," *Economic and Political Weekly* (Bombay) 23 (1988).

21. Ibid.

M. BAHATI KUUMBA

ONA ALSTON DOSUNMU

Women in National Liberation Struggles in the Third World

No society has accomplished the full liberation of its women. However, it can safely be argued that the status, opportunities, and general welfare of women in many Third World societies are dramatically improved following national liberation. Post–World War II anticolonial struggles have been fought in Asia, Africa, Latin America, and the Middle East.[1] Typically, their immediate goal is to wrest political control from the colonizer, a stage referred to as the national democratic revolution. It is sometimes followed by a process in which the working class and the peasants seize political power from the capitalists and landlords in a socialist revolution.[2] Women have been active in both levels of struggle.

The twentieth century has been replete with national liberation struggles. These struggles have led to the establishment of neocolonial states, bourgeois nationalist states, and socialist states boasting genuine changes in their socioeconomic and political structures. National liberation has been defined as a people's total control over their resources, the ability to provide food, health care, education, employment, and housing for the nation's population, and relative autonomy and independence in political affairs. Regardless of the immediate result, women have been key players in the process of national liberation and reconstruction because of their particular relationship to colonial regimes. They, along with their children, are generally the most oppressed and exploited by colonialism and its correlates, and they are certain to benefit the most from truly progressive change in their respective societies.

Most of this chapter's discussion of women in Third World liberation struggles focuses on the period from World War II to the late 1980s. Some of the struggles are of the classic anticolonial variety, such as those in Southern Africa; others strive to guarantee a minimum level of social welfare and self-determination, such as in Nicaragua. In both kinds of liberation struggles, it is through a recognition of the central role played by the women involved in them that their revolutionary nature can be discerned.

The national liberation struggles of the twentieth century have consistently expressed the dialectical relationship between the emancipation of women and the liberation of indigenous peoples from colonial and neocolonial oppression. They assert that, on one hand, national liberation is necessary for the true emancipation of women; on the other hand, the mobilization and participation of women is decisive for the success of the liberation struggle. Despite these historical facts, women's contributions to these efforts remain invisible and understudied because of the devaluation of women and their activities in both precolonial societies and colonial regimes.

This chapter seeks to address this void on the basis that women's participation and mobilization is indispensable for the success of the national liberation struggle. It seeks to examine not only the impact of women on the process of national liberation but also the transformative effects of the national liberation process itself on women. It can also be suggested that the extremely unusual circumstances brought about by war usually result in radical change in and among all sectors of society, including among women. Such a change may be short lived or it may be more rhetorical than real. Although temporary or rhetorical changes in the status of women cannot be equated with genuine institutional efforts to address the plight of women, they nonetheless provide an opportunity for women to continue to struggle for more fundamental transformations. As the nature and extent of women's participation and mobilization in the liberation struggle speaks to the true aims of the movement, the postnational liberation status of women is a litmus test for the truly liberating effects of the movement.

SOME THEORETICAL QUESTIONS

The proper evaluation of the participation of women in struggles for national liberation requires an examination of theoretical questions related to the status of women in society and the role of women in national liberation struggles. A balance must be struck between class, national, and gender oppression inasmuch as the oppression of women results from a combination of all three. Dual assumptions of gender as a material reality and the condition of women as historically determined will guide our analysis.

An examination of the historical development of society shows that while reproduction and its associated tasks create the conditions for a sexual division of labor, it is social definitions that make traditional women's work less important, less prestigious, and less deserving of recompense. While a sexual division of labor has been universal throughout human history, it has not always been hierarchical. Sexual stratification arose with increased production, occupational specialization, and the emergence of wealth and social classes. Although at the individual level the oppression of women operates through the actions of men, it is invariably linked to the existence of oppression in general. Consequently, the liberation of women is intricately connected to overall societal liberation from exploitative systems. Gender inequalities thus have their origins in the emergence and development of classes and exploitative relations of production. There is ample evidence that the subjugation of women preceded the emergence of capitalism and that the oppression of women has paralleled the development of class cleavages and class conflict.[3] Thus, the development of classes has been described as "the result of the revolutionary social changes which destroyed the egalitarian society of the matriarchal gens or clan and replaced it with a patriarchal class society which, from its birth was stamped with discriminations and inequalities of many kinds, including the inequalities of the sexes."[4] The oppression of women, then, is clearly linked to class oppression. This fact makes class analysis, which is necessary for the study of power and its distribution in a society where inequality exists, also necessary for an adequate understanding of the position of women in society.

Also implied is the need for an accompanying gender analysis. Socialist feminists argue that class oppression is a significant but not the sole determinant of women's position in society. By subsuming the woman question completely in the class question, they argue, important determinants of women's status are disregarded.[5] Ideological, cultural, religious, and various other social precepts and practices are viewed as important dimensions of social reality. Thus, according to Mohanty, "Women are constituted as women through the complex interaction between class, culture, religion, and other ideological institutions and frameworks."[6]

In approaching the question of women in national liberation struggles, clearly these other realms of women's subjugation have a significant impact on women's class exploitation and must therefore be treated as important dimensions of the general oppression of women. For example, religious and traditional beliefs often obstruct the full participation of women in society and in social movements. They can serve as significant barriers to women's liberation even after transformations on other planes have occurred.[7] This fact is apparent in Latin America and the Middle East, where Catholicism and Islam have arguably impeded the progress of women's liberation.

Finally, struggles for national liberation and for gender liberation are invariably linked. Because the oppression of women is used to perpetuate national oppression (and both have their basis in the continuation of colonial and neocolonial domination), the struggle for national liberation can be seen as a higher level of the struggle for gender equality. It also serves as a catalyst for the realization of gender equality.

Women's oppression and liberation must be placed in their broader, global context. The effects of imperialism as manifested in national oppression (i.e., subjugation of an indigenous society by an external power) must be treated as just as significant to an analysis of the woman question as considerations of capitalism and patriarchy are.[8] An understanding of the oppression and liberation of colonized women must incorporate an analysis of the emergence and status of their nations in relation to the world political economy.[9]

The systematic oppression of women, while having a particular character and form within various social systems, is an aspect of social divisions that exist within a society. Thus, the struggle that women have waged for the eradication of these systems can be argued to be the ultimate and highest expression of their fight for women's liberation.

The struggle for women's equality in a socialist context, and liberation in class society, is the struggle to reunify the familial and the social, the productive and reproductive processes, on the higher plane made possible by the advance of technology. Socialism and women's participation in production, necessary prerequisites to equality, are not sufficient in and of themselves. Political, economic, and ideological considerations simultaneously come into play. Similarly, national liberation and the participation of women in the struggle to bring it into being are necessary but insufficient components in the liberation of nationally colonized women. By viewing women's liberation as a process, rather than a fixed state or event, the national liberation struggle can more accurately be seen as one of its stages.

Both objective and subjective components affect women's success in achieving equality through the vehicle of national liberation. These components are dialectically related in sometimes complementary and sometimes contradictory ways. The national liberation struggle itself is a constant balancing act between the opposing forces of oppression and liberation. On one hand, it can provide a catalyst to such breakthroughs for women as the formation of women's organizations, the development of gender consciousness, and the opening of nontraditional roles and statuses. On the other hand, these same types of struggles have often proven incapable of maintaining the gains achieved during their most active periods. Evidence on this side of the issue includes the entrenchment of traditionally female roles that were politicized during the national liberation struggle, the assignment to women of subordinate positions in organizational and political party hierarchies, and reversals of progressive gains achieved after the success of the liberation struggle.[10] It is through the continual resolution and re-creation of these opposing tendencies on different levels that transformation in the conditions for women occurs.

What follows are case studies of national liberation struggles that exemplify the role women have played and continue to play in the struggle for national and sexual liberation.

SOUTHERN AFRICA

Nowhere has the participation of women in movements for national independence been more evident than in Southern Africa. The extreme nature of the apartheid regime that has controlled the region linked the African man, woman, and child in a commonality of oppression that has found expression in common struggle. In the independence movements of Angola (1961–75), Mozambique, (1964–75), and Namibia (1966–90), and the continuing struggle in South Africa, women have been active out of necessity. The intensity of these wars robbed women of the luxury of noninvolvement. They have been caught up in the struggle by virtue of their very presence in the region. Their roles have ranged from fully committed revolutionary activists, to supportive participants, to unintended participants involved because the conflict came to them.[11]

While the participation of these women spanned the continuum, it has often missed the limelight directed at more visible leaders, actions, and organizations. At the same time, however, women can be said to have been both the backbone and catalyst of the movements. This fact is succinctly summarized by Hilda Bernstein: "Although there is no doubt that the overt leadership has been dominated by men, the seemingly unacknowledged and informal segment of society controlled by women has been key to many of the most significant mass movements in South African history."[12]

Women's particularly active role in the region's national liberation struggles has been due in no small part to their direct relationship to the oppression experienced under the colonial regimes. While gender differentiation predated colonialism, existing differences became magnified and new ones were created under these regimes. In essence, national oppression found distinct expression among women.

The inseparable link between women's liberation and national liberation is highlighted in all of the Southern African struggles. All of the popular liberation organizations have shared the official position that the true emancipation of women can come about only through national liberation. In Mozambique they said, "it is against the system, that is, against colonialism and imperialism, that Mozambican women must direct their struggle."[13] In South Africa it was argued that "meaningful change for women cannot come through reform but only with the total destruction of the apartheid system."[14] In Angola "the interests of women are identified with the interests of the whole people of the nation."[15] The Namibian struggle for national independence was said to be "at the same time a struggle against racial, cultural oppression and dehumanization; against discrimination in all its forms including gender."[16]

Given the equally important emphasis placed by these movements on the other side of this dialectic—the necessity for mobilizing the women of the nation to insure the victory of the liberation struggle—the contribution of women to the struggle in these nations becomes decisive against a powerful enemy, for "constraints against women's full participation in the revolutionary process are clearly seen as detrimental to the advance of the whole people."[17] Both on a political and on a practical level, therefore, women's support for the national liberation process is viewed as crucial.

The framing of the woman question within that of national liberation is depicted by some as overlooking women's discrimination and oppression.[18] The Southern African case, however, has not been characterized by submerging or postponing the push toward women's equality. While definitely exhibiting uneven development, the gender and national liberation processes have tended to occur simultaneously. In the process of struggle, the status of Southern African women has been transformed. And in this, women's organizations and wings of the liberation movements have greatly facilitated the participation of Southern African women in their respective liberation movements.

Within the Southern African context of the liberation war, the traditional womanly roles, such as mother, nurturer, and cook, take on new meaning. To the extent that they sustain the struggle and maintain the nation, they become infused with revolutionary content and significance. The art of survival becomes revolutionary action.

The struggle also dictates that women perform new tasks often far removed from accepted female behavior. Participation in military activities is a prime example of this. In all of these societies, women in military combat stretched the limits of the traditional gender roles. The participation of women in armed combat required considerable alteration in the attitudes of both men and women. As Sandra Danforth points out, this level of activity in the liberation struggle "not only involves new roles and role relationships with men but brings about changes in the societal interpretations of the nature of women and of morally acceptable behavior."[19]

ANGOLA

The People's Movement for the Liberation of Angola (MPLA) recognized the need to mobilize all segments of the Angolan population to oust the Portuguese colonialists. The inclusion of women was inherent in this policy. As a result, women were encouraged to join the struggle very early in the liberation process. The formation of the Organization of Angolan Women (OMA) solidified this MPLA policy. Established in 1962, just a year after the initiation of armed struggle, its stated goals were to "mobilize Angolan women patriots for the tasks of national liberation, defining the ways in which they would participate, and establishing women's prospects in the Angolan context."[20]

The formation of the women's wing of the MPLA was supported by the official ideology of the MPLA, which stressed the linkages between the emancipation of society and the emancipation of women. In addition, the involvement of Angolan women in the struggle against colonialism had folkloric and historical support: "Angolan women could look to examples of heroines in their own history, particularly that of Queen Ginga, who in seventeenth-century Angola united a number of tribes and led the people's armed resistance against Portuguese colonialism for 30 years."[21] The popularizing of these ideological and historical references to women provided grounding for even more extensive participation by women in the liberation struggle.

The women's organization facilitated their involvement on all levels of the struggle and served as a link between women and other sectors of the movement. Charged with the mobilization and education of women around the liberation struggle, the OMA utilized many strategies in building popular support among women. One was to initiate a series of seminars, held in liberated zones at various periods of the liberation struggle. These seminars served the multiple purposes of increasing the mobilization and politicization of women, providing basic organizational training, and launching material aid and solidarity campaigns. These efforts also went a long way in developing grassroots skills and, at the same time, impacting the international community with information about the Angolan struggle.

The work and education brigades set up by the OMA, for example, concentrated on practical issues facing women and children in the liberated areas. Confronting matters ranging from child care and sewing classes to basic literacy and political education programs, the basic services and training offered to women often allowed them to make more intensive contributions to the movement. Most impressive was OMA's literacy campaign, for which the organization received UNESCO's Nadejda Krupskaya Literacy Award.

The contributions of women to the Angolan struggle that were facilitated by the OMA varied. While many of the roles played by women were in the realm of support, there was emphasis on viewing all contributions as equally necessary components of the struggle. OMA branches outside of Angola, for example, were active in the Voluntary Corps for Assistance to Refugees (CVAR); they provided health services and grew food for those displaced by the war.

Notable contributions inside the country, on the other hand, were made in the realms of medical assistance and telecommunications. Angolan women were active in the movement's Medical Assistance Service (SAM) as doctors, nurses, technicians, and first-aid assistants.[22] In addition to providing the masses with linkages to the liberation movement, as discussed earlier, Angolan women also provided the much-needed link between the movement and the international community. A large number of women received operator courses in the movement's Radio and Telecommunications Service. According to Marga Holness,

> women members of the MPLA and OMA performed all kinds of essential tasks. They wrote radio programs which were broadcast to Angola, prepared publications for distribution abroad, . . . and generally worked to make the Angolan people's struggle known throughout the world and to mobilize international humanitarian aid for the people in the liberated areas, particularly women and children.[23]

Women were also active in setting up agricultural cooperatives in the liberated areas. Again, an activity traditionally within the realm of women's work took on a political character in the midst of the struggle.

Angolan women actively engaged in military operations as well. March 2, 1967, marked the day when five female guerrilla soldiers of the Kamy column (an MPLA military detachment) were murdered. They had been "on an important mission in the MPLA's first military region in northern Angola . . . [and] were captured by the rival National Front for the Liberation of Angola (FNLA) and subsequently murdered in the notorious Kinkuzu camp in Zaire."[24]

This and other examples amply speak to the dedication of women within the Angolan liberation movement. The question then becomes how well the contributions of women have been reflected in the social life of postindependence Angola.

Upon close examination one finds numerous examples of discriminatory practices in Angola even after independence in 1975. A glaring disparity was the continued underrepresentation of women in the leadership bodies of the MPLA. By the time of the First Congress of the Organization of Angolan Women in 1983, there were only four women on the Central Committee of the MPLA.[25] An analysis of congress papers indicates that discriminatory legislation, women's inequality in the productive process, patriarchal and polygamous family relations, and a conservative view of the role of women still plagued postindependence Angola. While gender inequities continue to exist, the Organization of Angolan Women, both a creation of and actor in the liberation movement, provides a necessary vehicle to continue the process of women's emancipation into the reconstruction period.

MOZAMBIQUE

The involvement of Mozambican women in the liberation struggle began in 1966, just two years after the outbreak of armed struggle. At that time the Mozambican Liberation Front (FRELIMO) "decided that the Mozambican women should take a more active part in the struggle for national liberation, at all levels."[26] This heightened activity necessitated both political and military training for women, which began officially in 1967. While the number of women involved in the struggle at higher levels was relatively small, their contribution has been depicted as far out of proportion to their numbers.[27]

The first group of women to pass through training became known as the "Women's Detachment," which in 1969 merged into the Mozambican Women's League (LIFEMO). Militarily, many Mozambican women fought "shoulder to shoulder" with male guerrillas. However, the majority of women's military activity was "concentrated in the defense of the liberated areas, thus freeing the men for the offensive activities in the zones of advance."[28] Their position in the military aspect of the struggle also placed female fighters in closer proximity to the day-to-day survival struggles of Mozambican women. While facilitating women's military participation, the Women's Detachment also served important sociopolitical functions. From running orphanages to mounting literacy campaigns, the organization played a wide variety of roles in the struggle. Josina Machel, deceased wife of Samora Machel, first president of independent Mozambique, described the mission of the women's Detachment as follows: "Apart from its strictly military function the Women's Detachment has important political duties on two levels. At one level it is charged with the mobilization and education of the people. . . . We work at the next level of encouraging even more active participation by inviting people to follow our example."[29]

In 1972 the Organization of Mozambican Women (OMM) was formed. As part of the FRELIMO structure, it set out to enlist the broad masses of women and women's organizations in the Mozambican struggle. The very existence of women's organized participation in the Mozambican liberation movement served as a catalyst for their further involvement.

For Mozambican women, as with women in most liberation struggles, a major impediment to participation in the movement was internalized attitudes of inferiority resulting from the triple oppressions of nation, class, and gender that existed under colonial government. To contend with this internalized subservience, as well as the more objective barriers to participation among Mozambican women, the First Conference of Mozambican Women was held in 1973. The conference gave particular attention to the obstacles to the involvement of women in the movement and provided strategic direction to FRELIMO and the OMM for their eradication.

Postliberation Mozambique continues to harbor sexual divisions and inequalities. Much of the remaining disparities have been attributed to OMM's failure in "initiating, intervening and pushing the party in its formulation of policy toward women."[30] As a result, many of the policies and programs enacted since independence, such as agricultural reform, have had dire effects on women. Consequently, the potential strength of an organized structure through which women could influence governmental policy has not yet been fully realized. Despite this fact, Stephanie Urdang reminds us that "in Mozambique and other postrevolutionary societies, there are real gains that have been made by women. To ignore these and the kind of support—economic and political—that women get from their governments and political party is to ignore some real, tangible advances."[31]

NAMIBIA

In the Namibian struggle, surviving and maintaining the family and community structures in the face of constant onslaught was seen as a main form of women's resistance during the war of liberation.[32] Even reproduction took on added significance; women were seen as "reproducing the revolution." In fulfilling their function as life givers, they were actually giving birth to potential freedom fighters. Earlier days of resistance testify to the creative ways in which women utilized their particular resources toward the ends of liberation. In 1904–5 the Herero women of Namibia stopped bearing children and went on a "sex strike" to force the men into armed resistance against the German colonial occupiers.[33]

Other outgrowths of the nurturer role, such as the support that women gave to the freedom fighters, were also acclaimed. Not only was this practice extremely important for the success of guerrilla warfare, it was also very dangerous. For women in Namibia to shelter and feed SWAPO combatants or to store arms was to risk jail, torture, and death. As one Namibian solidarity group noted: "[O]ur fighters are very integral of course, but the women, even if they are very old, are the informers of our soldiers, the suppliers of food to our soldiers, the mobilizers of each other; they are just everything. Their active participation has cost so many of them so much."[34]

The degree to which the women of a community will physically support and protect its combatants is also a measure of the popular character and scope of the struggle. In this case, all of the Southern African struggles boast of this high level of support among the women of the communities.

The presence of women was felt from the beginning of the Namibian struggle against South African occupation in the late 1950s. They played a key role in the 1959 Windhoek protest against forced relocation into newly created reserves, an action that gave birth to the South West Africa People's Organization (SWAPO). So complete was their involvement in that protest that its date, December 10, was proclaimed Namibian Women's Day. The racist regime's violent reaction to the protest, which resulted in twelve protesters killed and thirty injured, gave an initial impetus to women joining the movement. This was especially the case among the young Namibian women who saturated the ranks of the militant SWAPO Youth League (SYL).[35]

The founding of the SWAPO Women's Council (SWC) in 1969 provided Namibian women a new avenue for participation. The SWC encouraged the active participation of Namibian women and, as a result, their involvement in SWAPO-organized demonstrations and meetings increased noticeably in the early 1970s. Their greater involvement, however, provoked greater repercussions from the Namibian government. But again the regime's violent reaction had opposite the intended effect; instead of stifling protest, it in fact fueled opposition. The detentions, torture, harassment, and arrests of women made the vicious nature of the government ever more obvious, bringing even more women into the struggle as well as sending more women into exile, where they continued their resistance work.

The important role played by organizations in facilitating women's participation in national liberation movements is clearly illustrated in the Namibian case. The SWAPO Women's Council was by far the most important vehicle for their integration into the struggle. Its stated goals were to "develop theory and accompanying policy to insure that women's demands for equality are heard."[36] The SWC branches outside of Namibia were initially the strongest. The SWC in exile successfully ran many services in the refugee camps. For the most part, these focused on the day-to-day educational, health, food, and shelter needs of these communities. The SWC's efforts were geared not only to support the struggle but also to prepare Namibian women for their role in national reconstruction.

> In order to alleviate the depressing conditions of exile life, SWAPO Women's Council (SWC) . . . worked out programmes for learning, for productive labour and cultural creativity. There are literacy campaign courses and formal correspondence courses at both primary and secondary levels. . . . Vocational training in the fields of weaving, tailoring, driving, typing, etc., is being conducted in order to keep exiled women busy preparing themselves for a fruitful and productive future in their country after independence.[37]

In the late 1970s, the SWC's presence became more visible inside Namibia. "By the 1970s, women inside the country had formed effective support networks, [and were] holding rallies, addressing meetings, and holding seminars to deepen their political understandings."[38] The fruits of their labor were clearly illustrated by a 1977 SWC-sponsored rally attended by over four thousand people.

To a much more limited extent, the presence of Namibian women was felt through the actions of the labor unions. Between 1950 and 1971, Namibian women in laundry, domestic, factory, teaching, and other occupations organized and participated in a series of strikes. Despite their small numbers in the unions, women were described as having "impressive militancy." Given the repressive nature of the regime, the very existence of these organizations constituted resistance.

As often noted in studies of women in wars of national liberation, their own internalized sexist notions are often the most formidable obstacle to their full participation. "Namibian women have also had to face their own feelings of inferiority, owing to the new roles that they were forced to assume under the apartheid regime."[39] To confront this reality, the SWC placed great emphasis on political education among both men and women. In numerous seminars and meetings the SWC engaged women in the communities in discussions of the roots of women's oppression and the importance of their involvement to the success of the movement. This process of education and political action has greatly transformed Namibian women. Moreover, in Namibia, women took a more direct role in the armed struggle than did women in other Southern African struggles. Female combatants participated in the launching of the armed struggle in 1966. By the 1970s "hundreds of Namibian women enlisted themselves into the guerrilla ranks of the People's Liberation Army of Namibia (PLAN).''[40] While remaining a small fraction of the forces, members of the SWAPO Women's Council exerted sufficient pressure to assure the full integration of women into the army.

While the participation of Namibian women in the national liberation struggle had profound effects on the society, barriers to gender equality remain. Take, for example, the position of women in the Namibian government since independence in 1989. Despite the fact that women were actively involved in SWAPO's military and political activities during the height of the independence struggle, they comprise only five of the seventy-two members of the postindependence SWAPO-dominated Assembly.[41] In addition, work discrimination and tenets of the Anglican Church have continued to slow the momentum toward women's liberation generated during the national liberation struggle. Nonetheless, as Lapchick relates, "Namibian women faced tremendous obstacles to equal participation with men in their society. However, their role in the struggle for national liberation from the Pretoria regime has forced the way for a new place for them and helped overcome the barriers imposed by both traditional African and colonial societies.''[42]

SOUTH AFRICA

In South Africa, women comprised the majority of the population in the "bantustans" and reserves, as the adult male population participated in the labor migration to the urban areas. The over five million African women in these bantustans suffered from a dearth of amenities and economic opportunities. Prevented by apartheid legislation from having lawful residence and employment in urban areas, women and children also formed the majorities in the illegal squatters' camps that have sprung up on the outskirts of South Africa's urban economic centers, where they remain vulnerable to forced removal. Arguing that these women and families were not South African citizens and that they had their own livelihoods on the reserves, the South African mining companies were able to pay male workers the lowest wages imaginable on the ludicrous assumption that they did not have families to support.

Attacks on the family and community life were among the first things against which women in South Africa organized and mobilized. According to Tessa Marcus, women constitute the backbone of resistance struggles at the local level in communities all across the country. Issues such as forced removals, rent increases, harassment of students and youth, child care, literacy, and education have been focuses of action for South African women.[43] Their strategies have varied, ranging from protests, boycotts, and demonstrations to community and workplace organizing. This "mobilization of women into local activities with immediate and limited demands has become woven into the total resistance to apartheid."[44]

Some of the most intense activity among women has occurred in response to two main threats to normal family existence: passes and forced relocation. Specifically, these policies meant that families could not live together, were forced to move repeatedly, and were subject to constant harassment. The apartheid government was held off from forcing women to use passes for over forty-eight years. From 1913, when the European settlers first attempted to have women carry passes, until 1960, when close to 75 percent of all African women were carrying them, and 1962, when it became obligatory to do so, South African women waged both spontaneous and organized actions. As early as 1913 South African women mobilized against the pass laws. Their actions included a 1956 march to Pretoria by more than twenty thousand women and the 1957 stoning of government officials by two thousand women in the northern Transvaal.[45] Forced relocations and the demolition of squatters' camps were also cause for anticolonial activity among South African women. The resistance at Crossroads, a camp outside of urban Cape Town, is a prime example.

The Crossroads Women's Committee emerged in response to the South African government's 1977 declaration that the Crossroads camp would be destroyed and its residents resettled. Being most impacted by such a threat, the women of Crossroads utilized a wide range of tactics to resist the proposed demolition. In June 1978, more than two hundred women demonstrated at the Bantu Affairs Administration Board. They followed up in the next month by organizing a mass prayer service for the camp's survival that was attended by approximately five thousand people. The women also organized themselves and kept twenty-four-hour vigils in an effort to forestall the destruction of their dwellings. The ultimate resistance was their sitting in front of bulldozers that were slated to destroy the community. "When the first lot of bulldozers arrived, the women sat down. Three people were killed. The women continued to protest. They sought and received international support."[46] This pressure led the South African government to cancel the proposed destruction of Crossroads in 1978.

These actions reverberated throughout the country. The women of the Nyanga squatters' camp, for example, took up the resistance. To forestall the confiscation of their homes, the residents of this camp would dismantle and bury their shacks every dawn, leaving only their beds. They were, therefore, labeled the "bed people." The desperation with which South African women protected these communities showed their understanding of the negative relationship between migratory labor and the quality of their family life.

Resistance was illustrated not only by the stubborn fight that South African women put up to protect their communities; it was inherent in the very existence of the camps, which challenged the very basis of apartheid's migratory labor system. Hilda Bernstein explains that, "one must understand the nature of the challenge posed by the women who refuse to rot in the bantustans, and form squatters' camps outside the towns where the male migrant workers are employed and where women have some hope of seeking work. In choosing to live together as families, they are challenging the basis of the entire cheap labour power in South Africa."[47]

South African women also have a long history of action in response to threats to their children's well-being. "The 1954 passage of the Bantu Education Act brought resistance from African women to having their children's education dominated by the Christian nationalist white supremacist philosophy."[48] To counter this, the women of the African National Congress led a school boycott and initiated the National Education Movement to provide alternative education under the guise of "cultural clubs." Concern for their children also prompted South African women to active involvement in the June 1976 Soweto uprising against the instruction of African children in their oppressor's language, Afrikaans.

Popular political organizations have been an important vehicle in the liberation struggle among South African women. The labor unions were some of the first organizations within which South African women participated. "The early women trade union organizers, though predominantly white, organized African, Indian, Coloured, and white women into multiracial unions—particularly the Food and Canning Workers' Union, the Sweet Workers' Union, the Textile Workers' Union, [and] the Garment Workers' Union."[49] These women united across national origins in a 1928 strike in support of three white union organizers threatened with losing their jobs. There is evidence, however, that strikes initiated by African union members did not receive the same level of support from their white sister members. Nonetheless, the involvement of African women in these unions contributed to their preparation for later organizing efforts. Many of the women involved in South African trade union organizing in the 1920s and 1930s would later form the leadership in organizations such as the Federation of South African Women (FSAW), which emerged in 1954, and the ANC Bantu Women's League.[50] Although males composed the leadership in the most popular liberation organizations (e.g., the African National Congress, the Pan-Africanist Congress, and the South African Indian Congress), there was a great deal of reliance on women to organize and participate in the various resistance campaigns, demonstrations, and boycotts.

There has been great endurance among South African women in their fight against apartheid. For example, they made persistent efforts to form organizations. Upon the banning or dissolution of one, others would soon emerge to carry on the work. Banned and imprisoned leaders would be soon replaced by younger, emerging leaders. Despite the countless South African women who have suffered imprisonment, banning, torture, death, and exile as a consequence of their political activities, women have maintained a presence in the struggle against apartheid and on behalf of national liberation.

THE MIDDLE EAST AND NORTH AFRICA

Women in the Middle East and North Africa have a long history of struggle. The juxtaposition of this political activism against the limitations to women's activities ostensibly prescribed by Islam makes their participation in national struggles particularly significant. Specifically, women's active role in such struggles has the potential to challenge the relegation of women's endeavors to the private realm. It also confronts norms about acceptable types of male-female relationships.

While the struggles in the Middle East and North Africa have, for the most part, been male dominated, the involvement of women in political struggles has had an impact on prevailing social arrangements and perceptions. Their involvement has necessarily confronted traditional perceptions of acceptable characteristics and behavior of women. For instance, the belief that men were superior to women in courage and intelligence was challenged in the face of countless acts of revolutionary commitment expressed by women. In addition, the integration of both men and women into action made Islamic codes of gender separation more difficult to enforce.[51]

The spectrum of possible effects of women's participation in national liberation struggles in this region is illustrated well by the Palestinian and Algerian revolutions.

ALGERIA

Perhaps one of the earliest instances wherein the heroism of women in a national liberation struggle captured the attention of the world is the case of Algeria. The Algerian war of independence against French colonialism was the only struggle of its kind in the region. It was a protracted war of resistance against an occupying European power that lasted nearly a decade

(1954–62). As is the case in most modern wars of national liberation, Algerian women struggled heroically, and Algerians point to several exceptional women as national revolutionary heroes.

The National Liberation Front (FLN) was composed of anticolonial organizations active at the time. Although lip service was paid to the establishment of a socialist state, particularly by Algerian expatriots in France, conservative Islam was used to appeal to the general population, and progressive forces lost the political day to more conservative nationalist elements. The FLN had no clear ideological position aside from opposing French colonial rule, and it had a heavily "petit bourgeois and socially conservative character."[52]

> The new middle peasantry and the new urban petty bourgeoisie were the new social classes most profoundly threatened by French insistence on cultural assimilation and the emancipation of Algerian women. . . . Members of this new national petty bourgeoisie thus became the first converts to the conservative program of the *ulama* [Muslim theologians]. . . . The *ulama*'s achievement of ideological ascendancy over the Algerian national petty bourgeoisie was critical to the persistence of patriarchy during the Revolution and afterwards. Most of the revolutionary leadership was recruited from the middle peasantry or from the urban petty bourgeoisie.[53]

A fundamental feature of French colonialism in Algeria was the attempt to "Frenchify" Algeria. This entailed an attack on Islam, an attempt to educate the Algerian national and petty bourgeoisies in the French tradition, and, eventually, overt appeals to Algerian women. Every major scholar on the subject, including Frantz Fanon, observed that the French considered women the key to breaking the Algerian resistance. One of them described the hoopla surrounding a public unveiling of Algerian women by the wives of French military officers in these terms: "French women, to applauding crowds, lifted the veils from the heads of a number of Moslem women who gratefully smiled at the cameramen. Behind this drama were the wives of some of the generals and top officers of the French army."[54]

The nationalist response to this campaign was to embrace the veil as a symbol of defiance. Women became the symbols of a romanticized past and of independence. French attempts at assimilation, therefore, actually strengthened the conservative Islamic forces in the anticolonial movement. Despite the overtly Eurocentric assumptions of his study, David C. Gordon captures the situation well when he writes:

> The revolution was conceived of as a struggle for two different sets of values, each contradictory to the other on many points. On the one hand,

the revolution sought to bring into being a modern nation along socialist lines; on the other hand the revolution sought to resurrect and restore a culture which the French were accused of having disparaged and disrupted—a culture that was essentially Arabic and Islamic.[55]

It is not known when women became active participants in the FLN and the National Liberation Army (ALN). However, most observers agree that the participation of women resulted primarily from the danger various missions posed to men. Women were recruited as the sisters, wives, and mothers of men who were members of the FLN, not as autonomous individuals in their own right. "In earlier stages, they were not even kept informed of what was being done; the clandestine meetings, the secret councils only involved men who made the decisions."[56] Because of the all-inclusive, mass nature of the war, the FLN and ALN were forced to accept the participation of women. However, according to Peter Knauss, even then women held no substantive decision-making positions in these organizations. Men made the decisions and women carried them out, without input. Women were segregated into separate cells within the FLN and separate military units within the ALN.[57]

Although women's participation in the liberation struggle is certainly undercounted, at least eleven thousand women officially claimed to be former militants. Of this number 84 percent participated in the civil organizations of the FLN and 16 percent served in the ALN.[58] The fact that official veteran status was more difficult to attain for women contributed to the undercount of women who participated in the struggle.

One way in which Algerian women contributed greatly to their nation's eventual victory over the French was by carrying messages and, less often, bombs. Women could move more easily through the streets, whereas men were more subject to searches and detention. "Protected by the veil and considered by the authorities to be too bound by tradition to participate in such activities, they were able to penetrate into places where men could not go."[59] Some of the women involved in the FLN were assigned the responsibility of placing bombs in French areas. "They thus played a highly spectacular role and have left a particularly deep impression on people's memory."[60]

The majority of women who participated in the liberation struggle in the urban areas via the civil organizations were married women between the ages of thirty and forty-nine. However, those who participated in the ALN tended to be younger, with 51 percent under the age of twenty and almost 84 percent under thirty.[61] One reason suggested by some for the relative youth of the female ALN militants is that it was easier for young women to break away from their families and join the underground resistance; another is that they might also have joined as a means of escaping early, arranged marriages.[62] (In the resistance the ALN essentially took the place of the family patriarchy by approving—or infrequently disapproving—marriage among the militants. However, the circumstances under which relationships developed between men and women were much more liberal. People got the opportunity to grow, to know, and to come to like one another.) Another possibility is that families sent their daughters to the underground to avoid the sexual violence of French soldiers.

According to one study, "One out of every five female revolutionaries suffered imprisonment or death."[63] Among the women touted as national revolutionary heroes in Algeria, the two most famous—Djamila Bouhired and Djamila Boupacha—were arrested, imprisoned, and tortured for alleged bombings. The well-educated, middle-class Bouhired was twenty-two years old when she was arrested, tortured, and sentenced to death (a sentence that was never carried out). She was working as a liaison agent at the time and was charged with planting bombs that exploded at two restaurants. "On May 25, 1959, *El Moudjahid* (the organ of the FLN) declared her to be the best known Algerian woman, and indeed, for anyone concerned with the Algerian revolution her name became a household word."[64] Boupacha's situation was similar to that of Bouhired. Her portrait, drawn by Picasso, appeared in many magazines, and she was given extensive publicity in France. She was accused of having thrown a bomb near the University of Algiers.[65]

The 1991 victory by Islamic fundamentalists in preliminary elections (the results of which were thrown out) can be seen as part of the continuing reaction of traditionalist forces. While the first postcolonial president of Algeria, Ahmed Ben Bella, at least gave lip service to ameliorating the status of women, after Ouari Boumedienne took over the presidency in 1965, under the popular pressure of rising Islamic fundamentalism, even the rhetoric of women's emancipation came to an end.

At the advent of liberation, the Algerian economy was in shambles. Unemployment was extremely high, and men received priority for what few employment opportunities existed. Although in the early days of the revolutionary government a few women deputies were elected, they had little impact on women's legal status. In the intervening period little progress has been made to ameliorate the inequalities between men and women, and Algerian women continue to be treated as second-class citizens. The status of women in Algeria does not seem to be improving. In fact, despite all the improvements in their lives since the end of colonial rule in the early

1960s, Algerian women may, with respect to their sexual liberation, be worse off today than they were over two decades ago.

PALESTINE

The participation of women in the Palestinian struggle for national liberation has matured in step with the larger national movement. Women have been consistent contributors to the struggle, but their level and forms of participation have varied in accordance with historical developments and conditions confronted by the movement. The strong patriarchal values inherent in the Islamic faith and feudal traditions have, at times, thrown up serious impediments to women's participation. However, the imperatives of the struggle are, in great part, overruling these barriers. In other words, the increasingly integral role of women in the struggle is steadily chipping away at traditional sex-role expectations.

Nevertheless, the Palestinian national liberation struggle remains gender qualified. As Hamida Kazi notes, "the patriarchy that dominates the social system also shapes the political structure of the movement."[66] Thus, a situation has been created where, although women are dispersed throughout the various levels of struggle—military, political, and social—they are underrepresented in those areas traditionally thought to be men's work. According to Julie Peteet, "There is, however, a sexual division of labor within the Resistance; women tend to be most concentrated in the social field, and least in the military. Women are also actively involved in administrative aspects of the Resistance."[67] The other side of this coin, she relates, is the closer connection of women to the grassroots or the masses that these positions encourage. In this semipublic, semiprivate realm of struggle, which only barely conflicts with prescribed norms of female behavior, women provide the link between the community and the broader movement.

The role played by women in forging this connection is facilitated by the significance given to the image of the heroic mother or "the mother of the martyr."[68] This sentiment has politicized everyday women's activities such as nurturing and protecting their children and families: "This form of participatory nationalism through 'motherhood' is an active and innovative form of struggle. . . . By expanding her mothering role to encompass all other children, she has dissolved herself in the wider nation."[69] It is significant that the Palestinian mother has used her reproductive and productive capabilities to sustain the nation, maintain and promote the Palestinian culture, and fuel the sense of nationalism necessary to insure the continuation of the liberation struggle. Mothering the resistance has also entailed more tangible activities such as feeding and hiding freedom fighters, nursing the wounded, and sustaining political prisoners. The role that women play in mourning and assisting dispossessed families has also contributed directly to the struggle. Many gatherings at the gravesites of martyrs, initiated by the women of the community, have turned into large protests.[70]

Referred to by Peteet as "politicizing domesticity," this process of framing motherhood in the context of resistance has its pros and cons. On one hand, adding political significance to these acceptable female activities can be seen as an affront to society's traditional devaluation of such roles. On the other hand is the contention that, rather than insuring the emancipation of women as a part of the national liberation struggle, this process may in fact serve further to entrench gender-role differentiation, leading to the continued suppression of women after the victory of the national liberation struggle.

The involvement of Palestinian women in "official" aspects of the national liberation movement has developed in stages. Whereas they were initially limited to auxiliary and supportive positions, their roles were later expanded and made more substantive. The extent of their involvement and the forms their struggle took were influenced both by general social conditions and the needs of the struggle and by the consciousness of the Palestinians, and Palestinian women in particular.

In the earlier days of the struggle, Palestinian women took part in the protests and demonstrations, but in a spontaneous, unorganized manner. For instance, Palestinian men and women together protested the first Jewish settlements in the late nineteenth century and the Balfour Declaration of 1917. During this stage of involvement, women, while relegated to specific spheres of struggles, were often catalysts to action. Organized expression of women's resistance emerged at this time. It took the initial form of the Palestinian Women's Union, established in 1921, which was essentially a coalition effort of various Palestinian women's groups.[71]

At this point, the movement took two related but autonomous forms. One, led by educated, middle-class, urban Palestinian women, manifested itself in boycotts, demonstrations, and the collection and distribution of funds and other resources to the needy. The other, mainly expressed by women in the rural areas, was more militant: "Peasant women transported weapons and messages, hid fighters from authorities, provided food for them and nursing care to the wounded, and as an omen of the future, a few women fought alongside the men."[72] These women actively participated in both the 1929 and 1949 rebellions, but roles for women remained greatly limited in the movement.

The establishment of the Israeli state in 1948, and the subsequent extreme disruption of the Palestinian community, shifted women into their next phase of involvement. Palestinian women organized themselves into self-help groups that administered needed services, especially among the refugee population. Conforming to the mandates of the movement, "they organized soup kitchens, and campaigned increasingly for donations to administer to the needs of the refugees. During this period, and until the UN Relief and Work Agency was established in 1950, the women performed the crucial function of substituting for the state services."[73]

A new phase of women's involvement in the Palestinian struggle began in 1967. "At this time it became the movement's policy to recruit women. The defeat of the Arab forces in 1967 once again strengthened the idea in the Palestinian mind that women's participation was essential for the success of their struggle."[74] During this period of intense armed struggle, women became more active in the military aspects of the liberation struggle. While their participation on this level was sporadic and often relegated to support roles, the provision of military training for Palestinian women was a significant step in the process toward more intense political involvement.

The late 1970s saw the emergence of a more secure grassroots base in the involvement of women in the Palestinian struggle; it signaled the birth of the Women's Work Committee (WWC), the first of four mass women's committees to emerge in the Occupied Territories. These committees were more effective in merging the urban-rural and middle–working class factions that characterized much of the previous participation of women in the movement. The WWC, "set up in Ramallah in 1978 by a group of highly educated and ideologically and politically motivated women," had the stated objectives of increased political education and mobilization of women in the context of the broader national movement.[75] While admittedly more political than "charitable," their actions still closely resemble those of their predecessors—responses to the day-to-day realities of women in the Occupied Territories, such as education, child care, training, and health care.

These committees not only conform to the dictates of living conditions in the Occupied Territories, they also manifest the prevailing political conditions. The four women's committees that form the Federation of Women's Action Committees also represent specific ideological factions within the Palestinian struggle. The result is "a factionalism which created competition and occasionally hampered their attempts to respond to local conditions and women's needs."[76] Nevertheless, they remain viable vehicles for continued and enhanced female participation in the struggle.

The increased political consciousness, activity, and organization among women during this phase of the struggle was reflected by the activities of women even outside the committee structure. In Neve Tirza Prison, for example, female inmates struck for nine months for better conditions. Their victory in March 1984 was both a milestone for the movement and a testimony to the expanding political space of Palestinian women in the national movement.

The Intifada (uprising) that began in the Occupied Territories in December 1987 occurred when Palestinian women's participation in the struggle was at its peak. According to Kitty Warnock, "Palestinian women's massive participation in the Intifada provides a unique case for a potential real Arab feminist movement in contemporary Arab and Middle Eastern history."[77] The forms of struggle in which Palestinian women are currently engaged is, to a great extent, a reflection of the heightened level of struggle inherent in the Intifada itself. Since the beginning of the uprising, numerous Palestinian women have been killed, imprisoned, and harassed in the course of their higher level of involvement.

The women's committees have proven especially important during this phase. They have taken the initiative in building the grassroots structures of the mass movement. These structures are, in effect, creating the foundation upon which the future Palestinian state will rest. And if women's participation in the political and public life of the Palestinian people follows the pattern that has been established thus far, Palestinian women are likely to play an unprecedented role in the new state and be a source of inspiration for women throughout the world.

CENTRAL AMERICA

Throughout Central America women have played and continue to play key roles in their nations' struggles against the poverty and violence that have long plagued the region. Women in Nicaragua, El Salvador, Guatemala, Honduras, and Costa Rica face similar historical, cultural, and economic circumstances, including the cultural legacy of machismo and Catholicism, massive levels of militarization, political violence, and economies still largely dependent on cash crops for export.

Central America, colonial and post-colonial, shares with much of Latin America a brand of patriarchy and chauvinism known as machismo. Historically, machismo has entailed the strict relegation of women to the domestic sphere: public activities are men's domain; child rearing and keeping house are women's. Another cultural factor affecting the status of women in Central America is the near hegemonic influence of the Catholic Church. However, the Catholic hierarchy's traditional interpretation of the Bible and the personality of Mary has encountered a stiff challenge from what has become known as "liberation theology." This progressive interpretation of

Biblical teachings is opening political and social space for Latin American women through the church.[78]

In Central America, the slavery and genocide of the indigenous populations at the hands of the conquistadores has resulted in large percentages of mixed-race or mestizo people. In Guatemala, where the majority of the population is indigenous, local languages are still spoken, along with the official Spanish, and original customs are still practiced, indigenous dress, language, and culture have been a form of resistance throughout the region, marking people as peasants and therefore enemies of the oligarchic and military regimes. Perhaps the most recent example of a Central American state's attempt systematically to eradicate indigenous people is the case of Guatemala, where the government targets indigenous communities for death and destruction. It is out of these communities that Guatemala's political resistance has arisen. The involvement of women as traditional guardians of culture and teachers of children has fueled the resistance both in the armed guerrilla movements and in the numerous political organizations, such as unions, that lead the challenge to state power there. Perhaps the best-known popular leader of Guatemala is Rigoberta Menchú, the subject of the film *When the Mountains Tremble*, based on her autobiography. Menchú is an organizer of the Peasant Unity Committee (CUC), which was part of the early January 31 Popular Front, "founded in January 1981 to commemorate the massacre of a group of Quiche Indians who occupied the Spanish embassy in Ciudad-Guatemala in order to draw attention to their plight."[79] Menchú is now international coordinator for the CUC and a member of a group of prominent exiles called the Representation of the United Guatemalan Opposition (RUOG).

Honduras has not been spared the militarization and economic problems of the region. Its use by the United States government as a staging ground for its counterinsurgency campaign against the Sandinista government of Nicaragua during the 1980s contributed greatly to the influx of men with guns, adding to the already tenuous social situation there. Throughout the region military, paramilitary, and police forces were involved in disappearances, murder, rape, and torture—acts that almost always occurred with impunity.

Added to these physical insecurities were economic ones. Most of Central America is plagued by neocolonial economic arrangements that leave the nations dependent on the export of cash crops, principally cotton and coffee. Preexisting disparities in income and land distribution are exacerbated, while the demise of the smallholding peasant and the migratory nature of employment have wreaked havoc with the traditional family structure, leading to a plethora of female-headed families. This, in turn, has forced women to work outside the home and to respond politically to economic situations that threaten their ability to provide for their families.

The armed guerrilla fronts were perhaps the most dramatic expression of opposition to the status quo in Central America. However, labor unions, consumer and peasant groups, organizations of relatives of the disappeared, and Christian organizations all played an important role in the eventual victory of the Sandinista National Liberation Front (FSLN) in Nicaragua and in the social changes brought about by the Farabundo Martí National Liberation Front (FMLN) in its negotiations with the government of El Salvador. Women played key roles in all of these aspects of struggle against the status quo. Each of these opposition organizations contributed to the revolutionary processes in their nations. The demands and pressures put on the respective governments by strikes, land takeovers by peasants, and the denunciation of human rights abuses contributed to the delegitimization of these states and the creation of a political situation conducive to struggles for revolutionary change.

It is generally agreed that the integration of women into the guerrilla armies of Central America was unprecedented. Norma Chinchilla suggests, "They also seem to represent a qualitatively new stage in the history of women's participation in revolutionary movements, not only in this hemisphere but perhaps in the world."[80] Several factors have contributed to this, including: the historic and political contexts of the civil wars; the transformation of the Latin American guerrilla strategy from one of *foquismo* to protracted "people's wars"; increased awareness of women's issues and their political implications, and societal contradictions that directly impact on women's daily lives, thereby politicizing them.[81]

Perhaps the best-known revolutionary struggles in Central America are those of El Salvador and Nicaragua. In the remainder of this section we focus on the role of women in these two liberation struggles and examine their experiences in more depth.

NICARAGUA

The Sandinista National Liberation Front was founded in 1961 by Carlos Fonseca, Tomás Borge, and Silvio Myorga. Named after Augusto César Sandino, the Nicaraguan national hero famed for leading a guerrilla war against the United States from 1926 to 1933, the FSLN matured and by 1977 was a serious contender for power in Nicaragua.[82] In July 1979, its troops marched into the capital city of Managua and seized state power. At this point women constituted at least 30 percent of the guerrilla forces. "They were fully incorporated into the actual fighting forces of the FSLN not only in transportation, communications and logistics, but in combat and positions of command, something unprecedented in Latin American history.''[83] Although women were used initially in support positions, by 1979 "everything from small units to full battalions," were commanded by women, and during the final battle in Managua, four of the *comandantes* were women.[84]

Motives for joining the FSLN were undoubtedly as varied as the women who joined. However, some generalizations can be made. First, the day-to-day reality of women, a great number of whom found themselves single heads of households, flew in the face of the dominant ideology propagated about women. Instead of the dependent domestic beings portrayed by bourgeois ideology, a great number of women had to work outside the home to support families abandoned by their husbands. Helen Collinson reports that as many as 85 percent of Nicaraguan single mothers worked outside the home prior to 1979. Often this work was an extension of their domestic role and almost invariably it paid poorly, but it was work nonetheless.[85] They had a stake in national economic policies and were especially affected by the absence of social welfare policies. They were personally touched by the political violence (in the form of disappearances, assassinations, and torture) carried out by the Somoza regime. Often mothers became politicized through the involvement of their children.

> In urban areas, young people proved to be the easiest recruits for the early FSLN due to their concentration in schools, relatively greater "leisure" time (if unemployed), and ability to get through the streets without attracting attention. As a result, it was often sons and daughters who first exposed their parents, usually their mothers, to the ideas of the anti-Somoza movement. When sons and daughters were captured, it was mostly mothers who went to jails, penitentiaries, and public offices to demand their release, partly because mothers tended to be more sympathetic to the activities of their children and partly because adult men were vulnerable to being arrested themselves. Mothers who got involved in the struggle against the dictatorship because of their children did so for the most traditional of reasons—protection or defense of an immediate family member.[86]

Another factor facilitating the participation of women in the Nicaraguan revolutionary process was the close relationship between the Catholic Church, Christian base communities (CBCs), and the FSLN. In most of Latin America the Catholic Church is split between the hierarchy, which allies itself with the status quo, and the priests, nuns, and layworkers who have adopted the "preferential option for the poor" recommended by the 1968 Latin American bishops' conference in Medellín. In Nicaragua during the 1960s, small study circles were set up to discuss the Bible and its relevance to daily life. Out of these circles came the CBCs. Composed of poor and working-class people in both the city and countryside, these communities were drawn into the anti-Somoza struggle in the 1970s. They participated in the occupation of churches and collaborated with and joined the FSLN.[87]

The Catholic Church provided another vehicle for women's participation in the revolutionary movement. Due to a shortage of priests in the countryside, lay people were trained as catechists called "delegates of the word." Although women could not be ordained priests, they could be lay catechists. This experience provided women with crucial leadership training and a forum for social expression.[88]

Middle-class and upper-class women were also exposed to liberation theology through their religious education, which was often much more formal, and encouraged to accept the preferential option for the poor. For some middle-class women, their Christian beliefs were the starting point in becoming involved in the struggle against Somoza. Nora Astorga, who before her death in 1987 was the Nicaraguan ambassador to the United Nations, became a Catholic activist in the marginal barrios of Managua soon after leaving convent school. Another radical middle-class Catholic who took a position in the new FSLN government was María del Socorro, who gave up a private business to work for a relatively low wage as general secretary for the Ministry of Housing.[89]

Whatever the reasons that eventually led women to join the ranks of the FSLN, once in they faced the same tough physical conditions, separation from loved ones, and constant risks that their male counterparts suffered. As we said earlier, women first began working in support positions with the front, but by the end of the guerrilla era they shared full combat duties. However, the importance of support activities to a clandestine guerrilla organization should not be underestimated.

> Women can play important revolutionary roles in support positions because of sex stereotyping by the opposition. Using data compiled from news sources on 350 terrorists from around the world, Russel and Miller argue that women attract less suspicion than men. Women as a group can operate safe houses or store weapons without attracting as much suspicion as a gathering of males. Women are able to pose as wives or mothers in order to gain entrance to restricted areas. They can also act as decoys and distract males' attention in hit-run assaults, as was frequent in the Tupamaro movement [of Uruguay]. Guerrillas may thus place women in support roles more out of strategic utility than sexism, because they can manipulate patriarchal images to the movement's advantage.[90]

Although far from any feminist ideal, life within the ranks of the FSLN offered Nicaraguan women significantly more freedom and opportunities than they were likely to have at home with their families.

Unlike the Cuban revolutionary movement, which did not seek to organize women until victory had been achieved, the FSLN founded an organization specifically geared toward recruiting more women to the anti-Somoza movement. Called the Association of Women Confronting the National Problem (AMPRONAC), it was begun in 1977 by Lea Guido and Gloria Carrión, among others, at the behest of *comandante* Jaime Wheelock. The organization denounced human-rights abuses, educated the population about their legal rights, organized rallies and protests, and at one point occupied the local offices of the United Nations in Managua. Initially many bourgeois women were involved, which probably allowed the organization to get away with more than it would have had all its activists been poor and working people.[91]

After the Sandinista triumph in 1979, women continued to play a large role in public life in Nicaragua. AMPRONAC changed its name to the Luisa Amanda Espinosa Nicaraguan Women's Association (AMNLAE) to honor the first woman member of the FSLN to die fighting. The FSLN was transformed from a guerrilla movement to a national government. In addition to a new constitution, new laws were passed aimed at ameliorating the status of women. However, the Sandinistas' social programs were difficult to sustain in the face of the war that soon broke out with the U.S.-backed "contras" or counterrevolutionary forces. Although the contras never made much headway militarily, the war, coupled with a U.S. trade boycott, ruined the nation's economy. An agreement to demobilize the contras was finally reached in 1989. National elections, which brought about the presidency of Violeta Chamorro, were part of that agreement. Thus, another chapter in the long saga of Nicaraguan history began.

EL SALVADOR

Prior to the end of Javier Pérez de Cuellar's tenure as secretary general of the United Nations at the end of 1991, the government of El Salvador and the Farabundo Martí National Liberation Front (FMLN) agreed to a cease-fire. Negotiations preceding the cease-fire and subsequent talks were aimed at ending the decade-long civil war and at transforming the struggle for power in El Salvador from a military to a political one.

The political history of El Salvador is a labyrinth that includes coups, countercoups, and fraudulent elections. Unlike the dictatorships of Anastasio Somoza in Nicaragua and Fulgencio Batista in Cuba, El Salvador had no single arch-villain. Rather, that role has been filled by a variety of men, often through sham elections. El Salvador was run by an oligarchy of fourteen families who owned and controlled the majority of the country's resources at the expense of the masses of people.

As was the case in Nicaragua, women played leading roles in all aspects of the Salvadoran opposition movement.

> The massive incorporation of women into the political process in El Salvador has profound implications both for El Salvador's revolution and for women's liberation throughout the world. Salvadoran revolutionaries have long understood the importance of incorporating women into the movement and have encouraged the development of separate women's organizations for that purpose. This has enabled large numbers of women to break through the traditional obstacles to activism. Grassroots organizing and political participation have had far-reaching effects on women's everyday lives, opening the possibility of redefining their roles as women in society and in the home.[92]

A variety of organizations make up the Salvadoran opposition, but the main opposition force in El Salvador—virtually a second government—is the FMLN. Named after Augustín Farabundo Martí, a Communist Party leader and martyr, the front comprises the five major opposition groups active in El Salvador in the late 1970s. The FMLN was organized in October 1980, and because women were already leaders of some of its component organizations they held leadership positions in the FMLN from the outset. Melida Anaya Montes, now dead, and Ana Guadalupe Martínez, now part of the FMLN diplomatic corps and a chief negotiator, were among that original leadership.[93] Montes was second in command for the Forces of Popular Liberation (FPL), and Martínez is a member of the Central Committee of the Popular Revolutionary Army (ERP) and military commander for an entire province. Another woman who has represented the FMLN in its negotiations with the government is Nidia Díaz, a *comandante* and political leader in the front. In 1985 she was captured and tortured by government forces. She was subsequently released and continues to be active in political life. Inasmuch as women constitute 40 percent of the FMLN and 30 percent of its combat forces, it seems clear that Montes, Martínez, and Díaz are not unusual but rather are increasingly becoming the norm in the FMLN.[94] Moreover,

> The fact that women such as Ana Guadelupe Martínez, Melida Anaya Montes, Nidia Díaz and Eugenia [Ana María Castillo Rivas] have been active members of the FMLN since its inception has encouraged other

women to join and participate fully, and to challenge the stereotypes of women as unfit for military tasks. Their presence has ensured that the FMLN's stated commitment to the goal of sexual equality is translated into reality.[95]

There is no real Salvadoran equivalent to AMNLAE, the Nicaraguan Women's Association. There are, however, women's commissions for most unions and other organizations. Women have organized as never before in response to the deterioration of their standard of living and other economic hardships, in protest of the attack on the family, and in protest of the terror to which the poor in El Salvador are subjected. "By 1988 there were dozens of groups with the prefix 'COFE' (standing for *comisión femenina* or women's commission)."[96] Individually, these organizations are often small, but most belong to a larger coordinating committee or association. One woman leader who became a martyr for El Salvador was Febe Elizabeth Velásquez, killed in the October 31, 1989, bombing of a trade-union federation office. Valásquez was general secretary of the federation known by its Spanish acronym, FENASTRAS (standing for the National Trade Union Federation of Salvadoran Workers). The same day a bomb exploded in the offices of COMADRES (standing for Committee of Mothers of Political Prisoners and the Disappeared), a predominantly women's organization of relatives of the disappeared. Some observers believe that these events provoked the last major offensive by the FMLN, which altered the balance of power in the country to an extent sufficient to force the government back to the negotiating table.[97]

If shifting the struggle to electoral politics succeeds in diminishing the political terror inflicted by the oligarchy and those that serve them, then one can be optimistic that just as women in El Salvador participated in the guerrilla movement in unprecedented numbers, so too they will participate in national politics and press forward with the struggle for social justice and national liberation.

CONCLUSION

Modern national liberation struggles have altered the status of women in different and often complex ways. Sometimes this alteration has consisted of a small step forward, as in Chile during the Allende years or in Mozambique after the victory against colonialism; sometimes it is a great leap forward, as in Cuba and China; and sometimes it is a step forward and then back again, as in Algeria. Sometimes this process entails fundamental changes in traditional female roles, or a breaking free of these roles altogether, as women come to play a part in directing their future and the future of their nations.

The scope, form, and content of women's participation in the national liberation struggle has both quantitative and qualitative dimensions. On the quantitative level, the sheer numbers of individuals and organizations actively promoting national liberation influence the degree of change that results. In qualitative terms, the particular form of women's involvement is of great importance. For instance, the tendency for traditional female roles to be infused with political content has caused controversy with respect to the subsequent effect of these changed roles on women's liberation. Some have proposed, for example, that creating a web of revolutionary symbolism around the woman as mother, as in the Palestinian case, only serves to fortify existing gender differences.[98] Generally, however, women in revolutionary struggles are forced out of their traditional roles and pushed to a new and more powerful political level.

Economic, political, and cultural factors influence the size of the step toward true emancipation that women take through their participation in national liberation struggles. Many of these factors also determine whether subsequent advances occur. Others influence the sustainability of their progress. The most influential factors include the scope, form, and content of women's participation in the liberation process; the political ideology of the liberation movement; the presence of autonomous women's organizations; and political structures and the socioeconomic situation of the postliberation nation-state.

The ideology of the organization(s) leading the struggle, and the extent to which those ideologies are internalized by both cadre and the masses, are other important determinants. The degree to which the dominant ideology links the liberation of women to that of the nation is especially important.

The ideological position that the liberation movement takes toward women's liberation is most often reflected in the existence of a women's wing or through its encouragement of autonomous women's organizations. The extent of women's participation has been shown to be influenced by the degree to which they can autonomously coordinate and initiate their resistance activities. These women's organizations raise the consciousness of both women and men to the factors underlying and contributing to women's oppression. They also monitor and increase the levels of women's participation in the liberation struggle, which is important to its success. The form that these women's organizations take is also significant. Whether they are autonomous or linked to the state or to the liberation movement influences the positions they take and the kinds of activities they carry out.

Many of these women's organizations and wings focus on local issues.

These seemingly narrowly focused efforts in fact constitute resistance to oppression and therefore assist the broader liberation effort. Clear sight must not be lost of these broader issues and implications of women's activities, however. The women's committees in the Palestinian struggle and the numerous women's organizations in South Africa are good examples of success in combining the survival concerns of women with broader national objectives. The degree to which conscious links to and coordination with the broader objectives of the liberation struggle are maintained determines the degree to which these same organizations can be vehicles for women's emancipation after independence.

The struggle for women's equal rights to participate in the national liberation struggle is a prelude to their struggle for equality in the liberated nation-state. However, while this is a necessary precondition, it is not the sole determinant of liberation within the new independent nation. A change in status for women in the throes of the national liberation struggle is almost inevitable. What is less certain is the degree to which these changes can be maintained and enhanced after the achievement of national liberation. Many objective conditions influence the extent to which this is possible.

As was clearly exemplified in the Algerian case, the culture and traditions of a society prior to liberation, especially with respect to religion, greatly impact the status of women in the new society.

The economic situations of newly independent nations greatly affect their continued attention to women and their concerns. Economic issues largely determine a state's ability to provide education and social services to women and strongly influence the degree to which women will become integrated into its workforce. These factors, in turn, have great bearing on women's progress toward genuine equality and full integration into the new nation.

In addition, the class interests of those who come to hold state power in the postindependence period also influence the continued liberation of women. The degree to which the new government goes past its nationalistic objectives and continues to the next level, that of alleviating class, ethnic, and gender divisions, has great bearing on the subsequent status of women.

The participation of women in any struggle for national liberation is a necessary precondition for its success. In turn, the depth and breadth of female participation in the struggle has direct bearing on the role of women in nation building after independence. The degree to which women's participation is complete throughout the various phases of national liberation and reconstruction is thus indicative of the movement's commitment to equality for all its citizens.

NOTES

1. Ben Turok, *Revolutionary Thought in the Twentieth Century* (London: Zed Books, 1980).

2. Ibid.

3. Frederick Engels, *The Origin of the Family, Private Property, and the State* (New York: International Publishers, 1972).

4. Evelyn Reed, "Women: Caste, Class, or Oppressed Sex," in Alison M. Jaggar and Paula S. Rothenberg, eds., *Feminist Frameworks: Alternate Accounts of the Relations between Women and Men* (New York: McGraw-Hill, 1984), p. 133.

5. Michele Barrett, *Women's Oppression Today: Problems in Marxist Feminist Analysis* (London: Villiers Publications, 1980); Heidi Hartmann, "The Unhappy Marriage of Marxism and Feminism: Toward a More Progressive Union," in Jaggar and Rothenberg, *Feminist Frameworks*, pp. 172–89.

6. Chandra Talpade Mohanty, "Under Western Eyes: Feminist Scholarship and Colonial Discourses," in Chandra Talpade Mohanty, Ann Russo, and Lourdes Torres, eds., *Third World Women and the Politics of Feminism* (Bloomington: Indiana University Press, 1991), p. 64.

7. Johanna Brenner and Nancy Holmstrom, "Women's Self-Organization: Theory and Strategy," *Monthly Review* 34, no. 11 (1983): 34–46.

8. Mohanty, Russo, and Torres, *Third World Women and the Politics of Feminism.*

9. Monica Bahati Kuumba, "Sisters in Struggle: A Historical Materialist Analysis of Women in National Liberation Movements" (Ph.D. diss., Howard University, 1993).

10. Julie Peteet, "Women and National Politics in the Middle East," in Berch Berberoglu, ed., *Power and Stability in the Middle East* (London: Zed Books, 1989); Nora Benallegue, "Algerian Women in the Struggle for Independence and Reconstruction," *International Social Science Journal* 35, no. 4 (1983): 704–6.

11. Sandra Danforth, "The Social and Political Implications of Muslim Middle Eastern Women's Participation in Violent Political Conflict," *Women and Politics* 4 (Spring 1984): 35.

12. Hilda Bernstein, *For Their Triumphs and for Their Tears: Women in Apartheid South Africa* (London: International Defence and Aid Fund for Southern Africa, 1985), p. 81.

13. Liberation Support Movement, *The Mozambican Woman in the Revolution* (Toronto: Liberation Support Movement Information Center, January 1974), p. 3.

14. Richard E. Lapchick, "The Role of Women in the Struggle against Apartheid in South Africa," in Filomina Chioma Steady, ed., *The Black Woman Cross Culturally* (Rochester, Vt.: Schenkman Books, 1981), p. 231.

15. Marga Holness, "Introduction," in Organization of Angolan Women (OMA), *Angolan Women Building the Future: From National Liberation to Women's Emancipation*, trans. Marga Holness (London: Zed Books, 1984), p. 13.

16. Tessa Cleaver and Marion Wallace, *Namibia: Women in War* (London: Zed Books, 1990), p. 86.

17. Holness in *Angolan Women Building the Future*, p. 13.

18. See, for example, Fatima Meer, "Organizing under Apartheid," in Miranda Davis, ed., *Third World—Second Sex* (London: Zed Books, 1987), pp. 20–29.

19. Danforth, "The Social and Political Implications of Muslim Middle Eastern Women's Participation," 40.

20. Ruth Neto, "Report of the National Committee," in OMA, *Angolan Women Building the Future*, p. 87.

21. Holness in *Angolan Women Building the Future*, p. 14.

22. Neto, "Report of the National Committee," p. 90.

23. Holness in *Angolan Women Building the Future*, p. 15.

24. Ibid., p. 23.

25. Marga Holness in *Angolan Women Building the Future*, pp. 11–24.

26. Josina Machel, "The Role of Women in the Revolution," in *The Mozambican Woman in the Revolution* (Richmond, Va.: Liberation Support Movement, 1974), p. 5.

27. Ibid., p. 6.

28. Ibid., p. 5.

29. Ibid., p. 8.

30. Stephanie Urdang, *And Still They Dance: Women, War and the Struggle for Change in Mozambique* (New York: Monthly Review Press, 1989), p. 26.

31. Ibid., p. 28.

32. Cleaver and Wallace, *Namibia: Women in War*, p. 86.

33. Ibid.

34. SWAPO Women's Solidarity Campaign (UK), "Women in Namibia: The Fight Goes On," in Davis, *Third World—Second Sex*, p. 74.

35. Ibid., p. 71.

36. Cleaver and Wallace, *Namibia: Women in War*, p. 77.

37. SWAPO, "Women in Namibia," p. 72.

38. Cleaver and Wallace, *Namibia: Women in War*, p. 82.

39. Richard E. Lapchick and Stephanie Urdang, *Oppression and Resistance: The Struggle of Women in Southern Africa* (Westport, Conn.: Greenwood Press, 1982), p. 111.

40. SWAPO, "Women in Namibia," p. 71.

41. Cleaver and Wallace, *Namibia: Women in War*.

42. Lapchick and Urdang, *Oppression and Resistance*, p. 110.

43. Tessa Marcus, "The Women's Question and National Liberation in South Africa," in Maria van Diepen, ed., *The National Question in South Africa* (London: Zed Books, 1988), pp. 96–109; Bernstein, *For Their Triumphs*; Lapchick, "The Role of Women in the Struggle against Apartheid."

44. Bernstein, *For Their Triumphs*, p. 109.

45. Ibid.; Lapchick, "The Role of Women in the Struggle against Apartheid."

46. Lapchick, "The Role of Women in the Struggle against Apartheid," p. 251.

47. Bernstein, *For Their Triumphs*, p. 26.

48. Nancy Van Vuuren, *Women against Apartheid: The Fight for Freedom in South Africa, 1920–1975* (Palo Alto, Calif.: R & E Associates, 1979), p. 45.

49. Ibid., p. 11.

50. Lapchick, "The Role of Women in the Struggle against Apartheid"; Van Vuuren, *Women against Apartheid*.

51. Danforth, "The Social and Political Implications of Muslim Middle Eastern Women's Participation."

52. Juliette Minces, "Women in Algeria," in Lois Beck and Nikki Keddie, eds., *Women in the Muslim World* (Cambridge, Mass.: Harvard University Press, 1978), p. 161.

53. Peter R. Knauss, *The Persistence of Patriarchy: Class, Gender, and Ideology in Twentieth Century Algeria* (New York: Praeger, 1987), p. 34.

54. David C. Gordon, *Women of Algeria* (Cambridge, Mass.: Harvard University Press, 1968), p. 56.

55. Gordon, *Women of Algeria*, p. 83.

56. Minces "Women in Algeria," p. 163.

57. Knauss, *The Persistence of Patriarchy*, pp. 83–84.

58. According to Nora Benallegue, "almost half of the 205 ALN militants on whom accurate information has been obtained were nurses, as were about 2 percent of the 3,066 [women who participated in the] Civil Organizations." Nora Benallegue, "Algerian Women in the Struggle for Independence and Reconstruction," *International Social Science Journal* 35, no. 4 (1983); 704–6.

59. Ibid.

60. Ibid., p. 707.

61. Knauss, *The Persistence of Patriarchy*, p. 77.

62. Ibid.

63. Ibid.

64. Gordon, *Women of Algeria*, p. 54.

65. Ibid.

66. Hamida Kazi, "Palestinian Women and the National Liberation Movement: A Social Perspective," in Khamsin, ed., *Women in the Middle East* (London: Zed Books, 1987), p. 35.

67. Julie Peteet, "Women and National Politics in the Middle East," p. 143.

68. Nahla Abdo, "Women of the Intifada: Gender, Class and National Liberation," *Race and Class* 32, no. 4 (1991): 25.

69. Ibid.

70. Kitty Warnock, *Land before Honour: Palestinian Women in the Occupied Territories* (New York: Monthly Review Press, 1990).

71. Noha S. Ismail, "The Palestinian Women's Struggle for Independence: A Historical Perspective," in *Third Wave: Feminist Perspectives on Racism* (forthcoming, Women of Color Press).

72. Peteet, "Women and National Politics in the Middle East," p. 142.

73. Ismail, "The Palestinian Women's Struggle for Independence," p. 4.

74. Kazi, "Palestinian Women and the National Liberation Movement," p. 31.

75. Ibid., p. 34.

76. Rita Giacaman and Penny Johnson, "Palestinian Women: Breaking Barricades and Breaking Barriers," in Zachary Lockman and Joel Beinin, eds., *Intifada: The Palestinian Uprising against Israeli Occupation* (Boston: South End Press, 1989), p. 159.

77. Warnock, *Land before Honour*, p. 20.

78. It should be noted that the cultural constraints of machismo and Catholicism described above are often much less applicable to women living in traditional indigenous communities because of the relatively more egalitarian nature of those societies.

79. Elisabeth Burgos-Debray, ed., *I. Rigoberta Menchú: An Indian Woman in Guatemala*, trans. Ann Wright (London: Verso, 1983).

80. Norma S. Chinchilla, "Women in Revolutionary Movements: The Case of Nicaragua," working paper no. 27, Michigan State University, East Lansing, Mich., June 1983, p. 1.

81. Linda Lobao, "Women in Revolutionary Movements: Changing Patterns of Latin American Guerrilla Struggle," in Guida West and Rhoda Lois Blumberg, eds., *Women and Social Protest* (London: Oxford University Press, 1990), p. 184; Chinchilla, "Women in Revolutionary Movements," pp. 2–4. The *foco* theory of revolution was formulated by Che Guevara. It held that a small, mobile band of revolutionary fighters in the countryside could create, through their activities and very existence, the conditions necessary for revolution to take place.

82. George Black, *Triumph of the People: The Sandinista Revolution in Nicaragua* (London: Zed Books, 1981), p. 21.

83. Chinchilla, *Women in Revolutionary Movements*, p. 6.

84. P. Flynn, "Women Challenge the Myth," *NACLA Report on the Americas* 14 (September–October 1980): 29; Victoria Schultz, "Women in Nicaragua," *NACLA Report on the Americas* 14 (March–April 1980): 38.

85. Helen Collinson, ed., *Women and Revolution in Nicaragua* (London: Zed Books, 1990), p. 28.

86. Chinchilla, *Women in Revolutionary Movements*, p. 7.

87. Collinson, *Women and Revolution in Nicaragua* p. 84.

88. Ibid., p. 85.

89. Ibid.

90. Lobao, "Women in Revolutionary Movements," p. 190.

91. Margaret Randall, *Sandino's Daughters: Testimonies of Nicaraguan Women in Struggle* (Toronto: New Star Books, 1981), p. 2.

92. New America's Press, ed., *A Dream Compels Us: Voices of Salvadoran Women* (Boston: South End Press, 1989), p. 8.

93. Ibid., pp. 123, 14.

94. Lobao, "Women in Revolutionary Movements," p. 198; New America's Press, *A Dream Compels Us*, p. 126.

95. Ibid., p. 126. Ana María Castillo Rivas, known as "Compañera Eugenia," was a member of the FMLN leadership. Her story is recounted in a biography by Claribel Alegría entitled *They Won't Take Me Alive*.

96. Ibid., p. 17.

97. William M. Leogrande, "After the Battle of San Salvador," *World Policy Journal* 7, no. 2 (Spring 1990): 341.

98. Kazi, "Palestinian Women and the National Liberation Movement."

II

The National Question in the Advanced Capitalist Countries

Puerto Rican Nationalism and the Struggle for Independence

This chapter analyzes the origins and development of the Puerto Rican struggle for national self-determination. After a detailed historical account of the independence movement in Puerto Rico from the early nineteenth century through its various stages in the twentieth century, the chapter focuses on recent nationalist movements and struggles against U.S. imperialism in the post–World War II period and examines the successes and shortcomings of these struggles during the 1960s and 1970s. The chapter concludes with an extended analysis of Puerto Rican nationalism in the 1980s and early 1990s and provides projections on the future of the Puerto Rican national question in a world in transformation.

ORIGINS OF THE PUERTO RICAN NATION AND THE STRUGGLE FOR INDEPENDENCE IN THE NINETEENTH CENTURY

The earliest manifestations of Puerto Rican nationalism can be traced to the beginnings of the nineteenth century, coinciding with the period of Latin American struggles for independence. Some of the same factors that led to the pro-independence revolts in the continental territories of the Spanish Empire in America affected the stability of colonialism in Puerto Rico: the worldwide turmoil that the French revolution initiated, the sociopolitical consequences of the French occupation of Spain, the slow but increasing maturation of a new self-identity among the *criollos* or creoles (the white American-born colonial elite), and the worsening conflicts between *criollos* and *peninsulares* (the Spanish-born residents of the new world).

The kinship between Puerto Rican and early Latin American nationalist expressions can be seen in such events as the "instructions" given by the city of San Germán to Ramón Power. This leading member of the landowning creole elite was selected in 1810 to represent Puerto Rico in the Spanish Cortes (parliament) at Cádiz, a city still free from Spanish occupation forces. The main municipalities of the island gave Ramón Power written instructions concerning the points of view he, as representative of Puerto Rico, should defend and push forward in the Spanish Cortes. In the instructions of the city of San Germán in the southwestern part of the island it was argued that the inhabitants of Puerto Rico were loyal to the imprisoned Spanish king, but if the king were unable to regain the throne Puerto Rico should consider itself independent.[1] This apparently simple argument was widely used throughout the continental territories of Latin America in the earliest stages of the struggles for independence. The links between Puerto Rican and Latin American pro-independence efforts were not only ideological. In the 1810s colonial authorities in Puerto Rico were deeply worried about real and not so real separatist conspiracies, and they became increasingly distrustful of the loyalties of the local creole elite. Among the reasons the colonial authorities had to be worried were the different plans advanced on the continent to extend the Simón Bolívar liberation project to Puerto Rico. One of these unrealized plans involved the figure of Antonio Valero, a Puerto Rican–born general in Bolívar's armies.[2]

Unlike the rest of the territories of the Spanish Empire, Puerto Rico, together with Cuba, failed to achieve independence from Spain in the early nineteenth century. In the case of Puerto Rico, a number of reasons explain this failure. First, one has to consider the socioeconomic backwardness of the island society.[3] During the first three centuries of its existence Puerto Rico was a neglected military outpost within the vast Spanish Empire—an island with a very small population, most of whom lived in a subsistence, noncommercial economy. In 1765 the total population of the island was only forty-five thousand. Not until the late eighteenth century did the population and the economy of the island start to grow.

Against the possibility of achieving independence early in the nineteenth century also weighed the militarist character of colonialism in Puerto Rico. For Spain, the importance of holding the island had always been determined by military considerations. As a consequence of this, San Juan, capital of the island, became by the late eighteenth century the strongest fortified position in the Spanish American Empire.[4] One of the few places in the empire where the presence of regular troops of the Spanish army was a historical constant, the island was used as a base of military operations against the rebels in South America.

Another factor that also weighed strongly against possible pro-independence actions was the arrival in significant numbers of royalist and slave-owning refugees to Puerto Rico in the first decades of the nineteenth century. Colonial elites escaping the revolutionary turmoil in places such as Santo Domingo and Venezuela became pillars of the colonial regime in Puerto Rico.

Throughout the nineteenth century there were numerous pro-independence revolts. The most important armed insurrection against Spain was the so-called Grito de Lares in 1868.[5] The historical significance of the Grito (insurrection) de Lares for Puerto Rican nationalism is enormous, for it was in the town of Lares that the island's independence was proclaimed. The socioeconomic and political background to the various insurrections included frustration arising from repeated failures to achieve political reforms in the island, added frustrations brought by the failure of the Junta Informativa of 1867 (a metropolitan-initiated reformist project that after raising expectations was tabled), oppressive social conditions linked to slavery, the suffering of the peasantry under forms of extraeconomic coercion such as the so-called *libreta* system,[6] and finally, the mid-1860s conditions of economic depression and declining prosperity among the creole landed elite.[7]

The intellectual author of the Grito de Lares was Ramón Emeterio Betances, a French-educated medical doctor whom latter-day Puerto Rican nationalists consider to be the father of the country (*padre de la patria*).[8] The original plans called for an island-wide revolt coordinated with the arrival to the island of a ship carrying weapons. Early detection of the conspiracy by colonial authorities forced changes in the original plans. Instead of widespread revolt, the insurrection was limited to the town of Lares, where on September 23, 1868, the Republic of Puerto Rico was proclaimed. The next day the rebellion moved to the town of San Sebastián, where Spanish troops succeeded in defeating the rebels. In the following weeks an island-wide hunt for the insurgents and systematic repression completed the suppression of the revolt.

The historical and symbolic importance of the Grito de Lares for Puerto Rican nationalism belies its small military significance. For the colonial authorities, this was an event of scant importance. But for future Puerto Rican nationalists, the event became the necessary point of reference in the forging of an outlook that argues that there is a Puerto Rican nation which is rightly struggling to obtain its liberty through independence. Lares became part of the national foundation myth.[9]

It was illegal to express pro-independence political positions throughout the period of colonial rule. The late nineteenth century featured perpetual conflict between the creole-based political leaders who were pressing for political reforms and the *peninsulares,* for whom petitions favoring reform were synonymous with treason. Their own loyalty to Spain was absolute. The first political parties to appear in Puerto Rico, the Liberal and Conservative Parties, were founded in 1870. The Liberals evolved toward a semi-nationalist autonomist position, while the Conservatives expressed their reactionary inclinations through a form of mindless Spanish patriotism. Socioeconomic and nationalist aspects of the liberal-conservative dichotomy were expressed in struggles, at times lacking clear-cut boundaries, between *hacendados* (landowners) and merchants, between *criollos* and *peninsulares.*[10] Autonomism was the predominant political expression of the Puerto Rican creole elite, while unconditional acceptance of colonial status was embraced by sectors linked to the resident peninsular elite. Notwithstanding some forceful-sounding elements among the creole elite, their expressions in favor of self-rule had strong ambivalent qualities.

By the late nineteenth century elite creole politics was increasingly influenced by a new leader, Luis Muñoz Rivera. For him independence, while a glorious ideal, was unattainable because of limitations of island society related to the size of the island and its socioeconomic backwardness. Muñoz Rivera argued that if Cuba, with its more abundant resources, had been unable to achieve independence from Spain, similar struggles in Puerto Rico were necessarily utopian and doomed to failure.[11] A more pragmatic strategy was called for (one described as opportunistic by rivals) wherein the achievement of autonomy in a gradual, step-by-step process was the only goal that could realistically be achieved.

The timid anticolonial opposition expressed by the legal political organizations of the creole bourgoisie contrasted significantly with clandestine separatist activity carried out on the island and among the New York–based Puerto Rican section of the Partido Revolucionario Cubano (Cuban Revolutionary Party). Throughout the second half of the nineteenth century there were many links between Puerto Rican and Cuban anticolonial efforts. Many Puerto Ricans participated in the Cuban struggle for independence, both in the foundation of the party that Jose Martí created and in military combat against the Spaniards in Cuba. One of the programmatic goals of the Cuban party was to help in the achievement of Puerto Rican independence, and various plans were drawn up to send an expeditionary force to Puerto Rico to open a second front in the struggle against Spain. One of these plans involved an important Puerto Rican–born general in the Cuban rebel armies named Juan Ruis Rivera. The failure of these efforts is explained by some of the same factors responsible for the neocolonial outcome of the Cuban nationalist struggle: contradictions within the anticolonial organizations successfully resolved in favor of the more conservative sectors, and the decisive intervention of the United States in the whole affair completely changing the balance of forces.

PUERTO RICAN NATIONALISM IN
THE EARLY TWENTIETH CENTURY

Through its victory in the Spanish-American War, the United States demonstrated that it was a world power. With the U.S. victory, the course of Puerto Rico's historical development was also radically changed. U.S. military forces invaded Puerto Rico on July 25, 1898. Armed resistance to the invasion was limited, in part because Spain had for all practical purposes already lost the war. Spain surrendered when two-thirds of the island was still in Spanish hands. Local Puerto Rican response to the invasion was characterized, with some exceptions, by passive acceptance and even active collaboration with the American forces.[12] The invasion started in the southwest part of the island, an area traditionally dissatisfied with Spanish colonial rule. There the U.S. forces were well-received because the invaders presented themselves in their propaganda as liberators from Spanish colonial oppression. The contrast between the invaders and the old colonial masters, in both socioeconomic and political terms, favored the United States. Replacing an archaic and decadent metropolis with backward economic and political features (Spain) for a modern, democratic, and technologically advanced one (the United States) initially seemed a positive exchange. The military government that ensued for two years after the invasion was accompanied by the collapse of the nineteenth-century pro-independence project and a brief political honeymoon between Puerto Rico's mainstream political leadership and the U.S. colonial government.

The Puerto Rican political leadership expected great benefits to follow the change of colonial masters. While a substantial degree of autonomy had been achieved under Spain in 1897, the more democratic traditions and institutions of the United States were expected to offer greater opportunities for achieving local self-government. Anticipating a rapid granting of U.S. citizenship and political integration, two political parties formed shortly after the invasion, the Federal and Republican Parties, favored making Puerto Rico a state of the union. There was some naïveté in these expectations; some leaders in the Federal Party thought that the United States was a kind of "republic of republics" where every state was sovereign and that in such a framework the autonomist ideal could be realized under the U.S. constitution.[13] Early expectations devolved into disillusionment when in 1900 the reality of U.S. colonial rule became evident.[14] In that year a civilian government was established under the congressionally decided Foraker

Act.[15] Local self-government was reduced to almost meaningless dimensions in a political framework where the executive and judicial branches were controlled by directly appointed metropolitan officials (e.g., a U.S.-born appointed governor) and the legislative branch was divided into two spheres, only one of which was composed of people selected through an electoral process. U.S.-imposed limitations on the right to vote in the first two elections were another shock, and to make matters worse, U.S. citizenship was denied. An ersatz "Porto Rican" citizenship was established, recognized only by the United States.[16] Puerto Rico became, according to a U.S. congressional decision ratified by the Supreme Court, an "un-incorporated territory" defined by the fact that it "belongs but does not form part of the United States." The U.S. government had decided to have colonies without acknowledging the fact.[17]

The frustrations that the Foraker Act provoked among the Puerto Rican political leadership led to the formation of the Unionist Party in time for the elections of 1904. Independence figured as a possible alternative to self-rule in the programmatic declarations of the party, and some groups within the party began to campaign in favor of independence. What is today the flag of Puerto Rico was first used at this time by the pro-independence sectors within the Unionist Party. The flag was designed in New York by the Puerto Rican section of the Cuban Revolutionary Party. Since 1952 it has been the flag of the so-called Commonwealth of Puerto Rico, the current name for the colonial reality, but before that it was an emblem identified with the independence cause.

After 1904 the Unionist Party was the main political party on the island. Opposing it was the Republican Party, which demonstrated early sentiments in favor of the new American colonial rulers, defending without hesitation the goal of statehood for Puerto Rico and the complete annexation of the island by the United States. This political movement had complex social roots: on one hand, its leadership was drawn from those sectors of the Puerto Rican bourgeoisie most capable of benefiting from an early accommodation to the interests of U.S. capital; on the other hand, its constituency was based in the grass roots, a result of the particularities of the socioeconomic effects of the invasion. The possible extension to Puerto Rico of an American form of governance that would be far more progressive than anything the island had seen before created a local base of support for the colonial authorities.[18]

The regressive qualities of the early American colonial regimes led to an increasing radicalization in the national political postures of the Unionist Party, the dominant party on the island in electoral terms. Recurrent petitions for colonial reform pushed by the Unionist Party were met with metropolitan rejection. By 1913, the Unionist Party had independence as its final strategic goal and autonomy as its immediate tactical objective. This might seem an important clarification of means and ends, but there were significant contradictions in the national project that the Unionist Party tried to carry out. The national political radicalization of the party was first slowed and finally stopped by the successful political maneuvers of Luis Muñoz Rivera, who favored a more conservative approach to the achievement of self-government and still considered as utopian the party's goal of national independence. The expressed positions of the Unionist national project embodied the class contradictions of the whole endeavor.

A factor further compounding the contradictory features of the national project of the Unionist Party took form by the mid-1910s. In 1915, after many missed opportunities and difficulties, a nationwide Socialist Party was finally founded in Puerto Rico. On the island a labor movement had been forming since the 1880s, and the first efforts toward the formation of a labor party were made in 1899.[19] After many difficulties, the party entered the political arena in 1915, growing so rapidly that the traditional power structure felt threatened. Unfortunately, a series of problems accompanied these early manifestations of proletarian consciousness. The ideological and political character of the early Puerto Rican labor movement evolved, with the aid of conservative elements within the Unionist Party, toward a particular form of pro-Americanism that had U.S. statehood as its political goal.

In 1917 the United States imposed changes in the colonial arrangement through the Jones Act. Specifically, U.S. citizenship was imposed upon the Puerto Rican population. During the first years after the invasion, the attainment of U.S. citizenship for Puerto Ricans was a major goal of local political parties, but this had changed in part because of the colonial authorities' arrogant rejection of the continual petitions for colonial political reforms put forth by the Puerto Rican political leadership.[20] By 1917, the Unionist Party had independence as its final programmatic goal and as such was opposed to U.S. citizenship, which was seen as creating obstacles to independence. In spite of local political opposition, the population of the island was collectively naturalized as U.S. citizens, but Puerto Rico's relationship to the United States as an "unincorporated territory" remained unchanged.

The 1920s witnessed a realignment of political forces in the island with concurrent ideological changes.[21] Various factors caused the Unionist Party to renounce its independence objective in 1922, and it came to favor as its final goal a special type of autonomy called the "free associated state" (*estado libre asociado*). Among the factors that led to this change, besides the tenuous character of previous nationalist loyalties, were changes in the U.S. colonial policy toward Puerto Rico, which promised further reforms while emphasizing the impossibility of independence. Another important factor was the growing electoral strength of the Socialist Party. The traditional political parties of the island began to forge a bourgeois alliance to block the proletarian threat: in 1924 the Unionist and Republican Parties joined forces to form the Alianza, with local self-government and opposition to the growing "socialist menace" as common objectives.

In the meantime, the most pro-independence section within the Unionist Party left that organization to form the Puerto Rican Nationalist Party in 1922. During the 1920s the political impact and electoral participation of the new party was of minor importance. The socially conservative political orientation of the party, plus the bourgeois character of its leadership, meant a limited popular following for the would-be opposition party.

NATIONALIST CHALLENGES DURING THE GREAT DEPRESSION AND THE SECOND WORLD WAR

The Great Depression of the 1930s found an impoverished Puerto Rico facing increased material deprivation. U.S. federal antidepression measures were not always extended to Puerto Rico, and when they were, they were often inadequate because of the depth of the social problems on the island. Local social conflicts were sharply intensified; labor struggles and nationalist agitation typified the 1930s period.

As a consequence of the elections of 1932 a coalition composed of the newly reconstituted Republican Party and the Socialist Party became the leading government entity. From the beginning it was a contradictory alliance. The party of a bourgeoisie linked to the sugar corporations joined forces with the party whose main constituency was the proletariat of the sugar plantations. Their alliance was initially possible because of pro-statehood positions that became dominant in the Socialist Party, but the class contradictions of the alliance made it a short-lived one that was mainly detrimental to its proletarian component. From that point on the Socialist Party entered into a persistent decline until its total disappearance in 1952.

Throughout the 1930s the major electoral party in the island, despite being second in strength to the Republican-Socialist coalition, was the Liberal Party, the new name adopted by the reconstituted Unionist Party. Under its new leader, Antonio Barceló, independence became the declared political goal of the party. The Liberal Party became especially significant not only because of its electoral strength but also because of its links to the growing New Deal programs in Puerto Rico. Also to become important was Luis Muñoz Marín, son of the late nineteenth-century creole leader, as a Liberal Party leader in the political struggles of the period.

The U.S. government's economic transfers to the island in the 1930s were of an amount larger than the total of all funds it had previously expended there. The New Deal organizations that were established, such as the Puerto Rico Emergency Relief Administration (PRERA) and Puerto Rico Reconstruction Administration (PRRA), had budgets that in practical terms made them a parallel government in a country where political clientelism was the norm. The Liberal Party, although in opposition, was the main local beneficiary of metropolitan patronage. Luis Muñoz Marín's links with the Roosevelt-era liberal establishment were of enormous importance in enhancing the Liberal Party's status.[22]

Important changes occurred in the character of Puerto Rican nationalism during the 1930s. The election in 1930 of Pedro Albizu Campos as president of the Nationalist Party radically changed the political organization and tactics of that party.[23] A new militant, anti-imperialist outlook increasingly modified the objectives of the Nationalist Party. A confrontational style came to dominate the party's behavior toward the colonial authorities. A massive island-wide campaign of national affirmation was carried out. Old national symbols were rescued and new ones were created. The town of Lares became the site of an annual pilgrimage to celebrate the birth of the nation and commemorate the heroic efforts of the nineteenth-century rebels. Under the slogan "the fatherland is valor and sacrifice" (la patria es valor y sacrificio) a new heroic mystique was sought. The presence of the United States in Puerto Rico was declared illegal, and the right of armed resistance to colonial control was proclaimed. Armed confrontations with U.S. colonial authorities followed shortly thereafter.

The colonial authorities in Puerto Rico were alarmed by these new expressions of radical militancy. Their potential populist appeal, given the severely depressed socioeconomic conditions on the island and the social tensions and conflicts they provoked, accentuated the alarm felt by the colonial power structure. Metropolitan fears were well-founded because in 1934 a massive, island-wide strike broke out among workers on the sugar plantations, the center of the main industry of the country, and these workers, in open challenge to their traditional socialist leaders, sought the help and guidance of Pedro Albizu Campos.[24] Notwithstanding the failure of this strike, its massive scale, coupled with its potential to become the focus for a radical petit bourgeois and proletarian alliance, established the need for a rapid and forceful metropolitan response. Repression subsequently became the order of the day; it escalated step by step because of the violent armed responses the nationalists could carry out after every colonial attack. By 1935, Albizu Campos and most of the top leadership of the Nationalist

Party were in federal prisons on the U.S. mainland. In 1937 a peaceful party-sponsored march and demonstration in the city of Ponce was stopped with machine-gun fire, with scores of deaths and wounded, in what became known as the Ponce massacre. Throughout the rest of the decade the campaign of repression continued. On the ideological front, one of the tactics the colonial authorities used, given the wider realities of the period, was to accuse the nationalists of being fascists.[25]

The political figure who eventually benefited from the vacuum in social change expectations that was created by the successful repression of Albizu's party was Luis Muñoz Marín, scion of the old political patriarch of the Puerto Rican political elite. Significantly, Muñoz Marín was born in 1898, the year of the U.S. invasion. Part of his childhood and adolescence were spent in Washington, D.C., where his father was resident commissioner (delegate) for Puerto Rico in the U.S. Congress. Some of his early years as a young adult were spent in New York City, where he became associated with various liberal circles in the area. These experiences made him the first important Puerto Rican political leader completely fluent in the language and idiosyncrasies of the new colonial rulers. His earliest political orientation, while in his twenties, was toward socialism, and he briefly participated in the activities of the Socialist Party in the 1920s.[26] In later years, he cited this experience as evidence of his deep concern for the poor.

It was in the 1930s that Muñoz Marín fully began a political career. He started out as a leader of the most radical and nationalist wing of the Liberal Party. In his many newspaper articles of the period, both in Puerto Rican and in U.S. newspapers and magazines, he defended independence as the only possible solution to the island's problems. In spite of his youth, his importance in the party was great, in part because of his father's political prominence but also because of links he established with the Democratic Party of FDR during his years on the mainland. These links were translated locally into considerable influence for him and his followers in the parallel government that the U.S. New Deal established on the island. After 1936 these links were partially broken because of his refusal openly to condemn the violent expressions of the Nationalist Party's armed resistance and to applaud the violent response of the colonial authorities. By the late 1930s, he led a rebellion within the Liberal Party and took away most of its young, pro-independence leadership to create a new party that became known as the Popular Democratic Party (PPD). This new party had as its slogan "Bread, Land, and Liberty," a slogan stolen from the Puerto Rican Communist Party, which was founded in 1934 as a pro-independence organization. Despite this fact, independence was placed on the back burner as something to consider only after the alarming social problems of Puerto

Rico were addressed. Benefiting from the political turmoil of the period and the death or retirement of the old, traditional political leadership, the populist rhetoric of the son of Luis Muñoz Rivera was quite effective, and his newly formed party was successful in the elections of 1940.

PUERTO RICAN NATIONALISM IN THE EARLY POSTWAR PERIOD

The first Popular Democratic Party administration coincided with the Second World War, and the party was able to benefit from that coincidence. As in the United States, the Great Depression was finally over, economic conditions on the island began to improve, and the PPD was able to claim credit for these changes. The PPD asserted that the improvements were the consequence of the many reformist economic measures that the party had carried out. Politically, the PPD benefited from a new metropolitan willingness to allow political changes in the island (a willingness that the current international situation imposed). In 1941 Rexford Tugwell was named governor, the last American-born, U.S.-appointed governor of Puerto Rico and the first one with knowledge of the island and a reformist, liberal outlook who did not work against the efforts of the elected Puerto Rican political leadership. By the second half of the 1940s two things were happening: changes in the world system, which included metropolitan support for Muñoz Marín's reformist policies, and his open abandonment of the pro-independence political goal.

In the late 1940s important colonial reforms that during previous decades had seemed impossible to achieve were rapidly carried as part of the decolonization era that followed World War II.[27] In 1947, a Puerto Rican–born governor was appointed, Jesús T. Piñero, and in 1948 the people of the island were allowed to elect their own governor; in this way Luis Muñoz Marín became the first elected governor in the history of the island society. In 1952 the so-called Commonwealth of Puerto Rico was established, officially ending the colonial status of the island. The United Nations was informed by the United States of Puerto Rico's new noncolonial status. The island was to be called in U.S. Cold War propaganda a "showcase of democracy," but in fact it was all window dressing.[28] Significantly the Spanish term for the putative new political arrangement was different from its designation in English: in Spanish, it was *estado libre asociado* (free associated state). Basically the most significant structural features of the colonial relationship remained unchanged, with the important symbolic difference that the administration of the colony was delegated to the local political elite and that some of the basic symbols of the nationalist movement, such as the flag and the national anthem, were incorporated into the new colonial state.

To limit political opposition to the new colonial arrangement, which was worked out in complicity between the U.S. colonial authorities and the PPD, severely repressive legislation inspired by the McCarthyism then sweeping the United States was passed that practically made it illegal to be in favor of independence. To be seen at a pro-independence rally could be sufficient cause for prosecution. These laws were in force until the mid-1950s.[29]

Militant pro-independence agitation had increased on the island since the return of Pedro Albizu Campos in 1948. In 1950, shortly before a referendum to approve the new colonial status, members of the Nationalist Party carried out armed actions throughout the island and in the United States. For two weeks armed confrontations between nationalists and local police and National Guard forces took place throughout Puerto Rico. An attempt was made on the life of the governor, and the town of Jayuya was taken by the nationalists, where they proclaimed the Republic of Puerto Rico and where they were expelled by a combined air and land attack carried out by units of the National Guard. The revolt included an attempt to kill President Truman during which a nationalist was killed and another was wounded, and a Washington, D.C., policeman was also killed.[30] As with Lares in 1868, the military significance of this episode was substantially less than its symbolic importance. It was from the start a suicidal endeavor, provoked by circumstances of political persecution. Tactically, it was a total failure, but in traditional nationalist fashion the revolt was intended to lay the groundwork for a national revival; it was part of a persistent effort to create a heroic tradition. Pedro Albizu Campos went back to jail to continue his self-designated role as martyr and symbol of an ''irredentist'' Latin America in struggle against the U.S.[31]

In the late 1940s the legalist expression of Puerto Rican nationalism was concentrated in the Partido Independentista Puertorriqueño (PIP). Founded in 1946 as a breakaway faction of the PPD, this party was made up of the group that refused to follow Muñoz Marín in his rejection of the independence goal. Its main leader was Gilberto Concepción de Gracia, a former defense lawyer for Pedro Albizu Campos. The party first participated in elections in 1948, and by the elections of 1952 it was the main opposition party to the PPD. Subsequently, the party declined to the point that in the elections of 1960 it lost its electoral franchise because of the limited votes it received. In the early 1960s the party struggled to regain its right to participate in local elections. In spite of its legalist outlook, the PIP was hurt by the McCarthyist political repression of the 1950s. To explain the change of fortunes of the PIP in the electoral arena the socioeconomic transformation of Puerto Rico and its political consequences must be taken into account. Social tensions that previously had created a basis for a populist-nationalist appeal were eased. A massive emigration of Puerto Ricans toward the United States began in the 1950s. During those ten years half a million emigrated, a significant number considering that the total island population was slightly above two million.[32] Aided by this massive migration plus the favorable position of the U.S. economy during the 1950s, the socioeconomic condition of the Puerto Rican population steadily improved throughout the decade. The program of government-sponsored ''industrialization by invitation,'' the so-called Operation Bootstrap, was declared a success and a model that other less-developed countries could emulate.[33] The window-dressing of the new colonial arrangement was economically validated. The new Commonwealth was propagandistically defined as ''the progress that we are living'' (*el progreso que se vive*). Independence, on the other hand, was actively discredited. The PPD carried out a campaign that identified independence with hunger, poverty, and a political instability that was presented as typical of independent Latin American countries. Under the broad frontal attack of real and imagined conditions, the PIP began to experience a rapid electoral decline in the 1950s.

The main beneficiary of the changing socioeconomic conditions and the massive and intense antinationalist campaign carried out by the PPD was the pro-statehood movement, which favored total annexation and had bases of popular support among both high-income and low-income sectors of the island's population.[34] In 1968 a newly formed pro-statehood organization, the New Progressive Party (PNP), won the elections, breaking the twenty-eight-year PPD hegemony. Although the PNP lost the 1972 elections, the PPD has been unable to regain its former absolute electoral majorities. With a bourgeoisie that in its dependency lacks national aspirations, U.S. statehood signifies a guarantee of the privileges they enjoy through their direct access to the U.S. market. For the proletariat that in Puerto Rico has historically suffered massive unemployment and that has become accustomed to U.S. federal welfare subsidies, statehood is the cherished promise that these handouts will continue and increase. Carlos Romero Barceló (grandson of Antonio Barceló), the main pro-statehood leader throughout the 1970s and 1980s and governor of Puerto Rico in 1976–84, wrote a short book in the 1970s that had as its title *Statehood Is for the Poor*.

THE "NEW STRUGGLE FOR INDEPENDENCE" OF THE 1960s AND 1970s

In 1959, foreshadowing the electoral debacle that the PIP suffered in the elections of 1960, the Pro-Independence Movement (MPI) was formed as a nonelectoral partisan organization whose founding members came from a broad spectrum of previously formed nationalist and radical organizations. The MPI combined an Albizuist refusal to participate in "colonialist" elections with a political outlook and an interpretation of island social conditions that borrowed elements from the early Socialist and Communist Parties. The victory in Cuba of the Fidel Castro–led revolution, with its combination of socialist and nationalist themes, served as inspiration and a point of reference for what was enthusiastically proclaimed as the "new struggle for independence." The U.S. intervention in Vietnam and the draft of thousands of young Puerto Ricans to fight in that war, plus the worldwide radicalization that characterized the period, helped to push the MPI increasingly leftward. Under the leadership of Juan Mari Brás, a lawyer of Corsican descent who started his political career as one of the main leaders in the University of Puerto Rico student strike of 1948, the MPI strongly impacted and challenged the political ambiance on the island. The new organization concentrated its activities in extraparliamentary struggles that emphasized passive resistance and mass demonstrations without renouncing the right of armed resistance and struggle. The MPI played a significant role in various extraparliamentary struggles in the 1960s: the campaign against the colonial plebiscite of 1967, the struggle against the ROTC and the military draft, successful campaigns against ill-informed, anti-ecological, government-sponsored development projects to exploit the island's copper mines and to establish a "super-port" on the island of Mona for processing foreign oil.

The 1960s witnessed the radicalization of pro-independence propaganda, as different forms of Marxism came to inform the social outlook and rhetoric of Puerto Rican nationalism. The ideological roots of this new perspective lay in positions expressed in several publications and speeches by César Andreú Iglesias, one of the leaders of the Communist Party, in the late 1940s and early 1950s.[35] He argued that the pro-independence movement had failed to achieve the massive popular support it needed because of the class character of the political project Puerto Rican nationalism had been sponsoring. The bourgeois and petit bourgeois nature of Puerto Rican nationalism had failed to attract the proletarian masses of the island. The bourgeoisie had demonstrated its incapacity to lead Puerto Rico toward independence; only the proletariat had the potential to achieve that goal, and only if independence were combined with socialism would the working class have any reason to struggle to achieve this political goal. To implement this new reasoning became the raison d'être of the "new struggle for independence."

The PIP, too, was affected by the radical atmosphere of the period. Its protracted troubles made it fertile ground for political and ideological change. During the beginning of the 1960s the PIP spent much of its time struggling to regain its lost electoral franchise. Once having done so, the party lost it again in 1964, and only after the elections of 1968 were they able to maintain their electoral franchise. However, the party has been unable to win more than a precarious 6 or 7 percent of the total votes for governor, although they have been able to obtain more votes for individual legislative candidates and win representation. By the mid-1960s a new leadership was successfully challenging the old guard, and with these changes came new political identities and ideological positions. Socialism, in its different varieties, increasingly colored the party's self-identification. The search for a new definition of the party's project led to a consideration of positions ranging from Swedish-style social democracy to "Guevarist" and "Third-World" styles of radical socialism. The 1968–72 period was the climax of this process, as the MPI and the PIP competed to see who was more radical while failing to establish significant long-range collaborative efforts. After 1972 a political struggle within the PIP leadership ensued, and the more radical elements in the party were defeated and expelled. Rubén Berríos, a gifted public speaker and lawyer educated at Yale and Oxford Universities, became the undisputed leader of the party (almost in the style of a traditional Latin American *caudillo*), and a social-democratic political orientation, including affiliation with the Socialist International, began to guide the party from that moment on.

The radicalization of the nationalist movement was intensified by the victory in 1968 of a pro-statehood party, the New Progressive Party (PNP). During the governorship of Luis Ferré, the predominant analysis among nationalists called for an increasing political polarization that would reincarnate an old Albizuist maxim: "It is the hour of supreme definition: Are we Yankees or Puerto Ricans?" ("Está sobre el tapete la suprema definición—¿yanquis o puertorriqueños?"). The defeat of the pro-autonomy forces of the PPD in 1968 was seen as a permanent feature in a new political situation that would lead to the solution of Puerto Rico's colonial problem through a direct confrontation between Puerto Rican nationalists and the more deeply Americanized defenders of the U.S. presence in the island.

The growing radicalization of the period led in 1971 to the programmatic transformation of the MPI into the Puerto Rican Socialist Party (PSP), a self-defined Marxist-Leninist organization. To carry out the project of attaining a "workers' republic," an active campaign was initiated to win influence and strength in the labor movement. These efforts had some early successes, but the economic downturn of the mid-1970s, combined with several private and government-sponsored union-busting activities that were carried out in an atmosphere of anticommunist hysteria, prevented the growth in PSP influence. The introduction to the island after 1974 of the federal Food Stamp Program also had an effect on Puerto Rican politics. This program, which in the United States was established to benefit the 11 percent of the population considered to have incomes below the poverty line, was introduced to a society where, according to U.S. standards, 80 percent of the population was poor. It meant a sharp increase—of billions of dollars in a few years—in U.S. federal handouts on the island, with important political consequences.

During the early 1970s the PSP started an ambitious campaign of organizing and propaganda activities throughout the island. Branches of the party were organized all over Puerto Rico, and the party's weekly newspaper, *Claridad,* became for a few years a daily publication. Convinced of their growing influence, the PSP leadership decided to participate in the elections of 1972. First, they tried to convince the PIP to join forces on a common ticket. When the PIP declined the offer, they proceeded alone. The results of this electoral foray were disastrous, and the victory of the PPD under Rafael Hernández Colón—like Luis Ferré, a member of the Ponce bourgeoisie—contradicted previous analyses and led to widespread confusion among political activists.

The political radicalization of the period included the appearance of groups that tried to carry out what state authorities classified as "terrorist" acts, although the groups involved would most likely have classified their activities as armed propaganda. In the late 1960s and early 1970s these groups had names such as the Comandos Armados de Liberación (CAL) and Movimiento Independentista Revolucionario Armado (MIRA). Their activities consisted mostly of placing bombs in U.S.-owned commercial establishments, causing millions of dollars in material damage but scant bodily harm. For the FBI, these groups and the MPI-PSP and related political groups were the same people, and police action was correspondingly directed against all of them. Together with radical mainland groups, such as the Black Panthers and the Weather Underground, radical Puerto Rican nationalists were targets in the most important antisubversion operations the FBI carried out throughout this period.

PUERTO RICAN NATIONALISM IN THE 1980s

The new decade began with the death of Luis Muñoz Marín in 1980. In this and in many other ways Puerto Rican society was entering a situation very different in economic, political, social, and cultural terms from the previous epoch. After the partial victories and failures of the 1970s, and the demonstrated practical limitations of the political strategies of the 1960s, Puerto

Rican nationalism entered the decade of the 1980s without a clear sense of its political options and of the tactical and strategic changes that could improve on them. The previous decade ended with the 1978 murders of two young radical nationalists in a police entrapment set up by an agent provocateur. The deaths were followed by a government cover-up that intensified what came to be called the "Cerro Maravilla affair," taking its name from the location of the murders.[36] This incident was highly publicized through public hearings the PPD-controlled legislature carried out in 1983, which helped them in their victory in the elections of 1984.

The mixed outcomes of previous nationalist struggles affected the behavior of the pro-independence movement during the 1980s. The extraparliamentary agitation that was carried out by the MPI-PSP and other radical groups helped to expand the legally acceptable areas of public political dissent. Democracy was in this sense expanded, an important victory that created conditions favoring the growth of the movement. This process, together with the public discussion that ensued around the Cerro Maravilla affair, led to a partial decriminalization of the pro-independence movement. The decades-old practice of keeping in the police files a list of "subversives" focused on Puerto Rican nationalists was declared illegal by the local courts. On the other hand, the political project that guided the "new struggle for independence" found itself exhausted and overcome by events. In the late 1970s the PSP began to break up into factions, and by the late 1980s was a sad semblance of its former self. The PIP, although it has effective representation in the Puerto Rican legislature and a program of social advocacy that is nationally known and respected, seems unable to expand beyond its narrow partisan core. The defeatist attitudes that the confusing conditions of the 1980s fostered have led to a revival of old nationalist illusions of salvation through the autonomist wing of the PPD. In the elections of 1984 and 1988, won by the PPD, the traditional hegemonic party in the island was able to benefit from the votes of many pro-independence followers who had concluded that their most important priority was to stop the advance of the annexationist forces. The illusions that were created by the entrance of Luis Muñoz Marín's daughter into the political arena, proclaiming her father's populist rhetoric, also helped to gain pro-independence votes for the PPD. Victoria "Melo" Muñoz became the focus of a political phenomenon that has been named *melonismo,* which was responsible for channeling some of the electoral expressions of Puerto Rican nationalism toward the PPD.

The shape of Puerto Rican nationalism in the 1980s was directly related to the characteristics of the island society during this period. The economic crisis of the 1970s was partially resolved with the consolidation of a new model of economic development based on increased dependence on transnational corporations. This model benefits so-called 936 corporations, that is, U.S. corporations operating in Puerto Rico under a federal tax law that allows them to repatriate their profits tax-free to the mainland after several years in Puerto Rican banks. Their only cost is a "toll-gate" tax paid to the Commonwealth government.[37] U.S. transnational corporations are able in this way to save billions of dollars, and the colonial government of Puerto Rico earns millions of dollars from the collection of the toll-gate tax. In recent years this evident loophole in the U.S. tax system has come under attack in the U.S. Congress, but up to now it has survived. This new model of economic dependency has led to a deepening of tendencies that began in the mid-1970s and had as one of their basic features welfare income subsidies for the poorer sectors of the Puerto Rican population. Some Puerto Rican economists began to describe the island as having a "ghetto" economy similar to inner-city areas in the United States and with similar social problems.[38]

Puerto Rican society has also changed in recent years as a result of a socio-demographic transformation that is affected by the new dynamics of the emigration-immigration process. Since the 1970s the number of people involved in a "return migration" of Puerto Ricans born or raised in the United States has continuously increased. The growing importance of so-called Neo-Ricans in the island homeland and their possible political significance and meaning for the Puerto Rican national identity have until now not been considered sufficiently.

Despite a social context that militates against the development of a collective nationalist identity among the Puerto Rican people, there are many indicators of the strength of the Puerto Rican national identity, which overrides political, partisan, and geographical distinctions. Within Puerto Rico, even many followers of the pro-statehood movement assert a strong Puerto Rican identity. One sector within this movement argues that Puerto Rico will be a Spanish-speaking state and as such culturally nothing will change.

The strength of the Puerto Rican national identity is also demonstrated by its expressions among the Puerto Rican population in the United States (about two million today). Many second- and third-generation Puerto Ricans living in the United States continue to identify themselves as such and have proportionally among them as many pro-independence sympathizers as is typical in Puerto Rico itself. The desire to display basic national symbols such as the flag may even be stronger among the Puerto Rican population living on the U.S. mainland than it is on the island of Puerto Rico.

The decade of the 1980s was very hard for Puerto Rican nationalism.

The main pro-independence organizations during that decade were the PIP, which had stabilized but not succeeded in expanding its base, and the PSP and other radical leftist organizations, which were in perpetual crisis. The component of the pro-independence movement favoring armed struggle went through a similar process in the 1980s: In the early years they exulted in their initial successes, but by the middle of the decade they were practically crushed by the FBI. The first important group to be neutralized was the Chicago- and New York–based FALN (Fuerzas Armadas de Liberación Nacional). Before their elimination they had been the most prominent "terrorist" group operating in the U.S. mainland, responsible for many bombings, jail breaks, and different forms of armed provocations. In Puerto Rico itself, a group called the Macheteros was very active throughout the late 1970s and early 1980s.[39] One of their most successful operations was the dramatic destruction in 1982 of most of the U.S. fighter jets at the Muñiz U.S. Air National Guard base in Isla Verde, Puerto Rico, called hyperbolically (even when it is true) the most damaging attack on a U.S. military base in American territory since Pearl Harbor. The Macheteros' string of successes, however, was over by the mid-1980s. In 1985, a massive FBI operation in Puerto Rico practically decapitated the organization. By the late 1980s, the futility of conventional armed struggle was becoming evident.

In the early 1990s, three important events shaped the course of political development in Puerto Rico: a referendum in 1991 on Puerto Rican identity; general elections in 1992; and a "status" plebiscite in 1993. Issues common to these events were the meaning and importance of Puerto Rican culture and the Spanish language; the question of loyalty to the U.S. as opposed to forms of Puerto Rican affirmation; and changes in the pro-statehood discourse and in the positions of the PPD and the PIP.

The first of these events was the 1991 referendum. Its background was the failure of negotiations with the U.S. Congress to carry out a "status" plebiscite in the same year. The fear in the Congress of a pro-statehood victory was one of the factors leading to the rejection of plebiscite proposal. The PPD government followed this rejection with an attempt to form a united Puerto Rican front to press Congress for a resolution of the colonial problem. Puerto Ricans were to be asked to vote in a referendum, in a yes or no fashion, to a set of conditions that would lead to a solution of Puerto Rico's colonial status. Among the items to be guaranteed was the Spanish language and Puerto Rican culture. The PPD government played the cultural nationalist card by passing a law proclaiming Spanish as the only official language of the Puerto Rican government. Not all *independentistas* favored voting in this referendum, but the PIP and many others did. A PPD-

PIP alliance was practically, if not officially, achieved in what some called the "referendum on identity." The results of the referendum were a victory for the PNP, and U.S. colonial hegemony reasserted itself in a contest it was originally projected to lose.

The general elections of November 1992 resulted in the worst defeat ever for the PPD. The PIP retained its precarious electoral presence with slightly more than 4 percent of the vote, although some of its candidates as individuals were able to obtain sufficient votes to represent their party in the legislative bodies. This was the greatest victory for the pro-statehood forces. It was accomplished in spite of the internal differences and tensions within the PNP. Perhaps as a concession to the more militant right wing of the party, the new administration of Pedro Rosselló immediately began to carry out a plan for the early achievement of U.S. statehood. The Spanish-language law was eliminated, and a new law was passed that was euphemistically called "English Also." A law to carry out a "status" plebiscite for 1993 was proposed and approved in spite of the opposition—a plebiscite that would be a final blow against the PPD and force the U.S. Congress finally to express itself on the political status of Puerto Rico vis-à-vis the United States.

Despite their two previous victories, as well as the resources they had as the party in control of the government, the pro-statehood forces fell short of victory and their movement was stopped. Although none of the propositions gained a clear majority, the option of retaining Commonwealth status won a plurality with 48 percent of the vote. As a result the possibility of incorporating Puerto Rico into the United States has become ever more remote.

THE FUTURE OF PUERTO RICAN NATIONALISM

The immediate political future of the Puerto Rican struggle for national independence is extremely difficult to foresee. Much will depend on factors that are external to the Puerto Rican social formation. For example, what will be U.S. imperial policy toward Puerto Rico in the present context of its global economic decline and its attempts to reverse this by military means such as intervention in the Middle East and Somalia? Will a United States in hegemonic decline favor a neocolonial solution to the Puerto Rican national question through the so-called associated republic approach that some Puerto Rican political analysts envision, or will a particular form of retrenchment be in order?

Despite the outcome of the 1993 plebiscite, the possibility of U.S. statehood is something that must be acknowledged in analyzing the national question in Puerto Rico. After more than ninety years of U.S. colonial rule, statehood is favored by very close to half of the Puerto Rican electorate. From the nationalist point of view, the possibility of U.S. statehood threatens the very survival of the Puerto Rican nation. Given the present disarray in the nationalist movement, some analysts argue that priority must be given to reaffirming the Puerto Rican national and ethnic identity.[40] Another urgent task for Puerto Rican nationalism is a deep analysis of the conditions of survival of the Puerto Rican nation, in spite of the persistent failure to achieve national independence. Puerto Rico may not become the fifty-first state of the United States because, among many other reasons, of the political problems that incorporating a "minority" state imply for a nation that is already uncomfortable about becoming ethnically more diverse. But nations are not eternally fixed objects, and the survival and development of the Puerto Rican nation—the persistent objective of Puerto Rican nationalism—is part of an agenda whose final results are yet to be seen.

Historically, Puerto Rican nationalism has experienced, on many previous occasions, very difficult moments from which it has later recovered. The consistency and cohesion of a local culture that meets the requisites to qualify as a nation continue to serve as strong obstacles to any metropolitan design to absorb the Puerto Rican nation via U.S. statehood. On the other hand, the campaign for Puerto Rican nationalism has to confront the challenging economic conditions that exist for small countries within the context of the present-day political-economic arrangements in the world capitalist system. A new strategy capable of visualizing a feasible niche in the global geopolitical system is called for—a strategy attuned to the present conditions, acceptable to the United States, and capable of making possible the independence of Puerto Rico.

Pro-independence forces may benefit from Puerto Rico's chronic economic crisis and the exhaustion of once successful economic models there, as the socioeconomic bases of legitimation of the present colonial order are being increasingly undermined. It is significant that during U.S. congressional hearings held in January 1991, the then-governor of Puerto Rico, Rafael Hernández Colón, an advocate of reforms to the present colonial status quo, attacked statehood while defending the national characteristics of the Puerto Rican population and emphasizing the importance of protecting the cultural particularities that define Puerto Ricans as a nation.[41] Also of significance is the fact that on April 5, 1991, the PPD-controlled legislature, with the support of the PIP delegation, passed a law declaring Spanish the official language of the Puerto Rican government. This was a measure of national affirmation that overruled a 1902 U.S.-imposed law that gave parity to the English language, side by side with the Spanish tongue that

U.S. colonial authorities initially thought would be reduced to a folk dialect. But the Puerto Rican national entity is deeply divided. It is of interest to note that the first law passed in 1993 by the newly elected PNP governor, Pedro Rosselló, was to reestablish English as one of the official languages, in spite of the fact that 80 percent of Puerto Ricans cannot converse fluently in English.

There are signs that some leading sectors in the U.S. government are beginning to understand that to push Puerto Rico toward statehood would bring long-range problems for the United States that are better avoided. The persistent strength of nationalist sentiments in Puerto Rico presents very important obstacles to the sociocultural assimilation that would be necessary to prepare the way for statehood. Although the future of Puerto Rico is still uncertain, it is clear that in the years ahead the Puerto Rican people will play a central role in defining themselves and their relationship with the United States. Independence, the goal and ambition of Puerto Rican nationalism may finally arrive as a testament to the persistent will to be Puerto Rican.

NOTES

1. For details about the early pro-independence struggles in Puerto Rico, see Germán Delgado Pasapera, "Orígenes del independentismo puertorriqueño" (The origins of the Puerto Rican independence movement), *Revista de Historia* 1, no. 1 (January–June 1985): 58–75.

2. Two useful books about nineteenth-century Puerto Rican "separatism" are Germán Delgado Pasapera, *Puerto Rico: Sus luchas emancipadoras* (Puerto Rico: Its struggles for emancipation) (San Juan: Editorial Isla, 1984) and Harold J. Lidin, *History of the Puerto Rican Independence Movement,* vol. 1, *Nineteenth Century* (Hato Rey, P.R., 1981).

3. A recent account of Puerto Rico's economic history can be found in James L. Dietz, *Economic History of Puerto Rico: Institutional Changes and Capitalist Development* (Princeton, N.J.: Princeton University Press, 1986).

4. J. H. Parry, *The Spanish Seaborne Empire* (London: Penguin Books, 1973), p. 307.

5. For a detail explanation of what happened in Lares, see Olga Jiménez de Wagenheim, *El Grito de Lares: Sus causas y sus hombres* (The Lares insurrection: Its causes and its people) (San Juan: Ediciones Huracán, 1986).

6. Concerning some of the precapitalist features of the nineteenth-century Puerto Rican social formation, see: Labor Gómez Acevedo, *Organización y reglamentación del trabajo en el Puerto Rico del siglo XIX* (Labor organization and regulation in nineteenth-century Puerto Rico) (San Juan: Instituto de Cultura Puertorriqueña, 1970); Angel G. Quintero Rivera, "Background to the Emergence of Imperialist Capitalism in Puerto Rico," in Adalberto López and James Petras, eds., *Puerto Rico and Puerto Ricans* (Cambridge, Mass.: Schenkman, 1974), pp. 87–117.

7. For the socioeconomic background of the revolt, see Laird W. Bergad, "Toward Puerto Rico's Grito de Lares: Coffee, Social Stratification, and Class Conflict," *Hispanic American Historical Review* 60 (November 1980): 617–42; Olga Jiménez de Wagenheim, "Características y motivaciones de los rebeldes de Lares" (Characteristics and motivations of the Lares rebels), *Revista de Historia* 1, no. 1 (January–June 1985): 76–88.

8. A recent biography of Betances can be found in Ada Suárez Díaz, *El antillano: Biografía del Dr. Ramón Emeterio Betances 1827–1898* (The Antillean: Biography of Dr. Ramón Emeterio Betances, 1827–1898) (San Juan: Centro de Estudios Avanzados de Puerto Rico y el Caribe/Revista Caribe, 1988).

9. The importance of symbolic and mythical factors in the formation of nations has been emphasized by Anthony D. Smith, *The Ethnic Origins of Nations* (New York: Basil Blackwell, 1986). An indispensable aspect in the symbolic construction of a nation is finding an historically based heroic point of reference. In the words of Smith: "Finally, nations need heroes and golden ages. . . . The incommensurability of nations requires a distinctive culture, and this is best founded upon a heroic past" (p. 213). Olga Jiménez de Wagenheim in her important study of the revolt of 1868, *El Grito de Lares,* emphasizes the historical symbolism of Lares in terms of the emergence of the Puerto Rican nation: "Alrededor del Grito de Lares se han tejido mitos y símbolos de nacionalismo, que a su vez han contribuído a inmortalizar aquella gesta y a nutrir el convencimiento de que con el Grito de Lares Puerto Rico emergió como nación" ("Around the Grito de Lares nationalist myths and symbols have been woven that have contributed in turn to immortalizing that feat and to nurturing the conviction that with the Grito de Lares Puerto Rico emerged as a nation") (p. 231).

10. Angel G. Quintero Rivera, *Conflictos de clase y política en Puerto Rico* (Class conflict and politics in Puerto Rico) (San Juan: Edicioines Huracán, 1976).

11. Bolívar Pagán, *Historia de los partidos políticos puertorriqueños* (History of Puerto Rico's political parties), 2 vols. (San Juan, 1972), 1:149.

12. For an account of the local social context of the U.S. invasion of Puerto Rico, see Fernando Picó, *1898: La guerra después de la guerra* (1898: The war after the war) (San Juan: Ediciones Huracán, 1987).

13. In 1899 Luis Muñoz Rivera and other leaders of the Federal Party issued a proclamation in which they argued, among other things, that: "La América del Norte es un Estado de Estados y una República de Repúblicas. Uno de estos Estados, una de estas Repúblicas debe ser Puerto Rico en el porvenir. Y a que lo sea cuanto antes, dirigirá sus empeños el Partido Federal" (The United States is a state of states and a republic of republics. One of these states, one of these republics, ought in the future to be Puerto Rico. And the Federal Party will direct its efforts toward ensuring that this may come about as soon as possible). Quoted in Pagán, *Historia de los partidos políticos puertorriqueños,* p. 1:46.

14. For a detailed analysis of the first two years of U.S. colonial administration of Puerto Rico and the issues involved, see Edward J. Berbusse, *The United States in Puerto Rico, 1898–1900* (Chapel Hill: University of North Carolina Press, 1966).

15. For an analysis of the congressional debate that led to the Foraker Act, see Lyman J. Gould, *La ley Foraker: Raíces de la política colonial de los Estados Unidos* (The Foraker Law: Roots of U.S. colonial policy) (San Juan: University of Puerto Rico, 1969).

16. In a demonstration of imperial arrogance the U.S. colonial authorities decided to change the name of Puerto Rico to make it more easily pronounceable to the English-speaking colonial rulers. Although Puerto Ricans continued to use the traditional name for the island territory, Porto Rico was its official name until the 1930s.

17. A comparative analysis of the imperial policy of the United States toward the colonial territories it acquired in 1898 can be found in Whitney T. Perkins, *Denial of Empire: The United States and Its Dependencies* (Leiden: A. W. Sythoff, 1972).

18. Angel Quintero Rivera in *Patricios y plebeyos: Burgueses, hacendados, artesanos y obreros* (Patricians and plebeians: Bourgeoisie, landowners, artisans, and workers) (San Juan: Ediciones Huracán, 1988) argues that the U.S. invasion of Puerto Rico meant, in contradictory fashion, the external imposition of a "bourgeois democratic revolution," with significant political consequences.

19. For a short history of the labor movement in Puerto Rico, see Gervasio L. García and Angel G. Quintero-Rivera, *Desafío y solidaridad: Breve historia del movimiento obrero*

puertorriqueño (Challenge and solidarity: Brief history of the Puerto Rican workers' movement) (San Juan: Ediciones Huracán, 1982).

20. Manuel Maldonado Denis, *Puerto Rico: Una interpretación histórico-social* (Puerto Rico: A socio-historical interpretation) (Mexico City: Siglo XXI, 1969), p. 99.

21. A useful discussion of political changes during this period is found in Truman R. Clark, *Puerto Rico and the United States, 1917–1933* (Pittsburgh, Pa.: University of Pittsburgh Press, 1975).

22. For an analysis of problems in implementing New Deal legislation in Puerto Rico, see Thomas Matthews, *La política puertorriqueña y el Nuevo Trato* (Puerto Rican politics and the New Deal) (San Juan: University of Puerto Rico, 1970).

23. Juan Mari Brás, *El independentismo en Puerto Rico: Su pasado, su presente y su porvenir* (The independence movement in Puerto Rico: Its past, its present, and its future) (San Juan: Editorial CEPA, 1984).

24. Taller de Formación Política, *La cuestión nacional: El Partido Nacionalista y el movimiento obrero puertorriqueño* (The national question: The Nationalist Party and the Puerto Rican workers' movement) (San Juan: Ediciones Huracán, 1982).

25. An early example of this type of reasoning can be found in Luis Muñoz Marín, "Alerta a la conciencia puertorriqueña," *El Mundo* (San Juan), February 7–10, 1946; the persistence of these accusations can be seen in a recent book: Luis Angel Ferrao, *Pedro Albizu Campos y el nacionalismo puertorriqueño* (Pedro Albizu Campos and Puerto Rican nationalism) (San Juan: Editorial Cultural, 1990).

26. Carmelo Rosario Natal, *La juventud de Luis Muñoz Marín: Su vida y pensamiento 1898–1932* (Luis Meñoz Marín in his youth: His life and thought, 1898–1932) (San Juan, 1976).

27. For a discussion of the issues involved in the colonial reforms of the late 1940s, see Surendra Bhana, *The United States and the Development of the Puerto Rican Status Question 1936–1968* (Wichita: University Press of Kansas, 1975).

28. In the words of one of the founders of the "Commonwealth," it was all a farce. See Vicente Geigel Polanco, *La farsa del estado libre asociado* (The farce of the free associated state) (San Juan: Editorial Edil, 1981).

29. For a detailed analysis of these laws and their political effect in Puerto Rico, see Ivonne Acosta, *La mordaza: Puerto Rico 1948–1957* (The muzzle: Puerto Rico, 1948–1957) (San Juan: Editorial Edil, 1987).

30. An account of the nationalist rebellion of 1950 can be found in Miñi Seijo Bruno, *La insurrección nacionalista en Puerto Rico—1950* (The nationalist insurrection in Puerto Rico—1950) (San Juan: Editorial Edil, 1989).

31. In a speech in the United Nations in 1964 Che Guevara said: "Albizu Campos es un símbolo de la América todavía irredenta pero indómita" (Albizu Campos is a symbol of an America still irredentist but indomitable). Ernesto "Che" Guevara, *Obra revolucionaria* (Mexico City: ERA, 1967), p. 468.

32. An account of the importance of the emigration process for Puerto Rico is found in Manuel Maldonado Denis, *The Emigration Dialectic: Puerto Rico and the USA* (New York: International Publishers, 1980).

33. For an account of the historical significance of Operation Bootstrap see Emilio Pantojas García, *Development Strategies as Ideology: Puerto Rico's Export-Led Industrialization Experience* (Boulder and London: Lynne Reinner Publisher, 1990).

34. Marcia Quintero, *Elecciones de 1968 en Puerto Rico: Análisis estadístico por grupos socio-económicos* (The 1968 elections in Puerto Rico: Statistical analysis by socioeconomic groups) (San Juan: CEREP, 1972).

35. César Andreú Iglesias, *Independencia y socialismo* (Independence and socialism) (San Juan: Librería Estrella Roja, 1951).

36. For accounts of the Cerro Maravilla affair see Manuel Suárez, *Requiém en el Cerro Maravilla: Los asesinatos políticos en Puerto Rico y el encubrimiento por el gobierno de*

EE.UU. (Requiem in Cerro Maravilla: Political assassination in Puerto Rico and the U.S. government cover-up) (Maplewood, N.J.: Waterfront Press, and San Juan: Editorial Atlántico, 1987); Anne Nelson, *Murder under Two Flags: The U.S., Puerto Rico, and the Cerro Maravilla Cover-Up* (New York: Ticknor and Fields, 1986).

37. The economy of Puerto Rico is brilliantly analyzed by Richard Weisskoff, *Factories and Food Stamps: The Puerto Rico Model of Development* (Baltimore: Johns Hopkins University Press, 1985).

38. Elías Gutiérrez et al. *Inversión externa y riqueza nacional: ¿Un dilema?* (External investment and national wealth: A dilemma?) (Buenos Aires: Ediciones SIAP, 1979).

39. Ronald Fernández, *Los Macheteros: The Wells Fargo Robbery and the Violent Struggle for Puerto Rican Independence* (New York: Prentice Hall, 1987).

40. José Enrique Ayoroa Santaliz, "Acentuar el criterio diferencial" (To emphasize the distinguishing criterion), *Claridad (en Rojo)* (San Juan), July 22–28, 1988, pp. 16–17.

41. Salomé Galib Brás, "Ante el Congreso la batalla por la nacionalidad puertorriqueña" (Before Congress the battle for Puerto Rican nationality), *El Nuevo Día* (San Juan), January 31, 1991, pp. 12–13.

□ 7 □

The National Question
and the Struggle against British
Imperialism in Northern Ireland

Northern Ireland is a product of the opposing forces of imperialism and nationalism. Ireland was England's first colony, and it has been said that the conquest of Ireland was the model for British imperialism. As a consequence of England's attempt at domination, Ireland has been home to a variety of nationalist movements. The two nations' mutual history offers many insights into the relationship between imperialism and nationalism, and the impact of class, ethnicity, social consciousness, and national movements on this relationship. This chapter examines the origins and development of the conflict between British imperialism and Irish nationalism and analyzes the effects of this conflict on Northern Ireland as well as the nature and dynamics of the Irish struggle against British imperialism.

THE HISTORY OF UNITED IRELAND

Even before the arrival of the Anglo-Normans, the Gaelic Irish were the product of a series of migrations and invasions. From various points in Western Europe, the Gaels came to the island in relatively small groups. There they encountered aboriginal peoples, also of mixed descent, with whom they merged.[1] The organization of the Catholic Church by St. Patrick in the fifth century and the Danish invasions between the eighth and eleventh centuries also left their mark upon Irish history. The influence of Christianity served to break down tribal prejudices, to centralize authority, and establish market relations.[2] The "Danes" (Scandinavian traders and pirates) founded the cities of Dublin, Wexford, Waterford, Youghal, Cork, Bantry, and Limerick and furthered the development of trade.[3] In addition, these invasions lead to the militarization of the Gaelic chiefs, who triumphed over the Danes in 1014.

The English attempt to dominate Ireland began in the twelfth century when Henry II, acting with papal authorization, installed himself as Lord of Ireland. While the Norman invaders succeeded in occupying the towns and imposing their will within the "Pale" (the area in the vicinity of Dublin), the countryside remained largely the possession of the Gaels and Gaelicized Normans. For centuries, English hegemony was marginal at best. Because there was no centralized government in medieval Ireland, the English monarchy had no unified opposition to its nominal claim of authority. Nevertheless, individual Irish chieftains held out for centuries.

THE ORIGINS OF BRITISH IMPERIALISM

The most important episode leading to the partition of the island was the Ulster Plantation of 1609. About half a million acres of arable land were confiscated from the original inhabitants and turned over to settlers from England and Scotland. Thus, "the Ulster Plantation . . . laid the foundation for . . . a new conquest."[4] Rising in 1641 against the settlers, and subsequently drawn into the cause of English counterrevolution, the Irish were defeated by Cromwell's army in 1652. This led to further confiscations and settlements; Catholic land ownership fell from 59 percent to 22 percent.[5] Following the defeat of the Catholic James II by William of Orange in 1690 at the Battle of the Boyne, the Dublin Parliament began in 1692 to pass a series of acts known collectively as the Penal Code. These prohibited Catholics from voting, holding office in Parliament, possessing arms, and entering the professions. The rationale for these acts was not simply religious persecution: they provided the legal basis for an Angelican ascendancy.[6] While serving the cause of English domination, they fueled the growth of Irish nationalism.

The eighteenth century witnessed the development of a new phenomenon. Increasingly, Catholics and Protestants (and especially Presbyterians, also subjected to religious and political persecution) united in their contempt for British interference:

> During the seventeenth and eighteenth centuries, Ireland's economic development was deliberately retarded and distorted by England's colonial policies. Growth in any branch of trade or manufacture which presented a

threat to English economic expansion was promptly curtailed. . . . By the second half of the eighteenth century many Protestant settlers had begun to develop a spirit of independence . . . the germ of a new Irish nationalism.[7]

The emergence of this united Irish nationalism led to two significant developments during the eighteenth century. These were Theobald Wolfe Tone's formation in 1791 of the Society of United Irishmen and the establishment in 1795 of the Orange Order.

The Society of United Irishmen was a republican nationalist movement led by Protestant manufacturers. Inspired in part by the success of the American and French Revolutions, the United Irishmen attracted considerable support from Catholics as a result of their commitment to Catholic emancipation and Irish independence. Although they sought and achieved legislative reforms (such as the Catholic Relief Act of 1793, which repealed parts of the Penal Code), the United Irishman did not rule out the use of more militant tactics. Seeking to exploit the conflict between England and France, the United Irishmen sought French aid for an armed uprising. When the promised assistance failed to materialize, a 1798 rebellion was quickly crushed.

The other important development occurring at the end of the eighteenth century was the formation of the Orange Order in 1795. The Orange Order, "established to drive a wedge between Catholics and Presbyterians who had occasionally managed to make common cause in attacking Anglican landlords,"[8] was in large part a response to the United Irishmen. This organization, which survives to the present day, continues to be one of the most important players in the Northern Irish conflict.

Following the abortive rebellion of the United Irishmen and determined to settle the "Irish question" once and for all, the English parliament at Westminster passed the 1801 Act of Union: "The 500-year old Dublin Parliament was abolished; Ireland was directly bound to Great Britain in a 'United Kingdom'; and the Government in London was designated the first and last recourse for all matters involving this supposedly equal component of a single nation."[9] In 1817 the Irish Exchequer, the last relic of Ireland's independent existence, was combined with that of England. Since 1801, Irish politics have been shaped by the opposing movements of Unionism and Irish nationalism.

With the political and economic union of Britain and Ireland, Ireland was poised for an industrial revolution. Development proceeded unevenly, however, so that by the turn of the century only Ulster—and particularly Belfast—had become industrialized. The rest of the island's economy continued to be centered around agriculture. The reason for this uneven development was the Ulster Plantation two centuries earlier. In the south and west, landholdings were quite large, employed native labor, and were capital intensive. In the northeast, however, confiscated lands were turned over in relatively small parcels to colonists who had insufficient capital to engage in large-scale agriculture. These settlers, seeking to supplement their income, provided the basis for an emerging linen industry.[10] By 1900, linen production had been complemented by textiles and shipbuilding and the area around Belfast had become the site of a modern but export-oriented industrial economy.

The most widely known event in Irish history is also widely misunderstood—the "Great Famine" of 1846–47. Although this incident is commonly understood as a natural disaster, akin to an earthquake or volcanic eruption, it is more accurately portrayed as a result of the ruthless exploitation and domination of a predominantly Catholic agricultural proletariat by Protestant Irish and absentee English landed capital. Concurrent with the industrialization of Belfast, the rural population in Ireland was being subjected to the transformation from feudal to capitalist relations of production. The dynamics of this transition and their exploitation as a class put the majority of the Irish in an extremely vulnerable position:

the fact that ownership of the land remained in the hands of a small minority of landlords in search of maximum profit meant that the agricultural proletariat brought into being . . . was from first to last pitifully vulnerable—a vulnerability underlined in the most tragic fashion when the profit indicator began to swing away from tillage and point once more to [a less labor-intensive] pasture farming, with the implication that the best economic interests of the landlords lay in the elimination of a large part of this rural proletariat. That elimination the Famine itself was to achieve.[11]

While the failure of the potato crop as a result of disease was clearly a natural occurrence, the place of the potato as the staple of the rural Irish diet was no accident. Three-quarters of Ireland's arable land was used in the production of grain and livestock, but most of this was shipped to England, at a profit, for English consumption. Given that the vast majority of the Irish population was forced to subsist on whatever could be grown on the remaining land, the potato was the obvious choice. "Wheat would have taken three times the acreage to feed the same number of people."[12] And although the potato crop failed throughout the island in the summer of 1846, grain and livestock production were unaffected. The total value of agricultural production in Ireland in 1847 was just under 45 million pounds sterling, enough to feed twice the island's eight million people (albeit at subsistence levels). But because of the nature of the capitalist political economy, this output was a commodity destined for the marketplace. Those who suffered from the potato blight were those who lacked the wherewithal to purchase food on the market. At least two million Irish men, women, and children—a quarter of the population—were in such a position. Over one million emigrated and possibly over one million died of starvation and disease. But as William Perdue points out, ironically, "as is often the case with the politics of food, the problem was not one of availability but structural inequality."[13]

The British state, as the representative of the ruling class, supported the economic interests of the landlords in reducing the population of the island. And the Irish population seems to have been well aware of this fact. As "death by starvation" verdicts became commonplace at inquests, one jury added a rider stating that "death was caused through the negligence of the [British] government in not sending food into the country in due time." Another jury foreman "would bring in no verdict but one of willful murder against [British Prime Minister] Lord John Russell."[14] While premeditation is probably too strong, the British government was certainly culpable:

> There is no historical evidence implicating the British government in a conspiracy to exterminate the population of Ireland, but many government officials, as well as those advising them, looked upon the famine as a God-sent solution to the so-called Irish question. One such was Nassau Senior, professor of political economy at Oxford and a staunch supporter of the views of the British treasury. Senior did not hesitate to express himself on the Irish question, and after doing so to an Oxford colleague named Benjamin Jowett, the latter remarked: "I have always felt a certain horror of political economists, since I heard one of them say that he feared the famine . . . in Ireland would not kill more than a million people, and that would scarcely be enough to do any good.[15]

The British government refused to interfere with the interests of the capitalist class or the principles of laissez-faire economics.

While the potato blight was a natural disaster, the famine was not. The famine was a decisive event in Irish history. The hatred of the British that it engendered and the exodus of Irish men and women that ensued have left their mark upon the character of Northern Irish society and Irish nationalism. "Almost a century and a half after the event, Irish people assess the catastrophe in these terms: 'God surely brought the blight, but it was England that caused the Famine.' "[16]

One of the most immediate and tangible effects of the famine was the emergence during the last half of the nineteenth century of a renewed movement for national autonomy in the form of a markedly different kind of Irish nationalism.[17] The "Fenians" or the IRB (the Irish Republican Brotherhood or the Irish Revolutionary Brotherhood, depending on the politics of the supporters), founded during this period, sought not only a break with Britain but increasingly a revolutionary transformation of Irish society as well. The Fenians were an underground military organization that prepared to liberate Ireland by force and expropriate the property of the landlords. While the group enjoyed the general support of the peasantry, "its main strength and source of inspiration" derived from Irish émigrés to England, Scotland, Australia, and particularly the United States.[18] While their attempts at insurrection suffered from miscommunication and infiltration, the Fenian movement did serve for nationalists as a model of a revolutionary nationalist movement and for Unionists as further proof of the disloyalty of the subject nation:

> To defenders of the Union in Ireland and to the reactionary press in England, "Fenianism" became a vile epithet. Gradually, too, it was extended to apply to all Irish Catholics, whether or not they practiced revolutionary warfare, so that "Fenian" and "papist" became interchangeable terms of derision. A century later, Protestants along the Shankill Road in Belfast still refer to Catholics in general as "Fenian bastards."[19]

Beginning roughly in the 1870s, Ireland's agricultural economy underwent a significant transformation. In response to the growth of international markets for agricultural products—that is, forced to compete with British and American agriculture—Irish agriculture underwent a further shift from tillage to pasture farming, and prices plummeted. Poor weather contributed to the misery by reducing the size of harvests. As a result, many smallholders lost their land. "In 1877, 980 families were evicted (a total well above the average). In 1880, there were 2,110."[20]

These economic developments led to the organization of the Land League by Michael Davitt, a Fenian convict, in 1879. "The League was comprised mostly of tenant organizations that had been formed after the Famine, although it included a few Fenians and other ardent nationalists and republicans."[21] The Land League sought reforms that would give tenants some security in their holdings and rights to improvements they made to them. Among their more effective and innovative tactics was the organized ostracism of those serving evictions. Through their efforts, the Land League forced from Westminster agrarian reform.

"Encouraged by the success of the land war, rural Ireland and its legislative representatives started, in the early 1880s, to press a demand for Home Rule."[22] These parliamentary struggles were led by Charles Stewart Parnell, a leader of the Land League. Most advocates of home rule (i.e., regional autonomy) sought simply the reestablishment of the Irish Parliament, although some supported this was a first step toward an independent republic. In the elections of 1885, supporters of home rule took 85 of the 103 Irish seats at Westminster. In 1886, a home-rule bill was introduced and defeated by the House of Commons. In 1893, the second home-rule bill passed the House of Commons but was vetoed by the House of Lords. In 1895, the Tories returned to power at Westminster and home rule would have to wait.

The final decades of the nineteenth century witnessed a renewed interest in Gaelic language and culture. The Gaelic Athletic Association and the Gaelic League engendered an appreciation of Ireland's lost heritage and a sense of national identity among the people. In 1899, the year after the hundredth anniversary of Tone's rebellion, Arthur Griffith founded his newspaper, the *United Irishman,* and in 1905 he established a political party, Sinn Fein. Sinn Fein (pronounced "shin fane," meaning, in Gaelic, "ourselves alone") sought an Irish Ireland. As its name implies, Sinn Fein embraced the Gaelic revival; it also advanced a policy of protective tariffs and was supportive of the development of indigenous Irish capital.

Alongside the development of Sinn Fein was the emergence of the working-class movement in Ireland. The formation of the Irish Socialist Republican Party in 1896 by James Connolly and the Irish Transport and General Workers' Union in 1907 by James Larkin were the most important organizational expressions of Irish socialism. While these movements met with some success (most notably Connolly's ability to articulate the language of nationalism with that of socialism and Larkin's leadership of the 1907 Belfast dock strike), they failed to overcome the two-hundred-year-old ethnic conflict between planter and gael. Whereas anywhere else in Europe their efforts would likely have led at least to the establishment of a socialist labor party, the character of Norther Irish society prevented this:

Capital as it developed in Ireland was sectarian capital, concentrated in Protestant hands in the northeast. Labour, when it emerged in Ireland was also sectarian; in the North specifically, this entailed a skilled Protestant proletariat and a Catholic proletariat that was unskilled and disproportionately performed the role of the North's reserve army of labour. Two class alliances thus emerged as a result of this history, the working class being split, half owing its allegiance to the Unionist alliance, half to the nationalist alliance. The bourgeoisie was also split, the Unionists winning Protestant working class support through clientelism, the Nationalists blocked by the Unionists in their attempts to become a fully-fledged bourgeoisie. Given these alliances, "proper class politics" did not emerge in Northern Ireland. The traditional British political format of Labour versus Conservative . . . did not emerge in Northern Ireland. In the place of proper class politics, history bequeathed sectarian class politics.[23]

Given these circumstances, the socialist enterprise has had formidable barriers to overcome.

As the threat of home rule and the threat of worker solidarity loomed, Protestants formed and revived movements aimed at preserving their privileges. In 1902, the Independent Orange Order was established. These "renegade Unionists . . . attacked establishment Unionism for failing in its duty to see that Protestant workers and small farmers received preferential treatment over Catholics in the political and economic life of Northern Ireland."[24] In 1905, the Ulster Unionist Party was established. And in 1912, following the introduction of the third home-rule bill after the return of the Liberals to power at Westminster (and given that the removal of the veto power of the House of Lords made passage a likelihood), Edward Carson composed a "Covenant" pledging its five hundred thousand signers to resist home rule (and, by implication, the duly elected government of the United Kingdom) by whatever means necessary. In 1913, the Ulster Volunteer Force (UVF) was established to prepare to back up Carson's covenant militarily. The Tories aided and abetted Carson and the UVF.

After a series of negotiations and attempts at compromise failed, and following the mass resignations of fifty-eight British officers unwilling to do battle with the "loyal" Unionists, the more militant nationalists responded with the formation and arming of the Irish Volunteers. With Ireland on the brink of civil war, World War I broke out. The third home-rule bill was passed with the stipulation that it would not take effect until after the war and unless the Unionists were satisfied with its provisions.

Some members of the Irish Volunteers, unwilling to wait for the end of the war, decided to force the issue. On Easter Monday, 1916, a group of about one hundred men led by James Connolly and a republican named Padraig Pearse occupied the General Post Office in Dublin and declared Irish independence. Only about sixteen hundred Volunteers answered the call to arms; thirteen hundred died in the fighting, and the Easter Rising was put down in a week. Connolly, Pearse, and several other commanders of the uprising were executed. While the majority of the Irish recognized this attempt at severing the link with Britain as an exercise in futility, the executions of these patriots enraged nationalist Ireland.

The outrage of the Irish took form in 1918 when Sinn Fein won 73 of 105 Irish seats at Westminster. As a further expression of the contempt with which they held British rule, 36 of the 73 were serving prison terms for their republican activities.

> True to their campaign pledges and to their popular mandate, the members of the *Sinn Fein* contingent would have nothing to do with Westminster. All of them declined to sit in the Parliament of a foreign oppressor, and they declared themselves the elected representatives of an Irish republic. Those *Sinn Feiners* who were not in gaol then met in Dublin in January 1919 and formed a secessionist legislature—*Dail Eireann*.[25]

With the declaration of independence, the Irish Volunteers dropped their name in favor of the Irish Republican Army (IRA) and have since served as the armed wing of Sinn Fein. Under the command of Michael Collins, the IRA initiated a highly effective guerrilla war for Irish independence.

It soon became clear that England had to do something to placate the rebels, so in 1920 the Government of Ireland Act was passed by Westminster. The island was partitioned and home rule was granted to both of the newly created states. The boundary between the two was determined in such a way as to ensure Protestant domination of the industrialized north:

> As to why six counties had been selected rather than four or nine or any other number, the reasons were unashamedly straightforward. The traditional nine counties of Ulster held 900,000 Protestants, most of whom supported the British connection, and 700,000 Catholics, most of whom wanted to end it. However, in the six counties which were later to become Northern Ireland, the religious breakdown was 820,000 Protestants and 430,000 Catholics. In 1920, C. C. Craig, brother of James Craig, the first Prime Minister of Northern Ireland, expressed the case frankly in the House of Commons: "If we had a nine-county parliament, with sixty-four members, the Unionist majority would be about three or four, but in a six-county parliament, with fifty-two members, the Unionist majority would be about ten."[26]

The Dail and the IRA regarded partition and home rule as unacceptable and continued the fight. In 1921, England offered a second treaty: while partition itself was non-negotiable, a commission would be set up to reevaluate the boundary. In addition, the southwestern twenty-six counties would be granted the status of "Free State" but would retain membership in the British Commonwealth. A slim majority of the Dail accepted this proposal with the idea that it might prove a stepping-stone to an independent republic. The majority of the IRA rejected this proposal for what it was—something less than unconditional Irish independence. The antitreaty forces then waged a bloody civil war for over two years until, in 1923, they declared a cease-fire.

Devolved government in six of the nine counties of Ulster as a province of the United Kingdom of Great Britain and Northern Ireland was a gift not sought by Protestants. They wanted to preserve the Union in its entirety. The British government, however, that it could no longer maintain control over the entire island, but it could justify its continued rule over the northeast of the basis of Protestants' desire to retain the Union. Furthermore, devolved administration would distance Westminster from both the excesses of Ulster's elite and the reaction of the Catholic minority. "Like it or not—and the Unionists would quickly learn to love it—there was going to be a Protestant-dominated, devoutly loyalist parliament with jurisdiction over a chunk of Irish soil."[27]

HOME RULE TO DIRECT RULE

After the establishment of Northern Ireland, "the Unionist government took steps to strengthen its own position in power and to ensure the continued support of the whole Protestant population, regardless of class."[28] As is frequently the case in capitalist societies, "in Northern Ireland, unionisn exploited existing divisions among the working class with sectarian policies on unemployment, security, housing, and education. Working class militancy was neutralized with threats that political divisions within unionism would ensure victory to Irish nationalism."[29]

One of the first measures undertaken by the Unionist government was to eliminate proportional representation and to gerrymander the local electoral boundaries.[30] Moreover, public housing was selectively allocated to ensure that the demographics of the various wards remained stable. In addition, the franchise was restricted to "rate-payers" (i.e., property-tax payers), and business property entitled the owner to as many as six votes. This effectively disfranchised a disproportionate number of Catholics and extended the Unionist margin of victory at the polls.

To further insure Unionist hegemony, the Special Powers Act was implemented. This gave the Royal Ulster Constabulary (RUC), Northern Ireland's police force, virtually unlimited powers to search premises and detain suspects.[31]

With partition, and despite the best efforts of the Northern Irish ruling class to ensure continued hegemony (efforts that only exacerbated the situation), the seeds of confrontation were already taking root. Because "the political structure within which Unionist hegemony was reproduced depended on continued sectarian polarisation for its survival,"[32] any division within the Protestant community would topple a government already weakened by its lack of legitimacy among the Catholic third of the population. But Protestants were already divided by class and confessional differences, and it was only a matter of time before these surfaced.

ECONOMIC DECLINE, INEQUALITY, AND SECTARIAN POLITICS

The rigidity of this political establishment made it unable to deal with Ulster's economic decline. Despite the six counties' stature as the most highly industrialized region of the island, theirs was still a predominantly agricultural economy both in terms of numbers employed and in value of the product. Furthermore, Northern Ireland's industrial base remained concentrated in shipbuilding and linen manufacture, both highly export dependent. All three of these areas of economic concentration were to become crippled by the economic developments of the twentieth century; with only brief respites, the economy of Northern Ireland has been in a state of decline. International competition and mechanization reduced agricultural employment. Competition and the introduction of synthetic fibers hurt the linen industry. Competition and reduced demand crippled shipbuilding. "Agriculture, linen, and shipbuilding have accounted for the loss of more than 120,000 jobs since 1949, presenting a formidable problem in a province where the total manufacturing employment was only 183,000 in 1969."[33] Thus, "the economic foundations of Ulster's claim to political autonomy had begun to crumble even before the State of Northern Ireland was formally established."[34]

During the worldwide economic depression of the 1930s, Northern Ireland's export-dominated economy was especially hard hit. Unemployment ran in excess of 25 percent. "A 1938–39 survey found 36% of the North's population to be living in conditions of absolute poverty—i.e., they did not have enough money to buy food, clothing and fuel. The mortality rate in the Six Counties was 25% higher than in England."[35] This crisis sparked a resurgence of political conflict—a renewal of both class solidarity and sectarianism.

One of the few examples of working-class solidarity in Northern Ireland was the Outdoor Relief strike of 1932. Estimates of the strength of this movement vary widely, but between fifteen and sixty thousand Protestants and Catholics more or less spontaneously took to the streets to demonstrate against reductions in relief or welfare rates. Terrified by the apparent collapse of sectarianism, the Unionist-dominated Northern Ireland Parliament at Stormont quickly doubled these welfare payments and redoubled its efforts to drive home the sectarian wedge.

Concurrent with the emergence of class solidarity was a resurgence of sectarianism. In 1931, the Ulster Protestant League (UPL) was established—ostensibly to "safeguard the employment of Protestants."[36] While this movement was not simply the creation of the Unionist establishment, the UPL enjoyed the active support of Protestant capital:

> It was obvious that the UPL had friends in higher places. James Kelly [an interview respondent] thought it "significant that they were always given the use of the Unionist Party headquarters in Glengall Street" for their meetings and socials; and, as it openly advertised these events in the *Ulster Protestant,* it was lost on no one that the UPL was acceptable to the Unionist establishment.[37]

Despite their professed objective—safeguarding the employment of Protestants—the not-so-hidden agenda of the UPL was the intimidation of nationalist and socialist organizations and the preservation of the Union with Great Britain.[38]

In 1949, the Irish Free State declared itself a republic. Westminster reacted by passing the Ireland Act of 1949.

> This legislation cemented the bond between the North and the rest of the U.K., guaranteeing that "in no event will Northern Ireland or any part thereof cease to be a part of His majesty's dominions and of the United Kingdom, without the consent of the Parliament of Northern Ireland."
>
> Here was a precise formal articulation of what republicans call "the loyalist veto." Any possibility of self-determination by the people of all 32 counties of Ireland was expressly ruled out by the Ireland Act of 1949. Because the Parliament of Northern Ireland would always be dominated by loyalists, it could never, by its very nature, accede to the unity of the whole island.[39]

Preserving the colonial relationship under the guise of the self-determination of the people of Northern Ireland has proven to be a convenient scheme for control of the island.

However, the declaration of the Irish Republic kindled a renewed nationalism, both north and south of the border. "By 1955, the original republican party [Sinn Fein] had resurrected itself to the point where it was able to run candidates for all 12 Northern Ireland seats at Westminster.''[40] Sinn Fein candidates received 56 percent of the Catholic vote, and two candidates were elected to Westminster. The IRA ''interpreted these election results as a mandate for it to renew armed struggle in the Six Counties.''[41] Although this ''border campaign,'' called off in 1962, was largely unsuccessful, it provided a training ground for future IRA leaders.

By the late 1950s, Northern Ireland's continuing economic decline was straining the Unionist interclass alliance. Between 1950 and 1962 some 106,000 jobs were lost. In 1960, the average wage was 78 percent of that of Great Britain, and the rate of unemployment was three times higher. In 1958, the Northern Ireland Labour Party won four seats to Stormont, seats they retained in the 1962 elections. ''Very slowly, the bonds of loyalty chaining Protestant workers to the Union gently were rusting and loosening.''[42]

In addition, the economic and social inequality and injustice experienced by the Catholic community was increasingly regarded as unacceptable, especially by a growing Catholic middle class. Since the beginning of industrialization in Ulster, Catholics have done the dirty work:

> Protestants hold most of the top managerial, professional, scientific, and technical jobs. Catholics are massively underrepresented in those positions and also in relatively well-paid areas like the security forces, and the metal and electrical trades. On the other hand, they are overrepresented in such notoriously low-paid occupations as construction and personal services.[43]

Furthermore, the unemployment rate among Catholics has been consistently at least twice that of Protestants. In the Catholic ghettos of Belfast, the unemployment rate has been as high as 50 percent.[44] In household income, standards of housing, and availability of health care, Protestants as a group have been in a more advantaged position in relation to Catholics.[45] By the late 1950s, this structured injustice was beginning once again to be challenged systematically.

FAILURE OF REFORM AND INCREASING RESISTANCE

In 1963, the fourth prime minister of Northern Ireland, Terence O'Neill, took office. Although a descendent of an old landed-gentry family, O'Neill was committed to the economic development of Northern Ireland and to the political and social reforms this would require. Because he spoke the language of reform, and because he would be prevented from delivering on his promises by the intolerance of more reactionary Unionists, O'Neill's tenure as prime minister was marked by the resurgence of sectarian conflict at its bloodiest.

Even the suggestion of reform was enough to enrage many Protestants. In 1966, following a peaceful march commemorating the fiftieth anniversary of the Easter Rising, a group taking the name of Edward Carson's Volunteer Force (UVF) began a series of random attacks upon Catholic civilians.[46] Also in 1966, Ian Paisley, the founder of the "Free Presbyterian Church" and the Ulster Protestant Volunteers, began attracting attention with a trip to Rome to denounce the meeting between the Archbishop of Canterbury and the Pope, the publication of a weekly newspaper, and a march on the Presbyterian General Assembly that sparked a riot. Paisley, committed to the preservation of the Union and opposed to any kind of reform, had nebulous contacts with the UVF. A man arrested for one of UVF's murders said, "I am terribly sorry I ever heard of that man Paisley or decided to follow him."[47] Well before O'Neill attempted to ameliorate the worst injustices of Northern Irish society, reactionaries were mobilizing to oppose change.

With the failure of O'Neill to implement reforms and in the face of mass Protestant opposition to even the suggestion of reform, the Catholic population was ready to force the issue. In 1967, the Northern Ireland Civil Rights Association (NICRA) was formed. Organized primarily by middle-class Catholic liberals, NICRA's agenda included reforming the electoral system, remapping gerrymandered electoral boundaries, enacting antidiscrimination laws, introducing a point system to allocate housing, and repealing the Special Powers Act. The issue of partition was not raised; the NICRA simply sought the extension to Northern Ireland of the civil rights enjoyed by all other British subjects.

In 1968, in defiance of a ban, the NICRA led a civil rights march of two thousand in Londonberry (or Derry, the name of the city itself being contested). At the Craigavon Bridge, the marchers were met by the Royal Ulster Constabulary (RUC), who ordered them to disperse. In compliance, the marchers were turning back when their passage was blocked by another group of the RUC who had sealed off the street from its other end. The RUC then proceeded to charge the marchers, batoning them as they tried to disperse. Among the injured was Gerry Fitt, member of Parliament for West Belfast. A television interview with Fitt at the scene of the march, his clothes bloodied, brought the reality of Northern Irish society to Britain and the world.

Pressed by an embarrassed British government to back up his reformist rhetoric with concrete policy, O'Neill acceded to some of the NICRA's demands. He instituted a point system for the allocation of housing, revoked the extra votes given to business owners, and agreed to a review of the Special Powers Act. While this was enough to appease moderate elements within the NICRA, many Catholics saw these measures as too little, too late. A group of students, radicalized by the brutality of the RUC at Derry, had formed a group called People's Democracy (PD). In its attempt to keep the pressure on O'Neill, PD sponsored a march from Belfast to Londonderry on January 1, 1969. With an RUC escort, about a hundred marchers proceeded uneventfully until a few miles from Derry, where they were set upon by a mob of about 350 armed with clubs. As the RUC stood by, the marchers were badly beaten. Those who could continued on to Derry. After their story was told, barricades went up in defense of the Catholic ghetto known as the Bogside. The RUC regarded this as provocative and attacked, "running amok through the area, smashing down doors, yelling sectarian insults and generally intending to finish the job begun earlier in the day by the loyalist mob."[48]

In the face of the civil rights movement, the interclass Protestant alliance was breaking down.[49] While O'Neill was able to hold the Unionist Party (UP) together after his initial reform package, his appointment of a commission to investigate the causes of the violence in the Bogside was too much for the right wing of the UP. In the next election, O'Neill barely held his seat against a challenge by Paisley, and almost a third of the members of the UP elected to the Stormont Parliament were opposed to O'Neill's policy of limited reform. After a series of bombings (which turned out to have been planted by the UVF in an attempt to implicate the inactive IRA and discredit O'Neill's moderation),[50] riots in Derry and Belfast, and the mobilization of loyalist vigilante groups, O'Neill resigned as prime minister and leader of the Unionist Party. He was replaced by James Chichester-Clark, who, although committed to the reform of Northern Ireland, was more conciliatory toward the party's right wing.

GROWING VIOLENCE IN THE NORTH

In August 1969, following a loyalist march commemorating the anniversary of James II's defeat at Derry, riots broke out at the Bogside. Residents of the Catholic ghetto proclaimed it "Free Derry" and held off an RUC and loyalist attack for several days. The British Army was called out. Rallying in support of "Free Derry," members of the community of the Falls, a Catholic ghetto in Belfast, were attacked by Protestant vigilantes who proceeded to burn over two hundred homes to the ground. The RUC followed the loyalists, firing machine guns indiscriminately. "Ten people were killed and about 100 wounded during the two day RUC and loyalist attack on the

Catholic slum."[51] By September, six thousand British troops were stationed in Northern Ireland.

With the conflict in the North growing increasingly bloody, and with the British Army once again active on Irish soil, a bitter debate within Sinn Fein and the IRA over the direction of the movement led to a split in the organization.[52] After the Border Campaign, the IRA had supported a policy that stressed the importance of promoting interethnic working class solidarity through reform as a precursor to reunification and socialist transformation. In light of the new realities, and perhaps especially in view of the reaction of the Protestant masses toward reform, a minority of the members of Sinn Fein and the IRA (but the vast majority of IRA commanders in the North, some of whom had sought arms to defend the Catholic ghettos against Protestant vigilantism) broke away from what would become known as the "official" movement and established the Provisional Sinn Fein and the Provisional IRA (PIRA, often referred to as the "Provos"). The Provos renewed their commitment to militant republicanism and parliamentary abstentionism. The Provos sought to make Northern Ireland ungovernable by either Stormont or the British.

With the help of sympathizers, particularly in the United States, the Provos began arming themselves.[53] By the spring of 1970, they began bombing military and commercial targets. These bombings were accompanied by warnings, and no one was killed in this first series of attacks. In late 1970, the Official IRA joined the armed struggle (although they did not engage in the bombing of commercial targets on the ground that this merely deprived workers of jobs). "On the street level there was often close cooperation and friendly relations between OIRA and PIRA guerrillas."[54]

The escalating violence was taking its toll on the traditional character of Northern Ireland politics. Relatively feeble attempts were made to bridge the sectarian gulf. The Alliance Party (AP) and Social Democratic and Labour Party (SDLP) were formed and received increasing support, especially from the middle class, as nominally nonsectarian parties. Their positions on the border, however (the Alliance Party was pro-Union and the SDLP pro-reunification), presented an insurmountable obstacle to the development of interethnic solidarity. At the same time, the Provos' campaign was strengthening and radicalizing the right wing of the Unionist Party. Ian Paisley was elected to Stormont and, later, to Westminster. Chichester-Clark was forced to resign and was replaced by Brian Faulkner in 1971.

Because nothing Stormont or the British government tried was having an impact upon the effectiveness of the Provos, and with popular support for the organization at its peak, Faulkner decided to break the back of the movement by instituting a policy of internment. In August of 1971, the army raided the Catholic communities of Northern Ireland. Over 300 IRA members, civil rights activists, and ordinary citizens were held without charge, and of these 226 were interned without trial. Many were subjected to severe physical mistreatment and psychological torture.[55] Rather than crushing the IRA, internment worked to the political advantage of militant nationalism.[56] The Provos accelerated their bombing campaign, popular support increased further, and the barricades went back up. The Bogside and the Falls were effectively liberated by the Provos, who could recruit, train, and manufacture explosives free from harassment. "Far from being its salvation, internment actually marked the beginning of the end for Stormont."[57]

On Sunday, January 30, 1972, a march of fifteen thousand took place in Derry. As the procession wound its way through the Bogside, it encountered one of the roadblocks set up by the British Army to contain the demonstration. Most of the marchers turned away from the army, but several hundred demonstrators, mostly teenagers, approached the barrier and began shouting insults and lobbing rocks and bottles. After a few minutes, the army moved in to make arrests. As the crowd started to retreat, the army suddenly opened fire; thirteen were killed and twenty-nine were wounded.[58] "Bloody Sunday" led to international condemnation, another escalation of violence by both the Provos and the radical right, and, in March 1972, the suspension of Stormont and the imposition of direct rule.

DIRECT RULE AND THE FUTURE OF NORTHERN IRELAND

Since the British government took over the day-to-day affairs of Northern Ireland, it has sought to restore political control to the Irish. Content with economic domination (which it also enjoys over the Republic of Ireland), direct rule has become a political and economic liability. So far, however, the British government has been unable to wash its hands of its iniquitous creation.

The first attempt at this was the election, by means of proportional representation, of a Northern Ireland Assembly in June 1973, which was to negotiate the formation of a power-sharing government. In addition, this Assembly would participate in the formation of a Council of Ireland to address issues of concern to both Northern Ireland and the Republic. The Unionist vote was split, with a majority of these seats going to a coalition including Paisley's Democratic Unionist Party (DUP) and the Vanguard Unionist Progressive Party (VUPP) led by William Craig. This coalition was vehemently opposed to the idea of power sharing and refused to participate in the dilution of Protestant hegemony. However, a coalition including

Faulkner's Official Unionist Party, the Alliance Party, and the SDLP was able to put together a working majority. Faulkner was named chief executive. At a meeting at Sunningdale, England, agreement was reached on the formation of a (largely symbolic) Council of Ireland.

The same day that the Sunningdale conference convened, members of the coalition opposed to power sharing and the Council of Ireland met and formed the United Ulster Unionist Council (UUUC). It soon became clear that the majority of Protestants shared their agenda when, in February 1974, the UUUC won eleven of the twelve Northern Irish seats at Westminster. In May, the Ulster Workers Council, in support of the UUUC, called a phenomenally successful general strike. Within two weeks, the executive resigned and the Northern Ireland Assembly was suspended.

With the failure of Sunningdale, and the resumption of the Provos' bombing campaign, the British government held an election for a constitutional convention. As the UUUC won a majority of these seats, and as they would settle for no less than the restoration of Stormont, the convention quickly collapsed in 1976.[59]

In March of that year, the British government sought to criminalize the movement for Irish reunification.[60] Beginning in March 1976, all those convicted of political crimes were treated like common criminals rather than being allowed "special category status"—that is, treated as political prisoners, allowed to organize their own activities, wear street clothes, and so forth. The implication was that the "troubles" were the result of a breakdown of law and order and not a political conflict. In response, many of those arrested after this time "went on the blanket." They refused to wear prison uniforms and took to smearing the walls of their cells with their own excrement in a "dirty protest," and they organized a series of hunger strikes. The last of these was led by Bobby Sands. Before his death in May 1981, he was elected MP at Westminster. The death of ten strikers aroused nationalist sentiment, and in November reforms were instituted that partially met the prisoners' demands.[61]

Another instrument of repression used by the nationalist movement was the "supergrass" (informant) strategy. This entailed offers of immunity from prosecution and other inducements to attract accomplice evidence. Between 1981 and 1983, nearly six hundred were arrested based on the unsubstantiated accusations of informants to the RUC. While supergrass trials continued until 1986, they served only to further delegitimize the law: they did nothing "to prevent the continuation of the violence."[62]

While the British government did not moderate its position on IRA criminality, the 1980s in Northern Ireland were marked by a second tentative movement toward reform and a search for a resolution to the conflict.

Support for the Democratic Unionist Party and Sinn Fein shifted to the Official Unionist, Alliance, and the Social Democratic and Labour Parties. For its part, the British government found it in its best interests to seek "any set of policies which can hold out the prospect of eventually decoupling Northern Ireland from the United Kingdom."[63]

The two most important initiatives of the 1980s were the New Ireland Forum Report and the Anglo-Irish Agreement. In May 1984, the major moderate nationalist parties in Northern Ireland and the Republic issued the New Ireland Forum Report, which outlined three options for Ireland's future: joint authority, confederation, and reunification. Although Britain rejected these alternatives, the proposal led to a British dialogue with the Republic and, in 1985, to the Anglo-Irish Agreement. While this document reaffirms the "loyalist veto," it also pledges support for a devolved government acceptable to both Protestants and Catholics, promises an examination of human rights reforms, and establishes a permanent intergovernmental conference giving the Republic a consultative role in the administration of Northern Ireland.[64] In April 1991, discussions about the political future of Northern Ireland resumed, but these led nowhere.[65] Militant groups rejected the Anglo-Irish Agreement and these negotiations: right-wing unionists regarded any compromise as a betrayal; the IRA regarded the process as yet another attempt to perpetuate partition.

Over eight hundred years since the beginning of English involvement in Ireland, the "Irish question" remains unresolved. The IRA is once again taking the conflict to English soil and promising economic sabotage—they continue to engage in what they argue is a war of national liberation. Unionist vigilantees continue randomly to attack Catholics and to target nationalist activists.[66] The militancy of these groups and the centrality of the issue of partition makes a negotiated compromise virtually inconceivable.

Essentially there are four possible resolutions to the conflict.[67] First, Northern Ireland could continue to be ruled from Westminster directly or through the reintroduction of devolved government. Second, Northern Ireland might be granted independence. Third, Northern Ireland might be repartitioned to create a smaller province with a more highly concentrated Protestant majority. And fourth, Ireland might move toward reintegration in the form of joint British/Republican authority for Northern Ireland, confederation, or reunification. Each of these options would be bitterly opposed by the rival groups. But because conflict is built into the structure of Northern Irish society, it seems clear that change in some form will occur.

Although there will likely be no rapid or peaceful resolution of the national question in Ireland, the direction of change seems to point toward the increasing reintegration of the divided island. The restoration of devolved government has been attempted without success since 1972, and the British government's desire to disengage from the political conflict rules out the normalization of direct rule.[68] Because of its dependence on British security forces and subsidies, Northern Irish independence is not a viable alternative: "If forced to live within its means, Northern Ireland would experience a catastrophic fall in material living standards, which would fall to 60% of the present level or less."[69] Finally, a repartition of Northern Ireland could only be an interim resolution; the question of the British connection to this new, smaller Northern Ireland would remain. Furthermore, any repartition scheme would meet with strong opposition from those who found themselves on the wrong side of the new border, and its implementation would escalate sectarian violence.[70] While it would be naive to expect a permanent solution to the conflict soon, such a resolution will require the reintegration of Ireland through the implementation of joint authority, confederation, or reunification. This process will meet with violent opposition from loyalists as well as require the accommodation of Protestants by Catholic Ireland (beginning with the Republic's repeal of intolerant divorce and abortion legislation). Undoubtedly, as in the past, and making of Irish history will be difficult. Nevertheless, developments since the imposition of direct rule point in this direction. For the first time, British interests would be served by extrication from the conflict. In addition, the Anglo-Irish Agreement's legitimization of the "Irish dimension" to the conflict signals a willingness on the part of the British government to challenge loyalist intransigence. And British and Irish membership in the European Community would provide a neutral forum for the resolution of the conflict and should make the border increasingly irrelevant.[71] These developments provide some basis for optimism.

NOTES

1. T. A. Jackson, *Ireland Her Own: An Outline History of the Irish Struggle* (New York: International Publishers, 1970), pp. 24–25.
2. Ibid., p. 32.
3. Ibid., p. 34.
4. Ibid., p. 53.
5. Kevin Kelley, *The Longest War: Northern Ireland and the IRA* (Westport, Conn.: Lawrence Hill, 1982), p. 5.
6. Michael MacDonald, *Children of Wrath: Political Violence in Northern Ireland* (Cambridge: Polity Press, 1986), pp. 38–40.
7. Belinda Probert, *Beyond Orange and Green: The Political Economy of the Northern Ireland Crisis* (London: Zed Press, 1978), pp. 20–21.
8. Kelley, *The Longest War,* p. 10.
9. Ibid., pp. 11–12.

10. Peter Gibbon, *The Origins of Ulster Unionism* (Manchester, 1976), pp. 13–14, cited in Probert, *Beyond Orange and Green,* pp. 30–31.

11. F.S.L. Lyons, *Ireland since the Famine* (New York: Charles Scribner's Sons, 1971), p. 30; parenthetical comment mine.

12. Thomas Gallagher, *Paddy's Lament: Ireland, 1846–1847—Prelude to Hatred* (New York: Harcourt Brace Jovanovich, 1982), pp. 20–21.

13. William D. Perdue, *Terrorism and the State: A Critique of Domination through Fear* (New York: Praeger, 1989), p. 27.

14. Gallagher, *Paddy's Lament,* pp. 76–77.

15. Ibid., p. 85.

16. Kelley, *The Longest War,* p. 16.

17. Karl Marx, Letter to Frederick Engels, November 30, 1867, in R. Dixon, ed., *Ireland and the Irish Question* (New York: International Publishers, 1972), p. 147.

18. Jackson, *Ireland Her Own,* pp. 295–96.

19. Kelley, *The Longest War,* p. 20.

20. Jackson, *Ireland Her Own,* p. 320.

21. Kelley, *The Longest War,* p. 20.

22. Ibid., p. 21.

23. Bill Rolston, "Reformism and Class Politics in Northern Ireland: The Case of the Trade Unions," *The Insurgent Sociologist* 10, no. 2 (Fall 1980): 76.

24. Jim MacLaughlin, "Ulster Unionist Hegemony and Regional Industrial Policy in Northern Ireland, 1945–1972" (Discussion paper, Department of Geography, Syracuse University, Syracuse, N.Y., 1983), p. 10.

25. Kelley, *The Longest War,* p. 35.

26. John Darby, *Northern Ireland: The Background to the Conflict* (Belfast: Appletree Press, 1983), p. 20.

27. Kelley, *The Longest War,* p. 38.

28. Bob Rowthorn and Naomi Wayne, *Northern Ireland: The Political Economy of Conflict* (Cambridge: Polity Press, 1988), p. 29.

29. Ellen Hazelkorn, "Why Is There No Socialism in Ireland?" *Science and Society* 53, no. 2 (Summer 1989): 139.

30. Probert, *Beyond Orange and Green,* p. 60.

31. Alfred McClung Lee, *Terrorism in Northern Ireland* (New York: General Hall, 1983), pp. 61–67.

32. Probert, *Beyond Orange and Green,* p. 65.

33. Ibid., p. 67.

34. Ibid., p. 68.

35. Kelley, *The Longest War,* p. 65.

36. Mike Millotte, *Communism in Modern Ireland* (Dublin: Gill and Macmillan, 1984), p. 127.

37. Ronnie Munck and Bill Rolston, *Belfast in the Thirties: An Oral History* (Belfast: Blackstaff, 1987), p. 40.

38. Ibid., p. 40; Millotte, *Communism in Modern Ireland,* p. 127.

39. Kelley, *The Longest War,* p. 69.

40. Ibid., p. 72.

41. Ibid., p. 73.

42. Ibid., p. 74.

43. Rowthorn and Wayne, *Northern Ireland,* p. 107.

44. Ibid., pp. 110–18.

45. See, for example, Frank Gaffikin and Mike Morrissey, "Poverty and Politics in Northern Ireland," in Paul Teague, ed., *Beyond the Rhetoric: Politics, the Economy and Social Policy in Northern Ireland* (London: Lawrence and Wishart, 1987), pp. 149–51.

46. John F. Galliher and Jerry L. DeGregory, *Violence in Northern Ireland: Understanding Protestant Perspectives* (Dublin: Gill and Macmillan, 1985), pp. 22–23.

47. Ibid., p. 96.

48. Ibid., p. 110.

49. Katherine O'Sullivan See, *First World Nationalisms: Class and Ethnic Politics in Northern Ireland and Quebec* (Chicago: University of Chicago Press, 1986), pp. 118–21.

50. Patrick Buckland, *A History of Northern Ireland* (New York: Holmes and Meier, 1981), p. 127.

51. Ibid., p. 118.

52. Erhard Rumpf and A. C. Hepburn, *Nationalism and Socialism in Twentieth Century Ireland* (New York: Barnes and Noble), pp. 158–61.

53. For a discussion of the U.S. connection, see Adrian Guelke, *Northern Ireland: The International Perspective* (Dublin: Gill and Macmillan, 1988), pp. 128–52.

54. Ibid., p. 140.

55. John Magee, *Northern Ireland: Crisis and Conflict* (London: Routledge and Kegan Paul, 1974), pp. 145–47.

56. Ronald Weitzer, *Transforming Settler States: Communal Conflict and Internal Security in Northern Ireland and Zimbabwe* (Berkeley: University of California Press, 1990), p. 129.

57. Ibid., p. 160.

58. Kelley, *The Longest War*, p. 163.

59. Michael J. Cunningham, *British Government Policy in Northern Ireland, 1969–89: Its Nature and Execution* (Manchester: Manchester University Press, 1991), pp. 93–100.

60. Weitzer, *Transforming Settler States*, pp. 206–7.

61. Martin Wallace, *British Government in Northern Ireland: From Devolution to Direct Rule* (London: David and Charles, 1982), pp. 158–60.

62. Cunningham, *British Government Policy in Northern Ireland, 1969–89*, pp. 156–58.

63. Henry Patterson, "Ireland: A New Phase in the Conflict between Nationalism and Unionism," *Science and Society* 53, no. 2 (Summer 1989): 216.

64. Cunningham, *British Government Policy in Northern Ireland, 1969–89*, pp. 177–80.

65. Neil Collins and Frank McCann, *Irish Politics Today*, 2d ed. (Manchester: Manchester University Press, 1991), p. 122.

66. As this book was being prepared for press, new developments have revived hope. On August 31, 1994, the IRA announced a unilateral cease-fire. After continued attacks, including the September 5 car bombing of Sinn Fein headquarters in Belfast, failed to provoke a response, loyalist paramilitaries joined the cease-fire on October 13. Formal negotiations regarding the future of Northern Ireland will likely begin soon.

67. Rowthorn and Wayne, *Northern Ireland*, p. 126.

68. John McGarry and Brendan O'Leary, "Northern Ireland's Options: A Framework for Analysis," in John McGarry and Brendan O'Leary, eds., *The Future of Northern Ireland* (Oxford: Clarendon Press, 1990), pp. 298–99.

69. Bob Rowthorn, "Northern Ireland: An Economy in Crisis," in Teague, *Beyond the Rhetoric*, p. 118. See also Frank Gaffikin and Mike Morrissey, *Northern Ireland: The Thatcher Years* (London: Zed Books, 1990), pp. 48–49.

70. McGarry and O'Leary, "Northern Ireland's Options," p. 271.

71. Ibid., p. 298.

Basque Nationalism and the Struggle for Self-Determination in the Basque Country

After its defeat in the Spanish-American War in 1898, Spain experienced a decline in its national image and subsequently a call for regeneration. This new situation gave rise to the idea of a "center" around which different regions were to be organized, an idea that theoretically allowed for a kind of regionalism that would preserve the symbolic basis of traditional society—for example, in the Basque Country, the *fueros* or traditional Basque laws.[1] This regionalism could then be transformed into nationalism if a given region considered itself no longer part of a national whole but rather a whole in itself. Basque advocates of this type of thinking stood for a prenational policy based on the protection and preservation of the *fueros*.

During this period a great deal of wealth was generated in the Basque Country by exporting Vizcayan iron to England. The earnings were invested in the creation and expansion of an important steel and iron industry along the Vizcayan river inlet of Bilbao. By the end of the nineteenth century three Vizcayan companies were producing three-quarters of all iron forged in the Spanish state. The directors of these companies created the Bank of Vizcaya. This Vizcayan iron-and-steel financial oligarchy set the standards for protectionism in trade and in doing so forged the first economic nationalism in Spain.[2] The great demand for labor resulted in large concentrations of immigrant Spanish workers, and in the 1880s and 1890s the mining zone of Vizcaya became the main stronghold of Spanish socialism.

One of the most influential political parties in the Basque Country is the Spanish Socialist Workers' Party (Partido Socialista Obrero Español, PSOE). Since the late 1800s it has advocated cosmopolitanism, the creation of a proletarian Spanish nation, the worldwide unification of language, and the rejection of Basque regionalism or nationalism, which it labels reactionary. Facing these two types of Spanish nationalism (for economic protectionism of the Vizcayan oligarchy on the one hand, and the nationalism of the Spanish proletariat on the other), the Basque prenational movement of the *fueros* evolved into contemporary Basque nationalism.

THE EMERGENCE OF BASQUE NATIONALISM: ANTECEDENTS AND EVOLUTION TO THE SPANISH CIVIL WAR

Sabino Arana, born in Bilbao in 1865 and the son of a shipbuilding magnate, was responsible for fusing diverse elements of *fuerismo* and Basque prenationalism into a new nationalist ideology that viewed contemporary Basque society through a romantic filter of historical rights and the nationalist theories of his time.[3] In Arana's works, rural Vizcayan society was depicted in mythical terms and Basque society as a whole was characterized as having no class distinctions. According to Arana, industrial society had corrupted Basque tradition; the socialists and the Basque industrialists who had attracted them to the Basque Country were to blame. (Socialism was described as a foreign invention of the Spaniards.) The *fueros* were defined by Arana as the constitutions of each of the Basque provinces. The Basque language, Euskera, was seen as an ancient and perfect tongue. However, in Arana's formulation, the essential factor defining the Basque nation was race, a concept that encompassed all Basque characteristics and captured the essence of the Basque nation (more a feeling of moral superiority than a distinction based on biological connotations). This explanation, which was a product of the *fueros*-inspired myth of racial purity, was a factor in the exclusion of immigrants, who were referred to with the derogatory term *maquetos.*

Arana is credited with the creation of Basque symbols including the national anthem and the Basque flag. In 1894, he founded the Euskaldun Batzokia, a private society that served as the seed for the future Basque Nationalist Party (Partido Nacionalista Vasco, PNV). Beginning in 1898, a group of supporters of the *fueros* (led by Ramón de la Sota) and the followers of Arana joined forces. This new coalition achieved rapid electoral success, especially in Vizcaya. After the death of Arana in 1903, the PNV placed equal emphasis on the communitarian objective of independence and the restoration of the *fueros*-based rights.[4]

The fall of the Spanish monarchy accompanied the end of Miguel

Primo de Rivera's dictatorship (1923–30). It was replaced by the Second Republic, which felt threatened by the nationalist movements in certain regions and began to look for solutions. The PNV initiated federal proceedings to create a statute of autonomy beginning at the municipal level, but the new Spanish Constitution of 1931 condemned the Basque initiative as illegal. The Basque nationalists were then forced to pursue their goal through means approved by the Constitution. At the end of 1933 the proposal for autonomy was submitted to a plebiscite and was approved by 85 percent of the population of the Basque provinces. However, after the triumph of Spanish right in the 1933 elections the Basque statutory proceedings came to a standstill; right-wing Spanish leaders proclaimed that they preferred "a red Spain to a divided Spain."[5] Catholic nationalism was transformed; the idea that the Catholic tradition was the essence of Spain (and was based on a notion of "Spanishness" that condemned any other beliefs as anti-Spain) became linked to the ideology of fascism.[6] This paved the way to the Spanish Civil War and to Franco's accession to power. It was not ideological compatibility but rather the relentless opposition of the Spanish right wing led by the fascists that forced the PNV to join the Republicans at the onset of the military uprising in July 1936.

The Basque statute for autonomy was finally approved in September 1936, and the Basque government was formed. José Antonio Aguirre was elected president. All sectors of the Republican side participated in the Basque government except the anarchists. (Some pro-independence nationalist factions opposed the participation of the Basques in what they considered a civil war between Spaniards.)

The Basque government's social regime was the most moderate in the Spanish Republic, and private businesses were not taken over by the government. While the Basque nationalist clergy suffered repression in Francoist zones, the Catholic Church in the Basque Country was strongly protected. The myth of the Francoist uprising as a "crusade against communism and atheism" was shattered in the face of the Basque reality. One month after the beginning of the Francoist offensive against the Basque government, on April 25, 1937, the Nazi air force destroyed the town of Gernika (Guernica), an act that resulted in a division of opinion within the Catholic Church in Europe, which had previously supported Francoism. This situation prompted Spanish bishops to draft a letter in favor of Franco's crusade, while the Catholic leadership in Europe and in the Basque Country expressed dissent.[7] After the Francoist takeover of Bilbao in July 1937, incarcerations and executions ensued. Relentless persecution was carried out against any visible signs of collective Basque identity. This persecution began with the indiscriminate repression of the Basque people in their own territory, which were referred to as the "treasonous Basque provinces."[8]

The ideology of the PNV at the time combined the beliefs of Christian democracy with the defense of Europeanism. This ideology gained support for the exiled Basque government among a number of European states. However, the climate of the Cold War influenced the Allies, who were no longer willing to help put an end to the Franco regime. In fact, in 1955 the Franco regime entered the United Nations. As a consequence, the PNV found itself paralyzed.[9] But new social organizations that had fought on the Basque side took over in the Spanish Civil War and pushed forward with their demands.

BASQUE NATIONALISM DURING THE FRANCO YEARS

Under the Franco regime Basque social life was characterized by the presence of *cuadrillas*, informal peer groups formed by neighborhood residents according to ideological affinities that were in all cases anti-Francoist. The clergy provided refuge for clandestine groups and activities that promoted the Basque language.[10] Ekin was formed in the early 1950s by students of Bilbo University as a nationalist student group dedicated to political education. They broke away from the youth wing of the PNV in 1958 and became ETA (Euskadi ta Askatasuna, or Basque Country and Freedom) in 1959. In 1961, violent confrontations between ETA and the authorities led to the exile of the organization's top leadership. In May 1962, ETA held its first assembly in exile in France. There its leaders came in contact with liberation movements in the Third World, especially Algeria, and began to view armed struggle as a catalyst of nation building.[11]

In the 1960s, many workers and farmers joined ETA. During these years, the Basque Country underwent a new and intense process of industrialization that attracted a second wave of immigrants. Subsequently a new labor movement appeared, one that had to be self-organized and clandestine because of the Francoist prohibition of all collective bargaining and the ban on strikes. Francoist persecution gathered solidarity between these workers' organizations and new radical nationalist groups.[12] This solidarity transcended the ethnocentrism that was prevalent in the Basque Country at the end of the nineteenth century.

In the early 1960s, the new Basque nationalism created a syncretic platform by blending classic nationalist concepts with a new vision of armed struggle. In this plan ETA became the armed nucleus that would insure a permanent struggle. The absolute Francoist hostility to manifestations of collective Basque identity provoked a reciprocal hostility against the Francoist state that resulted in what became known as the "revolutionary war" led by ETA.[13]

According to *Insurrección en Euskadi* (Insurrection in the Basque Country), published by ETA in the mid-1960s, a revolutionary war should result from the fusion of three factors: psychological warfare, which aspires to win the enthusiasm of the people; guerrilla warfare; and social revolution. The militant fighter who carries out this revolution must firmly believe that his cause is a just one and must therefore be uncompromising.

ETA found itself in need of a nationalist community that would accept it as the vanguard of revolutionary war. Two essays published in 1965— "Carta a los intelectuales" (Letter to the intellectuals) and "Las bases teóricas de la guerra revolucionaria" (Theoretical basis of the revolutionary war)—served this purpose. The "Letter," influenced by Frantz Fanon, called on Basque professionals and intellectuals to make a commitment to the revolution through culture.[14] The objective of the revolutionary war was no longer destruction and expulsion of the enemy from Basque territory. The armed struggle was to reveal the true oppressive nature of the occupying state, so that its repression would descend upon the masses until they rebelled against it and were willing to aid and support ETA.[15] This concept of struggle was put into action during the ten years that followed until the death of Franco. The characteristics of Francoism made this goal attainable with little physical violence and few casualties. In this period, Marxist terms began to be used for the first time in reference to the class struggle.

In 1965 and 1966 some Marxists in the movement broke away and turned against the idea of revolutionary war. The political wing of ETA, established during the Fourth Assembly, analyzed the labor struggles within the Spanish context. They defined traditional Basque nationalism as "bourgeois nationalism" and advocated "nonreformist" or radical reforms in place of revolutionary war. At the beginning of the Fifth Assembly, ETA expelled the leaders of its political wing. Later, during the second part of the assembly, held in the spring of 1967, new structures were established and a new theoretical platform was formulated. ETA's anti-imperialist policy and proletarian internationalist solidarity were reaffirmed, and the Basque working class was presented as the leading force in the national and social struggle. In the following year, the military and labor wings of ETA participated in the intense labor struggles that emerged subsequent to the economic crisis of 1967. These members of ETA fought side by side with militant members of the labor unions and shared jail cells with them. Rivalry between the military and labor wings, however, would eventually provoke internal crisis in the organization lasting until the death of Franco.

In June 1968, a confrontation between ETA and the Spanish Civil

Guard resulted in the deaths of Txabi Etxebarrieta, the young leader of ETA's fifth assembly, and an officer of the Civil Guard. In response, the following August ETA assassinated Melitón Manzanos, a police officer from Irún known to torture prisoners. The government imposed martial law in Guipúzcoa, which suspended the few constitutional rights still recognized under the Franco regime. This situation lasted intermittently for four and a half years until the death of Franco. These circumstances led to the formation of a new antirepressive nationalist community. In keeping with the understanding that one is not suffering repression because of ethnic origin but because one lives in a territory governed by martial law—in this case the Basque Country—this new community promoted the integration of immigrants into the antirepressive struggle.

The Burgos trial of fourteen members of ETA and two priests, which took place in December 1970, was intended as a deterrent to the new nationalism. The prosecution requested six death sentences for the accused. However, the trial actually served to turn public opinion against Francoism. The victims of the trial became symbols of anti-Francoism and inspired strong solidarity with ETA throughout Spain. Clandestine groups, which had remained underground until that point, gained public support and fought openly against the Franco regime. Infuriated with the new developments, the Spanish nationalists emerged to swear allegiance to Franco in the Plaza de Oriente in Madrid. Concern for the "internal enemies" of Francoism shifted from communism and unionism to "communist and terrorist separatism." For the next five years military and police forces concentrated on the "war of the north" and did not oppose the gradual transition to democracy that was being led by the democratic opposition and moderate sectors of the Franco regime. The Burgos trial was seen as the rehearsal of an alternative to Francoism.[16]

The labor movement joined forces with the nationalist struggle as a result of the vision created by the Burgos trial, which left its impression on an entire generation. Massive numbers of members belonging to the youth branch of the PNV joined the military wing of ETA, which from this point on constituted the entire ETA organization. ETA left behind its earlier rural tactics and adopted urban guerrilla tactics similar to those of the Tupamaros of Uruguay, the Palestinian resistance, and the Irish Republican Army.

Beginning in 1973, two conceptions of armed struggle arose within ETA. The labor front maintained that armed struggle should complement the struggle of the masses, while the military front considered their mission as demonstrating the contradictions of the Spanish state and obtaining total autonomy of action for itself. During this time, the imminent end of Francoism provided a favorable environment for the employment of insurrectionary strategies. The assassination in December 1973 of Admiral Luis Carrero Blanco, second to Franco in the regime, gave free rein to those seeking an alternative to Francoism. It demonstrated the validity of the theory that armed struggle was a successful means of exposing the internal contradictions of the regime. ETA's military front reached the peak of its popularity among the nationalist youth of the Basque Country through this action.[17]

In 1974 the labor front broke away from ETA and formed the Patriotic Revolutionary Workers' Party (Langile Abertzale Iraultzaileen Alderdia, LAIA). It also created nationalist labor unions that would be the embryos of the future Patriotic Workers' Council (Langile Abertzaleen Batzordea, LAB). The Spanish opposition began to differentiate separation from Spain and disassociation from the regime and later formulated a reform agreement. The dissipation of the prospect of separation generated more violence of ETA; occasional assassinations turned into repeated anonymous acts of violence against members of the Spanish National Police Force.

In October 1974 ETA's military front split into two factions: ETA-M (military), a faction committed to armed struggle as the vehicle for independence; and ETA-PM (political-military), which adopted a Marxist class-struggle approach.[18] ETA-PM devised two plans of action: the first was a long-term plan with the objectives of independence, extension of the Basque language, and the creation of socialism; the second was a minimum program aimed at finding an immediate alternative at the end of the Franco regime. However, this would explicitly differ from the reform agreement of the Spanish opposition. During the second part of the sixth assembly in January 1975, ETA-PM reformulated the role of the armed struggle. Insurrection not being an option, a war should be waged on the enemy that would force it to accept political negotiation. At the same time, ETA-PM sought the support of other Basque groups for its minimum program.[19]

In April 1975, the Franco regime imposed the last and most severe measure of martial law in the Basque Country. Amnesty International attested to the fact that thousands of Basques were detained and tortured. During this period two militant Basque youths were executed along with three members of GRAPO, a Spanish leftist group. Intense reaction to these executions followed in the Basque Country and Spain and throughout the world. Several civil and armed groups from what is now known as the Basque Nationalist Left (Izquierda Abertzale) formed a socialist coalition called the Patriotic Socialist Coordinating Council (Koordinadora Abertzale Sozialista, KAS). This group rallied in favor of amnesty for all political prisoners and exiles.

After the death of Franco in 1975 and until the first democratic elections in June 1977, mass social movements of labor and Basque nationalist groups were on the rise. The worldwide economic crisis of the mid-1970s was felt in the Basque industrial monoculture, consisting of iron and steel production, metallurgy, and shipbuilding. The result was a drastic shift from the full employment of the 1960s to unemployment exceeding 20 percent in the 1970s. This situation also provided the environment for the emergence of a Basque rejectionist front that resulted from the radicalization and politicization of alternative social movements. After the middle of 1976, large demonstrations brought together proponents of amnesty and supporters of dismissed workers.[20] The organizational deterioration of ETA-PM, the result of numerous arrests carried out under martial law and of the new social radicalism, led the group to consider disbanding the armed component of the organization, which could give rise to another civil organization.

ETA-PM assigned an increasingly subordinate role to the armed struggle, which would have a dual function: that of dissuading the bourgeoisie and defending the interests of the people. ETA-PM's Seventh Assembly, held in September 1976, officially approved the creation of a new revolutionary party. While ETA-PM believed that the new party should lead KAS (and ETA-M as well), ETA-M proposed a new autonomous structure for KAS, whose authority prevailed over that of its constituent parties.[21]

In November 1976, through the initiative of Spanish president Adolfo Suárez, the Francoist parliament was dissolved and the transition to a parliamentary democracy was approved. The Spanish opposition and the PNV expressed disagreement, but in a December referendum the proposal was approved by a large margin, with more than 75 percent of votes affirmative, except in the Basque Country where KAS strongly opposed the reform. Affirmative votes totaled only 50 percent in Vizcaya and 42 percent in Guipúzcoa, thus revealing for the first time Basque discontent in the electoral sphere.

The reform agreement retained the coercive elements of the old regime (the police, judiciary, and especially the military). The military reluctantly accepted the legalization of the Communist Party of Spain (Partido Comunista de España, PCE) during the spring of 1977, and from that point forward antiseparatist attitudes prevailed over anticommunist ones. This was reciprocated by the acceptance of the monarchy, the flag, and the unity of Spain by the PCE.[22]

In spite of its more than eighty-year history, the PSOE reemerged as a "new" party in its twenty-seventh congress in December 1976. The moderate attitudes of its young leaders contrasted with some of the resolutions adopted during the party's earlier years. Hence, a country characterized by political extremes experienced the triumph of centrism and moderation, while radical Basque nationalism was forced out of the process and came to be identified as the "internal enemy" of the new parliamentary-democratic consensus.

The democratic opposition (including PNV) and the government negotiated a date and format for the general elections as well as for drafting a new constitution. KAS had to deal with the conflicting views of ETA-PM, which advocated participation in the general elections, and those of ETA-M, which emphatically opposed the elections.

In April 1977, a new political party, the Basque Revolutionary Party (Euskal Iraultzarako Alderdia, EIA), came into existence. The EIA defined itself as heir to ETA. On May 8, the Basque left-wing coalition known as Euskadiko Ezkerra (EE), consisting mostly of EIA members, put forward its candidacy. As a result of ETA-PM's negotiations with the Spanish government, the latter decided to banish the most recognized Basque prisoners, including those from the Burgos trial, to foreign countries. In a May assembly, EIA determined that EE would participate in the general elections while the remaining parties in KAS broke away from the coalition. In Spain, the Union of the Democratic Center (Unión de Centro Democrático, UCD), a party created by the Spanish government, triumphed with President Adolfo Suárez as its leader. PSOE came in second, therefore becoming UCD's opposition. The electoral results obtained by Basque parties reflected the historical influence of PNV and PSOE, which received considerably more votes than any other Basque party competing in the elections.[23]

BASQUE NATIONALISM IN THE POST-FRANCO PERIOD

After the elections of June 15, 1977, the pro-amnesty movement split into two groups. Through an initiative of PNV and PSOE (which together obtained twenty-seven of the forty-two parliamentary seats in the four provinces, including Navarre) a Basque parliamentary assembly was created with the intention of seeking amnesty and autonomy.

Influenced by the consensus of UCD and PSOE, in conjunction with the PCE, the Spanish Parliament proposed to facilitate national reconciliation through an amnesty law that would conciliate the effects of the Spanish Civil War. This proposal was approved in October 1977. However, the new law turned out to be more of a pardon for Basque political prisoners, who were still considered criminals, than an acknowledgment of the struggle of the Basque people for autonomy. The law was applied gradually, and its implementation was left to the courts. Hence, the Basque leftists did not accept this law as constituting true reconciliation.

The drafting of a new Spanish constitution, also initiated by consensus, would guarantee individual and collective liberties and give legal form to a "multinational and multiregional" state. However, the PNV and the EE were not represented by this consensus since they were not part of the project's preliminary planning process.

In November, with the participation of PNV and PSOE, the assembly of the Basque Parliament drafted a preautonomy proposal. The EIA, which attempted to counter the proposal together with KAS and two Basque parties to the left of PNV—Basque Nationalist Action (Acción Nacionalista Vasca, ANV) and Basque Socialist Convergence (Euskal Sozialista Biltzarra, ESB)—ended up approving it.[24]

In 1978, with socialist Ramón Rubial as its leader, the Basque General Council (Consejo General Vasco, CGV) was created as a pre-autonomy government. The disenchantment felt in the Basque Country was the result of several factors, including limitations of the amnesty law, the institutionalization of unions, which were previously independent and radical, and the monopolizing of political activities by the professional leadership of political parties. The resulting discontent spurred the creation of alternative popular movements, including feminism, an anti-nuclear movement, and others. These movements joined forces with radical Basque nationalists to form a strong alliance of anti-institutional resistance.

Beginning in October 1977, ETA-M began an offensive of fatal attacks with an intensity never seen before. This increased violence, however, tended to insure the survival of the community that identified itself with ETA-M. The sixty-ninth issue of *Zutik* (ETA-M's main voice), published in February 1978, proposed exchanging the tactic of armed struggle for negotiation with the Spanish state through the KAS alternative, which ETA-M considered to be inevitable. The five points of this alternative measure became the minimum conditions for a military cease-fire. They included amnesty; the legalization of pro-independence political parties; withdrawal of the Spanish police from the Basque Country; the right of self-determination, and the inclusion of Navarre within the Basque statute; and improvement of living conditions for workers. In the spring of 1978, Herri Batasuna (Popular Unity, HB)—a coalition of four parties, including HASI, LAIA, ANV, and ESB—was created. The desperate situation of the Basque General Council, which found itself deprived of real authority, and the radicalism that ETA-M's acts transmitted to the nationalist opposition, conferred credibility on the HB coalition.

From the beginning of the constitutional debates in 1978, the incompatability of the project sanctioned by the Spanish majority (as well as Catalonia) and the amendments proposed by the Basque Nationalist Party and Euskadiko Ezkerra, representing the traditional and radical factions of Basque nationalism, was apparent. Both Basque factions defended the sovereignty of the nations within the Spanish state, the Basque nation in particular. The substitution of the unitary Spanish center of Francoism with the complex Spanish center of post-Francoism was based on the concept of a state composed of autonomous regions on the basis of the dual premise of the ''indissoluble unity of Spain'' and ''the right of autonomy for the nationalities and constituent regions of Spain.'' Spain was seen as a ''nation made up of nations,'' an expression often used in debates; however, sovereignty only applied to the Spanish nation.[25] Within this hierarchy of nations there also existed a hierarchy of languages, the only condition being that one had to learn the official language, Spanish.

The model for autonomy was not truly federal because it did not recognize the sovereignty of autonomous communities. However, this model would create a sphere of political activity that in the future would permit the participation of the principal nationalist groups in the central government. Euskadiko Ezkerra's claim to the right of self-determination as defined by the United Nations was rejected by all Spanish parliamentary powers, which based their reasons on principles observed by the UN—that such rights were only applicable to Third World countries that had begun a decolonization process.[26] They also rejected the traditional Basque nationalists' claim to a constitutional amendment to restore their historical rights.

In December 1978, on the occasion of the referendum on the Spanish Constitution, all major Basque parties, including the PNV, EE, and HB, expressed their disapproval of the referendum by advocating abstention or rejection of the Constitution. While it was approved in the Spanish Parliament by a wide margin, affirmative votes in the Basque Country totaled only 42.3 percent, with 11.3 percent rejecting and 40 percent abstaining. The Spanish Constitution thus went into effect despite the fact that a majority of the Basque population had, in effect, rejected it. In the period that followed, there was a marked increase in the armed struggle, and legal and illegal repression proliferated.

The Basque general elections of March 1979 reflected the region's broad disapproval of the Constitution. To the surprise of many, HB, which had expressed vigorous opposition to the Constitution, won three seats in the Spanish Parliament. This success was repeated in Basque municipal elections in April. The breakthrough achieved by the Basque candidates provided the nationalists with strength superior to that of the Spanish forces in the Basque Country. The PNV rose to the top with 870 municipal council members, followed by HB with 297, PSOE with 167, and UCD with 129.

In March 1980, the PNV triumphed in the Basque parliamentary elections, while HB took second place ahead of the Basque Socialist Party (the Basque branch of the PSOE). Carlos Garaikoetxea became the first president of the autonomous government. To secure even greater autonomy from the center, the Basque government drew up a project for the creation of an autonomous police force, which by the end of a five-year period would number six thousand. This police force was to take the place of the Spanish police in the Basque Country.

In the meantime, the EIA joined a sector of the Basque Communist Party (Euskadiko Partido Komunista, EPK), which in its fourth congress in January 1981 approved the proposal of merging with Euskadiko Ezkerra.[27] However, given the attitude of PCE-EPK, which favored the "defense of the democratic state against terrorism," this merger could mean no less than the dissolution of the "political-military alliance" formed by EIA and ETA-PM.

The UCD government, formed by the fusion of the democratic opposition and powers of the Franco regime, had deteriorated during the transition to democracy, as had the prestige of its president, Adolfo Suárez. Discontent among the military leadership increased during 1980. The Spanish Army retained its old leadership and structure, which remained focused on the "internal threat" not only of terrorism but also of autonomous decentralization. Although the majority accepted the new order (though without much enthusiasm), a minority within the army opposed it.

After the resignation of Adolfo Suárez at the end of January 1981, a series of events during February revealed a weakness in authority at the highest levels of the Spanish government. First, representatives of HB expressed their opposition to King Juan Carlos's visit to Gernika by singing the Basque civil war song "Eusko gudariak." Then, ETA-M kidnapped the chief engineer of the nuclear plant at Lemóniz in Vizcaya, demanding the dismantling of the plant in exchange for his release. The engineer was killed, and an ETA-M militant was captured and shortly thereafter died in prison after being tortured. Finally, judicial action carried out against the police officers responsible for the prisoner's death, and the chain of resignations that followed, gave rise to plans for a coup d'état.

Three military conspiracies were planned at the same time: one by military officers who opposed the Constitution; another by those who wished to implicate the king in a coup; and one that planned to attract the PSOE to the idea of a coalition government headed by a military leader. Miscalculations led to the failure of all of these conspiracies. On February 23, some Civil Guards implicated in the first conspiracy occupied the Spanish Parliament under the orders of a Lieutenant Colonel Tejero. This provoked large demonstrations in Spain in which the Constitution was equated with liberty and democracy. Basque indifference to the new constitutional fervor, together with the widespread belief among Spaniards that Basque terrorism had led to the frustrated coup, brought about a change in attitude. Popular anger previously directed at the military was rechanneled toward the "Basque problem."

The consequence of the events of February 23 were immediately felt as the government assigned the army to patrol the borders of the Basque provinces. A law was passed in defense of democracy that stiffened antiterrorist measures and strictly repressed support of terrorism. Against general public opinion and that of the PSOE, the Congress approved Spain's entry into NATO as a political and military measure to prevent future coup attempts. At the same time, the UCD and PSOE collaborated on a bill that eventually became the Ley Orgánica de Armonización del Proceso Autonómico (Organic Law for the Harmonization of the Autonomy Process), or LOAPA for short. One of its provisions was to give preeminence to the organic laws of the central state over those of the autonomous communities.[28]

The Basque government voiced its disapproval of the bill, and in company with Spanish political groups that included the Communist Party, presented a high-court appeal, arguing that it was unconstitutional. The PNV, which had organized many protests against this law, adopted a policy of national resistance that lasted until 1985 and was embodied by Basque president Garaikoetxea. However, the law of economic agreement, which created a Basque treasury, allowed the self-financing of autonomous institutions for the first time. Given that the provincial governments of the three territories of the Basque Country were responsible for the collection of taxes, a conflict arose between the notion of "centralization" of the autonomous structure, which would give free rein to the Basque government (an idea supported by Garaikoetxea and his government), and "decentralization," which emphasized actions to be taken by each provincial council. The subsequent confrontation resulted in a split and the creation of Eusko Alkartasuna (Basque Solidarity, EA), led by Garaikoetxea.

Beginning in 1982, the cycle of subordination of HB to KAS came to an end. HB declared that it was willing to mediate the expected negotiations between ETA-M and the institutional representative of the Spanish state, in this case the army. ETA-M's strategy of "war of persistence" provoked the deployment of a long-term counterinsurgency strategy through the use of a militarized police force. ETA-M's insurgent slogan, "to resist is to triumph," was met with repressive military force of the Spanish state, which sought to isolate its armed nucleus. But these measures, directed against the Basque insurgents, provoked a strong negative response among the Basque population—a response specifically directed against the government's increased military intervention into the social life of the region in the name of fighting terrorism.

During the Spanish general elections of October 1982, PSOE obtained ten million votes and was recognized as the undisputed winner, as the masses considered it an alternative for real change and an agent for modernization. Spain's impending entry into the European Community created a need to modernize the obsolete Spanish industrial structure. Throughout Spain, and especially in the Basque Country where the industrial restructuring affected traditional industry, unemployment increased rapidly.[29] Economic hardship among the working class in Spain, and particularly in the Basque Country, perpetuated the notion of an internal enemy and identified in with radical nationalism.

PSOE's social model, based on the depoliticization of the masses and the plebiscitary character of public politics, was diametrically opposed to the ideas of the Basque nationalist left wing. At the same time, the changes that had taken place within the Spanish police forces since 1980 replaced Francoist hostility toward ETA and Basque nationalism with a democratic antiterrorist one.[30] Beginning in 1983, PSOE imposed the Plan de la Zona Especial del Norte (Plan for the Special Northern Zone), known as "Plan ZEN." (The "Zona Especial del Norte" is a euphemistic term used to refer to the Basque Country—Vizcaya, Guipúzcoa, and Alava, as well as Navarre—in order to avoid acknowledging the existence of a Basque problem in the officially non-Basque autonomous region of Navarre.) This plan had the effect of generalizing the hostility toward the radical Basque nationalists into suspicion against a large segment of the population of the northern zone and allowed coercive measures to be used against the radicals' sympathizers.

In the summer of 1983 the Supreme Court repealed LOAPA's Article 4 as unconstitutional. This was the article that established the supremacy of the state's organic laws over those of the autonomous communities. The PSOE, the only party that continued to support LOAPA, began to favor legislative agreements with the main nationalist parties. In the Basque Country, this project was incompatible with Garaikoetxea's "nationalism of resistance," but it was accepted by the leaders of PNV.

Euskadiko Ezkerra's second congress, held in January 1985, was dominated by self-criticism. Presentations stressed EE's weak electoral performance, its failure to create a hegemonic left-wing alliance, and the failure of the autonomy process to instill a Basque national democratic consciousness. Divisions within PNV that put an end to its dominance allowed EE to assume a more important role within Basque politics. EE's new project for modernization led to competition with the socialists and caused it to shift its opposition from PNV to PSOE.

In the early 1980s the socialist government opposed the legalization of

HB as a party. By the end of the decade, however, HB was finally recognized by the courts as a legal party. This, along with charges brought against its leaders and the persecution of refugees, convinced HB's voters that KAS was right in its statement that the Basque Country was in a state of war.

The armed nucleus formed by ETA-M lacked control over specific areas of the Basque territory; therefore, the sector of the community that supported it came to occupy a sociopolitical space having more and more in common with the rejectionist front that had disassociated itself from the elite political and civic groups that had taken their place in the autonomy process.[31] The autonomous community, which could have provided the opportunity to reclaim a collective identity, to participate in the self-determination of society, and to oppose the centralization of the nation-state, became a meeting ground for numerous elite groups. These groups rejected the initiatives of alternative movements because of the latter's identification with armed actions. Thus, a "front for peace" emerged in 1988 to coordinate the interests of elite groups, which agreed to share autonomous power among themselves while at the same time marginalizing those who continued to support armed struggle.

During the 1980s HB was the leading force in the struggle for self-determination. But following the dissolution of the USSR, the political forces supporting the Statute of Autonomy came to challenge HB's leading role as they attempted to make the right of self-determination part of their policy for Basque autonomy. Even if the substance of such a right, as understood by international law, was largely nullified in the new claims, the initiative of the Basque pro-autonomy parties created great anxiety in the PSOE and the Spanish state, which strongly rebuffed it.

In December 1989, the European Community supported German reunification on the basis of the right of self-determination. Immediately, the Catalan Parliament passed a resolution stating that it had not renounced self-determination. Taking advantage of the situation, the PNV announced that it would propose to the Basque Autonomous Parliament a nonbinding resolution on the right of self-determination for the Basque Country. Eusko Alkartasuna entered the fray demanding the creation of a Basque legal bloc that would demand self-determination from the Spanish Parliament. This forced Euskadiko Ezkerra to accept the Basque parliamentary debate on self-determination. All of this provoked a hostile reaction from the major Spanish institutions and political parties. The Spanish government declared its opposition to the parliamentary resolution; the PSE-PSOE stated that the debate provided justification for terrorism; the army disapproved the debate; and the king publicly acclaimed the indissoluble unity of Spain. The furor forced the PNV to accept PSOE's proposal to draft a document that reiterated its compliance with the constitution. This paradoxical statement (the Spanish Constitution had explicitly denied the right of self-determination) was not sufficient to dissipate the central government's misgivings toward the PNV.

Two alternative propositions were presented, one jointly prepared by the PNV and EE and the other by EA. HB made amendments to both texts, although it agreed with parts of them. Since one common goal of the three parties (PNV, EE and EA) offering parliamentary propositions was to take away from HB the banner of self-determination, they agreed on a common text in line with EA's pro-independence stance. On February 15, 1990, in a full session of the Basque Parliament in which the three signing parties aimed most of their attacks against HB, the right of self-determination of the Basque Country was approved by the absolute majority of the Autonomous Parliament, with PSE-PSOE voting against it. Even if HB did not back the resolution, popular institutions such as Euskaria, with strong representation of Basque nationalists close to HB, found positive aspects in the resolution, which exceeds the framework of the Basque autonomous institutions.

CONCLUSION

As to the possibility of a general accord among the various parties at present, the very attempt to delineate a specific agreement reveals the difficulty of the task; it would require profound transformations in the political attitudes of all the participants.

If such an agreement is to be reached, the parties involved will have to become much more receptive than they are today to the demands of alternative movements and radicalized sectors of Basque society, instead of stigmatizing their demands by linking them to "terrorism." Such a concession would change the present situation in which the dominant political forces partition among themselves political and social power, casting out as marginal whatever is beyond their control, in particular the HB. On the other hand, if the Basque patriotic movement led by HB is able to overcome its traditional characterization of the Spanish state as an internal enemy, then it could challenge the cohesiveness of the governing bloc united by its rejection of "violence" as well as open the political gridlock to the needs of Basque civil society in general.

One can and must hope for an end to the armed struggle, whose persistence hopelessly divides Basque society and whose actions in the Basque Country and in Spain defeat its own purpose. However, this process must be an outcome of negotiations that liberate national energies. Such an outcome will only be possible through a struggle against the central state *and* through the reciprocal recognition of national groups. This recognition would exclude mutual hostility and facilitate mutual enrichment. Only in this manner will the new triumph over the old in the Basque Country.

NOTES

1. These refer to the traditional Basque laws of the Middle Ages, which provided a degree of self-government to the Basque territories.

2. On the industrialization of Vizcaya at the end of the nineteenth century, see Manuel González Portilla, *La formación de la sociedad capitalista en el país vasco* (The formation of capitalist society in the Basque Country) (San Sebastián: Luis Haramburu, 1981).

3. The works of Sabino Arana have been published in his *Obras completas* (Complete works) (Bayona: Sabindiar Batza Beyris, 1965). For a biography of Arana, see Javier Corcuera Atienza, *Orígenes, ideología y organización del nacionalismo vasco, 1876–1904* (Origins, ideology and organization of Basque nationalism, 1876–1904) (Madrid: Siglo XXI de España, 1979). On the origins and evolution of Basque nationalism in the early twentieth century, see Beltza, *El nacionalismo vasco* (Basque nationalism) (Hendaya: Mugalde, 1974) and idem, *Nacionalismo vasco y clases sociales* (Basque nationalism and social classes) (San Sebastián: Txertoa, 1976). Also see Antonio Elorza, *Ideologías del nacionalismo vasco* (Ideologies of Basque nationalism) (San Sebastián: Haramburu, 1978) and Juan José Solozábal, *El primer nacionalismo vasco* (The first Basque nationalism) (Madrid: Tucar, 1975).

4. This led to a legal battle that resulted in the revocation of the Spanish Law of October 1839, which had affirmed the supremacy of the Spanish Constitution over the Basque *fueros*.

5. On the Second Republic and Basque nationalism, see José Antonio Aguirre, *Entre la libertad y la revolución, 1930–1935* (Between freedom and revolution, 1930–1935) (Bilbao: Verdes Achirica, 1935). Also see A. de Lizarra, *Los vascos y la república española* (The Basques and the Spanish Republic) (Buenos Aires: Vasca Ekin, 1944) and Juan Pablo Fusi, *El problema vasco en la II República* (The Basque problem in the Second Republic) (Madrid: Turner, 1979). On the Basque Statute of Autonomy, see José Manuel Castells, *El estatuto vasco* (The Basque statute) (San Sebastián: Luis Haramburu, 1976).

6. On the Catholic Church and fascism in Spain, see Raúl Morodo, *Los orígenes ideológicos del franquismo: Acción española* (The ideological origins of Francoism: Spanish Action) (Madrid: Editorial Alianza Universal, 1985) and Stanley G. Payne, *Historia del fascismo español* (History of Spanish fascism) (Paris: Ruedo Ibérico, 1965).

7. See Hugh Thomas, *La guerra civil española* (The Spanish Civil War) (Paris: Ruedo Ibérico, 1976). On the situation in the Basque Country during the Civil War, see Juan de Iturralde, *El catolicismo y la cruzada de Franco* (Catholicism and Franco's crusade) (Bayona: Egi-Indarra, 1965). Also see, Joseba Elósegui, *La guerra en Euzkadi* (War in Euzkadi) (Madrid: Plaza Janès, 1978) and Georges Steer, *El árbol de Gernika* (The tree of Guernica) (Bayona: Ediciones Gudari, 1963).

8. The repression of the Basque people under Francoism is documented in Basque Academy of Language, *El libro blanco del Euskera* (The white book of the Basque language) (Bilbao: Euskaltzaindia, 1977) and *El pueblo vasco frente a la cruzada franquista* (The Basques against Franco's crusade) (Bayona: Egi-Indarra, 1966).

9. On the ideology of PNV and the Basque government in exile in the 1940s, see José Antonio Aguirre, *De Gernika a Nueva York pasando por Berlín* (From Guernica to New York by way of Berlin) (Bayona: Vasca Ekin, 1944) and Iñaki Aguirre, *La coordinación de las nacionalidades europeas según José Antonio de Aguirre y Lekube* (Coordination of European nationalities according to José Antonio de Aguirre y Lekube) (Madrid: Siglo XXI, 1983). On the influence of PNV on the ideology of the Christian-Democratic parties, see Pierre Letamendía, *La démocratie chrétienne* (Christian democracy) (Paris: P.U.F., 1977) and Jean Marie

Mayeur, *Das partis catholiques à la démocratie chrétienne, XIX–XXème siècles* (From Catholic parties to Christian democracy, nineteenth to twentieth centuries) (Paris: Armand Colin, 1980). On the specific aspects of the Francoist repression, see José María Garmendía, "La resistencia vasca," (Basque resistance) in *Historia general del país vasco* (General history of the Basque Country), vol. 13 (San Sebastián: Haranburu, 1979–80).

10. On Basque society during the first Francoist period, see Alfonso Pérez Agote, *La reproducción del nacionalismo: El caso vasco* (The reproduction of nationalism: The Basque case) (Madrid: Siglo XXI de España, 1984) and Ander Gurutxaga, *El código nacionalista en el franquismo* (The nationalist code during Francoism) (Barcelona: Anthropos, 1985). On Basque nationalism during this period, see Itarko, *El nacionalismo vasco en la guerra y en la paz* (Basque nationalism in war and peace) (Bayona: Alderdi, 1971). On the role of the clergy in this period, see Pablo Iztueta, *Sociología del fenómeno contestatario del clero vasco: 1940–1975* (Sociology of the phenomenon of rebellion among the Basque clergy, 1940–1975) (Bilbao: Elkar, 1981) and Manu Lipuzkoa, *La iglesia como problema en el país vasco* (The Church as a problem in the Basque Country) (Buenos Aires: Editorial Vasca, 1973).

11. For a history of the ETA, see José María Garmendía, *Historia de ETA,* 3 vols. (San Sebastián: Haramburu, 1979) and Gurutz Jauregui Bereciartúa, *Ideología y estrategía política de ETA* (ETA's ideology and political strategy) (Madrid: Siglo XXI, 1981). Also see Ortzi [Francisco Letamendía], *Historia de Euskadi: El Nacionalismo vasco y ETA* (History of ETA: Basque nationalism and ETA) (Paris: Ruedo Ibérico, 1975) and idem, *Euskadi: Pueblo y nación* (Euskadi: People and nation), 7 vols. (San Sebastián: Kriselu, 1991), as well as Robert Clark, *The Basque Insurgents: ETA 1952–1981* (Madison: University of Wisconsin Press, 1984) and idem, *The Basques: The Franco Years and Beyond* (Reno: University of Nevada Press, 1979).

12. On Francoism, see Max Gallo, *Historia de la España franquista* (History of Franco's Spain) (Paris: Ruedo Ibérico, 1971). On the economic situation in the Basque Country during this period, see Milagros García Crespo, Roberto Velasco, and Arantza Mendizábal, *La economía vasca durante el franquismo: Crecimiento y crisis de la economía vasca, 1936–1980* (The Basque economy under Francoism: Growth and crisis of the Basque economy, 1936–1980) (Bilbao: La Gran Enciclopedia Vasca, 1981). On the labor movement in the Basque Country, see Pedro Ibarra Guell, *El movimiento obrero en Vizcaya: 1967–1977* (Labor movement in Vizcaya, 1967–1977) (Bilbao: Servicio Editorial UPV, 1987).

13. This "war" was theorized in two works of the period, one of them being *Vasconia,* written by Federico Krutwig (Buenos Aires: Norbait, 1962), and the other a 1963 ETA publication entitled *Insurrección en Euskadi* (Insurrection in the Basque Country). The latter was inspired by the writings and actions of Mao Zedong and Che Guevera.

14. See Fernando Sarrailh de Hiartza, *Estudio dialéctico de una nacionalidad: Vasconia* (Dialectical study of a nationality: Vasconia) (Buenos Aires: Norbait, 1962). The work that had the greatest impact on ETA during this period was Frantz Fanon, *Les damnés de la terra* (The wretched of the earth) (Paris: Masperó, 1968).

15. This new strategy, as defined in "Theoretical Basis of the Revolutionary War," was the spiral strategy of "action-repression-action."

16. On the Burgos trial, see Gisèle Halimi, *Le procés de Burgos* (The Burgos trial) (Paris: Gallimard, 1972) and Kepa Salaberri [Miguel Castells and Francisco Letamendía], *Sumarísimo 31-69: El proceso de Euskadi en Burgos* (Martial court 31-69: Process to Euskadi in Burgos) (Paris: Ruedo Ibérico, 1971).

17. On the assassination of Carrero Blanco, see Julen Aguirre, *Cómo y por qué ejecutamos a Carrero Blanco* (How and why we executed Carrero Blanco) (Paris: Ruedo Ibérico, 1974).

18. See Robert Clark, *Negotiating with ETA: Obstacles to Peace in the Basque Country, 1975–1988* (Reno: University of Nevada Press, 1990), p. 15.

19. The splits in ETA in the 1970s are examined in Angel Amigo, *Pertur, ETA 71–76* (San Sebastián: Ediciones Hordago, 1978).

20. See Crespo, Velasco, and Mendizábal, *La economía vasca durante el franquiso;* Guell, *El movimiento obrero en Vizcaya.*

21. On ETA-PM and KAS, see *Arnasa No. 1* (Hendaye: Editions Mugalde, 1976) and *Proyecto provisional de los partidos políticos del KAS sobre el período constituyente* (Provisional project of the KAS political parties on the constituency period) (n.d. [October 1977]).

22. For a history of the PCE, see Gregorio Morán, *Miseria y grandeza del partido comunista de España, 1939–1985* (Misery and greatness of the Spanish Communist Party, 1939–1985) (Barcelona: Editorial Planeta, 1976).

23. See Francisco José Llera Ramos, *Post-franquismo y fuerzas políticas en Euskadi* (Post-Francoism and political forces in Euskadi) (Bilbao: Servicio Editorial de la Universidad del País Vasco, 1984).

24. It should be pointed out that the self-exclusion of EIA resulting from the Mesa de Alsasua marked the beginning of the future coalition of Popular Unity (Herri Batasuna, HB).

25. On the constitutional debates, see Frank Moderne and Pierre Bon, *Les autonomies régionales dans la constitution espagnole* (Regional autonomies in the Spanish constitution) (Paris: Económica, 1981); Jordi Solé Tura, *Nacionalidad y nacionalismos en España: Autonomías, federalismo, autodeterminación* (Nationality and nationalisms in Spain: Autonomies, federalism, and self-determination) (Madrid: Alianza Editorial, 1985); and Pablo Lucas Verdú, *La singularidad del proceso constituyente español* (Singularity of the Spanish constitutional process) (Madrid: Centro de Estudios Constitucionales, 1978).

26. On the juridical aspects of the autonomy question, see Guy Heraud, ''Les communautés autonomes en Espagne'' (The autonomous communities in Spain), in Institut Européen des Hautes Etudes Internationales (IEHEI), *L'autonomie: Les régions d'Europe, en quête d'un statut* (Autonomy: The regions of Europe in search of a statute) (Nice: Presses d'Europe, 1981). On the right of self-determination, see S. Calogeropoulos-Stratis, *Le droit des peuples à disposer d'eux-mêmes* (the peoples' right to self-government) (Brussels: Bruylant, 1973); IEHEI, *Le droit à l'autodétermination* (The right of self-determination) (Nice: Presses d'Europe, 1980); José Antonio Obieta Chalbaud, *El derecho de autodeterminación de los pueblos* (The peoples' right to self-determination) (Bilbao: Publicaciones de la Universidad de Deusto, 1980); and Javier Villanueva, ''Autodeterminación de los pueblos: Un reto para Euskadi y Europa'' (Self-determination of peoples: A challenge for the Basque Country and Europe), *Herria 2000* (Bilbao), vol. 2 (1985).

27. On the Basque Communist Party (EPK), see Morán, *Miseria y grandeza.*

28. See Tura, *Nacionalidad y nacionalismos en España.*

29. On the PSE-PSOE, see the interview with the socialist leader Txiki Benegas in *Euskadi, sin la paz nada es posible* (Euskadi: Without peace nothing is possible) (Barcelona: Argos Vergara, 1984) and the article by Justo de la Cueva, ''El PSOE de Felipe González, 1974–1988'' (Felipe González's Spanish Socialist Workers Party, 1974–1988), in *Euskadi, la renuncia del PSOE* (Euskadi: The failure of the PSOE) (Pamplona: Editorial Txalaparta, 1988). On the Basque economic crisis in the 1980s, see Begoña Arrizabalaga, ''La industria vasca (1936–1984),'' *Euskal Herria,* vol. 2 (1985).

30. Changes in the Spanish Police Force in the 1980s are examined by Diego López Garrido, *El aparato policial en España: Historia, sociología e ideología* (The police apparatus in Spain: History, sociology, and ideology) (Barcelona: Ediciones Ariel, 1987).

31. On the urban character of the contemporary armed struggle, see Grabowsky, ''The Urban Context of Political Terrorism,'' in Michael Stohl, ed., *The Politics of Terrorism* (New York: Marcel Dekker, 1978).

Quebec Nationalism and the Struggle for Sovereignty in French Canada

As it has everywhere else, at least in Western history, the national question has evolved in Quebec in the context of the formation and transformation of the capitalist economy and the liberal democratic state.[1] The internal market and wage relations that tend to homogenize economic practices within a social formation (money, weights and measures, salaries, free circulation of individuals and goods) were becoming institutionalized at the same time as the modern state was becoming the center of regulation of social relations and relations of power that are now administered in the name of the nation within the framework of popular national sovereignty. In the meantime, the formation of national states and the development of national communities have resulted, in all societies including Canada, in a multitude of struggles and conflicts that are called "national questions."

The trend toward the affirmation of one single nation provoked the resistance of minority communities who refused to sacrifice their identity in the larger movement of assimilation since that movement most often took the form of oppression. In this way, the formation and reproduction of the Canadian nation has also functioned as a process of national domination that still today incites the resistance of the Acadian and Quebecois peoples, just as it does the Amerindian communities (who represent themselves increasingly as "nations").

In this chapter I will try to show how the national question is manifested in Quebec and is rearticulated through the evolution of capitalism, and transformations of the state, and the relations of power between the different social forces. After a brief historical survey, I will analyze at greater length the origins and development of the current national movement in Quebec, which go back to the 1960s.

ORIGINS OF THE QUEBEC NATIONAL MOVEMENT

The history of French communities in America begins in the seventeenth century when the French absolutist state, in struggle with the Dutch and the British, wanted to participate in the movement to colonize North America.[2] New France was founded on the shores of the St. Lawrence (present-day Quebec), in Acadia on the Atlantic coast (present-day Nova Scotia and New Brunswick), and in Louisiana. Canada constituted the center of French colonization. Its economy was founded on the fur trade with the Amerindians and on the seigneurial system, a feudal agricultural system. The Catholic Church, which owned significant amounts of seigneurial lands, held an important place in the regulation of social relations, for example, in its management of schools and hospitals and in its definition and diffusion of the dominant religious ideology. New France could therefore be considered a feudal society in the era of transition to capitalism, the colony of a nation that was still dominated by feudalism.[3]

New France was conquered by England in 1760. (All that remained of New France was Louisiana, which would be surrendered by Napoleon in the beginning of the nineteenth century.) This marked the beginning of the national conflicts that would be reproduced in different forms up until today. In the first years after the Conquest, it was the dominant classes in the French community that fought for the recognition of their interests and their distinctiveness. Having the intention of managing its new colony in the manner of its other colonies, England issued in 1763 the Royal Proclamation that abolished the seigneurial system, instituted measures that threatened the continued existence of the Catholic Church, and created an assembly chamber in which English was the only official language. The French nobility and the high clergy mobilized to demand the maintenance of the seigneurial system and the recognition of the Catholic Church. They obtained these rights when the Quebec Act of 1774 recognized French civil law and the seigneurial system while also tolerating the presence of the Catholic Church; the legal right of the seigneur to collect rents and of the clergy to tithe were thus reaffirmed. These first conflicts in the form of ethnic opposition (French against English) can be considered a feudal and premodern reaction to the inevitable reorganization of relations of power between the dominant classes in the new colony. One cannot speak in a strict sense of a national conflict because (besides the fact that it was limited to a conflict between the dominant classes) the seigneur and the high clergy, far from supporting a nationalist ideology, sought the restoration of their rights by declaring themselves to be loyal subjects of the British Crown.[4]

The first real national movement in Quebec developed at the beginning of the nineteenth century. One can briefly define a national movement as one that is nationalist, multiclass, and political. It is multiclass because the national movement involves the constitution of a social bloc that goes beyond the narrow interests of a single class. Even if it is most often placed under the hegemony of the bourgeoisie or petite bourgeoisie, this type of movement cannot develop fully without the support of the dominated classes (the peasantry and the working class). It is nationalist because such a social movement affirms clearly the existence of a distinct nation in the name of which it demands the political rights associated with the exercise of power (from autonomy to independence).

It was this type of movement that developed at the beginning of the nineteenth century and led to the Rebellions of 1837–38.[5] Its emergence was first encouraged by the Constitutional Act of 1791, which divided what would come to be called the Province of Quebec into two distinct colonies: Lower Canada (approximately what is now Quebec) and Upper Canada (present-day Ontario). In addition to insuring a very clear francophone majority in Lower Canada, the Constitutional Act created in each colony an assembly chamber without, however, according the latter ministerial responsibility. (The fundamental dimension of representative liberal democracy in the British parliamentary system is the selection of members of the executive from among the members of the assembly chamber and the fact that they are accountable to the latter.) These moves to divide powers, an effort by the Colonial Office to avoid a repeat of the American experience in 1776, nonetheless incited national and anticolonialist struggles. Multiple confrontations erupted rapidly between the elected representatives of the assembly, who could legislate and adopt the budget, and the members of the executive and legislative councils, which were not responsible before the chamber. In Upper Canada as in Lower Canada, the assembly chamber became the spearhead for the struggle of local bourgeois and petit-bourgeois interests against the colonial power.[6] In Lower Canada, the struggle essentially arrayed the petite bourgeoisie (doctors, lawyers, shopkeepers) supported largely by the peasantry against the colonial administration, the large merchants, the aristocracy, and the high Catholic clergy (primarily francophone) who controlled the executive and legislative councils.[7] While fighting the extortionist regime typical of colonial societies, the nationalists demanded, primarily, the right of ministerial responsibility. It was in the name of the Canadian nation that the fight was carried on in Lower Canada. The "Mouvement des patriotes" or Patriots' Movement thus fought for a separate nation, speaking a different language, largely in Lower Canada where the representatives could exercise their full democratic rights in their own assembly chamber. These confrontations led to an armed struggle in 1837–38 and the defeat of the Rebellions.[8]

After this defeat, London appointed Lord Durham to Canada with the goal of studying the situation and proposing a political solution. He proposed the union of Upper and Lower Canada with the double hope of encouraging the development of a market economy and resolving the national problem. In the latter case, he considered, like many administrators and large anglophone merchants of Upper and Lower Canada, that it was necessary to assimilate the francophones, "those people without a history and without literature." Favoring ministerial responsibility, he counseled London to wait until an anglophone majority was assured within the Union, which was created in 1840.[9]

FROM UNION TO CONFEDERATION

It was during the second half of the nineteenth century that the Canadian state was formed. The regime of the Union did not achieve the hopes that had been put in it, either on the economic level or in terms of the national question.

The adoption of free trade with England invalidated almost from the beginning the economic policy still dominant in colonial trade. The Canadian economy grew up around the trade of raw materials (fur and later wood and wheat) and was based on preferential duties with the mother country. Since the English conquest, the merchant bourgeoisie, profiting from its links with Great Britain and from the navigable St. Lawrence seaway, sought to play an intermediary role in the trade between the United States and England. The Union of the two Canadas was aimed at completing the canalization of the St. Lawrence in the hopes of developing this trade. However, the abolition of preferential duties in England and the construction of the Erie Canal in the United States tolled the end of the Canadian colonial economy.[10] In search of a new market, Canada looked more resolutely toward the United States, with whom it had signed the Treaty of Reciprocity in 1854. But the refusal of the United States to renew this agreement ten years later forced Canada to rely only on its own strengths.

It was then that the idea developed to reunite all the colonies of British North America within the same state and to create a vast market with Canada connected by railroads and supported by a protectionist policy. This project was not realized in all its dimensions until 1896 (after the crisis at the end of the nineteenth century). It permitted the settlement of the western provinces with an economy specialized in wheat at the same time as the industrialization of central Canada (Ontario and Quebec) was developing. But the economic development of Canada could occur only through an ensemble of political contradictions that appeared from the beginning and that have been reproduced right up to the present.

The creation of the Canadian state in 1867 occurred as part of the conjuncture of events in the second half of the nineteenth century that included the formation of numerous new states in the West, including Germany in 1871 and Italy in 1870. The creation of an internal market in Canada, shielded by protectionist policies and in which the different regions were connected by railroads, constituted the principal element of a strategy that was aimed at strengthening industrial capitalism.[11] The project of the creation of the Canadian state was imposed following the refusal of the United States to renew the Treaty of Reciprocity mentioned earlier. Supported essentially by the political circles linked to the grande bourgeoisie of Montreal and Toronto, the initial proposal consisted of uniting all the colonies of British North America, from New Brunswick to British Columbia, within the strongly centralized framework of a legislative union. The men called "the fathers of Confederation" met strong resistance from what was to become the Province of Quebec as well as the colonies of the east (New Brunswick, Nova Scotia, and Prince Edward Island) and the west (British Columbia). Cultural and economic reasons (the cultural distinctiveness of francophones, fear of economic domination in a united Canada) pushed the regional elites to demand a form of local autonomy.[12] That is why the federal regime that was finally adopted represented a political compromise that the initiators of the project accepted reluctantly.[13]

The British North America Act thus created a federal union that accorded to the central government large economic and repressive powers and to the provinces jurisdiction over their natural resources and social and cultural policies. Such a political regime was destined to contribute to the reproduction up to the present of the contradictions already perceptible during the debates concerning the formation of the Canadian state. Federalism contributed in effect to the deepening of regional and national contradictions that were growing in Canada. It is important to underline here that the political tensions in Canada were not limited only to national struggles;[14] regionalism, strengthened by the existence of provincial powers and at times allied to nationalism (for example, in the case of Quebec), also fed important federal-provincial struggles. The question of natural resources, the economic policy of the central state, the representation of the provinces in the

Senate are just some of the questions that regularly arise in current political debates, debates that deepen during periods of economic crisis. This linking of national and regional questions complicates political life and the resolution of the conflicts.[15] When they do not reinforce each other, as they do in the case of Quebec, the resolution of one of the conflicts (such as the nationalist opposition between Canada and Quebec) is blocked by the demands of another conflict (for example, the regional conflict between western Canada and central Canada). The current situation, which I examine later in this chapter, illustrates this point clearly.

The national question thus constitutes an inherent problem for the Canadian state. But once more I must insist on the fact that the national question cannot be reduced to a single opposition between Quebec and the Canadian state. It is important to underline the multiplicity of national conflicts because, as in the case of the overlap between regionalism and nationalism already mentioned, the attempts at solving one problem (the place of Quebec in the confederation, for example) are often complicated by increased demands of another nature (for example, the current struggle of Native Canadians). The analysis of the particularity of each of these national questions in Canada is impossible in this brief space, but one must still insist on the multiplicity of national struggles that have continued since the creation of the Canadian state: the French Canadian nation was a strong influence in the adoption of a federal regime rather than a legislative union; the Acadian people, who were deported by sea in 1754 by the British Crown, progressively resettled in New Brunswick and Nova Scotia, where they fought for recognition of their rights; the Métis allied to Native Canadians of the West were repressed militarily during the formation of Manitoba (1885) and Saskatchewan (1905); the diverse Native societies still struggle today for the recognition of their right to self-government; the French Canadians—that is, the francophones outside Quebec and Acadia—must fight daily to obtain respect for their fundamental rights—recognition of the French language, the right to education in French, and so forth.[16] Canada is thus characterized by the existence of a constellation of national realities even if, as we will see, the question of Quebec risks in the short term the partial dismemberment of the Canadian state.

THE QUEBEC NATIONAL QUESTION SINCE THE FORMATION OF THE CANADIAN STATE

The existence of a francophone majority in the regions of former Lower Canada (rejoined with Upper Canada in 1840 to form a united Canada) constituted one of the important factors in the adoption of a federal regime in 1867. Quebec, the only province with a francophone majority (currently more than 80 percent of the population), was therefore created at the moment of the creation of Canadian Confederation. To highlight the distinctiveness of the current national movement in all its dimensions, it is necessary to show how the articulations of the national reality of Quebec are modified by the fluctuations and transformations of the Canadian state.

The Canadian state that was created in 1867 presented itself as a democratic state of the liberal form. Ministerial responsibility had already been acquired in 1848 with the unification of the two Canadas. Industrialization and monopolization began to occur rapidly in 1896. The government, which favored the self-regulation of the market, intervened little in the market economy except to subsidize generously the private companies contracted to build the railroads and to establish customs tariffs aimed at protecting the young national industries. At the social level, the federal government intervened little because Canadian federalism conferred to the provinces jurisdiction in social and cultural matters.[17]

It is against this backdrop that the rearticulation of power relations in Quebec and the new dimensions of the national question must be considered. We have seen that between 1800 and 1840 a national movement developed that demanded the creation of a Canadian nation (the francophone community of Lower Canada); it proclaimed independence in 1838 but was defeated following the Rebellions of 1837–38. This movement, led by the petite bourgeoisie, had progressively imposed its hegemony within the community at the expense of the landlords and high Catholic clergy, who continued to collaborate with the colonial administration. But the defeat of the Rebellions, the attaining of a responsible government (1848), the abolition of the seigneurial system (1854), and, ultimately, the creation of the Canadian state (1867) provoked a reorganization of power relations within the francophone community of Quebec. The Catholic Church profited from this reorganization to reimpose its leadership, and the more moderate petite bourgeoisie accepted from that time on to participate politically in the Union, and then in Confederation.[18] It is in this way that what is called the traditional petite bourgeoisie in Quebec became the dominant political force. These local elites, composed of members of the liberal professions, the Catholic clergy, and members of religious orders, formed the personnel of the two major institutions of Quebec society: the Canadian democratic state and the Catholic Church.[19] The petite bourgeoisie, under the hegemony of different bourgeois factions, maintained their power through the support of the peasants.

Thus it was the joining of federalism and the liberal state that permitted the traditional petite bourgeoisie of Quebec to exercise so important a political role. Federalism conferred to the provinces the management of social and cultural areas at the same time that the liberal state attributed administration to private institutions. One can therefore understand why the traditional petite bourgeoisie of Quebec defended the liberal Canadian state until 1960. Whereas its secular representatives controlled the political system (the mayors, senators, federal and provincial deputies, and public administrators in Quebec were most often doctors or lawyers), its clerical members oversaw the administration of the greater part of private institutions run by the Catholic Church (schools, hospitals, asylums, charitable organizations, and the like).

At the same time, this class imposed a new definition of the national community. The Canadian nation of 1800 to 1840 became the Catholic, French-Canadian nation. This new definition developed in the face of the reorganization of power relations described above. Within the united Canada and then in Confederation, this definition allowed for the affirmation of the specificity of French Canadians in distinguishing themselves from English Canadians. In defining themselves as Catholic, they insured the power of the Roman Catholic Church. The French Canadians were thus distinguished by their culture (French language and Catholic religion) as the basis of a common political identity in the Canadian state.[20]

QUEBEC IN THE WELFARE STATE

The crisis of the 1930s, the strategy for the transition to a welfare state proposed by the federal government during the 1940s, and the acceleration of industrialization in Quebec after the Second World War all radically transformed the nature of the national question.

As in all other advanced capitalist societies, the economic crisis of the 1930s put liberalism and the liberal state in doubt. At the beginning of the thirties the Richard Bennett government in Ottawa was inspired by the New Deal programs of Franklin Roosevelt and initiated certain reforms favoring major state intervention. In 1937 the succeeding government of W. L. Mackenzie King created the Rowell-Sirois Commission (Royal Commission on Dominion-Provincial Relations) to study the role of the state and the division of powers between the different levels of government in Canada. The political will that was growing in certain federal circles to involve the state in the regulation of social relations was directly confronting the division of powers between the federal government and the provinces as defined in the Canadian Constitution. The first federal propositions met opposition from provinces that were trying to maintain their autonomy. In the name of the war effort, the central government was able to impose the federal programs of unemployment insurance (1941) and family allowances (1944). Immediately after the Second World War, during the Conferences on Reconstruction in 1945–46, the federal government again took the offensive in proposing a complete package of welfare-state programs characterized principally by the establishment of Keynesian economic regulation and a universal and integrated social security program (extension of unemployment insurance, old-age pensions, health insurance).[21] However, in Canada the transition to a welfare state was made in piecemeal fashion and was not realized everywhere and in all its dimensions until much later.

In Quebec, the National Union government (1936–39 and 1944–60) resisted fiercely the transition to the welfare state. Invoking provincial autonomy and traditions, it opposed the centralization of power that the federal programs implied. With its defense of provincial autonomy and its critique of state intervention, the regime clung to the maintenance of the liberal state. But at the end of the 1950s, the National Union lost the support of the Canadian grande bourgeoisie as well as of the Quebec bourgeoisie.

It was not until the election of the Liberal Party at the provincial level in 1960 that the systematic transition to a welfare state started. In the space of a few years, the role of the state was radically transformed. There was a multiplication of state-owned companies, reform of work codes, the nationalization of the provincial hydroelectric power companies, the creation of a ministry of education, and state programs of health insurance, social welfare, and so on.[22] However, the transition to a welfare state in Quebec did not ease relations between the federal government and the province. On the contrary, the essentially defensive and conservative nationalism of the 1950s, based on respect for provincial autonomy and the maintenance of the liberal state, gave way to an offensive nationalism that led to the demand for a sovereign Quebec. This paradox can be explained by several factors.

First, the acceleration of industrialization and urbanization in postwar Quebec and the development of a consumer society effected important changes in Quebec society. The consolidation of the working class, the rise of the new petite bourgeoisie, and the new Quebec capitalism constituted the most significant elements of this change. But it is without doubt its relation to the state that best explains the distinctiveness of the new Quebec nationalism. More precisely, it is the relations between the transformation of social structures resulting in the development of capitalism, the consolidation of the welfare state, and the situation of national domination that account for the rise of the sovereignty movement.

This is particularly clear in the case of the dominant classes. Since the Conquest, the Quebec economy has been controlled by a predominantly anglophone bourgeoisie. Very quickly a split occurred between an overwhelmingly anglophone grande bourgeoisie, who since the beginning of the twentieth century participated in the monopolization of the Canadian economy as a whole, and a francophone "middle" bourgeoisie, who controlled mostly small and medium-size businesses with principally local or regional orientations. If one looks at the composition of the Quebec bourgeoisie, one can see two major factions, one monopolist, predominantly anglophone, and unconditionally favoring Canadian federalism, the other nonmonopolist, predominantly francophone, and with a sphere of influence confined principally to the provincial level.[23]

Until the 1960s, the nonmonopolist bourgeoisie of Quebec had always supported the liberal policies and provincial autonomy of the governments of the province. But the recession of the second half of the 1950s and especially the acceleration of the monopolization of the economy provoked a series of bankruptcies and the absorption of small and medium-size businesses by monopolist interests. This caused a questioning of the liberal strategy, and a number of Quebecois employer associations called for state intervention. Several of the state-owned enterprises created during the early 1960s had the purpose of favoring Quebecois capital: these included the Caisse de dépôt et de placement du Québec (Quebec Deposit and Investment Fund), Société générale de financement du Québec (General Investment Corporation of Quebec), and the Société de développement industriel du Québec (Quebec Industrial Development Corporation), among others. The 1960s and 1970s also saw the formation of an economic network in Quebec linking the state-owned enterprises, banking capital, and small and medium-size businesses.[24] Even if the Quebecois nonmonopolist bourgeoisie did not become unanimously pro-sovereignty, it supported nonetheless a very strong autonomist position within the framework of promoting a decentralized federalism.

However, it was first and foremost among the new petite bourgeoisie that the new Quebecois nationalism was defined; it was essentially political and considered the Quebecois state the principal means to national liberation.

QUEBEC NATIONALISM IN THE 1960s

The new Quebec nationalism of the 1960s imposed a radical redefinition of the national community. From a primarily cultural definition of the Catholic, French-Canadian nation as referring to all francophones in Canada, the new nationalism switched to an essentially political representation of the Quebecois nation, identified with the Quebecois territory and state.[25] On the ideological level, such a definition provided the basis for an independence movement. It is not surprising that this new nationalism emerged first within the intelligentsia of the new petite bourgeoisie. Following the postwar baby boom and the acceleration of urbanization, this new salaried class, which did not consist of direct producers and which some authors have called "the new middle class," multiplied. In all monopoly capitalist societies in which a welfare state was imposed, these were the principal agents recruited by the public and private bureaucracies. In Quebec, the reality of the national domination of francophones reinforced this tendency, and the Quebec state became a privileged site for employment of the new francophone petite bourgeoisie.[26] It should be understood here that a systematic discrimination was practiced against francophones, who could only occupy subordinate positions in private enterprises as well as the federal bureaucracy (the only public bureaucracy developed in Canada).[27]

This new importance of the state can also be seen within the organizations of the workers' movement. The establishment of the regime of collective bargaining, which certain authors have called the "Keynesian compromise" in the process of the formation of the welfare state, is important.[28] State intervention into wage relations and social policies was, in Quebec as elsewhere, one of the principal demands of the workers' movement from the beginning of the twentieth century. In 1964 the welfare state brought about a reform of the work code favoring unionization, particularly in the public and parapublic sectors. The Quebecois union movement has thus become the sometimes-contradictory site of the defense of the interests of both the working class and the new petite bourgeoisie. The Quebec state much more than the federal government was from this point on considered the principal site for the defense of the interests of the labor movement, the new petite bourgeoisie, and of regional small and medium-size businesses.[29]

It is against this backdrop that different movements and political parties appeared during the 1960s promoting Quebec independence, which was considered an instrument for the liberation of the Quebecois nation. The new national movement could therefore be presented as a new political alliance emerging from the welfare state.

During the 1960s, the national movement was characterized by the multiplicity of its organizations and the diversity of its methods. Its principal organizations emerged from the petite bourgeoisie. The Assembly for National Independence (Rassemblement pour l'indépendence nationale, RIN) and the National Rally (Ralliement national, RN) were the first two significant political parties. The first, the most important politically, came out of the new petite bourgeoisie, making the Quebec state the principal instrument for national liberation; the second, linked to the traditional petite bourgeoisie, was born of a split within a right-wing federal party, the Social

Credit Party. The new national movement at the same time gave rise to the development of an armed struggle. The principal clandestine organization, the Liberation Front of Quebec (Front de libération du Québec, FLQ), whose young members came primarily from the new petite bourgeoisie, contained many diverse ideological tendencies.[30] Initially fairly close to the dominant wing of the RIN, the FLQ evolved little by little toward the positions linking independence and socialism defended by the left wing of the RIN. The movement became increasingly radicalized until the kidnapping in 1970 of a British diplomat and the execution of a provincial minister. These actions incited the adoption of the War Measures Act by the federal government under Pierre Trudeau and the occupation of Quebec by the Canadian Army. This was the last significant action by the FLQ.

The conjuncture had changed within the national movement. Following a division in the Liberal Party of Quebec, a group of dissidents formed the Sovereignty-Association Movement (Mouvement souveraineté-association, MSA) in 1968. Led by René Lévesque, the charismatic political leader who had participated in the "quiet revolution" at the beginning of the 1960s,[31] the MSA would soon dominate the national movement.[32] In fact, several months later the Parti Québécois was formed following a fusion of the MSA and the RN. The RIN, with whom Lévesque refused to negotiate because of distrust of the radicalism of its left wing, was dissolved and most of its members joined the Parti Québécois. This was the beginning of the second phase of the national movement. While the 1960s were characterized by a plurality of organizations (RIN, RN, FLQ, MSA) and methods of action (demonstrations, support of strikers, armed struggle, electoral campaigns), the 1970s saw the domination of the movement by one party, the Parti Québécois, and the focusing of the fight for independence solely upon electoral and parliamentary battles.

These changes are explained by the transformations in the class composition of the national movement and, more precisely, by the hegemony of the former dissidents of the Quebec Liberal Party united first within the MSA. René Lévesque, former minister of the Liberal government from 1960 to 1966, architect of the nationalization of electricity (Hydro-Quebec), and head of the left wing of the party, had united and continued to gather around him some of the great technocrats of the quiet revolution (for example, Jacques Parizeau, economist and current leader of the PQ, from a bourgeois Quebecois family and counselor to several premiers of Quebec). The group led by Lévesque affirmed its hegemony within the PQ and insured the party's adoption of its political project. Simply put, the goal of the PQ's economic policy was the development of Quebec capitalism through the coordination of the intervention of state enterprise, the cooperative movement, and regional private enterprise.[33] To quote René Lévesque, "We [Quebecois] will decide whether an enterprise will be private, public or mixed. But it must be Quebecois."[34] As Jacques Parizeau would repeatedly emphasize, for followers of the PQ the state would be the preferred instrument for the promotion of Quebecois capitalism.

The national movement, whose political instrument was from then on the Parti Québécois, appeared thus as a multiclass movement. Dominated by a circle dedicated to the promotion of Quebecois capital, its membership was recruited primarily from the new petite bourgeoisie. Even if the state was recognized unanimously as the special instrument of national affirmation, the party was crossed with contradictions that related to its two principal tendencies. The dominant one of technocratic inspiration aimed first and foremost at the promotion of Quebecois capitalism. From this perspective the realization of sovereignty was linked to the maintenance of an economic association with the rest of Canada with the goal of preserving access to the Canadian market for Quebecois capital. The second tendency, linked to the new petite bourgeoisie and more radical for being inspired by social democracy, favored independence (without association) and the expansion of the social reforms initiated by the welfare state.[35]

DEFEAT AND RESURGENCE OF THE NATIONAL MOVEMENT

After coming to power at the provincial level in 1976 and pursuing a Keynesian-inspired policy favorable to Quebecois capital and the protection of the French language in Quebec, the Parti Québécois held a May 1980 referendum on sovereignty, which if realized was to be accompanied by the maintenance of economic association with the rest of Canada. However, the referendum was defeated: only 40 percent of voters and 50 percent of francophones voted in favor. After the victory of the federalists, the central government began the process of repatriating the Constitution. Until then all constitutional amendments were required to have the formal endorsement of the British Privy Council. The government of Pierre Trudeau, which during the referendum had promised an in-depth reform of federalism that would be favorable in Quebec, used the PQ defeat instead to strengthen the powers of the central state. Under the initiative of the federal government, the Constitution was thus repatriated to Canada, at which time a Charter of Rights and Freedoms was enshrined in it. Since 1982, the Constitution has been interpreted by the courts according to the spirit and language of the Charter. A detailed analysis of the Canadian Charter of Rights and Freedoms and the political issues that it has raised are beyond the scope of this chapter.[36] Therefore, I will look only at what is essential to the present argument.

First, I would emphasize that the creation of a charter of rights and the amendment of the Constitution itself represent the recognition of a set of contradictory rights. Whereas the French and Americans limited themselves to the proclamation of rights of the individual citizen tied to universal principles of citizenship, the Constitution Act of 1982 contains a variety of diverse elements. In summary, it recognizes universal rights (e.g., "freedom of conscience and religion"), special rights (e.g., "equal protection and equal benefit of the law without discrimination based on race, national or ethnic origin, colour, religion, sex, age or mental or physical disability"), cultural rights (e.g., "[to] receive primary and secondary school instruction in the language of the English or French linguistic minority population of a province"), collective rights of a political nature (e.g., "the existing aboriginal and treaty rights of the aboriginal peoples of Canada"), and social rights characteristic of the welfare state (e.g., "essential public services of reasonable quality to all Canadians").

We must limit ourselves to exploring the two principal sources of tension in the relations between Quebec and Canada that have arisen from the adoption of the Charter. The Charter was viewed first as an instrument in the fight of the federal government against the promotion of French in Quebec. The Charter permits the Supreme Court to nullify laws or portions of laws adopted by a government of the federation (and thus that of Quebec) that in the area of language would have discriminatory effects on individuals belonging to the minority.[37]

It is important to grasp the fundamental issue of the debate and the problem posed by the demands of a national movement within a liberal democracy. The essential problem is the nature of the rights tied to the existence of a distinct national community. These rights can be recognized as political rights that should be inscribed in the Constitution and in the political regime itself. They are political rights that are conferred on a group as a whole, not on individual members of that group. For example, the Constitution Act of 1982 recognizes the "treaty rights" of aboriginal peoples (section 35). Conversely, it is possible to see these as essentially individual rights: that individuals are granted these rights on the basis of their membership in a particular community. It is from this perspective that the rights of anglophones and francophones in Canada are recognized in the Charter (sections 16 to 23).

What are the implications of such a choice? Before answering the question directly, we would emphasize that the inscribing of cultural rights in the Charter is the result of the struggle by francophones in Quebec, Acadia (francophone regions of the Maritime provinces), and the rest of Canada. In this section we will look only at the position of Quebec. The demands of the Quebecois always refer explicitly or implicitly to the struggle for the recognition of political rights tied to the existence of a particular nation, rights that should translate as specific powers for the state of Quebec: specific status within the Canadian federation, formation of associated states, or sovereignty. The Charter does not respond in any way to these demands, nor does the whole of the Constitution. As we have emphasized, it only recognizes the cultural rights of individuals that apply everywhere in Canada, to the anglophone and francophone communities.

So where is the problem? The problem lies precisely in the fact that the cultural rights inscribed in the Charter are in fact rights related to the protection of minorities. They protect against discrimination individuals belonging to the francophone minorities outside of Quebec and to the anglophone minority within Quebec. One can thus appeal to the Supreme Court to nullify provincial legislation judged discriminatory by individual members of a minority. However, the situation in Quebec is completely paradoxical in this respect. Its francophone majority perceives itself as a nation, the Quebecois nation. Moreover, it considers itself a threatened minority within Canada and, more generally, within the whole of the overwhelmingly English North America. The francophone majority in Quebec considers the anglophone minority an integral part of the English Canadian community as well as of the dominant English North American society.

From this perspective, it is not the anglophone minority that needs to be protected but the francophone majority on whom there are constant pressures to assimilate into the English North American whole. Therefore, the francophones of Quebec do not consider that their situation is different from that of other francophones in North America except that by forming a majority within a specific state (the province of Quebec), they can facilitate the adoption of political measures aimed at countering the trend toward assimilation.

This position is sustained with all the more firmness because the anglophones in Quebec constitute one of the most protected minorities in North America. For example, they possess their own system of education, their own media, and a health-care system. Nevertheless, the government of Quebec has since the mid-1970s adopted a series of laws on the question of language that are, either wholly or in part, objectively discriminatory, directly or indirectly, with respect to the anglophones. These laws were aimed at protecting and promoting the French language in Quebec. To understand the issues and the spirit behind these laws, we will look at two typical examples. The first is based on the fact that, historically, immigrants settling in Quebec overwhelmingly have assimilated into the anglophone community. The second example revolves around the problem that commercial signs, particularly in Montreal, Quebec's metropolis, were largely written in English. The Quebec government adopted two laws to counter these phenomena: children of francophones and immigrants coming from outside Canada were required to send their children to French preschools and primary and secondary schools (Bill 101), and external commercial signs were required to be written only in French (Bill 178).

Since the adoption of the Charter of Rights and Freedoms, however, several sections of Quebec's language laws have been overturned (e.g., the complete ban of other languages in provincial courts).

But this was not the case with the measures concerning school enrollment and commercial signs outlined above. It must be emphasized that within limits judged reasonable by the Supreme Court, any government can suspend the implementation of the Charter for five years (a period that is renewable) by invoking the "Derogatory Clause," which is what the Quebec government did. The use of the clause has serious political consequence as a government must then publicly admit that the law it wants to pass is objectively discriminatory.

At the risk of simplifying a complex problem that has provoked interminable debates since 1982, I would synthesize the issue as follows. Can the Quebec government, using the principle of affirmative action as a model, adopt laws aimed at protecting and promoting the French language and culture in Quebec? By applying the Charter, the Supreme Court of Canada has said yes, but within narrow limits judged to be "reasonable" and most often related to the use of the Derogatory Clause. This response is far from satisfying the traditional demands of the governments of Quebec, even the federalist ones.

I indicated above that the adoption of the Charter was the source of two major tensions in the relations between Quebec and Canada. The second was the result of the disparity in the Charter between the treatment of the question of Native peoples and that of Quebec. We have just seen that the Charter does not recognize the francophone majority in Quebec as a distinct society. In this respect there is a double standard: the Charter targets first and foremost individuals and not the national community; it refers to the whole of francophones and anglophones in Canada and not to a political community situated in Quebec. At the same time, the Charter and the section 35 of the new Constitution Act recognize the political and collective rights of Native peoples. This disparity of treatment is not without problems, even if the Quebec government itself recognizes the existence of distinct Native nations and their right to self-government. René Lévesque thus declared in 1983 at a constitutional conference aimed at defining the political rights of Native peoples recognized in the Constitution:

This is rather a supreme irony, at a time when we are considering the recognition of rights in the Constitution—not only individual rights, but collective rights, and national rights, as it were, of native peoples (and God only knows that they have toiled long and hard to merit this recognition)—in the same way, the specific existence or identity of another nation, as distinct as any other, whose homeland is Quebec, should have been and must be acknowledged. The Canada Bill has totally ignored our nation, as if it were a simple collection of individuals.[38]

Far from resolving these problems, the repatriation of the Constitution and the enshrining of the Charter of Rights and Freedoms heightened the conflicts between Quebec and Canada. These antagonisms were exacerbated by the fact that during the negotiations between Canadian provincial and federal governments that led to the repatriation, Quebec was isolated in such a way that it refused to sign the new Constitution, to which it is nonetheless tied at the legal level. Symbolically, these events were considered an affront by the vast majority of francophones in Quebec.

The Parti Québécois was reelected in Quebec in 1981. Its second term was marked, however, by a certain moroseness. The world economic crisis created pressures for it to break with the Keynesian strategy that it had adopted earlier.[39] On the social plane, it was led to "fire on its own troops" by attacking the public- and parapublic-sector unions. While undertaking certain measures of a neoliberal orientation, it put off its sovereignty project. The PQ finally lost power in 1985 to the Liberals, who were clearly oriented toward neoliberal policies aimed at dismantling the welfare state. Toward the end of the 1980s, the sovereignty movement seemed to have reached its last breath. Some observers declared its death definitively, particularly because the Parti Québécois (led by Pierre-Marc Johnson after the resignation of René Lévesque) was no longer fighting for sovereignty, the issue that had once been the essence of its program.

The Conservative government of Brian Mulroney took power at the federal level in 1984, in large part because of massive support from Quebec. This government, which in its term in office put into effect neoliberal policies (privatization of state-owned companies, deregulation, adoption of free trade with the United States), had promised "to reintegrate Quebec into the Constitutional fold with honor and dignity."[40] Negotiations were undertaken to satisfy the demands of Quebec and then to bring it to sign the Constitution. The provincial government of Robert Bourassa had formulated five minimal conditions for ratification, of which the principal one was the recognition of Quebec as a distinct society. In what was called the Meech Lake Accord (the proposed constitutional amendment of 1987), the distinct-society clause stipulated "that Quebec constitutes within Canada a distinct society" and consecrated "the recognition that the existence of French-speaking Canadians, centred in Quebec but also present elsewhere in Canada, and English-speaking Canadians, concentrated outside Quebec but also present in Quebec, constitutes a fundamental characteristic of Canada." This ambiguous clause, whose real weight could never be evaluated as it was never applied, was aimed at resolving the conflicts raised by the Charter. Its defenders maintained that by giving the Quebec government the mission to protect and promote the French language and culture, the accord could play a role in counterbalancing section 23 of the Charter on the language rights of French-speaking and English-speaking Canadians outlined above. Following a series of reversals, the negotiations ended in failure. The Meech Lake Accord was first accepted in 1987 by all principal premiers. It was then submitted to the legislatures of all provinces and to that of the federal government. The rule of unanimity had to prevail. Technically, it was because the provincial government of Manitoba did not ratify it that the accord was definitively rejected in 1990.

Canada found itself plunged into a profound crisis from which it has not yet recovered, one that threatens to explode under the weight of the multiple regional and national contradictions.

The failure of the Meech Lake Accord provoked a spectacular push for sovereignty in Quebec.[41] The Parti Québécois, now led by Jacques Parizeau and with its program once again centered on sovereignty, came to power in September 1994. The Quebec national movement seems stronger than ever. A great part of the francophone Quebecois population seems now convinced that it will be impossible for Quebec to reach an accommodation with the rest of Canada. How can this be explained?

In order to do this we must try to understand why it has so far been impossible for the rest of Canada to satisfy Quebec's basic demands and for the federalist forces to develop a satisfactory compromise. It is the conjuncture of Native demands for self-government, the regionalism of the western provinces, and Canadian nationalism that has led to this situation. At the symbolic level, it is important to note that the Meech Lake Accord was ultimately blocked by a Native deputy, Elijah Harper, member of the provincial legislature in Manitoba, one of Canada's western provinces. Far from being opposed to the interests of the Quebecois, the representatives of the Native peoples claimed only their own constitutional rights. From 1983 to 1987 federal-provincial conferences were held aimed at defining the concrete political scope of the rights of Native peoples recognized in the Constitution. These conferences ended in failure. Native people believed that, with the ratification of the Meech Lake Accord satisfying the demands of Quebec, finding a solution to the demands of Native people would be postponed indefinitely. While the Quebecois and Native people seemed to advance relatively similar demands, the constitutional intricacies tend to oppose them. Thus, at present, representatives of Native groups fear that sovereign Quebec would become an obstacle to their achieving the right to self-government.

At the provincial level, on the other hand, the current economic crisis, like the ones that preceded it, had provoked a resurgence of regionalist claims, principally in the western provinces. Since the beginning of Confederation, Canadian federalism had traditionally been accused, particularly in the West but also in the Maritimes, of favoring the industrialized central provinces (Ontario and Quebec). During the 1980s, this sentiment led to the proposal of a Senate reform that would give each province an equal number of representatives. Not surprisingly, this reform was resisted as much in Ontario as in Quebec, as these two provinces, by far the largest, would see their political power diminish within the federation. Here again, just as in the case of the Native Canadians, the West refused to amend the Constitution to accommodate Quebec without satisfying at the same time the claims of the other provinces.

Finally, it must be recognized in the confrontation between (English) Canadian nationalism and nationalist (French) Quebec that a national oppression exists. This can be seen in English Canada's obstinate refusal to recognize the existence of a distinct national reality in Quebec, if not at an exclusively symbolic level.

The discussions on these proposals were solely based on the recognition of a highly ambiguous "distinct society" in Quebec and not a "nation."[42] In the Meech Lake Accord, for example, it was recognized that there exists in Quebec "a distinct society" because of its francophone majority and anglophone minority, while everywhere else in Canada there is an anglophone majority and a francophone minority. In addition, the accord gave responsibility for promoting this distinct society to the government of Quebec. A large number of constitutional experts argued that if this clause were included in the Constitution, far from favoring the promotion of French, it would force the government of Quebec to adopt a policy of bilingualism. The distinct-society clause would have been interpreted by the courts in terms of the provisions of the Charter of Rights and Freedoms. Because the clause was drawn up on the basis of relations between the majority and minority in Canada and in Quebec, it risked reinforcing the Charter, which on the linguistic level was oriented principally to individuals and the defense of their minority rights. One should note here that the use of the notion of a distinct society helps avoid the use of the term "nation." Thus it also avoids recognizing the reality of the Quebecois nation and eventually of its right to self-determination because at the international level the exercise of this right is linked to the existence of a national community. In addition, the federal strategies are tenacious in their search for a formula that, while recognizing symbolically the existence of a distinct society in Quebec, would not confer on that province any new specific powers that would not at the same time be accorded to the other provinces and that would not be subject to interpretation according to the Charter of Rights.[43]

Whatever the result of this discussion, in the final analysis it will be the Supreme Court judges who will have to evaluate the relative weight of individual rights and collective rights. Without a doubt, it is the Charter and the rights of individuals that will continue to prevail since the Meech Lake Accord attempted to ensure that the (interpretive) clause of the distinct society would be compatible with the Charter. In such a context, the precedence of individual rights did not seem to satisfy fully the demands of measures aimed at countering the national oppression.

Here again a satisfactory demonstration of this argument would require long development; thus I will be very schematic. First, let us start with the existence of a very small linguistic community, the Quebecois, within the vast English society that is North America. Add to this that we are faced with advanced capitalist societies within which a mass culture has developed based on a media system capable of invading the daily life of all people. In a situation of absolute laissez faire, individuals belonging to the francophone minority would be exposed everywhere to pressures to assimilate: at work they would have to speak English; they would be deluged with English advertising; they would be strongly urged to read English newspapers; they would watch English-Canadian and American television; they would enroll their children in English schools to prepare them for their future in the English world. In other words, the French-speaking minority would become assimilated into and immigrants would identify with the English-speaking majority.

The full and free deployment of economic and cultural institutions in the liberal capitalist society of North America tends to produce a cultural oppression for the francophone minority. American readers unfamiliar with this problem can confirm this by looking at the current situation of francophones in Louisiana, where in a similar situation of laissez faire the original French majority has been almost entirely assimilated.

I argue that in such a context only political intervention aimed expressly at protecting and promoting the French language and culture can counter the pressures on a minority group to become assimilated. I also maintain that only actions inspired implicitly or explicitly by affirmative action and collective rights is capable of meeting the demands of such a policy. The invocation solely of individual rights would not suffice since the promotion of French in such a perspective necessarily implies limiting certain individual rights.

The law mentioned above that requires francophone and immigrant children to go to French schools constitutes a seemingly coercive measure. It was adopted because free choice tended to favor enrollment in English schools and to reinforce assimilationist pressures.

It is clear that the application of affirmative action programs must be strictly controlled. These types of measures must still respect the fundamental rights of citizenship, those for example that are the basis of all democratic capitalist states and that are inscribed in section 2 of the Canadian Charter. Moreover, in a case like that of Quebec, the adoption of these types of measures would not exclude the necessity of preserving and maintaining the institutions of the anglophone community. The debates on the Canadian Charter and the distinct-society clause illustrate the difficulty of the problem of the relation between individual rights and collective rights in a capitalist democracy.

The case of Quebec illustrates how the application of a charter centered essentially on the rights of individuals does not suffice in countering the trend toward cultural homogenization, assimilation and, in short, national oppression characteristic of the free development of a capitalist market economy. This is without doubt why the application of the Canadian Charter can be temporarily suspended in certain cases by invoking the "Derogatory Clause," as was done by the Quebec government regarding the language of signs. The necessity of using such a clause has tended to render the defense of certain collective rights politically suspect.

CONCLUSION

It is this squaring of the circle that the Canadian political elites attempted to resolve at the end of 1992. Following long and painful negotiations, the federal and provincial first ministers as well as aboriginal leaders agreed on proposals for constitutional reforms that were put to the Canadian people during a referendum held on October 26, 1992.[44] The Charlottetown accord, which attempted to satisfy the demands of all parties present simultaneously, ultimately failed to convince anyone.

The initiative centered on the following: (1) the affirmation of the right of self-government for the First Nations, which was to be negotiated with each aboriginal community; (2) the recognition of Quebec as a distinct society within Canadian federalism (recognition that did not, however, confer new powers on the province); (3) a reform of the Senate that assured each province equal representation but that gave the upper chamber new powers.

The constitutional initiative was soundly defeated in the referendum in Quebec and in the Native communities, as well as in the rest of the country. Thus, Canada appears presently to be a blocked society within which citizens and the different communities cannot agree on a new Constitution.

Meanwhile, the national movement in Quebec has grown stronger and stronger, revitalized not only by the failures of the Canadian constitutional negotiations but also by the transformations of the sociopolitical conjucture. As I have outlined above, the 1980s were dominated in Quebec by the neoliberal credo, the success of which helped in the regression of the national movement that had been strongly associated with the welfare state. The hour of euphoric neoliberalism, which promoted privatization and sang the glory of entrepreneurship, was short-lived. The deepening of the economic crisis, the spectacular bankruptcies of certain Quebec capitalists, plant closings, and the increase in unemployment and poverty have shown the failure of neoliberal solutions. In their place we are currently witnessing the emergence of a new policy that rehabilitates the role of the state based on the cooperation between private companies and the central unions. Such a strategy could lead to the development of a new wage relation that allows the unions to intervene at the level of the organization of labor in companies. In the welfare state, collective agreements have focused primarily on salaries and have left under the control of employers the management of work itself. With respect to the organization of work, unions could only intervene secondarily through the definition of jobs in the collective agreement, jobs that are conceived of in Taylorist terms by the company management.[45] The economic crisis is currently provoking in Quebec as elsewhere a questioning of the Taylorist organization of work. In such a context, union organizations can intervene directly in these transformations by demanding from management direct participation in the organization of work, most often in exchange for greater flexibility in the division of tasks and fewer demands with respect to wages. A climate of cooperation between management and unions could favor in Quebec the development of such an alternative to neoliberalism, which Danièle Leborgne and Alain Lipietz call the Kalmarist model (referring to Sweden and Germany).[46]

Almost the entire union movement in Quebec has formally announced that it favors sovereignty. It is important to note that contrary to what has happened in the rest of North America, the union movement has not declined but has increased its membership since the beginning of the crisis. The unionization rate of the workforce in Quebec is 47 percent (in Canada it is 38 percent and in the United States 16 percent). On the management side, many executives of the Mouvement Desjardins, one of the most important financial and banking institutions in Quebec, are in favor of sovereignty. Similarly, a poll of the heads of small and medium businesses in Quebec revealed that a significant majority favor sovereignty. In addition, the leaders of the major state-owned enterprises are generally recognized as favoring sovereignty. Jean Campeau, former president of the Caisse de dépôt et de placement du Québec, one of Canada's largest financial institutions, is now Minister of Finance in the Parti Québécois government.

It is among the monopolist bourgeoisie and the anglophone population of Quebec that one finds the greatest opposition to sovereignty. Leaders of Quebecois businesses, francophone as well as anglophone, fear that sovereignty will lead to a break with the Canadian market within which they are solidly placed.[47] For its part, the anglophone population refuses any division of Canada that would place it in a minority position in a new state.

To conclude, the sovereignty of Quebec or at the very least a profound reform of Canadian federalism seems increasingly possible given the nature of power relations that I have outlined here. It is difficult to predict what political transformations may happen within the Canadian state in the short term, but a victory of the sovereignty project in the next referendum would certainly have a determining influence. However, such a victory would not necessarily mean full and complete sovereignty for Quebec. We must emphasize here that sovereignty supporters themselves propose maintaining economic union with Canada as well as using the Canadian dollar and the Bank of Canada. It is far from impossible that negotiations would begin between the federal government and Quebec following a victory of the pro-sovereignty option. Negotiations could lead not to sovereignty but to a different solution—for example, the creation of associated states or the attainment by Quebec of a redefined status within the Canadian federation. It must be remembered that the expansion of the welfare state after the Second World War permitted an important centralization of powers at the federal level. As just one example, the adoption of universal social policies permitted the intrusion of the federal government into areas formerly under provincial jurisdiction. The importance of the public debt and a transformation of the role of the state under the influence of neoliberal policies may favor an important devolution of powers to the provinces.

The factors that I have outlined above may provoke in the short term a significant transformation of public institutions in Canada. But there will not be a long-term solution to the Canadian political crisis as long as there is no recognition of a distinct Quebecois nation and as long as no satisfying political solution is found for the demands of Native peoples.

NOTES

1. In order not to weight down this brief essay unnecessarily, I have often referred to my own works on Quebec written over the past twenty-five years. The reader can consult them to find more detailed explanations of theses I present here only briefly as well as more complete bibliographic information. See, for example, Gilles Bourque, *L'Etat capitaliste et la question nationale* (The capitalist state and the national question) (Montreal: Presses de l'Université de Montréal, 1977).

2. Denys Delâge, *Le pays renversé* (The inverted country) (Montreal: Boréal Express, 1985).

3. Perry Anderson, *L'Etat absolutiste* (The absolutist state), vol. 1 (Paris: Maspéro, 1978). On the feudal character of society in New France, see Gilles Bourque and Anne Legaré, *Le Québec, la question nationale* (Quebec, the national question) (Paris: Maspéro, 1979).

4. Gilles Bourque, *Classes sociales et question nationale au Québec: 1760–1840* (Social classes and the national question in Quebec: 1760–1840) (Montreal: Parti Pris, 1970).

5. Ibid.

6. Fernand Ouellet, *Histoire économique et sociale du Québec: 1760–1850* (Economic and social history of Quebec: 1760–1850) (Montreal: Fides, 1971).

7. Bourque, *Classes sociales et question nationale.*

8. Bourque and Legaré, *Le Québec, la question nationale,* pp. 61–72.

9. John George Lambton, Earl of Durham, *Le rapport Durham,* ed. Denis Bertrand and André Lavallée (Montreal: Editions Sainte-Marie, 1969).

10. Jean Hamelin and Yves Roby, *Histoire économique du Québec (1851–1896)* (Economic history of Quebec, 1851–1896) (Montreal: Fides, 1971).

11. S. B. Ryerson, *Unequal Union* (Toronto: Progress Books, 1968).

12. Ibid.

13. Gérard Boismenu, Gilles Bourque, et al., *Espace régional de nation* (Regional space and nation) (Montreal: Boréal Express, 1983).

14. Leo Panitch, *The Canadian State* (Toronto: University of Toronto Press, 1977).

15. Bourque and Legaré, *Le Québec, la question nationale.*

16. Michel Brunet, *Québec, Canada anglais, deux itinéraires un affrontement* (Quebec, English Canada, two itineraries one confrontation) (Montreal: HMH, 1968), pp. 164–76.

17. Gil Rémillard, *Le fédéralisme canadien* (Canadian federalism) (Montreal: Québec-Amérique, 1985).

18. N. F. Eid, *Le clergé et le pouvoir politique au Québec* (The clergy and political power in Quebec) (Montreal: HMH, 1978), pp. 255–79.

19. Nicole Laurin-Frenette, *Production de l'état et formes de la nation (Production of the state and forms of the nation) (Montreal: Nouvelle Optique, 1978).*

20. Gilles Bourque, "Traditional Society, Political Society and Quebec Sociology, 1945–1980," *Canadian Review of Sociology and Anthropology* 26, no. 3 (May 1989): 394–425.

21. Yves Vaillancourt, *L'évolution des politiques sociales au Québec* (The evolution of social politics in Quebec) (Montreal: Presses de l'Université de Montréal, 1988), pp. 79–118.

22. Kenneth McRoberts and Dale Posgrate, *Développement et modernisation du Québec* (Development and modernization of Quebec) (Montreal: Boréal Express, 1983), pp. 115–45.

23. It is important not to confuse the question of the ethnic composition of the bourgeoisie with the issue of its division into factions (which, however, is often done in a case like that of Quebec). There does not exist, for example, an exclusively anglophone, monopolist bourgeoisie and an exclusively francophone, nonmonopolist bourgeoisie. Thus, one can speak of an anglophone bourgeoisie and a francophone bourgeoisie only in extremely general and essentially descriptive terms. It is not the national identification that determines the chief practices of the bourgeoisie, as the francophones of the monopolist bourgeoisie generally

adopt the federalist positions of that fraction of Canadian capital. Similar confusion surrounds the concepts of the Quebecois bourgeoisie and the Canadian bourgeoisie. It is the nature of capital and the base of accumulation that fundamentally distinguishes the different bourgeoisies and not their national identification. The practices of the Quebecois bourgeoisie, certainly predominantly francophone, are explained first by its nonmonopolist character and the regional extension of its capital. This does not mean that the national question has no place in the analysis, but it is important to situate it correctly. For example, the anglophone, monopolist grande bourgeoisie of Toronto and Montreal has since the beginning of the century maintained practices to exclude francophones, whom they have always considered outsiders. However, as I point out below, this did not prevent the francophone monopolists from being ardent defenders of Canadian federalism.

24. Pierre Fournier, *Capitalisme et politique au Québec* (Capitalism and politics in Quebec) (Montreal: Albert Saint-Martin, 1981).

25. See Bourque, "Traditional Society, Political Society and Quebec Sociology, 1945–1980."

26. Jean François Léonard, ed., *La chance au coureur: Bilan de l'action du gouvernement du Parti Québécois* (The luck of the runner: Action plan of the government of Parti Quebecois) (Montreal: Nouvelle Optique, 1978).

27. The first important manifestation of *indépendentisme* came at the beginning of the 1960s, after the president of Canadian National, a large railroad company controlled by the federal government, declared that no French Canadian was competent enough to be in the management of that company. We should emphasize that during the 1960s francophones occupied the bottom rungs of the income ladder of the salaried workforce among different ethnic groups in Quebec. A difference of 50 percent existed between the English Canadian and French Canadian communities in Quebec. The most recent census indicates that this difference in favor of anglophones has been considerably reduced but has nonetheless stabilized at about 15 percent. We should stress that a comparison between the anglophone and francophone communities today still favors the former on all the usual indices—income, level of education, unemployment rate, and so forth. Thus, if one compares French Canadians and English Candidates across Canada, the difference is significantly widened in all areas.

28. Gérard Boismenu and Daniel Drache, *Politique et régulation* (Politics and regulation) (Montreal: Méridien, 1990).

29. J. M. Piotte, *Le syndicalisme de combat* (Combative syndicalism) (Montreal: Albert Saint-Martin, 1977).

30. Louis Fournier, *FLQ: Histoire d'un mouvement clandestin* (FLQ: The history of a clandestine movement) (Montreal: Québec-Amérique, 1982).

31. The period is associated with the welfare-state policies implemented by the Liberal Party government in the 1960s. See Kenneth McRoberts and Dale Posgate, *Quebec: Social Change and Political Crisis* (Toronto: McClelland and Stewart, 1976); Bourque and Legaré, *Le Québec, la question nationale.*

32. Graham Fraser, *PQ: René Lévesque and the Parti Québécois in Power* (Toronto: Macmillan, 1984).

33. Gilles Bourque, "Class, Nation, and the Parti Québécois," in Alain G. Gagnon, ed., *Quebec, State and Society* (Toronto: Methuen, 1984).

34. René Lévesque, *La passion du Québec* (The passion of Quebec) (Montreal: Québec-Amérique, 1978), p. 202.

35. Vera Murray, *Le Parti Québécois* (Montreal: HMH, 1976).

36. Jeremy Weber, *Reimagining Canada* (Montreal: McGill-Queen's University Press, 1994); Peter H. Russell, *Constitutional Odyssey* (Toronto: University of Toronto Press, 1993); Charles Taylor, *Rapprocher les solitudes* (Bringing together the solitudes) (Sainte-Foy: Presses de l'Université Laval, 1992); Charles Taylor, *Multiculturalism and the Politics of Recognition: An Essay* (Princeton: Princeton University Press, 1992).

37. Under pressure of the national movement, the Quebecois governments since the

1970s have adopted diverse legislation with the aim of promoting the use of the French language. The existence of a pro-sovereignty provincial government in Quebec allowed the creation of a policy that through the introduction of a number of bills would promote the use of the French language. For example, Bill 101 of the PQ required the use of French in business and required francophone and immigrant children to attend French-language primary and secondary schools; Bill 178 under the Liberal government imposed unilingual French commercial signs on the outside of businesses. These measures effectively allowed the promotion of French in Quebec and principally in Montreal, where the anglophone community is concentrated. These language laws are still in effect.

38. Province of Quebec, *Statements and Interventions by Québec Delegates, Canadian First Ministers' Conference on constitutional matters respecting aboriginal peoples* (Ottawa, March 15–16, 1983), Québec, Direction générale des publications gouvernementales, 1984, pp. 11–12.

39. Gilles Bourque and J. G. Lacroix, "Du duplessisme au lévesquisme" (From "Duplessism" to "Levesquism"), *Les Cahiers du socialisme*, no. 12–13 (Spring 1983).

40. François Houle, "Réflexions sur la restructuration de l'état au Canada" (Reflections on the restructuring of the state in Canada), *Interventions économiques*, no. 18 (1987): 73.

41. Hubert Guindon, "Du désarroi à la remobilisation" (From disarray to remobilization), *Bulletin d'information de l'Association des sociologues et anthropologues de langue française* 13, no. 1 (February 1991): 7–8.

42. Dossier du Devoir, *Le Québec et le lac Meech* (Quebec and Lake Meech) (Montreal: Guérin, 1987).

43. Lise Bissonnette, "Le volet Québec" (The Quebec aspect) *Le Devoir* (Montreal), March 3, 1992, p. A-8.

44. The Bélanger-Campeau Commission, created by the Quebec government following the failure of the Meech Lake Accord, proposed holding a referendum either on sovereignty or on any federal proposals that dealt with a thorough reform of Canadian federalism and that would confer many more powers on Quebec. The Liberal government of Robert Bourassa fixed the date for the referendum as October 1992. This referendum was to have been held, of course, exclusively in Quebec. Bourassa argued, however, that the accord agreed on between the first ministers satisfied the demands of Quebec. This is why Quebec participated with the other provinces in the referendum held on October 26, 1992.

45. Alain Lipietz, *Choisir l'audace: Une alternative pour le vingt et unième siècle* (To choose audacity: An alternative for the twenty-first century) (Paris: La Découverte, 1989); Robert Boyer, eds., *Capitalisme fin de siècle* (Capitalism at the end of the century) (Paris: Presses universitaires de France, 1986).

46. Danièle Leborgne and Alain Lipietz, "L'après-fordisme: Idées fausses et questions ouvertes" (After Fordism: False ideas and open questions) *Problèmes économiques* 2, no. 260 (January 29, 1992).

47. Accordingly, the francophone leaders of large monopolist enterprises have recently formed a special group to defend Canadian federalism.

Socialism and the Nationalities Question

□ 10 □

The Nationalities Question in the Former Soviet Union

Transcaucasia, the Baltics, and Central Asia

The Bolsheviks seized power in 1917 at the high point of a revolutionary drama full of ambiguity. Three aggregate forces soon contested Bolshevik power, whose future was far from secure. First, the Bolsheviks were faced with indigenous counterrevolutionary forces whose armies sought to overturn the revolution. Second, the armies of various Western capitalist states, including the United States and Japan, invaded the fledgling Bolshevik state. Finally, the Bolsheviks found themselves face to face, as the czars had been, with the problem of the non-Russian nationalities. By the mid-1920s, Soviet leaders had overcome the first two obstacles and firmly established state power. The national question, by contrast, was never brought to an entirely satisfactory resolution.

SOVIET NATIONALITIES POLICY AND ITS IMPACT

The Russian Empire had been created through centuries of expansion and conquest of non-Russian peoples. The confusion and turmoil of World War I, the events of 1917, and the ensuing period of counterrevolution and reaction offered the non-Russians an opportunity to break away from the multinational state and create independent national entities. Finland declared independence and maintained its status outside of the Russian/Soviet state. Estonia, Latvia, and Lithuania maintained independence during the interwar period and were brought into the Soviet Union in 1940. Other initiatives

227

were shorter-lived. In the Transcaucasus, Georgia, Armenia, and Azerbaijan established independent national states until they were sovietized in 1920–21. Other short-lived states were established in Byelorussia, the Ukraine, Crimea, among the Volga Tartars, and in parts of Central Asia. Some lasted less than a year, others longer.

Lenin and the early Bolsheviks understood the dangers confronting them, and they acted boldly to cut their losses and to insure the safety of the revolution. An early and separate peace was negotiated with Germany in which Russia made major territorial concessions as the price for its withdrawal from the war. Finland, the Baltic states, Poland, and the Ukraine were ceded along with former Armenian territories in the south, which were granted to Germany's ally, the Ottoman Empire. These concessions were followed by initiatives to secure friendly borders with neighboring states beginning with Kemalist Turkey. Likewise, the New Economic Policy (NEP), which incorporated market incentives in the 1920s, should be seen in part as an attempt by a relatively weak state to win over the peasantry at a time when it was dependent on rural support and incapable of imposing collectivization in the face of peasant resistance.

In their relations with national minorities, the Bolsheviks similarly adjusted the logic of theory to bring it into line with the political reality. For the Bolsheviks, ethnic identification and its collective expression, nationalism, were forms of false allegiance promoted and encouraged by bourgeois leaders. Lenin and other early Bolsheviks opposed any type of federative system based on ethnic geographic units; instead, they proposed nonethnic geographic units that would serve as the basis for an ethnically neutral, universalistic identity rooted in class consciousness. The intent of this assimilationist policy was to replace the false consciousness of nationalism, which had led to hostility and bloodshed, with a scientific foundation for social and cultural development.

Breakaway nationalism by the minorities of the erstwhile Russian Empire forced the new Bolshevik leadership to tailor its policies on the national question.[1] Lenin came to promote the position that the national minorities should have political and cultural autonomy within a Soviet Union dominated by the Communist Party. The largest minorities were organized into union republics, such as Ukraine and Azerbaijan, and in return for the loss of political independence, they were guaranteed territorial status as well as cultural and linguistic rights. The smaller minorities were organized into subrepublic units including autonomous republics and regions within the Russian SSR and, in some cases, within other union republics. The Checheno-Ingush Autonomous Soviet Socialist Republic within Russia and the Nagorno-Karabakh Autonomous Region within Azerbaijan are examples.

The impact of Moscow's policies on the constituent republics was complex and textured. There was, without a doubt, repression, often severe, but successive Soviet leaders over seven decades also made important concessions to minority peoples. Each of the republics thus came to possess many of the symbols of independent states, including flags, anthems, national political parties, and parliaments. Republics had their own film studios, television stations, newspapers and printing presses, dance troupes, national museums, and opera houses. Schools were built and students received instruction in local languages. Alphabets were developed for peoples who lacked them, and national cultures were encouraged within politically defined limits. At the same time, the Soviet Union underwent a process of modernization and secularization that undermined traditional centers of power and allowed new national centers of power to emerge. Whatever one may say of the motivations of the former Soviet leadership, the impact of concessions to the republics and the success of Soviet educational and cultural policies strengthened national identity and consciousness among the peoples of the former Soviet republics.

HISTORICAL BACKGROUND

Each major nationality brought its own particular history and culture to the Soviet Union. Each was also defined by its specific geographical location and resources and population base. While overall Soviet policies, if not the specific details, have historically been the same for all of the minority republics, they were filtered through unique political cultures that shaped and gave rise to different national problems, ambitions, and strategies. That uniqueness is expressed in the Transcaucasus, the Baltics, and Central Asia, which are the focus of this inquiry, as well as within each region where significant variations are found.

THE TRANSCAUCASUS

Georgia, Armenia, and Azerbaijan are located in the Transcaucasus, a mountainous and high-plain land bridge between the Black and Caspian Seas about eight hundred miles south-southeast of Moscow. Georgia occupies the eastern Black Sea coast. Armenia is in the south of the region and landlocked, bordering Turkey and Iran, and Azerbaijan is in the east, on the Caspian Sea. As part of ancient trade routes between East and West, these areas were coveted and subject to invasions and conquests at various times by the Romans, Byzantines, Arabs, Mongols, Persians, Turks, and Russians.

The present-day Georgians and Armenians are descendants of ancient indigenous populations who converted to Christianity in the fourth century. At times, they have been able to consolidate power to form empires of their own. For most of their history, however, both peoples have had to preserve national and linguistic identity through their national churches and other institutions that operated within vassal states of larger empires. In the nineteenth century, both peoples were influenced by ideas of nationalism and experienced literary and cultural revivals that carried with them growing ideas of national independence.[2]

There had been a Muslim presence in the Transcaucasus even prior to the tenth century A.D., and with successive invasions from Central Asia, the eastern plains of the Transcaucasus became populated by Muslim peoples who were linguistically linked with Turkic peoples in northwestern Persia. Today these peoples are called Azeris. They are Shiite Muslims and they speak a Turkic language. They were primarily herders and agriculturalists and had no proper state formations. The Russians referred to them as Tatars or Caucasian Tatars. A small intellectual group among them explored various possibilities for national state identity formation around the turn of the century, and most of these leaned toward ties with the Young Turk movement of the Ottoman Empire and the ideology of Pan-Turkism, the plan for the unification of Turkic-speaking peoples from Istanbul, through Central Asia, to the Chinese border. For most turn-of-the-century Azeris, however, such ambitions had little meaning: their consciousness remained Islamic rather than national.[3]

The Russian Empire, expanding southward, conquered Georgia at the end of the eighteenth century and absorbed Caucasian Armenia and Azerbaijan in the early nineteenth century. By the beginning of the twentieth century, the social and political worlds of the three major nationalities of the Transcaucasus had taken quite different paths that would bear on their later histories. The majorities of all three communities were peasants, but patterns of social development were different. Armenians were the most urban of the three groups, with large national populations in Tiflis (Tbilisi) and Baku. The community was dominated by bourgeois and petit bourgeois social strata who played important roles in the industrial wage labor sector of the region. This was centered in the manufacturing sector in Tiflis and the oil industry of Baku. The Georgians were dominated by their nobility and the Azeris by their clerics. Both had more concentrated settlement patterns than the Armenians. In Baku, which was to become their capital, the Azeris occupied the lowest rung in the wage labor sector and were often in the employ of Russians and Armenians, an arrangement that created an explosive overlay of ethnic identities and class resentments.[4]

After the Bolsheviks took power in 1917, the Georgians, Armenians, and Azeris formed nation-states under different political movements. Georgia had been the center of Menshevism in the Russian Empire, and the Georgian Mensheviks headed the government of the Georgian Republic in 1918. They occupied a unified territory and had a long history of national identity as a people. Furthermore, the war had not ravaged their territory, and they had economic and political resources at their disposal, including support from the European socialist movement. The Azeris had the support of Ottoman Turkey and later of the emerging Kemalist Republic. The Muslim Azeris were attractive to the Bolsheviks, who saw the Islamic world to the south as a fertile ground for revolutionary recruitment and expansion. Least viable was landlocked Armenia with a poor resource base and its population of hundreds of thousands of refugees from the 1915 Ottoman Turkish genocide of Anatolian Armenians.

In the end none of the three nations would survive past 1920–21, when they were sovietized. The Armenians rebelled in 1921 and the Georgians in 1924, but the resistance was quelled. For a decade and a half the three formed a Transcaucasian Federation. In 1936, with the new Soviet constitution, they were separated into individual Soviet republics, a status they maintained until the dissolution of the Soviet Union in December 1991.[5]

Beginning in 1988 these three republics were centers of activism in the Soviet Union over a complex range of issues involving conflicts within and between the republics as well as with the central government.

THE BALTICS

The former Baltic republics of Estonia, Latvia, and Lithuania range north to south along the Baltic Sea. Estonia is separated from Finland by the Gulf of Finland and is bordered by Russia to the east and Latvia to the south. Latvia is bordered by Estonia to the north and Lithuania to the south with Russia and Belarus to the east. Lithuania shares borders with Latvia, Belarus, and Poland.

Estonia was occupied by Germanic conquerors in the thirteenth century, and several Estonian towns were members of the Hanseatic League. The area converted to Lutheranism in the sixteenth century. Sweden became the dominant foreign power in the seventeenth century, and Estonia was part of the Russian Empire from the eighteenth century to 1918. In 1918, Estonia declared independence, which it was able to maintain against Bolshevik forces with aid from the Western bloc. The Soviets withdrew in 1920 and recognized Estonian independence. The country was ruled by a series of coalition governments, excluding the Communists. The latter were outlawed in 1924 and the party leadership was placed under arrest. Parliamentary forms were abolished in 1934 in favor of an anti-Soviet authoritarian regime.

Latvia was subject to foreign occupation from the twelfth to the twentieth centuries. Germanic rule lasted until the sixteenth century and was superseded by Polish domination. The Russian Empire held sway from 1795 until 1918. The Latvians defeated Soviet forces, also with foreign assistance, and the Soviets recognized their independence in 1920.[6] The independent republic abolished its parliamentary forms in favor of a fascist-style dictatorship in 1934.

Lithuania's history differs from that of its Baltic neighbors in several respects. Lithuania maintained its independence later into the Middle Ages than its northern neighbors. Foreign influences were Polish and Catholic as opposed to Protestant, German, and Scandinavian. Lithuania was also the only one of the three to build an empire of its own. The Grand Principality of Lithuania was one of the largest states in Europe in the fourteenth and fifteenth centuries, encompassing lands running southeast from the Baltic Sea nearly to the Black Sea. In the sixteenth century, Lithuanian statehood was merged with Poland and then, in the eighteenth century, subordinated to Russia, where it remained until 1918. The Lithuanians also successfully fought against Bolshevik forces, also with Western aid, to establish their independence.[7] They were not successful in foiling Polish ambitions, however, and were forced to cede a third of their territory, including the capital of Vilnius, to Poland in 1920. Lithuania moved to the right earlier than its Baltic neighbors. A putsch in 1926 brought fascistic nationalists to power. They proceeded to dissolve the national assembly, impose martial law, and persecute both the Western democratic and the socialist opposition.

In recent years the linguistic, religious, and historical differences between the Baltic states have been less important than their shared history of forced entry into the Soviet Union in 1940. This came about as a result of the Molotov-Ribbentrop pact, which opened the way for Soviet penetration of the independent Baltic nations of the interwar period. Popular armed resistance to sovietization, still within the living memory of Baltic peoples, as well as repression by the Soviet authorities in establishing their rule over the territories, left the Soviet leadership with a lower level of legitimacy here than in most other regions of the former Soviet Union. When sanctions for dissent decreased under Gorbachev, the area became one of the most persistent centers of protest—first in favor of autonomy and later in support of secession from the Union.

SOVIET CENTRAL ASIA

Soviet Central Asia was the Soviet portion of a larger Central Asian land mass that includes western China and parts of Iran and Afghanistan. The area can be divided into four geographic regions that run roughly in east-west bands across this territory. Steppe covers the north. This gives way to semidesert. The third and largest region consists of desert with fertile oases and irrigated croplands. The southeastern region is rimmed with mountains along the Afghan and Chinese borders.

Because the majority of people in this territory are Asian and Muslim, these have become the region's defining characteristics. However, owing to its historic position as an east-west trade route and to Russian and Soviet settlement policies, the region's demographic makeup is complex. The five largest indigenous nationalities enjoyed full republic status in the former Soviet Union. The largest Central Asian nationality, the Uzbeks, were the third largest nationality (after Russians and Ukrainians) in the Soviet Union and made up approximately 6 percent of the total population. The Kazakhs, Turkmens, Tajiks, and Kirghiz also enjoyed republic status in the former USSR.

The largest territory is Kazakhstan. It runs in a wide east-west band south of Russia, from the northern and central Caspian to the Chinese border. The territory is heavily settled by Russians and other Slavs whose percentage of the population rivals that of the Kazakhs. Uzbekistan is south of Kazakhstan and runs in a southeasterly band. It borders Turkmenistan and Afghanistan on the south and runs to Tajikistan and Kirghizia in the east. Turkmenistan borders the southeastern Caspian and runs south of Kazakhstan and Uzbekistan. It shares international borders with Iran and Afghanistan. Tajikistan and Kirghizia are located in a mountainous region in the southeast and share borders with Afghanistan and China. The Tajiks are linguistically related to Persia while the other titular minorities are Turkic. The region's other inhabitants include Karakalpaks, Baluchis, and other indigenous minorities; deported groups such as Koreans, Germans, Crimean Tatars, and Meskhetian Turks; and Slavs who came as conquerors and settlers and in some cases as exiles. The Slavic population is largest in Kazakhstan but sizeable in all the former Central Asian republics. A final feature of the region's demographic terrain is found in the fact that significant numbers of large Central Asian groups live outside their native territories. Nearly a quarter of Tajikistan's population is Uzbek, and Uzbeks make up roughly a tenth of the population of Turkmenistan and Kirghizia. Sizeable percentages of Kazakhs and Tajiks live in Uzbekistan.

The traditional economy of the region was based on nomadic herding and subsistence agriculture along with trade in areas having water resources. The Arabs converted the area to Islam in the seventh and eight centuries, and the cities of Bukhara and Samarkand flourished as part of the east-west trade. The Arabs fell in the tenth century and were followed by the Turks and then the Mongols. Tamerlane established his capital at Samarkand, which served as the base for invasions westward into Persia and the Transcaucasus. The region prospered as a trade route between the East and the West until the sixteenth century, when it declined because of the West's deployment of modern weaponry, the discovery of sea routes to the East, and the encroachment of the Russian, Chinese, and British Empires.

In the mid-nineteenth century, the area was conquered by the Russians, who encouraged cotton production. The 13,200 hectares under cotton production in 1886 increased to 597,200 hectares in 1914.[8] The large-scale commitment of land, labor, and water resources required for such an enterprise resulted in the region's dependence on Russian grain and textile imports. Colonial settlement of the area by Russians and other Slavs also began in earnest.

Soviet policies further increased cotton monoculture and accelerated Slavic settlement through deportations and the open encouragement of settlers as with Khrushchev's "virgin lands" policy in Kazakhstan in the late 1950s. The Soviets also encouraged the settlement of nomads, introduced the Cyrillic alphabet for local languages, fostered a degree of industrialization, and discouraged but did not outlaw the practice of Islam.[9]

In 1916, Central Asians revolted against wartime famines and czarist conscription policies. After the war, the region was a center of anti-Soviet rebellion led by the Basmachis, who were originally bandits but later transformed into politicized anti-Soviet forces. This conflict lasted from 1918 to 1923 and was revived in the late 1920s to protest collectivization.

Since the mid-1980s, the area has been the scene of a series of protests and clashes, first in Kazakhstan in 1986, then in Uzbekistan in 1989 and Tajikistan in 1990. At times these conflicts have pitted indigenous ethnic groups against one another, but there have also been clashes between indigenous peoples and Europeans—the settlers and deportees and their descendants. People's fronts were formed later in this region than in the Baltics and the Transcaucasus and were not as fully developed. The main sources of opposition and protest, centered among intellectuals, were reluctant to challenge central-state authority until much later, when it became evident that the dissolution of the Soviet Union was imminent. This is evident in the voting pattern on Soviet President Mikhail Gorbachev's Union Treaty proposal. In a futile effort to preserve the Soviet Union as a semblance of itself, Gorbachev offered the republics broad autonomy within a national union. All five Central Asian republics ratified Gorbachev's union proposal, but only one of the three Transcaucasian republics and none of the Baltic republics did so. Nevertheless, the region merits careful attention for numerous reasons including its rapidly growing population, its Islamic base, and its proximity to the larger Muslim world. Of even greater importance, the region is home to political, economic, ethnic, and ecological issues that have served as the basis for mass-based social movements elsewhere in the former Soviet Union and worldwide.

SOVIET NATIONALITIES POLICY: ITS ACCOMPLISHMENTS

A balanced presentation of the position of the various nationalities in the former USSR calls for a discussion of the achievements of Soviet policy rather than an exclusive focus on national grievances. This is not to promote balance for its own sake but to acknowledge that these nationalities lived the Soviet experience in all of its dimensions. The numbers of people who define their experiences in particular ways is one important ingredient in the possibility for mobilization and in the intensity, perseverance, and direction of that mobilization. The precise and shifting balance of popular thought is and will remain an important matter for careful investigation. While the general conflict that evolved in the last years of the Soviet Union opposed the republics and the center, there was also an awareness, at least in some quarters, that the Soviet system brought benefits to the average person and that independence, including a move to an alternate economic system, could undermine social welfare benefits and workers' rights throughout the newly formed Russian Federation and the former minority republics.

Soviet economic and social policies brought real and substantial benefits to Russians and other nationalities throughout the former Soviet Union. In some cases these advances stemmed from specific policies directed at particular republics and regions, and in other cases they were a result of broader social policies designed to protect workers, women, and other sectors of society. The impact of these policies on national minorities may be measured through comparisons with prevailing conditions at the time of sovietization, and in the case of the Transcaucasian and Central Asian republics, with current conditions in the neighboring independent states of Turkey, Iran, and Afghanistan.

EDUCATION, HEALTH CARE, AND HOUSING

Soviet authorities, over the past seven decades, constructed and staffed thousands of schools throughout the former USSR, including institutions of higher education in all of the former republics. Education was made available to males and females without cost from primary through graduate and professional levels. In contrast to the United States, students in Soviet higher education did not have to work and, in fact, received modest government stipends whose levels were pegged to academic achievement.[10] In addition, education in local languages was made available to students in all of the former Soviet republics, and the majority of students attended such schools. For certain minorities, participation in higher education was high. The Georgians and Armenians were the leading national groups in the former Soviet Union in students in higher education per capita. In Central Asia, the rate of participation in higher education was double the rate in the neighboring nations of Iran and Turkey.[11]

Similarly, the Soviet authorities made large investments in health care, which produced substantial improvements in quantitative and qualitative indices of performance by the Soviet health care system between 1917 and the mid-1970s. By 1977, the Soviet Union had achieved the world's highest number of doctors and one of the highest numbers of hospital beds per capita.[12] Life expectancy steadily increased and infant mortality continued to decline during Soviet rule; by the mid-1970s they were not far divergent from standards in the most advanced nations of the West. In addition, health care and most prescriptions were available without charge to the client.

Housing is another good, along with education and health care, that was considered a basic human right by the Soviet system. Millions of housing units were built in the post–World War II period. Apartments were often small, and newcomers and newly started families often had to wait long periods to obtain housing. Yet, once a family was assigned to an apartment, it became that family's permanent home.[13] The apartments were electrified and contained indoor plumbing and were often nicely furnished and decorated by inhabitants who took pride in them. Severe housing shortages, however, prevailed in parts of Central Asia and in Armenia, which never fully rebuilt after the 1988 earthquake. Most important, in the post-Soviet era, there are now over a million homeless refugees resulting from armed conflicts in Georgia, Armenia, Azerbaijan, and Tajikistan.

INDUSTRIALIZATION AND WORKERS' RIGHTS

The former Soviet republics underwent significant industrialization during the past several decades. Central Asia benefited from fiscal policies that allowed it to keep nearly 100 percent of locally generated taxes while receiving subsidies for industrial investment from the center.[14] The Transcaucasus and the Baltics also received central-government subsidies for infrastructure and industrial development. Workers received professional and blue-collar training at government expense, and they benefited from government medical policies. They also received government subsidies for housing, basic food commodities, mass transit, and recreation and vacations, all of which were provided at below cost.[15] Three weeks of paid vacation was standard for Soviet workers. Most important, Soviet workers have had a legal right to their jobs, making them immune to layoffs. The burden of proof for dismissal rested with management, which made employment termination difficult.[16]

THE POSITION OF WOMEN

Before 1917, illiteracy among Russian women was 88 percent and for Muslim women nearly 100 percent. In 1926, literacy rates in Central Asia ranged from a low of 3.8 percent in Tajikistan to a high of 16.5 percent in Kirghizia, with a substantial percentage of the literate population accounted for by Slavic immigrants. By 1959, the Soviet Union had achieved near universal literacy for males and females, with rates exceeding 90 percent even for Central Asian women.[17] Partly as a result of government-imposed quotas going back to the 1920s, women had records of achievement in such fields as economics, law, physics, and chemistry. Soviet law guaranteed women equal access to professional training, employment, pay, and promotions.[18] In addition, women benefited from labor provisions that were among the world's most advanced. Workers in their seventh month of pregnancy were given fully paid leave lasting until the child's first birthday. At the end of that period, a woman could claim an additional year's unpaid leave. Regardless of whether she returned to work after one or two years, the employee was guaranteed her job plus raises and promotions she would have received had she been employed. Women workers were eligible for pensions at age 55 (60 for men) with twenty years of service.[19]

CULTURAL DEVELOPMENT

Despite "Russification" policies, state censorship, and the purges of writers, artists, and other cultural workers in the 1930s and after, national cultures in the former republics flourished within boundaries established by the central state. Thousands of cinemas, theaters, opera houses, galleries, and libraries were built, many of them in Central Asia where few existed before. All of the former minority republics produced electronic and printed mass media in local languages, with the percentages of Russian and local-language media roughly corresponding to the percentage of the titular nationality in the republic's population. The publication of books in local languages is particularly striking in Central Asia, where such resources were virtually nonexistent before 1917. While there were charges of Russification by native and outside critics, including hostile exile groups, over 90 percent of the nationalities of these republics did in fact identify the titular language as their native language.[20]

In the early years of the revolution, the Bolsheviks attacked those features of Islam they considered backward in nature, such as the veiling and seclusion of women, polygamy, child betrothal, the bride price, and pilgrimage to Mecca.[21] These changes opened the way to fuller participation in society by women in numbers consistent with prevailing Western, socialist, and human rights standards. Because Islam is an important part of the national and social identity of Muslim peoples, the Soviets hoped that the combination of education, urbanization, industrialization, and the technological progress would lead to assimilation, but this did not occur and the relationship between Islam and socialism developed into a fluid and uneasy truce. Nevertheless, the impact of Soviet policy in this area was progressive in the ways outlined above, particularly for women.

SOVIET NATIONALITIES POLICY: THE PROBLEMS AND THE PROTESTS

The expression of nationalist discontent and protests in the former Soviet Union since the late 1980s was an outgrowth of felt grievances and the less authoritarian nature of the Soviet state after 1985.[22]

As mentioned earlier, the organization of internal Soviet borders on a national basis provided the territorial and institutional basis for the development and strengthening of national consciousness. While not in and of itself a source of protest, the national context served as the framework for the expression of discontent, even where the issues were economic or political rather than specifically national in character. At the same time, the internal boundaries of the Soviet Union were drawn with an eye to political considerations, so that some territories that would have been assigned to particular republics on the basis of historical claims or population majorities were assigned elsewhere. This policy set the stage for prolonged territorial conflicts within and between a number of republics.

There are perhaps as many as two dozen cases where republics had claims on the territories of other republics or where majorities of various subrepublic regions desired full republic status or assignment to another republic. These conflicts have been deeply troublesome in the Armenian enclave of Nagorno-Karabakh in Azerbaijan, as well as in the Abkhaz, Ossetian, and Adzhar territories in Georgia, and in various parts of Central Asia.

Numerous territorial questions in Transcaucasia, for example, proved explosive, and none has been satisfactorily resolved. Nagorno-Karabakh has an Armenian history going back at least to the fourth century B.C.[23] While the territory did not always have Armenian rulers, it had an Armenian majority throughout its recorded history, and this majority exceeded 90 percent when it was ceded to Azerbaijan in 1921. The terms by which Azerbaijan received Karabakh called for local autonomy, but this too was denied, and the Armenians of Nagorno-Karabakh experienced chronic discrimination in economic allocations, cultural policies regarding language, religion, and education, and access to higher education, employment, and housing.[24]

Similar problems existed in former Georgian lands now in northwestern Azerbaijan, another area assigned to Azerbaijan in 1921. After seventy years of Azeri rule, the former Georgian majority (known as Ingilos) now constitute only a third of the population. Their numbers were reduced by pressure to migrate to Georgia and by forced assimilation.[25]

Other troublesome territorial questions are found in Georgia and Central Asia. The Georgian minorities, the Abkhaz, the Ossetians, and the Adzhar, the indigenous, and all had subrepublic territorial status within Georgia. They complained of linguistic and cultural persecution and of discrimination in monetary allocations. The Ossetians wished to leave Georgia and join their coethnics in North Ossetia, a part of Russia, while the Abkhaz sought full republic status. In Central Asia there have also been serious clashes between ethnic groups over territorial issues, particularly between Uzbeks, Kirghiz, and Tajiks in the fertile Fergana Valley.

These complexities have been compounded by the peculiar problems stemming from the distribution of responsibility in centralized states. The centralized Soviet power structure made all key decisions, altering them only to fit specific local conditions, based on its own interpretation of those conditions, and to meet its own needs. Thus, people were taught that wisdom emanated from the center. When things went badly, it was a short step for people to conclude that blunders emanated from the same place.

With the diminution of sanctions by the Soviet state since the mid-1980s, an outpouring of protest was leveled at the center and its local representatives, the republics' Communist parties. In this section we will examine the nature and forms of protest movements in the Transcaucasus, the Baltics, and Central Asia and explore the various demands of these movements upon the former Soviet state.

THE TRANSCAUCASUS

In Georgia, the protests in the 1970s, including activities of the Georgian Helsinki Watch Committee, founded in early 1977, focused on questions of language and history. Mass demonstrations in 1978 protested proposed constitutional changes that would have made Russian the official language. The proposal was withdrawn. There were also protests against the falsification of Georgian history.[26] These public protests gave way to the growth of underground groups advocating Georgian independence in the early 1980s.

Demonstrations in November 1988 brought out hundreds of thousands of protesters, and some students went on hunger strikes. Their targets were draft amendments to the Constitution that were seen as infringing upon the rights and sovereignty of the republics.

In April 1989 Interior Ministry and army troops attacked peaceful pro-independence demonstrators, killing nineteen and injuring hundreds. Intended as a show of government force that would create a climate of ''reason'' as defined by the authorities, the move backfired badly. The Georgian nationalist movement drew strength from the repression and in the fall 1990 elections, pro-independence forces led by former Helsinki Watch Committee dissident Zviad Gamsakhurdia swept to power.[27] But as Georgian nationalism gained in power, tensions with Georgia's minorities increased. In the summer of 1989, Georgia's Supreme Soviet called for increased use of the Georgian language in all spheres. In September, the Supreme Soviet of the South Ossetian Autonomous Oblast (SOAO) declared its independence and called for unification with the Russian federation. In December the Georgian Supreme Soviet voted to abolish the SOAO as an administrative unit. Meanwhile Gamsakhurdia proclaimed ''Georgia for the Georgians,'' and the Georgian Supreme Soviet moved to disenfranchise minorities by declaring areas that were home to a single group to be ineligible to vote. There were clashes between Georgians and Georgian minorities in South Ossetia and Abkhazia, and twenty-five persons were killed in 1989 alone.

The Georgians refused to hold elections on the Union Treaty, arguing that the sovietization of independent Georgia in 1921 was illegal and, therefore, Georgia was exempt from Soviet law. On the other hand, fearing for their future in an independent Georgia, South Ossetia and Abkhazia voted overwhelmingly in favor of the treaty.

As early as the late 1940s, Armenians were calling for the unification of Nakhichevan and Nagorno-Karabakh, which had been ceded to Azerbaijan, and lands that had been lost to Turkey between 1915 and 1920.[28] From 1963 to 1966, the Union of Armenian Youth played an active political role, organizing the mass April 24, 1965, demonstration commemorating the fiftieth anniversary of the 1915 Ottoman Turkish genocide against the Armenian people. In 1966, the National Unification Party was founded and called for independence and the reunification of lost Armenian lands. Its founders and members were arrested and jailed. The Armenian Helsinki Watch Committee was established in April 1977. It called for Armenian membership in the United Nations, the reunification of Armenian lands in Azerbaijan, and the use of the Armenian language in all spheres of life.[29] Within a short time, the Helsinki Watch Committee members were arrested and sentenced to prison terms.

Armenian protests gathered momentum in the summer and fall of 1987 by means of public gatherings calling for action on the issues of Nagorno-Karabakh, corruption in party circles, and environmental issues—specifically a nuclear power plant, which opponents said had been built on an earthquake fault, and a heavily polluting chemical plant in Yerevan. All of these issues would play a role in toppling Communist power in Armenia, but it would be Nagorno-Karabakh that would play the dominant role.

In January 1988 Karabakh Armenians sent a petition containing a hundred thousand signatures to Moscow, asking for a referendum on the territory's future. On February 13 demonstrations began in the regional capital of Stepanakert. Soon after, support rallies began in Yerevan. From the twenty-second to the twenty-eighth of February, massive demonstrations took place in Yerevan, with reports of up to one million participants in a single day. Methods of nonviolent resistance included marches, demonstrations, rallies, hunger strikes, and general strikes, but they were to no avail. Armenians were strongly attacked in the Soviet press as antisocialist and nationalist tools of imperialism. Soviet authorities refused to consider a territorial transfer. Meanwhile, Azeris in the industrial city of Sumgait, near Baku, carried out a pogrom against local Armenians, brutally murdering nearly forty persons.[30]

By mid-July 1988, the Armenian and Azerbaijani party chiefs had been sacked, Karabakh's economy was paralyzed by continual general strikes, and Armenian protesters seized and held the republic's international airport for two days until they were routed by the army. In the fall, Armenians in Azerbaijan were subjected to renewed persecutions. During this entire period, the central government and local Communist Party leaders in Armenia steadily lost legitimacy.[31] Their place was taken by a group of Armenian intellectual activists known as the Karabakh Organizing Committee (KOC). But soon thereafter, in early 1989, members of the committee were arrested and imprisoned in Moscow until late May. Subsequently, the committee was reorganized as the Armenian National Movement, and one of the original members of the committee, Levon Ter Petrosian, was elected head of state. The government declared Armenia sovereign in August 1990. This leadership refused to hold the official referendum on the Union Treaty because it made no provision for the self-determination of subrepublic territories such as Nagorno-Karabakh. Armenia held its own referendum on independence on September 21, 1991, and an overwhelming majority of Armenians voted in favor of independence.

In Azerbaijan, the Azerbaijani Popular Front (APF) was founded in early 1989. It had a broad platform of reform that included cultural, environmental, political, and economic issues. But the centerpiece of its program remained Nagorno-Karabakh. The front organized mass rallies throughout 1989 in response to Armenian resistance in the autonomous region.

In January 1990 a final round of anti-Armenian pogroms, including murder, rape, and pillage along with forced deportations, cleared Azerbaijan of nearly all Armenians except those in Nagorno-Karabakh. Gorbachev declared martial law and invaded with Soviet troops, but only after the anti-Armenian violence had peaked. Hundreds of Azeris were killed in the process of restoring order.

Though challenged by the Popular Front, the republic's Communist Party remained in power, handily winning elections in 1989, 1990, and 1991. Despite calls for a boycott by the front, the Union Treaty was also approved. In return for its cooperation Moscow placed Soviet troops at the disposal of the Azeris and lent tacit approval for their deployment in Azeri-Armenian border areas, where Armenians were again forcibly removed in the spring of 1991.[32] After Soviet forces were withdrawn, Azeri forces were deployed, and armed conflict continued in Nagorno-Karabakh.

THE BALTICS

Sharing similar twentieth-century histories and confronted by similar problems, the Baltics are free of the intraregional conflicts that plague the Transcaucasus. It suffices, therefore, to focus on one republic to represent the region. We will pay closest attention to Lithuania because its protest movement was the most highly developed. While it resembles Estonia and Latvia in many respects, Lithuania differs from its Baltic neighbors on two dimensions, its Catholicism and its demography. The activism of the Catholic Church was specifically Lithuanian and had little in common with the less activist Protestant churches of Estonia and Latvia. Furthermore, Lithuania's population is the most homogenous of the three nations and contains the smallest percentage of Russians. This gave the Lithuanians greater freedom of action and made it the boldest of the Baltic republics in challenging Soviet authority. Estonia ranked second and Latvia third on this dimension of demographic homogeneity and in the boldness of their challenge to Moscow.

National, religious, and cultural opposition throughout the Baltics began slowly to take shape in the early 1970s. Historical, literary, and folk-lore groups sprang up to study, revive, and promote traditional national culture. Folk music festivals were a popular means of exploring past traditions and forging a sense of national solidarity.

The largest volume of samizdat literature in the Soviet Union was produced in the Baltic republics, especially in Lithuania. These writings reflected a broad range of opinion including neo-Marxist, conservative, ecological, and Western liberal-democratic perspectives.

The Lithuanian Helsinki Watch Committee was established in November 1976. It sought to define ethnic rights as a type of human right. The group's writings reflected a broad range of concerns including the transfer of Lithuanian lands to Byelorussia, the destruction of pre-1940 books, illegal house searches, psychiatric imprisonments, and religious persecution.[33] The group was decimated in a wave of arrests in 1981.

The largest and best-organized group in the 1970s was the Catholic Committee for the Defense of the Rights of Religious Believers. In 1972, it began publishing the *Chronicle of the Catholic Church in Lithuania*, which documented arrests, restrictions on religious practice, and other repressive government policies.[34]

On August 23, 1979, the fortieth anniversary of the Molotov-Ribbentrop pact, forty-eight prominent signatories, most of them Lithuanian, called for the publication of the full text of the pact and the secret addenda that served as the basis for sovietization in the Baltics. In 1981, there was a call for a nuclear-free Baltic and Scandinavian zone.

In the fourth year of the Gorbachev era, protests accelerated dramatically. In April 1988 the Lithuanian Writers Union proposed Lithuanian as the national language. On May 23, the authorities broke up a demonstration in Vilnius to commemorate the deportation of two hundred thousand Lithuanians forty years earlier. On August 24, tens of thousands marched in the three Baltic capitals on the anniversary of the 1939 pact, and a quarter of a million demanded publication of the pact and the opening of the historical archives.[35] In October, the Inaugural Congress of the Lithuanian Movement for Support of Perestroika was held, and the popular movement Sajudis was born. Sajudis was founded by intellectuals with the goals of achieving sovereignty within the Soviet Union, guaranteeing Western-style civil liberties, and eradicating Stalinism. It soon developed a mass base and adopted the objective of independence. Another organization, the Lithuanian Freedom League, was founded by former dissidents, partisans, and political prisoners. Its demand for immediate independence served to radicalize Sajudis.

Perestroika defined by Moscow rather quickly became reform defined by Lithuania. By the end of 1988, one-half million people had turned out to protest a proposed third nuclear reactor, the flag and anthem of independent Lithuania were officially recognized, Lithuanian history and geography were introduced into the school curriculum, Russian language instruction was postponed until the third grade, nearly all political prisoners were released, and Christmas was declared an official holiday.[36]

In the March 1989 elections, the Communist Party, despite endorsing many Sajudis positions, lost 36 of 42 districts to Sajudis. On May 18, the Lithuanian Parliament declared Lithuania sovereign. Soon thereafter they declared Lithuanian veto power over Soviet law, and on August 23 they rejected the legality of the 1940 annexation.[37]

On August 24 hundreds of thousands from Tallinn to Vilnius via Riga joined hands in a human chain in a dramatic rejection of the Molotov-Ribbentrop pact. In December, Parliament voted to abolish the monopoly of the Communist Party. Before the end of the year, the Lithuanian Communist Party declared its independence from Moscow and endorsed the concept of an independent and democratic Lithuania.

On March 11, 1990, Lithuania declared unilateral independence from the Soviet Union. Gorbachev quickly rejected the move as "illegitimate and invalid" and imposed sanctions that cut Lithuania off from its Soviet markets and sources of energy and raw materials. The border with Poland was sealed. Soviet troop presence was increased, and some buildings were seized. In January 1991, coinciding with the U.S.-led invasion of Iraq, Soviet forces cracked down on Lithuania and to a lesser degree on Estonia and Latvia. The Lithuanian leadership withstood the attack but retreated on its claim to independence.

This was to be a temporary setback. Sentiment in favor of independence remained high, and the opportunity to act was provided by the abortive August 1991 Moscow coup. The three Baltic states seized the moment to declare independence, this time with success as recognition was extended by the central government and the Western capitalist states.

SOVIET CENTRAL ASIA

The five Central Asian republics represented a unique way of life within the Soviet Union, and the related ethnic, national, and religious issues found there lent a distinctive complexity to the region's relations with the central authorities.

Compared to the Transcaucasus and the Baltics, the popular-front movements in Central Asia arose as creatures of the intelligentsia without the same degree of mass-based followings. This does not so much represent a lack of popular sympathy with the issues as it does a lower level of mobilization and experience in employing institutional mechanisms for change. Coupled with the inability to challenge the center and a perceived lack of alternatives, Central Asia in the late Soviet years was characterized by the appearance of apathy interspersed with sporadic violent outbreaks. The weakness of the popular fronts was revealed in the region's vote on the Union Treaty, which was endorsed by the local party apparatus. Despite calls for a boycott by the popular fronts, voter turnout was heavy and the yes vote exceeded 90 percent in all five republics.[38]

The most active Central Asian state was Kazakhstan, which actually had taken the lead in popular demonstrations with the Alma Ata protests of December 1986. The central-state media attributed the disturbances to hooligans, but a Kazakh investigatory commission in 1990 indicted local and central-government authorities and confirmed the violent repression of protesters. Kazakhstan's declaration of sovereignty contained a ban on nuclear testing, which stood as the cornerstone of its test of sovereignty. Support for a nuclear test ban cut across ethnic and social groups in Kazakhstan. The same cannot be said, however, for assertions of Kazakh nationalism, which pit Kazakhs against the large Russian settler population. The 1989 language law was a compromise that declared Kazakh the official language of the republic and offered broad protections to Russian-language speakers.

In 1988 the Uzbek intelligentsia founded Birlik (Unity) under the leadership of Muhammad Salih, the first non-Communist head of the Uzbek Writers Union. Birlik sought independence over a five-to-six-year period. Two years later, Erk was established, which sought immediate independence. These initiatives had little popular support and seem to have had a limited impact on the party leadership, which remained among the most entrenched. Uzbekistan declared sovereignty, and the leadership criticized central government policies, but it was not assertive on a broad front. Proposals for economic change by the party and the popular front were limited. There was a commitment to privatization but also a fear of unemployment, already a serious problem. While Salih in the past criticized the republic's economic dependence on Moscow, no proposals were put forth to deal with this situation.[39] The Aral Sea in the west and the Fergana Valley in the east, where there were serious ethnic clashes in 1989 and 1990, symbolized the limitations of reform in Uzbekistan.

Turkmenistan, which likewise faces serious problems, including the highest infant mortality rate in the Commonwealth and a deepening ecological crisis, made little progress toward democratization and reform. Agzybirlik (Solidarity), the only significant informal group, was founded in 1989. The organization was weak and its program limited. It ran no candidates for the Supreme Soviet in January 1990, and 90 percent of those elected were members of the Communist Party.⁴⁰ The outer limits of reform in this republic were defined by the Supreme Soviet, which declared the titular language the official language (making Turkmenistan the last republic where this was done) and passed a sovereignty resolution affirming the republic's right to determine its social and political system.

Tajikistan was rocked by riots in 1989 and 1990, which left twenty-two dead and seven hundred injured. The immediate precipitant was the rumor that Armenian refugees would be given housing preference in a context of serious housing shortages for local residents. The underlying problems were long-neglected social and economic issues. Protesters demanded an accelerated rate of change that included resignation of the republic's leadership, the expulsion of all non-Tajiks, the closing of a polluting aluminum plant, the retention of all cotton revenues, and the release of those arrested during the rioting.⁴¹ Some members of the intelligentsia were concerned about the Turkic preponderance in the region and had reached out to Iran. As a result, there was stronger sentiment for Islamic fundamentalism and independence here than elsewhere in Central Asia. Tens of thousands, mostly Russians, left the republic after the disturbances in Dushanbe, the capital of Tajikistan. This accelerated the emigration of educated and skilled members of the labor force, including physicians, which had begun in earnest with the 1989 language law declaring Tajik the official language.

Kirghizia faces high unemployment and competition for land and housing among Kirghiz, Uzbeks, and Tajiks in the eastern Fergana Valley. The Kirghiz Democratic Movement was an umbrella organization and the largest informal group to gain recognition. It called for sovereignty, economic independence, universal suffrage, and a multiparty system. In 1989 and 1990 there were violent clashes over land and housing, and hundreds died.⁴² Large numbers of Russians, Germans, Uzbeks, Azeris, Tatars, and Tajiks left the republic, and the loss of skilled labor will certainly handicap the industries, health centers, and the overall economy of Kirghizia.

THE POST-SOVIET PERIOD, 1991–1994

The dual thrust of Mikhail Gorbachev's reform movement—economic reorganization with limited market incentives along with freedoms of expression and the encouragement of popular examination of past historical errors—led to an outpouring of criticism that bedeviled and then overwhelmed the center. What cannot be underestimated in this process is that Soviet policies had inadvertently strengthened national consciousness at the same time that they had aggravated and frustrated the aspirations of the nationalities and offended their sense of justice. Gorbachev raised national aspirations by speaking of redressing the grievances of many nationalities—the Crimean Tatars, Meshetian Turks, Karachai, Ingush, and Koreans, among others—but he never acted boldly on these matters. His equivocations on Nagorno-Karabakh, for example, quickly made him a deeply unpopular figure among Armenians and Azeris alike. Gorbachev's attempts to hold onto the Baltic republics similarly alienated the majority of people in that region. Each concession by Gorbachev was often seen in the republics as a self-serving half-measure, too little too late, and it was followed by new and greater demands. Gorbachev's show of force in Georgia in April of 1989, in Baku in January of 1990, and in the Baltics in January of 1991 further tied his hands. Neither cajolery nor concessions nor force could halt the momentum for change.

Gorbachev's last hope for preserving the Soviet Union as a reformed semblance of itself was the Union Treaty, which offered a broad range of autonomy to the republics. It had the support of the Slavic republics, Azerbaijan, and the Central Asian republics, which together incorporated the overwhelming majority of the Soviet land mass and population. But the matter of the future form of the Soviet Union was rendered moot by Gorbachev's arrest in the abortive August 1991 coup, on the eve of the signing of the treaty. The failed coup was followed by several months of political free fall that culminated in December with the Alma Ata accords, in which the Soviet Union was signed out of existence and replaced by the Commonwealth of Independent States (CIS).

In 1918 the major Soviet nationalities took advantage of the disorder of war, the revolution, and the weakness of a center spread out on numerous military, political, and economic fronts to break away from imperial control. Seventy years later, the center's decline and weakness presented a similar opportunity, and the national minorities again seized it. This time they shared seventy years of a common Soviet experience and brought with them a host of problems both old and new. The year 1991 was a watershed, representing both an end and a clouded new beginning.

THE TRANSCAUCASUS

The entire region has been engulfed by armed conflict since the early 1990s. Several of these conflicts continue to rage, but even where a semblance of order has been restored, as in South Ossetia, the underlying issues remain intact. They may flare on their own or be stirred out of dormancy by more powerful interests when there is something to gain from regional instability.

In Georgia, opponents of President Gamsakhurdia succeeded in driving him from office in early 1992. He was replaced by Eduard Shevardnadze,

Gorbachev's former foreign minister and a previous head of the Georgian Soviet Socialist Republic. At first Shevardnadze took a strong nationalist position, refusing to join the Commonwealth of Independent States. He was soon faced with two armed rebellions, one in Abkhazia and a second by forces loyal to Gamsakhurdia. In 1993 Abkhazian forces took half of Abkhazia including the Black Sea port and capital of Sukhumi. Meanwhile, Gamsakhurdia's forces won an impressive string of victories in western Georgia. Shevardnadze accused the Russians of supporting the rebel forces and threatening the collapse of the Georgian state. He appealed to the UN Security Council for intervention but to no avail. Desperate, Shevardnadze reversed himself in October 1993 and agreed to join the CIS and appealed for Russian help. With Russian assistance, Gamsakhurdia's forces were defeated and the Abkhazians were rolled back. The price was a weakened Shevardnadze and a disciplined Georgia, now made aware of its dependence on Russian power for survival.

As in 1918, Armenia was the prisoner of its geography, landlocked and bordered by stronger states either hostile or lukewarm toward the Armenian Republic. In this context the Ter Petrosian government has been an ardent supporter of Russia. For several years Armenia was the only state in the region to belong to the CIS and through the Russian alliance managed to survive under harrowing conditions.[43] Russia provided Armenia with military protection from Azerbaijan's ally Turkey, and Russia underwrote the devastated Armenian economy. Armenia attempted to distance itself from the conflict over Nagorno-Karabakh by renouncing a territorial claim and portraying the struggle as one between Azerbaijan and Nagorno-Karabakh. The latter held a referendum and voted overwhelmingly in favor of independence in December 1992. Unofficially, Armenia supplied volunteers and equipment to the Karabakh fighters, and for this the Azeris continued to subject Armenia to a withering economic blockade through the winter of 1994–95. Armenia has continued to be subjected to Azeri cross-border raids as well as shelling of its border areas.

Azerbaijan's politics continued to be dominated by the Nagorno-Karabakh issue. In June of 1992 Azeri elections brought to power the Azeri Popular Front under Abulfaz Elchibey. He renounced the pro-Russian policies of his Communist predecessors in favor of a pro-Turkish policy. This course of action proved disastrous to Azerbaijan because after an initial period of Russian support for Azerbaijan against the leadership of Nagorno-Karabakh and Armenia, Elchibey's policies tilted the Russians against Azerbaijan. Meanwhile, Turkey proved a major disappointment for, as the Azeris painfully learned, Turkey lacked the economic wherewithal to aid Azerbaijan substantially and the military wherewithal to stand up to Russia.

Azerbaijan needed more from Turkey than hearty expressions of Turkish-Azeri solidarity, joint Turkish-Pakistani UN resolutions condemning Armenia, and blustery, scarcely veiled threats directed at the Armenian government.

In the face of a weakened economy and military reversals, Elchibey was forced out of office by a mutiny of military forces a year after he had assumed office. Meanwhile, the Karabakh Armenians took advantage of the disarray in Baku to take control of nearly all of Karabakh from Azeri forces and to launch a series of attacks in western Azerbaijan that created as many as a million Azeri refugees and put a fifth of Azerbaijan's land under Karabakh Armenian control.

Elchibey was replaced by seventy-year-old Gaidar Aliyev, a Brezhnev protégé, former head of the Azeri KGB, and former Soviet Politburo member. In his new persona, he presented himself as an Azeri nationalist committed to a free-market economy. Aliyev took a number of initiatives designed to strengthen Azerbaijan's desperate situation. These included the hiring of Afghan mercenaries to fight for Karabakh.[44] But Aliyev's most important initiative was to repudiate Elchibey's pro-Turkish policy and to turn to Russia for support. Like Shevardnadze in Georgia, he brought Azerbaijan into the CIS and was rewarded with Russian aid accompanied by officers to train Azeri soldiers and advanced weapons. These allowed Azerbaijan to launch offensives against Karabakh Armenian forces by the end of 1993 and to reclaim some Azeri territories lost earlier to Karabakh Armenians.

The resolution of the Karabakh crisis is not yet at hand. What is clear, however, is that in the wake of failures by Iran, Turkey, the United States, the United Nations, and the Organization for Security and Cooperation in Europe (OSCE) to negotiate settlements, Russia emerged by the end of 1993 as the dominant force in the region. Although they have quite opposite objectives, the big losers here are Turkey and, perhaps, the Karabakh Armenians.[45]

THE BALTICS

The three Baltic nations remain heavily dependent upon Russia for industrial inputs, markets, and energy, which they must now pay for at world-market prices. The Estonians have been the most successful in redirecting trade to the West, with 35 percent of their trade in 1992 directed to Finland and Sweden. Lithuania has been much less successful, with 90 percent of its trade remaining within the former Soviet Union. Inflation and growing unemployment and shortages have plagued all three nations. In Lithuania, people's discontent over these problems has been so severe that Sajudis was voted out of office in the fall of 1992 and replaced by the Communist Party, which promised better relations with Moscow, better terms from the International Monetary Fund, and a reversal of the economic decline that was one of the most severe in the former Soviet Union for 1992.

Tensions with Russia have been high, especially in Estonia and Latvia where citizenship legislation prejudicial to Russian residents has been enacted.[46] While the Baltic peoples view most Russian residents as colonial settlers, the Russians see the situation very differently, prompting Russian President Boris Yeltsin to describe Estonian citizenship legislation as tantamount to apartheid!

Another important regional issue was the garrisoning of two hundred thousand Russian troops in the Baltic states and the insistence of the new governments that they be repatriated. The troops were removed from Lithuania by September 1993 and from the other two states over the course of the following year.

Relations with Russia continue to be tense, with the Baltic states subject to verbal threats and economic sanctions (for example, cutoffs in fuel supplies), but overall the region has suffered less than others in terms of economic hardship, and it has been free of the explosive violence that has rocked the Transcaucasus and parts of Central Asia.

CENTRAL ASIA

The Central Asian nations face problems of Islamic fundamentalism, and ethnic tensions. Uzbekistan, Turkmenistan, and Tajikistan are more conservative, repressive, and open to fundamentalism than Kazakhstan and Kyrgyzstan (formerly Kirghizia), which tend to be more pro-Russian, pro-Western, and open to reform.

In Kazakhstan, former Communist leader Nazarbayev has proven to be an adept politician in a nation with a significant potential for native Kazakh and Russian settler conflict. The country suffers from inflation, declines in output, and unemployment. Nazarbayev has made good on his commitment to follow the Korean model for development by offering major concessions to foreign investors in the form of duty-free imports, accelerated depreciation, and a 100 percent income-tax exemption for five years and an additional 50 percent exemption after five years for certain lines of production. Over fifty firms from Germany, the United States, China, Turkey, and Italy have so far set up shop in the country. There has been labor unrest among miners, who went on strike in 1992 over economic issues. The republic also faces the unhappy prospect of dealing with an estimated 8 million tons of high-level radioactive waste and 225 million tons of lower-level waste left over from Soviet weapons testing in the republic. Kazakhstan has been of particular interest to the United States because it is one of the spin-off nations with a nuclear arsenal—fourteen hundred warheads. In December 1993 the government agreed to dismantle these weapons in return for favorable treatment of its applications for Western aid and an $84 million U.S. disarmament subsidy to defray costs.[47]

Uzbekistan is closely tied politically and militarily to Russia (80 percent of its officer corps, for example, is Russian). The old Communist Party rules under the name of the National Democratic Party, and Birlik, the major opposition group, was not allowed to contest the 1991 national elections. The opposition remains centered on the intelligentsia and without a mass base, a factor partly related to the government's refusal to allow the opposition to hold rallies and occupy office space. The country has benefited, as has Turkmenistan, from the sale of energy at world prices, and the government's commitment to reform is limited to increasing mineral output and seeking to sell cotton at world prices.

Turkmenistan was the slowest of the former Soviet republics to embrace reform. The republic suffers from lower levels of inflation, unemployment, and other measures of economic distress than others in the region. Reform movements here, as in Uzbekistan, face numerous official obstacles.

Kyrgyzstan struggles to maintain a semblance of democratic political practice but does so in a depressed economy, without oil or natural gas resources, and with little Russian aid. High inflation and growing unemployment, along with high expenditures for energy and grain imports, are a few of the issues facing the republic's leadership.

Tajikistan, the most southeasterly of the Central Asian states, has an eleven-hundred-mile border with Afghanistan and China. The country has been the scene of the most violent war in any region of the former Soviet Union with estimates of as many as forty thousand deaths and over five hundred thousand refugees, close to one-fifth of them having crossed the border into Afghanistan.[48] President Ali Rakhmanov represents the old ruling Communist elite, now backed by reformist Russia. His government is opposed by a coalition of Islamic and liberal reformist forces whose character, agendas, and strengths relative to one another remain matters of debate.

A month after the fall of the Soviet/Russian-backed government at Afghanistan in April 1992, Tajik President Rakhmon Nabiyev, a former first secretary of the Tajik Soviet Socialist Republic, faced large-scale demonstrations calling for his resignation. He survived until the following September, when the opposition forced him from office. Before the end of the year, Rakhmanov assumed power. His government is heavily dependent on

Russia for political and military backing as well as for economic aid. He has been charged with media censorship and ethnically based persecutions, including summary executions of opponents.

Russia, Uzbekistan, and the other Central Asian states have provided troops to patrol the Tajik-Afghan border and to try to interdict troops, narcotics, and Islamic fundamentalist ideas emanating from the South. But their real fear is the challenge to the status quo posed by the Islamic/reformist coalition in Tajikistan proper, which is seen as an unwanted source of challenge and change for the region.

A NEW RUSSIAN EMPIRE?

The imperial impulse runs deep among Russians and predates the Soviet Union. We note that it also postdates the Soviet Union. In the West, the media, many scholars and politicians, and entrepreneurial types were quick to herald the demise of the Soviet Union as the triumph of capitalism and the true end of history. Such naive thoughts were bound to be disappointed, and indeed they have been for the following reasons:

1   Though no longer a superpower, Russia is not only the preeminent regional power but also a major world power. It commands a large geographical area and a large population. It is also heavily industrialized and possesses advanced weaponry and manufacturing capabilities. The opportunity for the minority republics to proclaim independence and for some of them to pursue truly independent policies by establishing ties with Turkey or vowing to stay out of the CIS parallels circumstances in the first years of the Bolshevik Revolution. The confusion and disarray of the revolutionary process after World War I allowed for initiatives by minority peoples that could not be sustained after an initial period of civil war and foreign invasion, when the Soviet Union emerged to flex its muscle. By 1994, the Russian Federation had similarly begun to assert its interests in the minority republics.

2   Not everyone in Russia was pleased with the 1991 collapse of the Soviet Union or with what was perceived as a series of Russian humiliations. The latter include the dependence of Russia on Western aid; the dictating of economic terms by the International Monetary Fund (IMF); discriminatory legislation and prejudicial practices against Russians living in newly independent minority republics; and the inroads of Turkey, Iran, and Afghanistan along the southern tier of what used to be the Soviet Union. Certainly many in the military feel this way, and there are also large numbers of civilians who are suspicious of the United States and the West. The idea of

a revitalized Russia reasserting its imperial prerogatives is attractive to many in such circles.

3 The first consequences of economic reform expressed as inflation, declining purchasing power, and layoffs have been attributed to the difficulties inherent in the transition to a market economy, but we ought to consider whether they are not more correctly seen as endemic to capitalism. In its campaign against the republic's referendum on independence, the Estonian Communist Party argued that a positive vote was a vote for the restoration of the bourgeois state and a vote for the private ownership of the means of production and all that it implied (unemployment; economic inequities; the sale of education, medical care, and housing; and so forth). The use of purely economic (as opposed to social) criteria in setting public policy has already led to the enrichment of some and the misery of many through the deterioration of employment, housing, education, health care, pension, and women's rights previously guaranteed by the Communist system. This economic crisis played out in the lives of millions of people makes those people open to nationalistic appeals as a way to salvation. Harking back to an earlier European catastrophe with similar roots, the term "Weimar Russia" aptly refers to the ominous implications of economic crisis in the context of fallen empires.

4 Political leaders in Western nations were far from unanimous about investment and aid to the Russian Federation. The United States, in particular, was severely limited by an enormous national debt largely acquired as a result of the anti-Soviet arms race. The same set of political and economic circumstances that allowed for a massive aid program to western Europe after the Second World War was simply not there for Russia. This factor has exacerbated the others by contributing to economic hardship and Russian humiliation.

During 1993 we saw the beginnings of the strategic and political coalescence of these four factors in ways that carry important implications for the former Soviet minority republics. Russia moved in the Baltics to defend the rights of Russians there by controlling the access of these states to energy, markets, raw materials, and component parts. In the Transcaucasus, Russia emerged as the primary arbiter of disputes, superseding the United States, Turkey, Iran, and the international bodies, the UN and the CSCE. Russia was also able to establish and strengthen its position in Georgia and Azerbaijan by selectively deploying military and economic resources to undermine political stability. In Azerbaijan, this took the form of promoting draft resistance and calls for secession by two Azeri minorities, the Lezghis and Talishes, as a way of weakening the Elchibey government and opening the way to a takeover by the more pro-Russian Aliyev. In Georgia, the government was not overthrown but rendered weak and desperate to the point that Shevardnadze had no choice but to throw his lot in with the Russians. Both countries joined the CIS, which is increasingly shaping up as an alliance of unequal partners for the promotion of Russian national security and economic agendas.

The primary advocate of economic reforms and a Russian-Euro-Atlantic alliance has been Russian president Boris Yeltsin. In October 1993 he responded to parliamentary opposition by shutting down the national legislature and militarily attacking and arresting his opposition (with only mild, perfunctory hand-wringing in the West). Yeltsin then called for parliamentary elections in December with results that were not so favorable to his agenda. The largest number of seats, though far from a majority, went to the supporters of the ultranationalist Vladimir Zhirinovsky. Yeltsin's supporters came in second, and other top vote getters were the Communist Party, a party representing collective and state farms trying to protect government subsidies, and a women's party advocating preservation of social welfare programs. The success of these anti-reform groups of the right and the left indicate the depth of people's unhappiness with Yeltsin's economic reforms and the distress they have caused in the lives of millions.

Many have labeled Zhirinovsky a fascist, and his stated program does, in fact, contain most of the essential features of fascism—that is, racism, militarism, and territorial expansionism. Zhirinovsky sees the Russians as the chosen people and the minorities as inferior peoples. He has called for the "ethnic cleansing" of Russia and the restoration of Russia's World War I boundaries (the Baltic states, Finland, Poland, and so forth).

Zhirinovsky's recent electoral success poses a deep threat to the former Soviet minority republics. The Baltic states immediately pressed for membership in the NATO alliance but were denied in favor of a weaker U.S.-sponsored partnership linkage. But even if Zhirinovsky never makes it to the Russian presidency, his substantial base of popular support and the military debts incurred by Yeltsin during the parliamentary clashes represent assertive nationalist forces that Yeltsin is compelled to consider.

The reassertion of Russian power has already curtailed the options open to the former minority republics, especially in matters of foreign policy. The question is what kind of empire will the new Russian empire be? If Zhirinovsky comes to power, the answer is a traditional empire. If Yeltsin or someone akin to him retains power, the answer is likely to be a neocolonial one in which there is formal independence and considerable autonomy on local matters along with Russian domination of foreign policy and the grand economic program.[49] The threat this poses to states that value their independence is real and substantial, though the eventual outcome in a fluid and shifting matrix of forces remains ambiguous.

NOTES

1. For a Soviet assessment of Soviet nationalities policy, see E. Bagramov, *The CPSU's Nationalities Policy* (Moscow: Progress Publishers, 1988).

2. Louise Nalbandian, *The Armenian Revolutionary Movement: The Development of Armenian Political Parties through the Nineteenth Century* (Berkeley: University of California Press, 1963); David Marshall Lang, *A Modern History of Soviet Georgia* (New York: Grove Press, 1962).

3. Ronald Suny, "The Revenge of the Past: Socialism and Ethnic Conflict in Transcaucasia," *New Left Review*, no. 184 (October–November 1990): 16–18.

4. Ibid., p. 18.

5. Zev Katz, Rosemarie Rogers, and Frederic Harned, eds., *Handbook of Major Soviet Nationalities* (New York: Free Press, 1975), pp. 145–46.

6. Ibid., pp. 98–99.

7. Ibid., pp. 122–23.

8. Michael Rywkin, *Moscow's Muslim Challenge* (Armonk, N.Y.: M. E. Sharpe, 1990), pp. 14–15.

9. Geoffrey Wheeler, *The Modern History of Soviet Central Asia* (New York: Praeger, 1964), p. 189; Geoffrey Jukes, *The Soviet Union in Asia* (Berkeley: University of California Press, 1973), p. 43.

10. Erwin Marquit, *The Socialist Countries*, 2d ed. (Minneapolis: M.E.P. Publications, 1983), p. 130.

11. Albert Szymanski, *Human Rights in the Soviet Union* (London: Zed Books, 1984), pp. 49–50, 74.

12. Ibid., p. 136.

13. Vic George and Nick Manning, *Socialism, Social Welfare and the Soviet Union* (London: Routledge and Kegan Paul, 1980), p. 154. Private-sector housing systems such as that found in the United States build better-quality homes for middle- and upper-class buyers and renters than the average dwelling provided by the former Soviet system. However, the capitalist system in the United States is market directed and excludes those who cannot participate in the market. The result is homelessness. What one thinks of Soviet housing and housing policy, therefore, is often class based. Affluent persons in the United States might well find the Soviet system anathema, whereas the millions of urban, suburban, and rural slum dwellers and the homeless in the United States might indeed find the Soviet model appealing.

14. Rywkin, *Moscow's Muslim Challenge*, chapter 4.

15. Marquit, *The Socialist Countries*, pp. 109–38.

16. Szymanski, *Human Rights in the Soviet Union*, pp. 137–40. The argument is sometimes made that the cost of benefits received by Soviet citizens contributed to bankrupting the system. A far better case can be made for Soviet military spending. From the early 1970s on the Soviets tried to match the United States in military expenditures on a GNP base one-third the size of that of the United States. This and not social spending proved catastrophic in the end.

17. Ibid., pp. 46–47, 118.

18. V. N. Tolkunova et al., *Soviet Legislation on Women's Rights* (Moscow: Progress Publishers, 1978), pp. 75–132; Marquit, *The Socialist Countries*, pp. 158–80.

19. Liudmila Rzhanitsina, *Female Labor under Socialism* (Moscow: Progress Publish-

ers, 1983), p. 49; Tolkunova, *Soviet Legislation on Women's Rights*, pp. 31–46; Szymanski, *Human Rights in the Soviet Union*, pp. 103–12.

20. Szymanski, *Human Rights in the Soviet Union*, pp. 52–53.

21. Wheeler, *The Modern History of Soviet Central Asia*, p. 189. Also see Jukes, *The Soviet Union in Asia*, p. 43.

22. Alexander J. Motyl, *Sovietology, Rationality, Nationality: Coming to Grips with Nationalism in the USSR* (New York: Columbia University Press, 1990), chapter 10.

23. Levon Chorbajian, Patrick Donabedian, and Claude Mutafian, *The Caucasian Knot: The History and Geopolitics of Nagorno-Karabakh* (London: Zed Books, 1994), pp. 51–54.

24. Ibid., pp. 58–64. The Armenians present their struggle as one for self-determination and argue that the three criteria employed in deciding the merit of such cases—history, present-day demography, and the will of the people—all favor the Armenians. The Azeris make their own arguments in support of their claim to Nagorno-Karabakh. These counterarguments, so diametrically opposed to the Armenian ones, clarify why the struggle for the territory has been so bitter, intractable, and, so far, immune to settlement.

Of particular importance in the debate over territorial claims are the Caucasian Albanians, an ancient and no longer extant people who predate the time of Christ. These Caucasian Albanians—unrelated to the better-known Adriatic Albanians—ruled over much of central and eastern Transcaucasia, including what is now Nagorno-Karabakh. They were converted to Christianity by the Armenians in the fourth century and later conquered by the Arabs, Islamicized, and eventually assimilated. Armenian historians acknowledge that the Caucasian Albanians in the eastern Transcaucasian lowlands were Islamicized and later Turkified, but they argue that those in the western Albanian regions, including what later became Nagorno-Karabakh, were largely absorbed by the Armenians and to a lesser degree by the Georgians. Azeri historians, in stark contrast, view Caucasian Albania, in toto, as the precursor of modern Azerbaijan, and on this basis, they lay claim to all erstwhile Caucasian Albanian territories including Nagorno-Karabakh. See Tamara Dragadze, ''Azerbaijanis,'' in Graham Smith, ed., *The Nationalities Question in the Soviet Union* (London and New York: Longman, 1990), p. 164, and Audrey Altstadt, *The Azerbaijani Turks* (Stanford: Stanford University Press, 1992), pp. xi, 2–6.

The Azeris also discount the importance of the Armenian majority in Nagorno-Karabakh by claiming that it dates only from the Armenian migration from Persia under the Treaty of Turkmenchai in 1828. The Azeris also employ formalistic arguments to bypass historical and demographic factors. For example, the claim is made that Nagorno-Karabakh rightfully belongs to Azerbaijan because it was part of the czarist Elizavetpol *guberniia* that was consolidated with the Baku *guberniia* to form Azerbaijan. It is further argued that the Armenians and Azeris agreed to what was essentially a pact in which the contested territory of Zangezur went to Armenia while Nagorno-Karabakh was ceded to Azerbaijan. The Armenians are seen as opportunistically seeking to break this implicit agreement without making any concessions to Azerbaijan. See Altstadt, *The Azerbaijani Turks*, pp. 100, 196.

The Azeris also reject the argument of Karabakh Armenians that the territory was economically exploited by Soviet Azerbaijan. The Azeris argue that pollution and shortages of material goods, including housing, were worse in other areas of Azerbaijan than in Nagorno-Karabakh. The territory is also said to have received a larger share of the republic's budget and greater subsidies than the larger and more populous Nakhichevan Autonomous Soviet Republic, Altstadt, *The Azerbaijani Turks*, pp. 127, 199.

25. Elizabeth Fuller, ''The Azeris in Georgia and the Ingilos: Ethnic Minorities in the Limelight,'' *Central Asian Survey* 3, no. 2 (1984): 75–85.

26. Yaroslav Bilinsky and Tonu Parming, *Helsinki Watch Committees in the Soviet Union: Implications for the Soviet Nationality Question* (Final Report for the National Council for Soviet and Eastern European Research, 1980), sec. 5, pp. 48–64; Ludmilla Alexeyeva, *Soviet Dissent: Contemporary Movements for National, Religious, and Human Rights* (Middletown, Conn.: Wesleyan University Press, 1985), pp. 106–17.

27. Suny, "The Revenge of the Past," 30–31.

28. Alexeyeva, *Soviet Dissent*, p. 124.

29. Ibid., pp. 123–25, 127.

30. Suny, "The Revenge of the Past," 27–31; Sanval Shahmouradian, ed., *The Sumgait Tragedy: Eyewitness Accounts* (New Rochelle, N.Y.: Caratzas Publishing Company, 1990); Pierre Verluise, *Arménie: La fracture* (Paris: Editions Stock, 1989), pp. 124–29.

31. In December 1988, Armenia was devastated by an earthquake that claimed tens of thousands of victims and caused heavy destruction in the republic's second- and third-largest cities and neighboring regions. Earthquake reconstruction has been severely hampered by recurring Azerbaijani rail blockades, which have prevented fuel, raw materials, foodstuffs, and construction materials from reaching Armenia. The inability of the party leaders to influence Moscow to put an end to Azerbaijani hostilities against Armenia and Armenians in Nagorno-Karabakh further contributed to the erosion of legitimacy of the local party leadership.

32. "Report of an International Delegation from the First International Andrei Sakharov Memorial Congress to Armenia and Azerbaijan" (May 25–31, 1991), passim; Caroline Cox, "Is Armenia Suffering Another Genocide," *Wall Street Journal Europe*, June 12, 1991. For more recent clashes in Nagorno-Karabakh, see Daniel Sneider, "Karabagh Clashes Reach Armenian Border," *Christian Science Monitor*, March 13, 1992; Caroline Cox, "Fighting in the Caucasus," *Washington Post*, January 31, 1992; and Caroline Cox and John Eibner, *Ethnic Cleansing in Progress: War in Nagorno Karabagh* (Zurich, London, Washington: Christian Solidarity International, 1993)

33. Bilinsky and Parming, *Helsinki Watch Committees in the Soviet Union*, pp. 5–41, a-82, a-109.

34. Ibid., pp. 72–75.

35. Bill Keller, "Thousands March in Baltic Capitals, Airing Resentment," *New York Times*, August 24, 1988, A1, A6.

36. V. Stanley Verdys, "Lithuanian National Politics," *Problems of Communism* 38, no. 4 (July–August 1989), passim.

37. Bill Keller, "Annexation Void, Lithuanians Say," *New York Times*, August 23, 1989, A1.

38. Francis Clines, "Gorbachev Given a Partial Victory in Voting on Unity," *New York Times*, March 19, 1991, A1.

39. Uzbekistan imports 90 percent of its consumer goods while exporting vast quantities of unprocessed raw materials.

40. Charles Carlson, "Turkmenistan: Inching toward Democratization," *Report on the USSR* 3, no. 1 January 4, 1991, 35–36.

41. Craig Whitney, "Riots Involving Ethnic Rivalries Erupt in Another Soviet Republic," *New York Times*, February 13, 1990, A1.

42. Francis Clines, "Death Toll at 148 in Unrest in Soviet Asia," *New York Times*, June 14, 1990, A16.

43. The fall in gross domestic product in Armenia for 1992 is estimated to be 50 percent. This is among the steepest drops for any country emerging from the Soviet Union. According to the IMF, "it is clear that most of the population is experiencing severe hardship." John Odling-Smee, *Economic Review: Armenia* (Washington, D.C.: International Monetary Fund, 1993), pp. 2–3.

44. Aliyev also invited back Megaoil, which had made its Azeri debut in 1991. This Marietta, Georgia (U.S.A.)–based firm, ostensibly an oil company, is staffed almost entirely by former U.S. military personnel. They are reported to be training Azeri servicemen at two sites in Azerbaijan. Megaoil's on-site director is none other than Richard Secord, a 1955 West Point graduate and retired Air Force general. Secord has a long history of espionage activities in Third World covert wars and destabilization programs. In the 1960s, Secord worked with Theodore Shackley, then CIA chief of station in Laos, and helped organize a covert war in

that country. During the Carter administration, he was deputy commander of the disastrous operation to rescue U.S. hostages held in Iran. In the mid-1980s, Secord was the operations head of an international weapons-trade network created under CIA director William Colby and national security operative Col. Oliver North to channel arms to Iran and the Nicaraguan contras, contrary to U.S. law and policy. See Jonathan Kwitney, *The Crimes of Patriots: A True Tale of Dope, Dirty Money, and the CIA* (New York: W. W. Norton, 1987), pp. 15, 43–52, 310–12, 315–16; "U.S. Army Veterans Train Azeris under Cover of Oil Firm," *The Observer*, December 4, 1993, 1; "North's Aides Linked to Australian Study," *New York Times*, March 8, 1987, sec. 1, 30; *Contra-Drug Connection* (Washington, D.C.: Christic Institute, 1987); Col. Moorad Mooradian, "Dirty Money, Willing Guns," *AIM* (Armenian International Magazine), January 1994, p. 30; Martha Honey, *Hostile Acts: U.S. Policy in Costa Rica in the 1980s* (Gainesville: University Press of Florida, 1994).

45. The UN and the OSCE both recognize the right to self-determination, but they undermine this principle by giving equal weight to the territorial integrity of existing states. Aside from interests based in alliances, it is worth noting that parties interested in the struggle for Nagorno-Karabakh—that is, the United States, Britain, Turkey, Iran, and Russia—all face threats of greater or lesser intensity from national minorities of their own who seek autonomy or even independence—the United States from Native Americans, African Americans, and Puerto Ricans; Britain from movements in Northern Ireland, Scotland, and Wales; Turkey and Iran from the Kurds; and Russia from a large number of groups who have only begun to mobilize around a broad range of issues including language rights, taxation, investment policy, environmental integrity, conscription, and the control of timber, energy, mineral, and water resources. An insistence on territorial integrity—that is, that Azerbaijan should keep Nagorno-Karabakh—therefore contributes to the ideological repertoire of the United States, Britain, and the regional powers for the discipline of minorities on their own turf. The failure of the Karabakh Armenians to secure recognition for their independence despite broad military successes over Azeri forces in 1993 places them in a more difficult position now that Azerbaijan has moved away from Turkey and closer to Russia while the latter has assumed the role of the key mediating power in the conflict.

46. The Estonian citizenship law required non-Estonian residents to apply for citizenship and learn Estonian or leave the country within two years. The Latvian law offered citizenship only to those Russians who had been residents prior to 1940. Jon Auerbach, "Moscow Is Pressured to Defend Rights of Russians in Baltic States," *Boston Globe*, July 5, 1993, 5.

47. "Kazakhstan Agrees to Dismantle Warheads," *Boston Globe*, December 14, 1993, 8.

48. Steve Erlanger, "Tajik Ex-Communists Prosecute Opposition," *New York Times*, January 10, 1993, 15.

49. Commentators in the West have touted freedom, democracy, and the free market, none of them ever very clearly defined, as the West's greatest contributions to post-Soviet Russia. In fact, freedom and democracy are little in evidence in Russia, and the free market operates in a deformed and unregulated fashion that has brought great hardship to millions of people. In the end the West's greatest contribution to Russia may be something entirely different, namely, neocolonialism along the lines of the United States's historic relationship to the Caribbean and Central America. The understanding that one can have an empire without the burdensome costs of direct ownership and administration is attractive to Russian leaders in a context of limited economic resources, assertive minority nationalism, and an international climate sympathetic to the formal independence of large former Soviet minority groups.

National Minorities and Nationalities Policy in China

At the center of China's modernization drive as it concerns national minorities are four core issues: social equality, economic development, cultural autonomy, and national integration. My aim in this chapter is to discuss some of the main implications of modernization for China's national minorities. The chapter begins by outlining the background to China's national minority situation, including a description of its minority groups, its historical experience with minority policies, and government provisions for varying degrees of autonomy in minority regions. Because of the great diversity that characterizes China's national minorities, I will emphasize China's western provinces, particularly Xinjiang and Tibet, where important changes are taking place.

NATIONAL MINORITIES: AN OVERVIEW

As the Chinese government defines national minorities (*shaoshu minzu*), they account for 90 million people.[1] Their population is increasing faster than that of the majority Han, partly due to a relaxed birth policy in the sparsely populated minority areas. China claims fifty-five national minorities, the largest group having more than fifteen million members and the smallest only about two thousand.[2] The reason these ninety million people, who account for only about 8 percent of China's population, occupy so critical a place is threefold. First, they inhabit over 60 percent of China's total land area. Second, over 90 percent of the interior border region of China is occupied by national minorities. And finally, the areas they occupy contain the majority of China's forest reserves, large quantities of mineral deposits, and most of the animals that supply milk, meat, and wool.[3]

Analyzing China's national minorities as a single entity is virtually impossible. Great cultural, regional, and developmental differences exist between them. Thus, the national minority policies espoused by the government are intended to be implemented flexibly so as to take account of the unique situation of each group. China's national minorities, referred to as "little brothers" (*xiongdi*) by the Han majority, can be differentiated according to a number of criteria.[4] These include population, group identification, regional variations, intergroup relations and migration, religious tradition, language, and cross-border nationalities.

POPULATION

The largest of the minority groups is the Zhuang nationality with over fifteen million members in the provinces of Yunan, Guizhou, Guangxi, Hunan, and Guangdong. The smallest of the minority groups is the Lhoba with about twenty-three hundred members in southwestern Tibet. The Hui, Mongolians, Tibetans, Uygurs, and Zhuang reside in provinces that have become designated as their respective autonomous regions. The minorities with comparable populations are the Manchu, Miao, Yi, and Tujia. Eighteen national minorities have over one million members, twenty-two have under a hundred thousand members, and seven have fewer than ten thousand members. The median group has about two hundred thousand members.[5]

GROUP IDENTIFICATION

Sun Yat-sen, who founded the Republic of China, saw China as having five nationalities.[6] In the 1930s the Guomindang government denied that ethnic minorities even existed in China, claiming that all groups were branches of the Han.[7] But soon after the founding of the People's Republic of China, some four hundred groups answered the call to register as national minorities. Not all claims to minority group status were recognized. Some groups were judged to be branches of the same minority nationality despite variations in dialects spoken or aspects of dress and custom. Other groups were too similar to the Han Chinese to merit separate status.[8] Although the official number of national minorities has been fifty-five since 1953, there are still over seven hundred thousand persons who have yet to be classified. Thus, the identification of national minorities has been a complicated problem. Nevertheless, Chinese scholars have long relied on Stalin's definition to identify national minorities: "A nation is a historically formed stable community of people arising on the basis of common language, common territory, common economic life, and a typical cast of mind manifested in a common culture."[9] Still, this definition presents China with many difficulties because some groups lack a common language, territory, economic life, or common culture, and therefore the definition is employed with flexibility.

REGIONAL VARIATIONS

National minorities inhabit virtually all regions of China, including rural, urban, mountain, coastal, and border areas. The proportion of members of a minority group that inhabit an autonomous area varies greatly. Some national minorities, like the Tibetans, account for over 90 percent of the population of Tibet, while others, like the Mongolians, account for less than 20 percent of the population of Inner Mongolia, although many Mongolians reside nearby in Xinjiang, Tibet, and Yunnan. Smaller groups have territorial jurisdiction over counties and prefectures rather than provinces. Others, like the Hui, who have an autonomous province, are scattered throughout most of the country. Finally, two groups may share jurisdiction over an autonomous county or prefecture.

INTERGROUP RELATIONS AND MIGRATION

Although most nationalities view themselves as minorities with respect to the dominant Han, others who live in proximity to a national minority larger than themselves may view these groups as the quasi-majority group. Still others, such as the Miao and Yao, who have lived in close proximity for thousands of years, have forged their own special relations.

Migration has also influenced national minority relations. Increasing numbers of Han have migrated to national minority regions, owing to such factors as the higher pay they receive for working in hardship areas, new opportunities to prosper, crowded conditions in the eastern cities, the stationing of army units, or mandatory job assignments after graduation from institutes of higher education.[10] Some of this migration has caused anxiety among groups. Whereas the Han composed 6.2 percent of the population of Xinjiang province in 1953, they numbered close to 40 percent by 1973.[11] Such trends are occurring in many minority regions, although harsh weather conditions in Tibet have prevented many Han from migrating there.

RELIGIOUS TRADITION

The main religions of China's minorities are Islam, Buddhism, and Lamaism, but others also have a following. Most of China's minorities have a strong religious tradition. For some, like the Muslim Hui, religion is the main attribute of their identity as a national minority. Members of the Hui, Uygur, Kazakh, Kirghiz, Tatar, Uzbek, Tajik, Dongxiang, Salar, and Bonan groups are adherents of the Islamic faith. The Tibetans, Mongolians, Yugurs, and Tus are adherents of Lamaism. The Dais, Bulangs, and Benglongs are adherents of Hinayana Buddhism. Shamanism is practiced by the Oroqens, Daurs, and Ewenkis. The Drungs, Nus, Vas, Jingpos, and Gaoshans practice polytheism as well as totemism and ancestral worship. A small number of adherents of Christianity can be found among the Koreans, Miao, Yao, and Yi.[12]

LANGUAGE

With the exception of the Huis and Manchus, who use the Han language, all of China's minorities have their own language and some have more than one. Most of the languages belong to the Sino-Tibetan and Altaic families, while some belong to the South Asian, Austronesian, and Indo-European families.

Before 1949, only twenty minorities had their own written language. Those in most common use were Mongolian, Tibetan, Uygur, Kazakh, Korean, Xibe, Dai, Uzbek, Kirghiz, Tatar, and Russian. Others included Yi, Miao, Jingpo, Lisu, Lahu, and Va.

The government helped to devise a written script for nine national minorities formerly without one.[13] Still, many minorities remain without a written script. While most of the Manchu are proficient in Chinese and have long since abandoned their written script and spoken language, other groups such as the Jingpo speak a variety of different languages, some of which are totally unlike each other. Other groups are trilingual, speaking their native tongue, the language of the nationality in closest proximity, and Han Chinese.

CROSS-BORDER NATIONALITIES

Mongolians, Koreans, and Russians, as well as the Kazakhs, Tajiks, and Kirghiz are the principal nationalities in the countries adjoining China. Other Chinese minorities belong to groups that are also minorities in the nations adjoining China. These include the Tatar, Mongolian, Uygur, Daur, Oroqen, and Hezhen populations. And the Miao, Hami, Dai, Jing, Jingpo, Lahu, Lisu, Va, Yao, Yi, and Zhuang live in Vietnam, Laos, Thailand, and Burma. Finally, some groups have had a tradition of relations with ethnic cousins of another region of the world. A good example are the Uygurs, who have strong ties with other Turkic groups in the adjoining states of Kirghizia and Kazakhstan as well as in Turkey and other areas of the Middle East.

HISTORICAL BACKGROUND

History shows that the Han majority resulted from an intermixing and fusion of many different peoples.[14] Chinese tradition recognizes that the yellow emperor of the twenty-seventh century B.C., chief of the league of tribes that ruled northwest China, brought the ethnic groups of the Yellow River Valley under unified control. This led to the gradual formation of the Xia people, the ancestors of the present-day Han.[15] Three thousand years of Chinese history have left evidence of at least eight thousand separate groups.[16]

Relations between the national minorities and the Han majority have gone through many stages. During much of China's history, the Han held other groups in contempt, and the distance of non-Han groups from the center often determined their levels of subjugation. These groups were simply referred to as Di, Yi, Rong, and Man, denoting the directions (north, south, east, and west) from which they came.[17] All groups were permitted to pay homage to the emperor, held a lower place within Chinese society, and were protected by the Han militia. In earliest times, the Chinese territory was a small area in the north plain of what is present-day China. The rest of the present-day area was ruled by other ethnic groups, many of whom were culturally and technologically equal to the Han and whose members held high positions in the Chinese state.[18] The Chinese state originated with the Qin dynasty (221–207 B.C.), which both unified the Han Chinese states and absorbed non-Han states. Non-Han groups were either assimilated into the empire or moved out of the area.

There have been wars throughout history between national minorities and the Han, in which an intricate web of relations evolved over time. Throughout history, there have been times when some of China's minorities were partially or fully assimilated.[19] Two of the present national minorities, the Mongols and the Manchu, ruled China for hundreds of years. Confucianism, the doctrine that ruled China for centuries, promoted the nonviolent assimilation of other groups.

The Qing, China's final dynasty (1644–1911), on the other hand, employed a full range of methods to control non-Han ethnic groups. Force was used both against the Yi rebellion in the seventeenth century and the two Muslim rebellions of the nineteenth century. Other forms of control included the tribute system; a court of colonial affairs that dealt with the large and powerful groups to the north and west; the native official system that dealt with smaller and more primitive groups to the south and southwest; Han migration to minority areas; and the incorporation of minority areas into the state administrative system.

In the early part of the twentieth century, minority territories often changed hands, and ethnic relations were very unstable. During the Republican era, decision-making processes were diffused among warlords, several foreign powers, and numerous factions of the Nationalist Party. Moreover, with many ethnic groups also involved, the situation became enormously complex. The national minorities had many reasons to mistrust the Nationalist government, including arrogant officials and the expropriation of national minority land. Except possibly in the cases of the Zhuang and Bai, the Nationalists' efforts toward rapid assimilation were disastrous, arousing deep resentment in the minorities. Generally, Nationalist assimilation policies were unsuccessful, but with the exception of Outer Mongolia they maintained the territorial claims of the Qing Dynasty.

Prior to liberation, Communist policies toward the minorities included "equality of nationalities, the right of autonomy within a unified state, a united front with nationalities, cooperation with upper class and religious leaders, respect for national minorities' cultural ways, the right to education in one's native language, and the development of a higher standard of living for nationalities."[20] In 1922 the Second Congress of the Chinese Communist Party (CCP) supported Lenin's formulation for the establishment of republics for national minorities.[21] Theoretically, these republics would have the authority to become independent if they chose. In 1935 the Communist Party moved in the direction of regional autonomy instead of federalism, although some of China's national minorities might have preferred the federal system suggested by Lenin.[22] While the CCP used the Soviet nationalities policy as a model, it was tempered by the party's view that the right of secession was incompatible with China's situation.

The early years of Communist government were characterized by moderation and flexibility.[23] Much infrastructure was built and and legislation for achieving equality was provided. Efforts were made to improve the economic position of minorities. Minority cadres were carefully trained. Every effort was made to promote the idea that each nationality had something to learn from and contribute to the others. The Communists, unlike the Nationalists, sought the minorities out.

CONSTITUTION AND REGIONAL AUTONOMY

All recent articles of the Chinese Constitution regarding national minorities are elaborations of the provisions of the Chinese People's Political Consultative Congress of 1949. Article 50 of the Constitution states:

All nationalities within the boundaries of the People's Republic of China are equal. They shall establish unity and mutual aid among themselves, and shall oppose imperialism and their own public enemies, so that the People's Republic of China will become a big fraternal and cooperative family composed of all nationalities. Great nation chauvinism will be opposed. Acts involving discrimination, oppression and the splitting of unity of the various nationalities shall be prohibited.[24]

Since the founding of the People's Republic, China has been a multinational unitary state. It currently has 141 autonomous areas, including 5 autonomous regions, 31 autonomous prefectures, 105 autonomous counties, and 3,000 nationality townships. Together they cover more than 63.7 percent of China's territory.[25] The total population of these regions is 142.5 million, of which 62.5 million are minorities. In fact, in only one-third of the autonomous regions is the dominant national minority group equal to more than one-half of the population. The Law on Regional Autonomy for Minority Nationalities was adopted in May 1984 at the second session of the Sixth National People's Congress.[26] It includes provisions for autonomous organizations and rights for self-governing organizations, help from higher-level organizations, training and assignment of cadres, specialists, and skilled workers among the minority peoples, and the strengthening and development of socialist relations among nationalities. The policy has been called one state/many nationalities or political integration with cultural diversification.

Nationality work is carried out at the national level through various governmental bodies. The Nationalities Committee of the National People's Congress is chiefly responsible for the state's handling of national minority problems. It evaluates regulations concerning autonomy and other issues submitted by the autonomous areas. These regulations are submitted to the National People's Congress or its standing committee for approval before going into effect.[27]

The State Nationalities Affairs Commission (SNAC) is under the State Council, that is, the Central People's Government, the executive organ of state power. The role of the commission is to supervise and inspect the administration of national policy in minority regions. It works to insure the principle of equality among nationalities, to strengthen unity among nationalities, to train national minority cadres, to improve socialist development among the minorities and to manage national minority work in general.

There are also divisions of ministries or commissions concerned with minority affairs. The people's congresses of some provinces and autonomous regions have nationality committees or sections. The governments of provinces, regions, and major cities also have nationalities affairs committees. Minority cadres are trained at one of the thirteen nationalities institutes, which are under the State Nationalities Affairs Commission.[28]

Problems remain regarding autonomy and self-determination. While formal laws allow for a great degree of autonomy, there is no provision for secession as there was in the Soviet Union. The problem is that all autonomy legislation is under the control of the central government. There has already been discontent on the part of national minorities regarding the handling of some matters by the government. For example, one area in Hainan province was classified as a national minority region but had that status revoked and reinstated three times over a period of several years.[29]

The idea of "autonomy within a unified state" is always defined by the principle of "democratic centralism," wherein there is subordination of the individual to the organization, subordination of the minority to the majority, subordination of the lower levels to the upper levels, and subordination of the whole party to the central committee. In theory, this still permits nationalities to enjoy an "equality of status." In reality, their autonomy is severely restricted from the outset. Finally, autonomy is tied to the territory, not the people. Autonomy comes not just by virtue of membership in a national minority but rather through residence within a national minority region. More than ten million members of national minorities live outside of national minority regions, and about five million others have no autonomy at all because of their settlement patterns.

NATIONALITIES POLICY

A variety of general policies toward national minorities have been in effect since 1949. The post-1949 period was distinguished initially by efforts not to alienate ethnic elites. The 1950–57 period was marked by the formulation of national policy directed at unification and consolidation, on one hand, and ethnic solidarity on the other. The formation of nationwide cooperatives strained relations between the Han and the national minorities. This, coupled with the failure of the Great Leap Forward and the split with the Soviet Union, led to a difficult period of national minority relations. After the Great Leap Forward, the government returned to granting more autonomy to its national minorities. This was short lived, however, because of the excesses of the Cultural Revolution.

During the Cultural Revolution, it was declared that nationality policy was no longer needed because it was denied that China was a multinational country. Minorities and their territories were no longer considered special.

This period dealt a severe blow to the cultural heritage and ways of life of minorities throughout China. The autonomous units in many regions were dissolved. Since the Cultural Revolution, the stated policy has been to emphasize the cultural distinctiveness of minorities and to respect their traditions and cultures. This was important in attempting to rectify the errors of the preceding period. Aside from the excesses of the Cultural Revolution, several major events have marked the national minority situation in China. Bitter feelings developed during the Tibet uprising of 1956–59, which resulted in the departure into exile of the Dalai Lama. In 1962, seventy thousand Kazakhs left the province of Xinjiang and crossed the border to the Soviet side. Also, bitter feelings have often surrounded Han migration to minority areas.

The four-modernizations policy (of agriculture, industry, national defense, and science and technology), initiated in 1978, increasingly opened China to the outside world, supported its participation in the global economy, and emphasized broad economic policies that focused on reducing central government influence. Following the June 4, 1989, tragedy in Tienanmen Square, severe constraints were imposed for a time on the economy and society. The building of a socialist market economy is still the government's central concern. Economic policy continues to be directed generally toward a more rapid development of the coastal regions, while investment in the interior, the region where most of China's minorities reside, must wait until at least the end of the century for the same focused economic development.

ECONOMIC AND REGIONAL DEVELOPMENT

The government has a program to develop minority regions, and while the minorities look forward to progress in this area, they are also apprehensive about what may accompany this development. In particular, the anxiety about "opening these regions" is growing due to large numbers of Han immigrants to these areas. For example, the Uygur have criticized efforts to exploit the deposits of raw material in their regions.[30] There have been demonstrations in both Xinjiang and Mongolia provoked by population migrations and Han control of factories that are responsible for ecological problems. Not surprisingly, some of the smaller minorities would like to remain isolated, and minority interest in preserving their culture and traditions has come into conflict with the drive for economic development.

According to state economic reform plans, development is to be guided by the local conditions of the national minority regions. Since 1949, economic development in these regions has been impressive. The gross value of agricultural and industrial output (GVAIO) rose from 3.66 billion yuan in 1949 to 68 billion yuan in 1984. Within that same period the gross value of agricultural output (GVAO) rose from 3.12 billion yuan to 33 billion. The gross value of industrial output (GVIO) rose from 540 million yuan to 35 billion yuan. If we compare 1949 with 1984, the GVAIO increased 18-fold, with GVAO having increased 10-fold and GVIO having increased 64-fold. Grain production increased 3.5-fold, and raw cloth production increased 16-fold. Between 1952 and 1983, forestry production increased 6-fold, cotton cloth production increased 2.5-fold, paper production increased 35-fold, coal production increased 37-fold, oil production increased 129-fold, electricity production increased 299-fold, and iron and steel production for roads and railways also increased greatly.[31]

However, when such development figures are placed in national perspective, they take on a different meaning. This is clearly evident when we compare the rates of development of national minority regions with other regions in China. The gap between the minority-dominated regions of western China and the largely Han eastern regions continues to widen each year.

CULTURAL AUTONOMY

The very survival of national minorities or ethnic groups is inseparable from their exercise of some degree of cultural autonomy. Of all of the ways that the government of the People's Republic of China has attempted to win back much of the support it lost during the Cultural Revolution, granting a greater degree of autonomy in cultural matters, especially religion and language, has been central.

RELIGION After the founding of the People's Republic of China, freedom of religion was formally guaranteed in the new constitution. During the early years of communist rule Mao Zedong argued that religion should not be prohibited, only restricted.[32] Religion was viewed as a historical product that could only be abolished under certain socioeconomic conditions. Thus, the practice of religion has come to be viewed as something that must be permitted to a limited extent. Also religion shares certain social concerns with socialism that permit mutual cooperation in some circumstances. For example, some religious leaders have joined educators in efforts to eradicate illiteracy. Nevertheless, only state-sponsored religious organizations are permitted; all others are severely suppressed.

Religion is pervasive among most of China's national minorities, and it is often blamed for their lack of social and economic progress. For instance, an autonomous region of Hunan Province spent 53 million yuan on educational expenditures, but among the fifty thousand peasant households, 50 million yuan was lavished on offerings to gods and on marriage and funeral expenses.[33] In the Ningxia Autonomous Region, there are 573 primary schools while the number of mosques is 473. School attendance rates are inevitably affected as parents send their children to mosques rather than schools for instruction. Among the Hui of this community in Ningxia, 60 percent of the children attend school and 40 percent go to mosques.

Nevertheless, there are reports of many varieties of cooperative relations that have developed between religious and party educational leaders to combat illiteracy and achieve basic education.[34] The official policy is that government authorities are not to interfere in the religious affairs of the minorities unless affairs of the state are affected. National minority cadres are not to be dismissed because they have religious beliefs but rather persuaded of the advantages of shedding their religious views, as cooperation between religious leaders and the Communists is still viewed as valuable.

LANGUAGE Since the beginning of the four-modernizations period national minority languages have also been emphasized. Groups without a written language have been helped to develop a romanized system. However, there are indications of a possible reversal of policy. There is a renewed call for Chinese to be the main medium of instruction in schools. This is justified by the fact that few scientific materials are published in national minority languages; therefore, it is argued that Chinese language, which is used nationwide, should be the main medium of instruction.[35]

The case of Xinjiang with a 62 percent minority population is illustrative. The Uygur, Kazakh, Mongolian, Kirghiz, Xibe, and Russians all have their own written languages, while the Hui and the Manchurians use the Han language system. Moreover, certain groups have dual or multiple languages, such as the Uygur, Kazakh, and Xibe, some of whom use each other's languages as well as their own. And some students of a minority nationality that lacks a written language take school examinations in the language of another national minority.

NATIONAL INTEGRATION

In China, the continued expansion of the national minority institutes is viewed as insuring the goal of national integration through training of high-level national minority cadres. There are thirteen national minority institutes, seventy-six institutions of higher education in national minority regions, and an increasing number of remedial classes (*minzu ban*) are organized for minority students in many of the key universities. Within universities in general, special emphasis is being placed on national minority language, culture, and historical traditions. Colleges of Tibetan medicine and Mongolian medicine have also been established. Within higher institutes, studies of ethnology, national minority history, and national minority arts have been set up. Minority languages are used as the medium of instruction. The state has supervised the translation, editing, and publication of textbooks, reference books, newspapers, and journals in national minority languages. Within national minority institutes or normal universities, students can major in the field of minority languages with specialties in twenty-one languages including Mongolian, Tibetan, Uygur, Kazakh, Korean, Yao, Yi, Zhang, Va, and Jingpo.

Since 1980, institutes of higher education in minority autonomous regions that teach in minority languages have been permitted to use regional entrance examinations so students need not sit for national-level examinations. Graduates of secondary schools in which minority languages are used need only sit for a modified version of the entrance examination for university. This exam, although in the Han Chinese language, is written to be less rigorous than the national exams in order to allow a greater number of national minority students to enter universities.[36]

Measures have been taken to accelerate the expansion of enrollment in higher education for national minorities. The government has assisted by allocating funds, personnel, and equipment, and groups of teachers from inland regions have been sent to frontier areas inhabited by national minorities. Cooperation has been increased between frontier institutes and those in the interior. In 1987 there were 91 universities and colleges in the autonomous areas with a total of 115,000 students and a teaching staff of 23,000. Since 1978 these figures have nearly doubled. A similar pattern exists in the thirteen minority institutes, where there has been more than a doubling of figures between 1978 and 1986. Beginning in 1988, the national minority institutes could begin awarding the doctoral degree in ethnology, the history of Chinese national minorities, and minority languages. The master's degree can be awarded in 31 fields and the bachelor's degree in 185 specialties. In a joint document issued in 1983, the State Nationalities Affairs Commission, the Ministry of Finance, and the Ministry of Education decided that minority cadre training should be full-time rather than part-time. Tuition was made free for those receiving regular training. The national minority institutes have set up evening classes with over six thousand students attending. Beginning in 1980 remedial classes for minority students have been run successfully in ten universities and five medical colleges, including Beijing University, Qinghai University, Beijing Normal University, and Beijing Medical College. In Xinjiang province, for example, three

thousand national minority students have been admitted to special prepara-
tory classes in forty-two institutions of higher learning.[37]

At the same time that efforts are being made to bring more national
minority students into the leading higher educational institutions, the issue
of activism among national minority students has caused increasing concern
to the government because of the threat it poses to national integration. In
1979 the Central Institute of Nationalities published a paper entitled the
"National Minorities and the May Fourth Movement," which championed
the role of national minorities in the democratization of China.[38] Several
members of the Hui nationality who actively took part in the movement
were held up as examples for all of China's nationalities. National minority
students also participated in the democracy movement of 1989 that culminated in Tienanmen Square.

National minority university students in autonomous regions have also
been active in nationalist movements, most notably in Xinjiang and Tibet.[39]
Such activism is an important issue because it raises the question of the
contribution of higher education of national minorities to national integration. At present national minorities are highly underrepresented in univer-
sity-level education, and the government has developed a variety of policies
to rectify this. However, increasing the university student population may
also increase the likelihood of student political activism.

TIBET

The most serious threat to national integration has been the case of Tibet.
Tibet was under martial law for long periods in 1989 and 1990. Before that
time, the authorities made strong efforts to integrate the population into the
national mainstream. The demonstrations that occurred in Tibet over the
last four years have focused considerable attention on the disputed region.
Tibet presents Beijing with one of its most challenging national minority
problems.

Tibet was unified by the Turfan Dynasty at the beginning of the seventh
century. The dynasty set up a system of official ranks, enacted laws, and
divided the territory into military and administrative zones.[40] The economy
and culture of Tibet continued to develop, and Tibet began to have frequent
contacts with the Tang Dynasty (A.D. 618–907). Royal marriages between
Tibetans and Hans occurred in 651 and 710, and cultural intercourse began
to flourish. After the collapse of the Turfan Dynasty several factions set up
their own independent regimes, which lasted for about three hundred years.
When the Mongols overran China and Tibet in the thirteenth century, they
established the Yuan Dynasty (1279–1368) and incorporated Tibet under

its rule. In 1253, Kublai Khan granted a title to the religious leader of Tibet and left him in control of the area. Between the thirteen and eighteenth centuries Tibet came under the rule of several dynasties. In 1751 the Gurkas of Nepal invaded Tibet, and the Qing court promptly sent an expedition to aid the Tibetan effort to drive out the invaders. Following this the central government further extended its control over the local Tibetan regime.

At the beginning of the twentieth century, Britain and Russia sought greater influence in Tibet, the former winning a trade agreement that the Chinese would only recognize with the acknowledgment of China's sovereignty over the region.[41] Armed conflict between the Tibetans and Chinese resulted in the eviction of the Chinese and a brief declaration of independence from the Chinese government by the thirteenth Dalai Lama.

During the 1920s and 1930s contact between the Llasa government and Beijing was minimal.[42] When the thirteenth Dalai Lama died in 1933, the Nationalist government held a memorial service in Nanjing and sent a special commissioner to Llasa to improve relations between Tibet and the central government. Eventually, the Tibetan government took a more conciliatory position toward the Chinese.

In October 1950 the Chinese Army entered Tibet again, and in 1951 Tibet officially became an autonomous region under the sovereignty of the People's Republic of China. Tibet provided the Chinese Communist Party with an enormous challenge. Its geographical distance from the rest of China and the potential for independence struggles presented obstacles. Soon after the People's Liberation Army arrived in Llasa, changes in the infrastructure began. The 1951 agreement provided for maintenance of the administrative status quo, although some administrative changes also began to take place. Road construction started immediately, and travel between Llasa, other Tibetan cities, and other parts of China soon became easier. Telegraphic and postal communications, newspapers, and radio stations linked Tibet with other parts of China.

In the period since liberation, Tibet has greatly benefited from the enormous amount of financial assistance and investment made by the central government. Without the help of Beijing, Tibet's development might not have been sustained. Highways, schools, and medical facilities have all been greatly improved. The Chinese state has become more open to issues of self-government and decisions have been made to prevent administrative interference in religious affairs. Yet, the Dalai Lama remains in exile and Tibetans favoring independence are imprisoned.

Within the Chinese constitution, all nationalities are entitled to make their own decisions on development, and the autonomy law of 1984 sets out the newest parameters of autonomy. However, all autonomous administrative organs are subordinate to those above them and ultimately fall under Han control because they are subordinate to the central bodies in Beijing where the Han are the majority.

In this sense, the case of Tibet is not only illustrative of the problem of other minorities in China but also of the problem of national minorities in other socialist societies as well. It is difficult for the local governments of autonomous units to resist the will of local party organizations. Under current political and administrative structures autonomy is greatly restricted. Economic decisions on how to exploit the natural resources of a minority region, or political decisions about the relative proportion of minority cadres in positions of power, or social policy decisions concerning the amount of Han migration to national minority regions, or military decisions as to whether nuclear weapons should be installed in minority border areas, all become encumbered by the restrictions placed on regions inhabited by China's national minorities.

EVENTS IN XINJIANG

In May of 1989, shortly before the democracy movement was suppressed in Tienanmen, a book published in Shanghai concerning Muslim religious practices offended Muslim sentiments and led to the storming of the Communist Party headquarters in Urumqi by hundreds of people.[43] Students at the Central Institute of Nationalities in Beijing also organized a protest that later dovetailed with the emerging student democracy movement. Immediately after June 4, the government list of the twenty-one most wanted student leaders contained the names of two minority students, one from Xinjiang who fled the country and another who was apprehended.[44] However, there was no indication that these students linked their participation in the democracy movement to their ethnicity.

Beginning in late January of 1990, the Chinese leadership expressed some concern over calls for autonomy in regions of the USSR bordering China.[45] The concern was serious enough to merit a special meeting on national minorities in Beijing.[46] In mid-February, a meeting of the State Nationalities Affairs Commission was convened. State Security Department officials also contributed to discussions concerning separatist movements. Despite these measures, anti-Han feelings intensified in Xinjiang and Tibet. A member of the commission stated that "separatist elements of various kinds are colluding with people both inside and outside China who are opposed to socialism and who insist on bourgeois liberalization. Maintaining stability in areas inhabited by minorities is the priority matter for this year."[47]

At the opening of the meeting, the national minorities commissioner, Ismail Amat, a native of Xinjiang province, admitted that the government had made mistakes and pledged to resolve the contradictions among China's nationalities. He stated that "the economic problems faced by national minority areas and the mistakes incurred by various levels of government in carrying out policies toward minorities may have engendered detrimental effects on relations among the nationalities."[48] To remedy these problems, the government committed itself to a number of measures, including more funds for infrastructural development, promotions for cadres of minority origin, and more flexible economic and trade policies at the local level to attract foreign investment. Local governments were given authority to set up trading offices in foreign countries, customs regulations were to be simplified to attract foreign commerce and investment into Xinjiang, and the province was to receive more federal funds to set up commodity export bases and to boost infrastructural facilities such as airports and railways.

At the time of the conference, there was growing alarm over political changes in Mongolia and the Soviet Union. Speaking at the meeting Premier Li Peng stated that "a minority of separatists have hoisted flags of nationalism and religious freedom in order to counter the socialist system"[49] and warned the minority cadres that the prosperity of the national minorities could only advance with the development of the country as a whole. The word "separatist" was increasingly employed regardless of the nature of the ethnic conflict involved.[50]

In line with efforts to refocus economic reforms in the national minority areas, the vice minister of the State Nationalities Affairs Commission, Jiang Jiafu of the Zhuang minority, urged Beijing to abolish the "east-central-west strategy" favoring eastern China over western sectors in the allocation of development funds. In March 1990, the vice chairman of Xinjiang, Huang Baozhang, welcomed economic aid from other countries as long as "religious favors" were not attached. But Xinjiang's regional congress chairman, Tomur Dawamat, told the National People's Congress that the Taiwan-based Nationalist Party was trying to split Xinjiang.

Soon after, an uprising took place in the border region of Baren adjoining Afghanistan in which twenty-two were killed. The clash between government security forces and Muslim minorities was said to be supported by mujahideen rebels.[51] The leader of the revolt, Abul Kasin of the Free East Turkistan movement, was killed. Shortly afterwards, the city of Kashgar was closed down as Chinese troops were dispatched to the region. Riots were reported there and also in Hotan, Kuqu, and the capital city of Urumqi.

In September, China's foreign minister, Qian Qichen, went to Turkey, where the separatist movements were said to be based, and asked for coop-

eration to prevent support for separatist movements in Xinjiang.[52] Party
secretary Jiang Zemin pledged more aid to Xinjiang but also demanded
tough measures to prevent separatism. This was followed in October by a
purge of party officials in Baren and the restructuring of ten party organizations including the youth league. In January of 1991, there was concern on
the part of the government that the Gulf War and China's neutral position
toward the war could have dire effects on stability in Xinjiang.[53]

These events in Xinjiang, which occurred within the short span of about
a year, reveal the complexity and sensitivity of national minority relations
in the region as well as discontent with government economic development
strategies that favor eastern China. The Xinjiang case also shows the difficulty of generalizing about China's national minority situation in various
regions of the country and the importance of looking in some detail at
particular cases.[54]

CONCLUSION

No other society has the ethnic contours of China, where as many as ninety
million minority people (constituting 8 percent of China's population) occupy over 60 percent of the total territory and 90 percent of the interior
border region. Their greatly differing populations, territories, histories, and
identities make both defining national minorities and comparing them a
formidable task indeed.

For a great many people, socialist policies in general and socialist nationality policies in particular have had desirable features. This was true
even though the specific patterns varied across time and place. Many minorities acquired equal rights in both economic and political arenas for the
first time. Negative cultural labels and discrimination became less potent
as national minority workers became empowered. More minority women
benefited from social policies designed to widen the opportunity and roles
available to them. National minorities were provided with opportunities to
eradicate illiteracy and were freed from many related handicaps. Unfortunately, the government's policies also came with tight centralized control,
restricted choices, and reduced autonomy in certain spheres of minority
decision making.

In China, socialist policy objectives toward minorities, especially in the
early period, seemed laudable. Great importance was placed on equality
among nationalities. The right of autonomy within a unified state was emphasized, as was respect for national minorities' cultural ways. The right to
education in one's native language and the development of a higher standard
of living were made central concerns. While the Communists have made

some major accomplishments and while it is difficult to bring about full ethnic harmony, especially in a developing country such as China and in view of its many minorities, the democratic centralism practiced by the socialist state has not dealt adequately with the autonomy issue.

The durability of ethnicity within the context of development is no longer a surprise. It remains a powerful axis of mobilization. Ethnic groups are likely to continue to want to retain a sense of group consciousness and control over their destiny. Yet, as the centralization of socialist societies loosens and national minorities are given the chance of increased self-government, other age-old problems may begin to emerge. Certain forms of ethnicity and certain economic conditions may lead to explosive situations and chronic interethnic friction. In this respect, the trumpeting of the demise of socialism that is occurring in the media and in scholarly circles may be premature. As economic difficulties intensify ethnic conflicts, rather than witness the terminal decay of socialism, we may hear calls for its rebirth in some places.

Autonomy will remain a sensitive issue in China, as it is in most multiethnic societies. What distinguishes national minority situations in different countries is the manner in which the various dimensions of social equality, economic development, cultural autonomy, and political integration interweave themselves historically, overlap, and remain interdependent. Moreover, different national minorities are subject to different combinations and weighting of these dimensions.

It is any government's task to juggle these four dimensions simultaneously. In China, the balancing act rests exclusively on the government's ability both to apply nationality policy in a flexible manner and, more importantly, to implement fully the provisions of the autonomy law of 1984, which empowers China's ethnic and national minorities to enact legislative protections for their customs and traditions, including education, language, and other social and cultural rights.

NOTES

1. The State Statistical Bureau, Department of Populations, *Population Census of the People's Republic of China, 1990* (Beijing: Statistical Publishing House, 1990), pp. 78–86.
2. *Beijing Review*, September 17–23, 1990, p. 23.
3. See Ma Yin, *China's Minority Nationalities* (Beijing: New World Press, 1985).
4. See Zhou Enlai, "Guanyu woguo minzu zhengcede jige wenti" (A few questions concerning our country's nationality policy), in Gansu sheng minzu yanjiusuo (Gansu Province Institute of Nationality Studies), *Zhonghuo minzu guanxishi lunwen xuanji* (Gansu: Gansu Minzu Chubanshe, 1983). This speech was originally delivered on August 4, 1957.
5. *Beijing Review*, September 17–23, 1990, p. 23.

6. See *Sun Zhongshan xuanji* (Selections of the writings of Sun Yat-sen) (Beijing: Renminchubanshe, 1981).

7. See Chiang Kai-shek, *China's Destiny* (New York: Macmillan, 1947).

8. See Fei Xiaotong, "Ethnic Identification in China," *Social Science in China* 1 (9180): 97–107.

9. Joseph Stalin, *Marxism and the National Question* (New York: International Publishers, 1934).

10. See Thomas Heberer, *China and Its National Minorities: Autonomy or Assimilation* (Armonk, N.Y.: M. E. Sharpe, 1989), chapter 6. Also see Du Wenzhan, *Renkou zongheng tan* (On the population) (Beijing: Zhongguo Qingnian Chubanshe, 1985).

11. Tian Hungmao, "Sinicization of National Minorities," *Current Scene* (Hong Kong) 11 (1974). Also see Leo Orleans, *Every Fifth Chinese: The Population of China* (Stanford: Stanford University Press, 1972).

12. See Ma Yin, "Religious Beliefs," in *Questions and Answers about China's Nationalities* (Beijing: New World Press, 1985).

13. See Ma Yin, "Languages," in ibid.

14. See Fan Wenlan, "Problems of Conflict and Fusion of Nationalities in Chinese History," *Social Science in China* 1 (1980): 71–82; Heberer, *China and Its National Minorities*.

15. See "Nationalities," in *Information China*, compiled and translated by the Chinese Academy of Social Sciences, edited by C. V. James (Oxford: Pergamon Press, 1988).

16. Wolfram Eberhard, "Kultur und Seidlung des Randvolkers Chinas," (Culture and Settlements in China), *T'oung Pao* (Countrymen), vol. 38 supplement (Leiden, 1942), pp. 412–19.

17. Heberer, *China and Its National Minorities*.

18. See June Dryer, *China's Forty Millions: Minority Nationalities and National Integration in the People's Republic of China* (Cambridge, Mass.: Harvard University Press, 1976).

19. See Fan Wenlan, "Problems of Conflict and Fusion of Nationalities in Chinese History."

20. Dryer, *China's Forty Millions*, p. 91.

21. Chu Zhihua, *Zhongguo geming yu zhongguo shehui ge jieji* (China's revolution and China's social classes) (Shanghai: Lienhou Shudian, 1930), pp. 259–60.

22. "Zhongguo Renmin Zhengzhi Xieshang huiyi" (China people's political consultative congress), *Zhongguo faling huibian* (A compilation of laws and regulations of China) (Beijing: Renmin Chubanshe, 1952).

23. Dryer, *China's Forty Millions*, chapter 5.

24. *The Important Documents of the First Plenary Session of the Chinese People's Political Consultative Conference* (Beijing: Foreign Languages Press, 1949), appendix C. Also see J. Xian, "China's 1982 Constitution and the Policy toward Nationalities," *Chinese Law and Government* 16, nos. 2–3 (1983): 67–87.

25. *Zhongguo Shaoshu Minzu* (China's national minorities) 12 (1988): 25; *Minzu Tuanjie* (Unity among nationalities) 2 (1989): 37.

26. "Autonomy for the Minority Nationalities of China" in *China News Analysis* (Hong Kong), August 15, 1989, p. 3.

27. See *Minzu Cidian* (Nationalities dictionary) (Siquan Minzu Chubanshe [Siquan Province Nationalities Publishing House], 1984), p. 260.

28. Ibid.

29. "Autonomy for the Minority Nationalities of China" pp. 41–42.

30. *Xinjiang Ribao* (Urumchi), August 4, 1988; *Minzu Tuanjie* (Beijing) 11 (1986): 1.

31. See *Xibu minzu digu jingji kaifa tansuo* (Investigations of economic development in nationality regions of western China) (Beijing: Zhongyang Minzu Xueyuan Chubanshe [Central Institute of Nationalities Press], 1986); *Zhongguo tongjizhaiyao 1987* (China's statis-

tical summary, 1987) (Beijing: Guojia Tongjiju [Statistical Bureau], 1987); and *Minzu gong-zuo tongjizhaiyao* (Statistical summaries of nationality work) (Beijing: Guojia Minwei Caijingsi [Nationalities Commission Finance Office], 1987).

32. Mao Zedong, *Collected Works*, vol. 1 (Beijing: Foreign Languages Publishing House, 1968).

33. Teng Xing, "Woguo shaoshu minzu diqu jiaoyu zhengti gaige guanjian" (The key to total reform of national minority education), *Qiu Shi* (Seek truth) 7 (April 1989): 22.

34. Ibid.

35. See Muhateer, "Jixu gaige minzu jiaoyu" (Continue to reform nationality education), *Xinjiang shehui kexue* (Social services of Xinjiang), no. 3 (June 15, 1989): 53–57.

36. Wang Tiezhi, "Shaoshu minzu jiaoyu de xinfazhan" (The new development of national minority education), *Jiaoyu jianxun* (Educational briefing), no. 4 (1987).

37. Ibid.

38. See Tong Li, "Wusi yundong yu shaoshu minzu" (The May Fourth movement and the national minorities), *Zhongyang Muinzu Xueyuan Xuebao* (Central Institute of Nationalities News), no. 1–2 (1979): 1–8.

39. "Five Students Arrested in Lhasa," *South China Morning Post* (Hong Kong), December 26, 1989. Between June 4 and late October 1989, Tibetan University president Ciwang Junwei confirmed that two university students had been arrested. One of the students was reportedly sent home while the other was sent to a labor education camp for three years.

40. "Nationalities in the Five Autonomous Regions" in Ma Yin et al., *About China's Minority Nationalities* (Beijing: New World Press, 1985).

41. Heberer, *China and Its National Minorities*, pp. 119–24.

42. Dryer, *China's Forty Millions*, pp. 33–38.

43. "Xinjiang minzu baoluan xunyinyou," (Insurrection movement among Xinjiang nationalities) in *Dangdai* (Contemporary World) (Hong Kong), April 21, 1990, pp. 13–14.

44. The list was published in a variety of newspapers in Hong Kong after June 4, including the *Ming Bao, Da Gong Bao*, and the *South China Morning Post*.

45. "China Fears Muslim Push for Autonomy," *South China Morning Post*, January 23, 1990.

46. "Zhonggong jinggao guonei shaoshu minzu buke fenli fangong zhizao dongluan" (The Chinese government warns the minorities against separatism and opposes disorder), *Mingbao* (Hong Kong), February 14, 1990, p. 10; "Shaoshu minzu chuxian fenli fangong" (Emerging separatism among national minorities), *Xianggong Shibao* (Hong Kong Times), February 4, 1990.

47. Willy Wo-Lap Lam, "Meeting on Minorities Called," *South China Morning Post*, February 12, 1990.

48. Willy Wo-Lap Lam, "Mistakes Made in Minority Policy," *South China Morning Post*, February 14, 1990.

49. "Li Peng Warns on Separatism," *South China Morning Post*, February 16, 1990.

50. The Chinese word *fenliefenzi* (used by Li Peng) literally translates in Chinese as "splittist," but the word "separatist" is the standard translation in this context.

51. "Mujahideen Guerillas Back Xinjiang Revolt," *South China Morning Post*, May 10, 1990.

52. "Jiang Woos Uygurs with Aid Promise," *South China Morning Post*, September 4, 1990.

53. "Fear of Hong Wars Spurs Beijing to Consider Threat of Ethnic Unrest," *South China Morning Post*, January 20, 1991.

54. National identity is a powerful rallying post in China. One manifestation has been the release and immediate censorship in 1990 of Turrun Almas's trilogy, which included *The Uygurs*. The book's argument is that China has never been a multiracial country, that it is a nation of Han people; that the Uygurs have always been an indigenous nation independent of China; and that various nationalities in Xinjiang are not strangers to each other, a view similar

to the pan-Islamic and pan-Turkic views of the 1930s and 1940s. Shortly after the publication of the three books, extensive refutations followed in the main local daily. See, for example, *Xinjiang Ribao,* May 18, 1991, June 3, 1991, and June 21, 1991. These were fortified by scathing front-page attacks on these books by the Xinjiang party leadership. The journal of Xinjiang University followed with more extensive commentaries. Nevertheless, the fact that these books even appeared on bookshelves indicates a certain amount of support for these views. See *Xinjiang Daxue Xuebao* (Xinjiang University Journal), no. 3 (1990): 31–44.

JASMINKA UDOVIČKI

□ 12 □

Nationalism, Ethnic Conflict, and Self-Determination in the Former Yugoslavia

The national question lies at the heart of the creation of Yugoslavia in 1918 and of its destruction in 1991–92. A vision of national liberation and modernization brought the various South Slav nationalities together after World War I; seventy years later, a retrospective, mythical, antimodernist vision tore them apart. The appeal to the concept of self-determination was used to justify both.

HISTORICAL BACKGROUND

The South Slav lands, a geographic and cultural gateway separating Eastern and Western Europe, were dominated for centuries by Hungarians, Ottomans, Venetians, and Hapsburgs.[1] Clashes between the great powers shaped the region into a large Balkan military frontier, a cordon sanitaire, and its people into the human buffer zone wedged between Istanbul on one side, and Budapest, Vienna, and Venice on the other. Two kinds of maps materialized as a result. The resident populations came to compose a cultural map, reflecting the intermingling of ethnic groups over time. The geopolitical divisions between the great powers formed another, a state map, evolving separately and independently from the existing ethnic configuration. Superimposed on the first, this second map divided and merged local populations, indifferent to the ethnic mix on the ground.

A strong deposit of foreign cultures and religions in the regions under foreign domination shaped life experiences and ways of thinking across the territory in crucial and diverse ways. Modes of land cultivation, legal structures and norms, urban administration, patterns of social interaction, work habits, and even modes of self-perception were all affected. In the west and north, Croats and Slovenes received Germanic, Central European, and Venetian influences and embraced Catholic Christianity as their religion. In Croatia and its northern, agriculturally rich part, Slavonia, an aristocratic land-owning class developed over time, residing in feudal castles and holding in its possession large estates.[2] Urban life developed in the nineteenth century in many Croatian cities. The literacy level was significantly higher than in Serbia, the birth rate lower, and in the early twentieth century the sons (and sometimes the daughters) of the land-owning families, even those of moderate means, were sent to the universities. Most of the existing industry in the early twentieth century was also situated in Croatia, and in Slovenia, the region in the northwest corner of the country bordering Austria. As a result, those regions had a better developed, though in comparison with the West European countries still rudimentary, middle class.

By contrast, Bosnia and Hercegovina retained a system of serfdom until late in the nineteenth century, and Montenegro was a tribal society of cattle breeders. Serbia inherited Greek Orthodox and Islamic traditions, alien to the influences of the Renaissance culture that had shaped many Croatian cities in Dalmatia. Serbian agriculture was inefficient, fragmented into small plots, tilled with the wooden plow, and producing at the subsistence level. Serbia lived on small trade and home industry, its small artisan class unaccustomed to the Western work ethic, business calculation, and planning.[3] Yet even within Serbia there were differences. Vojvodina, stretching to the north of Belgrade toward the Hungarian border,[4] enjoyed a level of development comparable to that of Croatia and Slovenia. Its capital, Novi Sad, was a thriving nineteenth-century cultural and economic center with an educated and cultured middle class.

These developmental disparities and diverse life experiences caused among the South Slavs a sense of cultural rift. Still, however great, the forces of separation were coupled with and tempered by two unifying forces. One stemmed from the common Slav historic origin and language. The other, equally strong, stemmed from the shared determination of the South Slav peoples to resist absorption by their colonizers and preserve their identities despite a millennium of foreign domination. Contrary to numerous misreadings offered today, the last one hundred and fifty years represented in the South Slav lands the period when attempts were made to bridge cultural gaps, overcome forces pulling the communities apart, and achieve national liberation, seen as tantamount to self-determination.

What made the pan-ethnic amalgamation of the South Slavs difficult was that the preservation of their identities as separate peoples was for them as important in the process of national integration as it has been during foreign occupation. The resolve to resist assimilation into the non-Slavic world of their colonizers had helped preserve ethnic pride, spirit, and a sense of the past history of each of the groups through time. But that same set of qualities, transferred into the domain of interethnic relations, became a source of conflict and strife and often nationalism itself.

The nineteenth-century project of South Slav unification was complicated because it did not imply self-determination of a single nation seeking liberation from another world power. Instead, the South Slav territories were at the time broken up into five zones: the first, encompassing Croatia and Slavonia, belonged to Hungary; the second, made up of Dalmatia and Slovenia, to Austria; the third, comprising Serbia and Montenegro, composed a semiautonomous Ottoman principality; the fourth, Macedonia, lived under Turkey; the fifth, Bosnia, belonged to the Ottoman Empire until 1878 and was subsequently occupied by Austro-Hungary and annexed in 1908.[5] The project of self-determination implied first two, and subsequently three, then five, and eventually seven self-determination efforts, as the Croats, Serbs, Slovenes, and eventually Macedonians, Montenegrins, Muslims, and Albanians, from the first half of the nineteenth century to the end of the twentieth, claimed their unique cultural, territorial, and political space. All those ethnic groups had a great deal of their own history to look back to. Most of them once had prosperous medieval states, the historical memory of which formed the core of their national identities, and they possessed distinct cultures shaped through centuries of cultural exchange with their different colonizers.

Yet the preserved sense of a common Slav origin, and a common Slav language, represented a strong and tenacious unifying thread. The two offered a firm basis to articulate "the Illyrian project" of national unification, first conceived in Croatia in 1835 as a drive for political emancipation of the South Slavs through a cultural renaissance. The Croat Ljudevit Gaj, and after him Josip Juraj Strosmajer and Franjo Rački (one a liberal Catholic bishop, the other a member of the Catholic clergy) stressed the linguistic kinship between the South Slavs as the foundation for their unification, hoping in the romantic nineteenth century tradition that a broad-based enlightenment effort would bring about spiritual integration of Croats, Slovenes, and Serbs. The "Illyrians" saw the pan-ethnic unification of Yugo-Slavs (South Slavs) as the only vehicle for achieving a degree of autonomy from Austro-Hungary and gaining self-determination. The unification, in their vision, was theoretically possible in two contexts: either within the

Hapsburg monarchy or within a sovereign Yugo-Slav state. While the second was more desirable, the first was more realistic. The Austro-Hungarian Empire, the ''Illyrians'' predicted, was unlikely to collapse any time soon. The most realistic solution, therefore, was a trinational one, unifying the Serbs, Slovenes, and Croats under the Hapsburg roof, with Zagreb as the center of unification.

But from the very outset the differences in their historic positions and needs prevented the Croat and Serb elites from joining forces. While all Croats lived together on the same territory, two-thirds of the Serbs lived outside the Serb principality, in Croatia and Bosnia.[6] Whereas unification under the Hapsburg Empire seemed better than no unification at all to the Croats, the Serbs perceived it as a fundamental obstacle to the unification of all Serbs and were therefore disinclined to accept Croatian proposals.

Hence the nineteenth century brought about two divergent conceptions of national renaissance. The Croatian idea, with Yugo-Slavism at the heart of the vision of national liberation, held out a promise of the eventual unification of all South Slavs. The Serbian idea focused above all on the retrieval of the historic Serbian territories and the unification of all Serbs, subjects at the time of three different states: Austria, Turkey, and Serbia itself. Serb elites promoted the concept of Balkan self-determination but did not see Yugoslavism as the focus of their integrative vision. Until the end of the nineteenth century there was not a single party in Serbia that advanced the idea of Yugoslavism as its program. The Serbian Radical Party, the strongest in the Serbian spectrum, rejected the idea as unrealistic. For the Serbs Yugoslavism was attractive only insofar as it helped Serbian national objectives. This suited Austro-Hungary well as it was eager to suppress pan-ethnic solidarity in the Balkans.

In both Croatia and Serbia the project of unification remained, however, an elite preoccupation. For the poor and uneducated peasant populations the ideas entertained by the liberal intellectuals were as alien as they were incomprehensible. Hence, not only was unification nothing but an idea at the time, it was also one without a grassroots base. When in 1904 the idea caught the imagination of the student youth in Belgrade, who founded their pro-Yugoslav club and launched the journal the *Slav South*, it was once again restricted to the elite circles of the enlightened.

Political circumstances favorable to implementing the idea in practice arose only in 1918, with the end of World War I and the disintegration of Austro-Hungary. Support for unification grew steadily among the common people as the war was drawing to a close. In 1918 it varied between 100 percent in Dalmatia and 60 percent in Croatia, Slavonia, and Bosnia-Hercegovina.[7] But the Serbs and Croats occupied rather asymmetrical positions at the end of the war; that fact would weigh heavily on the events following their unification into the Kingdom of Serbs, Croats, and Slovenes, declared on December 1, 1918. The Croats and Slovenes had been drafted and had fought on the losing, Austro-Hungarian side in World War I. Serbia fought on the side of the Allies, lost 23 percent of its total population, had half of its wealth destroyed, and inherited over half a million orphaned children to care for when the fighting was over. The Serbs thus considered their liberation from Austro-Hungary not only a military victory but also a moral victory that came at a very high price.[8] The Kingdom of Serbs, Croats, and Slovenes ("three tribes of the same people," as the Constitution stated) raised hopes of national equality, but in the new community the Serbs unambiguously felt superior to the others. This asymmetry, and the pronounced political self-righteousness of the Serbs—stemming from their perception that the new unified state was born of their blood and sacrifice—created between the two world wars a great deal of interethnic antagonism and resentment. For the first time in a thousand years, the Croats and the Serbs, who in the nineteenth century came to regard themselves as nations,[9] now in the twentieth century faced each other as sovereign subjects and found that there was a great deal to be worked out between them.

THE KINGDOM OF SERBS, CROATS, AND SLOVENES

In November 1918, only a week before the proclamation of the new kingdom, Vojvodina and Montenegro voted for immediate union with Serbia, and Serb areas (already significantly enlarged in the Balkan Wars of 1912–13 by expanding into Novi Pazar, Kosovo, and Macedonia) were once again increased. In the new kingdom, the Muslim, Macedonian, Montenegrin, and Albanian ethnic groups received no national recognition whatsoever. The kingdom was divided into thirty-three provinces of which twenty belonged to Serbia. This territorial asymmetry eventually exacerbated the tensions.

The newly formed kingdom was made up of people professing three religions, writing in two alphabets, and accustomed to a variety of patterns in the organization of everyday life and society as a whole. The kingdom inherited five different currencies, six different custom areas, four railway networks, and three types of banking systems.[10] The agrarian system also varied, including small property ownership in Serbia and Montenegro, residues of the Turkish feudal system in Bosnia, and large estates in Croatia.[11]

Ravaged during the war, the kingdom remained one of the poorest countries in Europe. In 1938 its population was 75 percent peasant, with over two-thirds of the people living on small, five-hectare plots. Only 2 percent of the population lived on plots larger than twenty hectares. Land was too fragmented for food to be produced in sufficient quantities. The peasant family owned no advanced agricultural technology and was continually indebted to the cooperatives, banks, or wealthy families. It had to borrow money to pay off former debts.[12] The cities were without urban traditions and without industry, save for lumber and brick making. Foreign capital owned and exploited the country's silver, copper, and coal mines. The working class was tied to the village, disunited and lacking in any trade-unionist traditions. Illiteracy varied from one region to the next, from 44 percent to 94 percent.

Yet great differences existed between different parts of the new monarchy. Its north and northwest (Croatia and Slovenia) were much better developed than the east and the south. The industrial output of Slovenia was twenty-two times greater than that of Macedonia and Montenegro. The paradox of the situation, however, was embodied in the fact that the Serbs, who lagged far behind the Croats and the Slovenes economically, owned slightly over one-fifth of the total capital, filled four-fifths of the political and administrative posts in the kingdom.[13] The Croats and Slovenes experienced this as another affront, indeed another form of domination, not entirely different from the earlier domination of Vienna and Budapest and in some ways even worse.[14]

Only a year after the proclamation of the new state the dissatisfaction of Croats and Slovenes with the new arrangement surfaced. Croats and Slovenes had hoped for a state that would allow what the Hapsburg monarchy did not: the affirmation of their own national identities in a federal unity with others. Instead, the Serbs had imposed on them a centralized state offering little room for national autonomy or the expression of national identity. These frustrations created strong tensions between the three groups, resulting in the formation of the Croatian Peasant Party under Stjepan Radić, who proclaimed his objective to be the preservation of Croatian national identity and tradition. The Croats were willing to accept Yugoslavia only as long as they did not feel that it curbed their national identity. Thus, while political bickering came to dominate political life in the kingdom, the ministerial crisis (twenty-three in total) and dismissals of the parliament heightened nationalist sentiments and blocked the search for economic solutions and political stability.

In June 1928 Radić and four other members of the Croatian Peasant Party were murdered in the parliament by a member of the Serbian Radical Party. King Aleksandar used this as a pretext to proclaim absolute monarchy in 1929 and to change the name of the country to the Kingdom of Yugoslavia, thereby wiping out any reference to the three separate nationalities that composed it. This move dealt the fragile alliance between the three nations an ominous blow, for which King Aleksandar paid with his life. In 1938 he was assassinated in Marseilles.

Prince Paul, the first regent who took over on behalf of the minor King Peter II, was from the beginning suspected by the Serbs of leaning toward the Croats and by the Croats of favoring the Serbs. In 1939, under Prince Paul's guidance, Croatia (including Slavonia, Dalmatia, and parts of Bosnia and Hercegovina) was granted the status of a self-governing *banovina* (province). Despite the complaints of Croat elites that what was gained was not enough, and the Serb elites who said it was too much, the self-governing status of Croatia could have represented the first step to federalism and reconciliation. World War II shattered all hopes that the differences between Serbs and Croats would be worked out. The invasion of Yugoslavia and its partition between Germany, Italy, Hungary, Bulgaria, and Rumania[15] gave rise to the internal forces that launched a civil war of astonishing proportions and brutality.

THE FIRST BREAKUP OF YUGOSLAVIA, 1941–1945

Two such forces occupied center stage: the Ustashe government of the Independent State of Croatia (NDH) and the Serb Chetnik army. There were smaller nationalist movements as well, but it was the clash of those two, and their mercilessly vindictive strategy aimed at the civilian population, that primarily account for the carnage brought about by the civil war. The Ustashe represented a much more powerful force, a ruling party in a state supported by the Axis. The Chetniks represented a guerrilla movement resisting the occupying German forces. They were supported until 1943 by Britain. Yet the groups shared two essential ideological features: fervent anticommunism and ultranationalism.

Hitler's aim was to destroy Yugoslavia and punish Serbia, the core of Yugoslavia, for the part it had played in World War I.[16] Germany counted on the ultranationalist forces on the ground to fan national antagonisms in the country and thereby fragment Yugoslavia internally. On April 10, 1941, immediately after the declaration of the war and the dissolution of Yugoslavia, Hitler created the Independent State of Croatia (NDH), which included all of Croatia (except for Dalmatia, which fell to the Italians) as well as a great part of Bosnia and Hercegovina. By creating a Nazi state under the Ustashe regime of Ante Pavelić in the midst of Yugoslavia, Hitler achieved a threefold objective: he satisfied the timeworn Croatian yearning for Great Croatia's independent statehood; he presented Germany as a force backing

Croatian national liberation; and he polarized the Yugoslavian nation internally.

NDH fell two days after the withdrawal of German forces from Zagreb in 1945. But during its four-year existence as an independent state, it was turned into a vast field for the extermination of Serbs, Jews, and Gypsies, as well as Communists and all Croats who expressed disagreement with the Croatian Nazi regime. The exact number of those who perished in the Croatian concentration camps will probably never be known. Just in Jasenovac, the largest concentration camp in Croatia run by the Ustashe government, the estimates vary between three hundred and seven hundred thousand. Serbs were declared a "foreign entity," the proven enemies of the Croatian people, immigrants who had to be removed. Of the 1.9 million Serbs who lived in Croatia at the beginning of the war, one-third were to be exterminated, one-third deported, and one-third converted to Catholicism.[17] Mass executions of the Serb civilian population started only a few weeks after the outbreak of the war, when 184 men, women, and children were slaughtered near the town of Bjelovar in northern Croatia. The massacres soon spread to Hercegovina, Lika, Kordun, and Banija and predictably led to an eruption of nationalist sentiment on all sides of the ethnic divide. Behind the massacres stood the Ustashe war machine. A part of the Muslim hierarchy known as *cvijet hrvatstva* (the best of the Croats) supported the Ustashe.[18]

The Chetnik movement headed by Draža Mihailović, a colonel of the royalist Yugoslav army,[19] was formed from among the army officers who refused to surrender their arms and who escaped mass deportation to Germany immediately following the outbreak of the war. The Chetniks represented the interests of the Yugoslavian monarchist government in exile. Mihailović's aim was to maintain the continuity of monarchist Yugoslavia and to create a "great" and "homogeneous"—that is, ethnically and religiously pure—Serbia. By virtue of this commitment, Mihailović was, unlike Pavelić, an antifascist, but, at the same time, like Pavelić, a passionate anticommunist.

Mihailović and the exiled government held the Croats, the Muslims, and the Kosovo Albanians responsible for the collapse of Yugoslavia in April 1941—the Croats and Muslims because they belonged to NDH, and the Kosovo Albanians because they supported the Italian fascists. The Chetniks did not make any distinctions between Croat, Muslim, and Albanian soldiers and civilians. Every Croat, every Muslim, and every Albanian was held accountable and was thus targeted.

Three wars played themselves out on the territory of Yugoslavia between 1941 and 1945: the war led by the forces of the Nazi and fascist occupation, the civil war between the Croat and Serb ultranationalists, and the war between all of them and the Yugoslav partisans—the antifascist, antinationalist, grassroots guerrilla movement organized by the Communist Party of Yugoslavia.[20] The Communists understood immediately that only a broadly based, pan-ethnic movement that would attract all strata of the population—the workers, the peasants, and the intelligentsia, including some prominent members of the prewar bourgeoisie—had a chance to prevail against a much stronger enemy. The Communists thus sought to form alliances with all patriotic forces willing to join the unified peoples' liberation front, irrespective of their creed, political allegiances, or nationality. The attempts of Josip Broz Tito, commander in chief of the Partisan forces, to form an alliance with the Chetniks never worked out. The reason was simple. The priority for the Chetniks was not the war against the occupiers but the war against the Communists themselves, whom the Chetniks perceived as their real, long-term rival. In this respect the interests of the Chetniks and the Axis powers converged, and eventually the Chetniks ended up collaborating in one way or another first with the Italians and then with the Germans.[21] Citing the German threat of mass reprisals as a reason for their passive attitude, the Chetniks developed a defensive war strategy, waiting for the eventual defeat of the Germans on the world fronts before launching their own attack.[22]

This strategy, designed to reduce civilian casualties in Serbia, had a demoralizing effect on the fighters, stunting the recruitment effort. In addition, because of their ultranationalism, the Chetniks were unacceptable to any non-Serb group and to all progressive political forces in the country.

It became clear as early as 1942 that the Partisans were the only force in Yugoslavia truly committed to fighting the enemy, foreign and domestic. This was reflected in the rapid growth of the Partisan forces. From a slim contingent of 7,500 barely armed men and women in June 1941, they grew into a force of 80,000 at the end of 1941 and of over 230,000 in the fall of 1943. By mid-1944 there were over 350,000 partisans under arms. The enormous casualties the Partisans were willing to suffer in order to weaken the vastly superior enemy won them great popular recognition and respect. In the decisive Sutjeska battle in the summer of 1943, for example, 7,000 Partisans lost their lives. In the battle on the Neretva River in Bosnia-Hercegovina in February and March 1943, 19,000 Partisans faced 117,000 Germans, Italians, and Nazi collaborators, including the Chetniks.[23] In an uneven battle, the Partisans effectively tied up ten German divisions, making them unavailable for dispatch on other Allied fronts. The fighting on the Neretva River went on for three weeks, ending not only with the destruction of the most dangerous German military contingent in the vicinity of Gornji

Vakuf but also with the rescue of the central Partisan hospital, situated between Prozor and Gornji Vakuf, with its 3,500 wounded. The Partisans won the battle, carrying all their wounded with them as they crossed an improvised bridge to the other bank of the river.[24]

In the end, the Partisans were the only force that triumphed in the Yugoslav War. Their success was contingent on three basic strengths: first, disciplined, tight, and skillful organization and high morale; second, the manifest inadequacy of their domestic, morally compromised, rivals; and third, the formula Partisans developed for the solution of the essential question of the civil war—the national question. Their formula reflected a realization that the solution for all Yugoslavs lies not in the escalation of ethnic hatreds but in national unification. The slogan "brotherhood and unity" expressed in a simple form a complex conception of national integration, the integration taking place within a framework of fratricide and chaos. In addition, the Partisans promised a new Yugoslavia as a federal state of peoples equal in every respect.

The shared experience of fratricide functioned on two levels. On one level, it served as a powerful agent of fragmentation, producing grievances so bitter and intense that the thought of their transcendence in any foreseeable future seemed altogether impossible. On another level, the same experience served as an agent of unification. Clearly, the way out of total mutual annihilation lay only in national reconciliation. The apocalypse thus carried within itself an undercurrent of rebirth. The Partisans were the only ones to recognize this undercurrent and to bet on the concept of a new order grounded in tolerance, equality, and unity. Their vision of the new Yugoslavia was based on the principle of national equality, and not the principle of the balance of forces. And they won, attracting overwhelming popular support at home and abroad, their Communist orientation notwithstanding.

YUGOSLAVIA UNDER TITO

Only a year or two after the most savage bloodshed was inflicted by the Croatian Ustashe regime on Serbs, Jews, Gypsies, and Communists, and by the Serbian Chetniks on Croat and Muslim civilians as well as the Communists, one could travel freely and fearlessly from one end of Yugoslavia to the other.[25] Yugoslavia, which retained its prewar configuration, was constituted as a Federative People's Republic of all of its nations and national minorities. In contrast to the Kingdom of Yugoslavia, the Federative People's Republic recognized not just Serbs, Croats, and Slovenes as separate and independent nations but also Macedonians and Montenegrins. The Kosovo Albanians in the south and the Hungarians in the north received the status of national minorities, granting them full civil and human rights. The Muslims, a national minority at first, were recognized as a nation in the reforms of 1967–68.

Tito recognized that the Partisan victory in the war afforded him a tremendous advantage. What every participant in the liberation struggle knew was that many of the decisive victories of the war were won without any outside help. The outcome was elating, and the aftereffects of the elation carried into the postwar years as a tremendous cohesive social force. That lent the kind of legitimacy to the Yugoslavian Communists that Communists of other Soviet bloc countries did not enjoy and allowed Tito to equate the wish of the Yugoslav nations for self-determination with the wish for a unified Yugoslavia.

Federative Yugoslavia was thus built on the hope that Yugoslav unification in 1945 meant something different than the 1918 unification. The Yugoslavism of 1945 had been forged through unimaginable hardships during the war, the national liberation struggle bonding the participating nations more powerfully than any decree or constitution could. The new Yugoslavia emerged from the solid foundation of a common purpose achieved through an enormous collective sacrifice of its nations. A firmer bedrock could hardly be imagined.

Tito's formula for the solution of the national question was, and remained until the end, the constitutionally guaranteed and vigilantly guarded equality of Yugoslavia's nations and national minorities.[26] Yet the new federal order suffered from the very beginning from an internal contradiction. It rested in the fact that to realize a project of national equality in a country as diverse as Yugoslavia, the new regime chose a federal, but centralized, unitary state. The new centralism was not the one practiced in the Kingdom of Yugoslavia, where it had worked in favor of Serbia. The nexus of Tito's centralism was not a nation but a political party: the League of Communists,[27] enjoying uncontested primacy in practically all spheres of life. In that sense Tito remained in at least a part of his complex personality the student of Soviet communism that he was in the 1930s, when the party sent him to Moscow to study. Tito did break with Stalin and the USSR in 1948, but he never fully abandoned the Soviet model. He saw the one-party system as the only viable form of socialist government and throughout his life veered between discipline and decentralization.

Yet of all Eastern European countries, Yugoslavia has in the postwar years been decidedly the freest, politically and culturally. By the mid-1960s, it required no visas for most European citizens, and its citizens could travel without visas to all countries of Western Europe. Contemporary Western philosophy, political theory, social science, literary theory, and fiction were being translated and were readily available. The foreign press was easily accessible in the main cities. A great deal of Western mass culture—films, television, and rock music—was imported regularly. Karl Marx was studied at the universities, but so were Martin Heidegger, Max Weber, and Talcott Parsons. In contrast to Czech or Rumanian communism, to name two, Yugoslav socialism had a pronounced hybrid quality.

Until the mid-1960s, the republics and autonomous provinces were all equal, but weak. The federation, which was strong, was involved in promoting rapid economic growth, hoping to dissipate the remaining tensions between the nationalities through an overall increase in the standard of living. The purge of the secret police in 1966 and the removal of the interior minister, Aleksandar Ranković, opened the way to a more significant decentralization, resulting in 1968–71 constitutional amendments giving much greater autonomy to the republics and the provinces. It was during this period that significantly greater autonomy was granted to the Kosovo-Metohija autonomous province of Serbia and that the status of Muslims in Bosnia-Hercegovina was changed from that of a national minority to that of a nation. This was one of Tito's calculated moves intended to secure multiple benefits: Yugoslavia was internationally recognized as a country on the cutting edge of reform in the Eastern bloc, and counterweights against possible Serbian political dominance were constitutionally installed.

The 1970s brought about a set of contradictory trends with respect to decentralization. The decade began with Tito's resolute suppression in 1971–72 of a massive resurgent nationalist movement in Croatia (the Maspok) led by the Croat Communist leadership. The members of Maspok argued among other things that the federation and Serbia had robbed Croatia of its fair share of foreign-exchange revenues from tourism and that Croatia should be granted economic autonomy and enabled to dispose of its revenue as it wished. This grievance remained unsubstantiated yet formed the core of Croatian nationalism until 1991. The Yugoslav system, although much more liberal than other Communist systems, nevertheless lacked the capacity of capitalist systems to neutralize through absorption opposing social and political trends, thereby removing them as threats to the system's own long-term survival. Consequently, Tito resorted to repression. The leaders of Maspok, many of them top government officials in Croatia, were purged from their state posts, and some were jailed.

To allay Croat public opinion, Tito a year later launched another crackdown, this time in Serbia. Only here the Serb politicians who were purged were not nationalists but an exceptionally strong and committed group of antinationalists and liberals actively engaged in seeking greater democratization in the country as a whole. By purging both Croat and Serb dissidents,

Tito formally acted as an evenhanded antinationalist. But by suppressing the strongest liberal movement Serbia had ever had, he precluded the possibility of decentralization on a wider, federal scale. Had the Serb liberals prevailed in 1972, the course of development in Yugoslavia could have been quite different.

In the early 1950s, the Communists hoped that an aggressive program of economic reforms would in time bring prosperity and thus dissipate the remaining tensions between the ethnic groups. In a way that eventually did happen, despite the vagueness, limited scope, and dogmatism of the economic vision of those who governed. They most often treated economics as a political, ideological matter, and, needless to say, this stifled growth. Yet Yugoslavia also had two essential advantages over the rest of socialist Eastern Europe that affected its economy in fundamental ways. The first was Tito's status in the West. His break with Stalin in 1948 won him the kind of respect abroad that as a Communist he would not have earned in any other way. Foreign aid and favorable loans were available to him when no other Eastern European country could get them. The second was the fact that at the peak of world prosperity, in the mid-1960s, Yugoslavia opened its borders and allowed its semiskilled and unskilled workers to migrate to West European countries that sorely needed a temporary, low-skilled workforce at the time. People of all nationalities went, and soon over 1.3 million Yugoslavs were working in West Germany, Austria, France, and Scandinavia. Living frugally, socializing little, and saving all their income in Yugoslav banks at home, these workers played a cardinal role in building up the country's foreign currency supply at the end of the 1960s and through the 1970s. One prudent domestic economic decision made investments in Yugoslav banks more attractive than keeping money abroad: Yugoslav banks offered interest rates that were double, sometimes triple, those paid by European banks. The banks also allowed their clients to keep their savings in foreign denominations.

The financial return was high. The standard of living in Yugoslavia rose rapidly, and the Yugoslav middle class expanded enormously. An expectation of continuing improvement prevailed among the population. By the early 1970s, the first postwar generation had come of age, and that generation was self-confident, vastly better educated than its parents, and much more "Yugoslav" than any preceding one. Despite the new buildup of nationalist tensions during the 1970s, Yugoslavism was becoming the predominant orientation of the country's young people.[28] One of the effects of official Yugoslavism was, inevitably, the fostering of a genuine climate of integration among vast portions of Yugoslav society, particularly among the new generation of Yugoslavs.

Although overall all regions of Yugoslavia were doing better in 1974 than in 1947, regional differences in the level of development—job opportunities, per capita income, as well as cultural development—were not narrowing but increasing. In 1947 the per capita social product (PCSP) in Slovenia was 2.4 times higher than that in Kosovo, while in 1974 it was over 6 times higher.[29] In 1953, the PCSP of Slovenia was 183 percent of the national average, compared to only 52 percent in Kosovo, the poorest region.[30] Macedonia, Bosnia-Hercegovina, and Montenegro also lagged far behind Slovenia and Croatia. This produced tensions both in the more developed and the less developed republics and provinces, for different reasons. The less developed ones complained they were being exploited by being reduced to suppliers of raw materials and cheap labor. The more developed ones voiced strong grievances against federal laws requiring them to share their capital inflow with the least developed regions, a requirement that slowed down their own economic development. In addition, it did not appear that the 3 percent of the total Yugoslav GNP that was transferred to Kosovo after the enactment of the Federal Fund for the Development of the Less Developed Regions was yielding any positive results. Fully 70 percent of all investment funds in Kosovo derived from the Federal Fund, yet Kosovo continued to experience economic stagnation and a de facto decline of its per capita income.[31] The political elites in Kosovo at the time were independent in their allocation of this capital. Much of it was mismanaged and misinvested.[32] The more developed regions saw their resources go to waste, and their elites insisted on the right to keep the capital at home and invest it for their own development. The burden placed on the more developed regions by the underdeveloped ones, which the federation allegedly sanctioned, became a powerful ideological tool to rally the Croatian public behind Maspok.

In their effort to gain popular support, the Croat and Slovene elites represented as relevant only one side of the overall picture: the draining of regional resources that crippled further economic growth in the northwest. They simultaneously chose to neglect, and indeed to obscure from public view, a crucial advantage of a commonly maintained Yugoslav economy. It was through the use of the economic infrastructure built since 1945 to support a federally organized economy that Croatia and Slovenia themselves made substantial strides in their economic development, surpassing by far other regions of the country. Between 1947 and 1974 Croatia increased its wealth 4 times and Slovenia almost 5 times, whereas Serbia's had risen only 3.7 times during this period.[33] This would not have been possible without the Yugoslav regional markets for their products, without common road and railway networks, and without shared supplies of electricity, natural gas, and gasoline. All this enabled them to capitalize on their initial economic advantage as the regions with traditionally the most developed industries, managerial skills, and work habits.

The 1974 Constitution had granted each republic and autonomous province an independent administration and economy as well as a veto power in the Federal Assembly. But while this looked democratic, authoritarian one-party structures were in reality simply transferred from the federal level to the local republic leadership. Instead of one centralized party, eight cloned ones now presided in each of the republics and provinces. What was introduced was pluralism and local self-determination without authentic democratization. Just as the federal party leadership had done in the past, the elites in the republics now curbed the development of any meaningful form of civil society. Without a civil society free to exert political pressure on the governing elites and powerful enough to be taken seriously, the establishments in the republics remained inert and in essence unassailable.

The republics and provinces also had veto power in federal decision making, guaranteed by the 1974 Constitution. This turned Yugoslavia into a de facto confederation of independent states, even though in name the country officially remained a federation. The federal government found itself gridlocked whenever any of the six republics and two provinces thought its local interests in jeopardy. No mechanism was left to reconcile existing particularistic interests and provide channels for the resolution of conflict. The result was a significant drop in the interrepublic traffic of goods, investments, and joint economic ventures, as well as cultural and scientific communication. Scientific research that would integrate country-wide resources was practically nonexistent.[34] The creation of eight autarkic, economically closed electric power systems resulted in substantial shortages of electricity in some areas of the country and surpluses in others. The railroads too became regionally fragmented and thus inadequate to serve interregional transportation needs. Decentralization of banks and investment contributed to regional duplication of industrial capacities. And while Serbia proper imported wheat, its autonomous province Vojvodina transferred its wheat across the territory of Serbia to the Croatian port of Split to be shipped abroad.[35]

If all this meant decentralization, its costs for the federal economy, as well as for the economies of the republics, were enormous, exacerbating the economic crisis. By the mid-1980s the Yugoslav people were generally worse off than ten years earlier. But the real causes of the malaise remained hidden under the increasingly open allegations of the Croats and Slovenes that federalism, Serbian economic supremacy, and the underdeveloped regions were to blame.

With the overall fragmentation of the economy and of the cultural sphere, the League of Communists itself split into eight independent regional parties. The fragmentation of the party, which had from the beginning functioned as the major roadblock to democratization, could possibly have created room for a genuine democratization in the republics and the federation as a whole. One condition was necessary for this to happen, however: the existence of a core of common interests pulling together the disintegrating union to everyone's benefit. Did such interests exist?

If the economic costs of disintegration can be considered, then they did. At the end of the 1980s Yugoslavia had behind half a century of construction of an economic infrastructure shaped to serve a closely integrated community, not a collection of hostile and self-protective duchies whose interests were local and exclusive. The economic cost alone of disintegration would have destabilized a country of much greater resources than Yugoslavia and with a much longer history of interethnic coexistence. In 1991, at the time when a major recession gripped Europe and the United States, the runaway Yugoslavian republics would have found abroad very few markets for the goods they once exchanged with five other republics and two autonomous provinces at home. The breakup of Yugoslavia represented a deeply irrational choice from the standpoint of its costs to each and every one of its nations, even under favorable economic circumstances.

The common interest, then, did exist. But three structural factors of great significance stood in the way: a deep economic crisis; a crisis of leadership; and the regionalization of economic and political concerns.

The internal roots of the economic crisis in Yugoslavia were discussed above. There were global determinants too. Like other Eastern European countries of the period, Yugoslavia found itself in the early 1980s burdened with a tremendous foreign debt. A period of reckless borrowing from foreign banks in the first half of the 1970s, when money was cheap, combined with a series of large-scale, heavy-industry investments that faltered, boosted national debt from roughly $6 billion in 1975, to almost three times as much ($17 billion) in 1979, to $19 billion by the end of the 1980s.[36] Merely paying off the interest on the debt triggered triple-digit inflation and a 60 percent bimonthly increase in the cost of everyday goods. The domestic economic and political fragmentation exacerbated the dire effects of foreign debt, precluding effective management of the borrowed funds on the federal level as well as the development of a sound long-term investment policy. Coupled with the wasteful distribution of borrowed funds, the foreign debt strongly destabilized the country's economy in the 1980s, producing a severe crisis.

Tito died in 1980, leaving behind him a vacuum of leadership that made it virtually impossible to deal with the crisis effectively. The "collective presidency" that succeeded Tito, made up of a representative from every republic and autonomous province and headed by a president elected for one year allowed every republic and autonomous province to take charge of governing the country once in every eight years. This cumbersome system of administration was justified as being antinationalistic and democratic. The only problem was that it did not provide leadership. A year was too short a period for a governing group to develop a viable strategy, much less implement it and follow it through. In place of a rigorous search for solutions to the worsening crisis came a series of half-baked experiments lacking any conceptual coherence and failing to yield any results.

THE RISE OF NATIONALISM IN SERBIA: THE SEEDS OF THE SECOND BREAKUP OF YUGOSLAVIA

The lack of top-level leadership and the resulting absence of any effective long-term strategies of economic recovery left ample room for the leadership in various republics to attempt to consolidate their political positions through regional initiatives. Two main strategies were developed in the second half of the 1980s, one Serbian and the other Croatian/Slovenian. Both turned out to be detrimental to the survival of Yugoslavia and in the long run polarized the country beyond reconciliation.

It was against this complex background of economic and leadership crisis, and the country's impending disintegration, that Slobodan Milošević, the president of the Serbian League of Communists from 1986 to 1989, formulated a policy aimed to protect and advance the interests of Serbia. His appeal to Serbian national interests to rally enormous popular support provided an effective justification for both Croatia and Slovenia boldly and aggressively to pursue their own national agendas—something that under different circumstances they would have done much more cautiously and less hastily.

The launch of nationalistic strategies at the end of the 1980s in three of six Yugoslav republics created a specific feedback loop. The contesting parties fed off of each other's nationalism. The more emboldened and aggressive Croatia and Slovenia became as the result of the moves of Milošević, the more they confirmed his claims that the disintegration of Yugoslavia was under way, and that the Serbian people, a great number of whom lived outside Serbia, were in imminent danger. It can be argued that beginning in 1990, if not earlier, Serbia on one hand, and Croatia and Slovenia on the other, functioned as each other's perfect enemies. Practically all moves on one side were used to justify countermoves on the other, a dynamic leading ultimately to war.

Milošević's initial success in Serbia was the result of his masterful articulation of some deep-seated national grievances and fears. Beginning in 1987 Milošević presented his issues to the Serbian public within a dual framework. First, he pointed to the disproportionate sacrifice of Serbia in the creation of Yugoslavia in World War I and II. He coupled this claim with the assertion that those who did not pay the price for unification (the Croats and Slovenes) now wanted to dismantle Yugoslavia, thereby threatening Serbs living outside of Serbia. Then Milošević warned of the weakened position of Serbia in relation to the federation as a whole and even in relation to its own two autonomous provinces, a consequence of the 1974 Constitution. This was a powerfully formulated set of grievances, and it touched the national nerve. Milošević's identification of national grievances and his alleged determination to correct the wrongs, something radically new on the Yugoslav political scene, struck most Serbs as bold and sincere.

Two issues were at the center of the populist strategy that brought Milošević to power: the Kosovo question (the question of the autonomy of the Albanian minority living in the Kosovo-Metohija autonomous province belonging to Serbia) and the Serb question (the question of Serbs living in Croatia and Bosnia-Hercegovina). It was the Kosovo question that provided the springboard for Milošević's nationalist populism. The reforms at the end of the 1960s had given the Kosovo Albanians a substantial measure of political and economic autonomy. As mentioned earlier, Tito's intention at the time was to curtail the strength of Serbia by granting its autonomous provinces much greater political and economic prerogatives. The Constitution of 1974 further strengthened Kosovo's autonomy, as well as that of Vojvodina, Serbia's other autonomous province to the north. As a result, the Serbian economy (like the rest of Yugoslavia's economy) was substantially fragmented. The Serbian government often found itself blocked by the local concerns of its two autonomous provinces and the veto power they could exercise at will. By the mid-1980s the perception had been created in the Serbian body politic that the republic was impossible to govern due to the virtual fragmentation of Serbia into three ministates.

Tensions intensified when massive student demonstrations shook Kosovo in 1981 with the Albanian demand to change the status of Kosovo to that of an independent republic. Serbia was in shock. Serbs have always considered Kosovo the heart of the medieval Serbian kingdom and culture, the site of a number of historical and religious monuments, including some of the most treasured medieval monasteries. Having the status of a republic would have constitutionally entitled the Kosovo Albanians to secede from

Yugoslavia and join Kosovo to Albania. This the Serbs could not and to this day cannot contemplate. In addition, most Serbs felt at the time that the Albanians already enjoyed a degree of autonomy unsurpassed by any other ethnic minority in the world: not only did they have their own economy, justice system, and police, but they also administered an entirely independent educational system that was free to import educational materials, including history textbooks, from Albania. What more did they want?

The Albanians, numbering today over 80 percent of the Kosovo population, are the only ethnic group besides the Gypsies remaining on the margins of Yugoslav society, just as they were in the Tito period.[37] The Albanian demonstrations of 1981 based the request for a separate republic on two claims: "a natural right" to the territory Albanians had occupied for five centuries or more, and "a demographic right" based on their numerical preponderance in Kosovo. Albanian claims for self-determination, however, clashed with those of the Serbs, who considered Kosovo an integral part of Serbia based on "a historical right" to the territory that was once the cradle of its medieval homeland and the center of its spiritual life. Two conflicting and deeply felt claims for self-determination were therefore at stake.

The federal leadership found it easier to call the problem by another name than to seek a compromise between two concepts of national self-determination that seemed to be mutually exclusive. The Albanian rebellion was declared a counterrevolution, the Albanian leadership was purged, and Azem Vlasi, an Albanian loyal to Yugoslavia, was installed as head of the autonomous province.

The Kosovo issue provided Milošević with the occasion to launch his rallying call to strengthen Serbia and the base to build his personal political authority. The issue was further complicated, and Milošević's position was buttressed, by the repeated attempts of ordinary Kosovo Serbs—most of them peasants—to alert both the Kosovo and the Belgrade governments to the pressures their Albanian neighbors placed on them to move out of the region.[38] Their demonstrations and pleas for help in the early and mid-1980s, however, were repeatedly ignored by both the Albanian leadership and, until 1987, the Serbian leadership, which was trying to dissipate tensions, defuse the situation, and avoid antagonizing the Albanian leadership in Kosovo.

Having pushed the moderate Serbian party leader Ivan Stambolić out of office in 1987 for being "soft on the Albanians," and having taken his place as president, Slobodan Milošević faced the situation head-on.[39] He did what no other Serbian leader before him had dared: he broke the taboo of Titoist Yugoslavia, harnessed the national question as the core of his policy, and used his high official position to declare that oppression of the

Serb population in Kosovo was the issue. While up until that point each spontaneous demonstration of the Kosovo Serbs was being suppressed by Belgrade, Milošević not only recognized their demands as legitimate but began to organize and officially promote the mass outpouring of Serb discontent, first in Belgrade and then in the Vojvodina capital, Novi Sad. Mass rallies—by that time no longer spontaneous and genuine but orchestrated from the top—were supposed to spread into Slovenia and Croatia as well. The Kosovo question was cast as an issue of Serbian national pride and integrity. Between 1987 and 1989 a climate was created in Serbia favorable to strong measures from the center to quell the upsurge of Albanian nationalism and protect the Serbs living in Kosovo. In June 1990 Milošević encountered no resistance when he enacted a new law authorizing Serbia to assume full powers in Kosovo. This law enabled him to crack down on Albanian dissidents, abolish the provincial government, take over the Kosovo media, and strip Kosovo of all autonomy.

THE RISE OF NATIONALISM IN CROATIA: THE MARCH TO WAR

Milošević's policy on Kosovo and his subsequent abolition of the autonomy of Serbia's northern province, Vojvodina, served to revive in 1989 and 1990 the old Croatian grievances against Serbia dating back to the period of the first Yugoslavia. Croatia accused Serbia of being expansionist, hegemonic, and antidemocratic. Franjo Tudjman, who became president in Croatia in 1990, buttressed his election campaign with a threefold promise: to end Serbian hegemony; to affirm Croatian identity and sovereignty; and to rid the Croats of their "Ustashe complex" (the stigma of being Nazi collaborators during World War II).

The desire for Croatian independence ("the thousand-year dream of every Croatian") as it was formulated in the electoral campaign of Tudjman's party, the Croatian Democratic Union (HDZ), had endured as a vital feature of Croatian political culture through the centuries of Austrian and Austro-Hungarian domination. Tudjman, who saw himself as an heir of the popular Croatian Peasant Party leader, Stjepan Radić, insisted that Croatia had been one of the oldest medieval states in Europe, that its modern culture was formed in the Western European, Roman Catholic tradition, and that among the South Slavs Croats represented a people apart, more cultured and worldly than the Serbs, who were Balkan in their politics, character, and manners. The Serbs, Tudjman insisted, defined the core of Yugoslav "Bolshevism" under Tito, and "Bolshevism" had robbed Croatia of its national pride as well as much of its money, which had been unjustly appropriated by the federation. The federation was controlled by the Serbs, he argued; hence the Serbs were responsible for stifling Croatia's prosperity.

Even though the appropriation of a large portion of Croatia's GNP by the federation had never been verified, Tudjman's rhetoric linked this accusation against "Bolshevik Yugoslavia" to the guilt the Serb-dominated Yugoslavia had attached to the Croatian people for the 1941–45 war period. Like the Germans, the Croats were indeed marked by the history of World War II. In the late 1980s the HDZ was trying to revise its past. Tudjman charged that "Bolshevik Yugoslavia" exaggerated the scale of Ustashe crimes in order to discredit the Croatian nation in the eyes of the world.[40] Casting Croatia as genocidal was a way for the Serbs to preserve for themselves the moral authority of victims when in fact they had their own ultranationalists in World War II. The time had come, Tudjman argued, to challenge the past as defined by Titoist Yugoslavia, to shake off the blame, and walk tall.

This issue of Croatian national pride allowed Tudjman to address two other significant national concerns: the legacy of anti-Serb sentiments and the newly awakened anticommunist sentiments. After he became president, Tudjman launched a campaign of reconciliation with the Croatian nationalists killed in World War II. The Croats must feel free, he insisted, to mourn all their dead equally, antifascist and nationalist alike. The fallen Croatian nationalists, he argued, should at long last be commemorated, and the surviving ones should receive earned pensions.[41] Emboldened by the lack of any reaction from the outside world, the HDZ and Tudjman did what would have been unthinkable in Germany: they effectively put reconciliation with the fascist past in the center of their agenda.

Another part of Tudjman's strategy was his pledge to "croatize" Croatia. He moved forcefully to fulfill his pledge soon after his inauguration. Under Tudjman's leadership, thousands of Serbs whose families had lived for generations in Croatia suddenly lost their jobs, not only in the state institutions but also in the health field, the tourist industry, and even in private firms. The Serbs, 12.5 percent of the Croatian population at the time, did occupy a disproportionate number of positions in the Croatian judiciary, police, and media. This was Tito's way of checking Croatian nationalism, and it was a cause of justifiable and long-lasting Croatian resentment. Wholesale dismissals of Serbs from all kinds of jobs in Croatia under Tudjman unnerved the Serb populations in Serbia and in Croatia itself.

The final blow was dealt when the new postelection Croatian Constitution of December 1990 changed the wording of the old socialist constitution regarding the "equal constitutive status" of Croats and Serbs. The new Constitution proclaimed the republic of Croatia to be "a national state of the Croatian nation, and the state of other nations and minorities who were its citizens." It was far from clear what the new wording meant in practice and how it affected the status of Serbs living in Croatia. But in the context of rising anxiety and frustration over the future of Yugoslavia, the new wording represented a strong provocation. The difference between the previous constitution of the republic of Croatia and the new one might have appeared subtle viewed from the outside, but from the vantage point of the Serbs it looked substantial. They felt they were being demoted from their status as a constitutive nation, one enjoyed now only by the Croat majority, and equated with the other, much less numerous "nations and minorities" living in Croatia; they did not know what this meant and were frightened.

All this was going on behind a veneer of liberalization and democratization following the first free elections in Croatia since 1945. In his "anti-Bolshevik" propaganda, Tudjman had joined the resounding anticommunist Eastern European chorus, heralded throughout the Western world as the dawning of the new era, the beginning of a "new world order." By using the same anticommunist vocabulary, Tudjman had placed himself among the liberating forces of Eastern Europe, effectively obscuring the fact that his nascent regime was a decisively right-wing one, indifferent to the issue of human rights and the liberal traditions his rhetoric evoked.

Meanwhile, Croatian paramilitary units, forming continuously since 1989, were arming themselves with weapons stolen from the federal army barracks, as well as with an increasingly massive import of arms from abroad. Tudjman embarked on completing the militarization of Croatia by building up a separate Croatian National Guard a full year before Croatia was to secede from Yugoslavia. Generously supported, as was Tudjman's electoral campaign, by funds supplied by Croatian ultranationalists who fled Yugoslavia after the end of World War II,[42] the Croatian drive to import weapons was swift and successful.[43] It was clear that the moves Tudjman aggressively pursued after his election (his revisionism regarding the Ustashe, the massive layoffs of Serbs, the changes in the new Constitution, the creation of the "National Guard," and the arms parade that followed) were not designed to effect a smooth disengagement from Yugoslavia. Instead of resolving it, Tudjman had radicalized the pivotal issue in the impending secession of Croatia and the fragmentation of Yugoslavia: the predicament of the Serbian population living outside of Serbia. Out of 8.1 million Serbs living in the former Yugoslavia, only 5 million lived in Serbia; the remainder were dispersed through Croatia and Bosnia-Hercegovina.

The "Serbian issue" had its bloody precedent in 1941, and that made all the difference. The only way to avoid bloodshed fifty years later was firmly and unequivocally to guarantee the Serbs their continued status in

Croatia, regardless of whether it separated itself from Yugoslavia or not, and to demonstrate that every effort would be made to assure their political, cultural, and human rights. By serving the Serbs a series of strong provocations instead, Tudjman fed into Serb nationalism, thereby undermining the chance for Croatia to secede peacefully.

Milošević's nationalism helped Tudjman win the elections. Tudjman's helped Milošević broaden his appeal beyond Kosovo and Serbia to Serbs throughout Yugoslavia. Tudjman's moves gave credibility to Milošević's claims that, should Yugoslavia fall apart and Croatia become a separate state, Serbia must demand the revision of the existing borders. This was already a war cry.

Prodded by Milošević, the Serbs in Croatia began to organize, arm, and set up barricades, preventing Croatian police from entering their communities. The Serbs insisted they would recognize Croatia as their homeland as long as Croatia remained a part of Yugoslavia. On October 1, 1990, in the southern region of Knin, the Croatian Serbs declared autonomy on the basis of their "geographic, historical, social, and cultural particularity." In case Croatia remained a part of Yugoslavia the Serbs would demand only cultural autonomy. But if Croatia were to secede, the Serbs would claim political and territorial autonomy. When in his electoral campaign, and later in June 1990, Tudjman said that in the future confederation it was necessary to think about the reorganization of Bosnia-Hercegovina—the land that had historically formed a geographic and political unity with Croatia—many Bosnian Serbs joined the Croatian Serbs in their determination not to be cut off from Serbia. By the fall of 1990 the leader of the Serbs in Croatia, Jovan Rašković, was advocating that an autonomous state of Croatian and Bosnian Serbs should be formed. Thus, the cross-regional alliance of the Serbs was initiated.

The Croatian war broke out in July 1991. Both Milošević and Tudjman hoped to gain from it. Milošević saw the war as the best vehicle to consolidate his power as the defender of all Serbs and to give him comparable stature to Yugoslavia's Tito. Tudjman counted on international recognition of Croatia as the victim of external aggression. Croatia's flagrant violations of the human rights of its Serb population faded next to the brutality of the war crimes being committed by the Serbian forces under arms. In the war, which cost upwards of ten thousand lives and lay waste to large swaths of Croatian land, the Croatian Serb paramilitaries, with the help of the Yugoslav People's Army and Milošević's regime, captured one-third of Croatian territory in Lika, Banija, and Slavonia. This substantiated Tudjman's warning that only international recognition could stop the war and save "anti-communist, democratic" Croatia. Had he tried to solve the Serbian question, Tudjman could have avoided the war. But it was precisely the war, in Tudjman's judgment, that would enable him to enter history as the first president of the internationally recognized independent state of Croatia.

THE DISINTEGRATION OF BOSNIA-HERCEGOVINA: THE GRAB FOR TERRITORIES

The January 1992 recognition of Croatia by the European Community and the United States—in contravention of international standards for recognition—left Bosnia-Hercegovina suspended in midair. To opt for staying in Yugoslavia meant joining Serbia, and to opt for independence meant opening the Bosnian "Serbian question." While in Croatia before the outbreak of the war the Serbs accounted for 12.2 percent of the population, in Bosnia the percentage of Serbs was more than 2.5 times that number, 31.4 percent (over 1.3 million).[44] Tudjman's electoral campaign and his subsequent strategy of reckless provocation of the Serbs, in particular his stated intention to partition Bosnia-Hercegovina, did more than any propaganda could have done to embolden Serb ultranationalists and to generate a climate of anxious anticipation among the common people. The prospect of the breakup of Yugoslavia and of the possible partition of Bosnia-Hercegovina seemed ominous in view of the ethnic mix on the ground: 43.7 percent Muslims, 31.4 percent Serbs, 17.3 percent Croats, and 5.5 percent those who declared themselves as Yugoslavs.[45]

In March and April 1992 tens of thousands of people of all nationalities and from all over Bosnia gathered in Sarajevo, carrying slogans—"We want to live together!" and "Yugo, we love you." This was a show of grassroots antiwar sentiment of a kind and magnitude that had never been seen in the former Yugoslavia. To be turned into a significant political force in the spring of 1992, this widespread antinationalist and antiwar sentiment needed to be channeled and sustained through a skillful and forceful organizing effort. But no organized pan-ethnic unifying force existed to counteract the determination of Serb ultranationalists to start the war and to inspire among the population a deeply felt sense of kinship and common belonging.

A history of latent and overt ethno-religious hostility and hatred among various groups in Bosnia is often cited as the background to the horrifying cycle of violence that ensued.[46] Yet, strife, hatred, and hostility represented only one thread of Bosnian history. After fifty years of life together in the former Yugoslavia, most Bosnians did not know or care to know until the war's outbreak the nationality of their neighbors, or even of all their kin—not because such inquiries were ever suppressed but because one's nationality had been a nonissue in the interpersonal relationships for fifty years.

Were it otherwise, it would be hard to explain the extraordinarily high rate of intermarriage in Bosnia, the highest in all of Yugoslavia.[47]

In the October 1991 session, with the Serb deputies having walked out in protest, the Muslim and Croat legislators approved a draft document working out the details of the secession of Bosnia-Hercegovina from Yugoslavia. This brought the conflagration one step closer. In November 1991 the Bosnian Serbs held a plebiscite, clearly demonstrating their full support for the republic to stay in Yugoslavia. In defiance of that plebiscite, Bosnian Muslims and Croats held their own referendum in February 1992, opting overwhelmingly for secession. The Constitution required, however, that to exact measures affecting the entire population, all three Bosnian nations must give their consent. Hence, neither the Serbian plebiscite nor the Muslim-Croat referendum was constitutional.

In December 1991 the Bosnian president, Alija Izetbegović, went ahead and applied to the European Community for recognition. When the European Community itself opted to consider the issue of constitutionality irrelevant and made international recognition of Bosnia-Hercegovina contingent on the outcome of the above-mentioned February referendum—in which only two of the three ethnic groups in Bosnia had participated—the EC too became a player in a deeply flawed, dangerous game. The EC considered the referendum crucial because it supposedly represented the expression of "the will of the Bosnian people." Yet the Serbs, one-third of the Bosnian people, had boycotted the referendum. In total indifference to that essential fact, the EC went ahead and on April 6, 1992, and recognized the independence of Bosnia-Hercegovina.

To the Serb nationalists in Serbia, Croatia, and Bosnia-Hercegovina, the specter of disintegration, now apparently imminent, offered an opportunity to advance a radical territorial program: the idea of a cross-regional linkage of the Serb-populated lands and the creation of Greater Serbia. This idea was implicit in Milošević's insistence that the disintegration of Yugoslavia made the revision of borders inevitable. By the fall of 1990, the same idea was being promoted by the Serb nationalist leader Jovan Rašković in Croatia and was being embraced by Radovan Karadžić in Bosnia. The notion that the Serbs outside of Serbia must not allow themselves to be cut off from the homeland gained overwhelming public support in 1991, as the war in Croatia ripped the republic apart and a massive influx of refugees from Croatia flooded Serbia.[48]

A powerful instrument in Milošević's strategy was his relentless insistence that Serbia itself was not at war with anyone. This appeased the moral conscience of the Serb body politic and spawned the belief that the real victims of the Croatian war were indeed only the Croatian Serbs. For the same thing to be avoided in Bosnia-Hercegovina, Milošević urged, Serbian enclaves had to form a federation and join Serbia proper.

This, of course, implied a carve-up of Bosnia, which, as events would show, was impossible to achieve without major bloodshed.

THE ROLE OF THE INTERNATIONAL COMMUNITY

In its efforts to find a solution to the crisis in Yugoslavia the international community was guided by two principles: the principle of national self-determination and the principle of the preservation of the internal borders of former Yugoslavia. The two principles were flagrantly contradictory and were based on the assumption that if it fell apart, Yugoslavia would separate as if it were a jigsaw puzzle, splitting neatly along the borders marking the republics and autonomous provinces. There was little understanding in London, Brussels, and Geneva, not to mention Washington, that the political map of Yugoslavia was superimposed on another, much older map established by history, former conflicts, wars, and lines of revenge and that the form of disintegration of a country like Yugoslavia depended more on the map lying underneath—because it had a much longer history—than on the one on top.

The international community also failed to recognize that the principle of self-determination, politically useful in the framework of colonization of one nation by another, becomes paradoxical when applied to territorial divisions between nationally intermixed populations. Under such circumstances, the principle of self-determination provides perhaps an unwitting legitimation, but a strong one nevertheless, for the bloody carve-up of territories and, ultimately, for genocide. It was thus precisely the principle of self-determination that both Serb and Croat ultranationalists used to justify their war aims. In their interpretation, the principle of self-determination fully sanctioned their objectives. The call for all Serbs to live in a single state was repeatedly presented as a call for the confirmation of the principle of Serb self-determination. Likewise, the call for the independence of Croatia was justified through a relentless reference to Croat self-determination. In the end, the principle of self-determination turned out to be the point of convergence for the international community in trying to stop the war and for the Serb and Croat ultranationalists in promoting it.

A sound, comprehensive solution treating Yugoslavia as a whole, and not as a sum of its parts, was the only way to avoid the tragedy. The only sensible path lay in upholding the principle of protection of minority rights, not the principle of national self-determination. The former—the protection of minority rights—would have accomplished what the latter could not. If the republics had been pressured to commit themselves firmly to safeguarding full civil, human, political, and cultural rights to their minorities before as states they would be eligible for international recognition, the principle of the protection of minority rights would have served all national minorities in the former Yugoslavia equally and would have crippled the expansionist projects of the Serb and Croat elites. Had the UN Security Council in the spring or summer of 1991 made the international recognition of Croatia nonnegotiably contingent on the solving of the "Serbian question" in Croatia (i.e., on steadfastly guaranteeing all political, cultural, and civil rights to Croatia's minority Serb population), the Croatian leadership would have had to face the fact that the appeal to "self-determination" was insufficient for Croatia to achieve sovereignty. It is reasonable, then, to assume that, to gain recognition, Tudjman would have tried to satisfy the condition of guaranteeing minority rights, had it been improved. Had such a condition been successfully enforced in Croatia, the ideology that rallied Serb public opinion behind Milošević (the core of which was the contention that with the loss of their rights as a nation in Croatia Serbs faced annihilation) would have been significantly undermined. There are no guarantees, of course, that in the excessively hot political climate of 1991 the war would not have broken out in any case. But with full constitutional guarantees of the unchanged status of the Serb minority in Croatia, the war would have been infinitely harder to justify and sustain.

What was lacking, then, were strict rules of peaceful disengagement imposed by the international community on all nations in Yugoslavia, the rules equally blinding for them and for the international community itself. Adequate measures, including military ones, should have been put in place to ensure compliance. Instead, the Security Council remained inactive well into the fall of 1991, and diplomacy remained in the hands of politicians lacking a sufficient grasp of the specific Yugoslav conditions.

The inaction of the international community may have been at least in part conditioned by an altogether different type of political motive: the eagerness to see communism finally and irrevocably dismantled in Europe. Had it survived, Yugoslavia may have remained a viable socialist alternative with a great potential of further liberalization, political and economic, a living challenge to the triumph of capitalism as a world system. To the EC and the United States this prospect could not have looked appealing. This may explain why the international community failed to give support to liberal socialist reformers in Yugoslavia in 1989–90, headed by then-Prime Minister Ante Marković. The reformers had launched an ambitious market-oriented economic program in 1990, encouraging private initiative as well as political pluralism while maintaining an essentially socialist orientation.

The economic reform showed positive results from the outset. But the Serb, Croat, and even Slovene elites saw Marković as a threat: he clearly stood for the transformation of the existing power structure and the preservation of Yugoslavia. The Serb, Croat, and Slovene leadership stood for the opposite. The Slovenian and Croatian leadership wanted the preservation of their own power structures and the dissolution of Yugoslavia. The Serb leadership wanted the preservation of its power structure and a Yugoslavia controlled by Milošević. Consequently, the Croat and Slovene leadership accused Marković and his reform program of being too pro-Yugoslav, while the Serb leadership accused it of being too market oriented.

Marković understood better than anyone that a way to preserve Yugoslavia at the time of its great turmoil was to hold federal elections in 1990. Separate elections in each republic he insisted, would only consolidate the gaping divisions and open the way for institutionalized nationalisms. Precisely for nationalist reasons, Croatia and Slovenia vehemently opposed federal elections. Serbia, by contrast, supported federal elections, not because of a genuine commitment of its leadership to the preservation of Yugoslavia but because pushing federal elections was a way to antagonize Croatia and Slovenia. A vicious propaganda campaign against Marković ensued in 1990 from all three national centers: Belgrade, Zagreb, and Ljubljana.

It was then that Marković badly needed determined international support, both economic and political. The future of Yugoslavia hung in the balance. Yet, even though the precariousness of the situation was clear, Marković received no support. The combined efforts of Serbia, Croatia, and Slovenia crushed the reform and with it the prospect of federal elections, the last chance for Yugoslavia to survive and avoid bloodshed.

By remaining inactive far too long, and by finally issuing their recognition to Croatia—despite its flagrant violations of minority human rights—the international community found itself supporting Tudjman's "anti-Bolshevism."[49] Tudjman's anti-Titoist rhetoric blended well with the new anticommunist thrust of Eastern Europe. That was what gave him legitimacy, Croatia's pronounced neofascist leanings notwithstanding. Eager to see communism rejected and defeated from within, the international community—as diverse as its various views on the Yugoslav crisis may have been in 1991—remained blind to the true character of Tudjman's regime and by recognizing it at the beginning of 1992 helped exacerbate the forces of ultranationalism.

The diplomatic response to the crisis was crucially affected by another exterior factor: the process of European unification taking place as the Yugoslav federation was disintegrating. The attempt to reach an agreement on the principles of peaceful disengagement in Yugoslavia could have provoked serious, unwanted ruptures between Germany, England, and France, to name only a crucial few, at a time when what they needed was consensus. The war in Yugoslavia has put the relationships between the European powers, and thereby also the whole project of European unification, to a significant test. The EC and the international community responded by giving a higher priority to their own unification than to developing a comprehensive solution for the crisis in Yugoslavia. The war was allowed to erupt and eventually to get out of control.

In the spring of 1992, following the principle of self-determination for the second time, the international community recognized the independence of Bosnia-Hercegovina. But what the EC gave Bosnia-Hercegovina on April 6 was a set of symbols—a state title and a flag—that should somehow have prevented total war between Serbia and Croatia over Bosnia-Hercegovina.

By recognizing a state whose independence was supported by only two-thirds of its people, the international community became a fourth party in the Bosnian crisis. The empty symbols of statehood turned out to be insufficient to prevent the deepening of the crisis and instead because a precipitating factor in the outbreak of war. The international community, having become a player in the crisis, committed itself to nothing and provided no safeguards whatsoever of peace in Bosnia-Hercegovina. In addition, the international community vastly underestimated the significance of the concentration of the Yugoslav Army in Bosnia-Hercegovina in the spring of 1992, after the war in Croatia had ended. As early as mid-1991 the army was made up of Serb recruits alone, other republics having pulled out their men after the collapse of the former Yugoslavia. The army was also controlled by an exclusively Serb officer corps. It no longer resembled the Yugoslav People's Army, whose pan-ethnic composition and World War II partisan legacy made it during Tito's time the cornerstone of Yugoslav unity. By 1991 the army had undergone a fundamental transformation and was committed to act in favor of Serb self-determination.[50] Milošević could not have realized his objectives without the top echelons of the army on his side.[51] After the war in Croatia, the army was transferred to Bosnia-Hercegovina to a new confrontation.

The European Community's support of Bosnian self-determination and the recognition of its independence turned into bogus acts in view of the fact that the Bosnian side remained unarmed and was encircled by a powerful war machine receiving its commands from Belgrade. The world that recognized Bosnia as an independent country remained unwilling to engage in any way to defend its independence. Bosnia-Hercegovina was consequently doomed.

THE ROAD AHEAD: THE PROSPECTS FOR PEACE AND NATIONAL COEXISTENCE IN THE FORMER YUGOSLAVIA

The war option prevailed in Yugoslavia not because its population was eager to settle old accounts and vent old loathing but above all because over a period of about three and a half years (1987–91), through their absolute control of the media, the political leadership had successfully induced fear for physical survival among all three ethnic groups.[52] Contrary to the myth generated by the Western media, neither fear nor hatred were there to begin with. The appeal to World War II collective memories had indeed played an important part in the propaganda that brought about the crisis and the war. But those memories are alive in other parts of Europe as well. It is hard to imagine that their calculated stirring elsewhere would have failed to cause profound anxieties and upheavals. Contrary to most claims, in the former Yugoslavia the passions awakened by the end of the 1980s were not the product of war memories stifled by the Communist gag, memories somehow destined to engulf the nations once the gag came off. The truth is that for half a century, the emotions attached to the memories, if not the memories themselves, had been gradually put behind, laid to rest—which was indeed the greatest achievement of Yugoslavia under Tito.

That did not mean, of course, that the memories could not be recharged and reactivated. Two conditions were necessary for this to happen: relentless evocations of the images of *new* holocausts, *new* genocides, coupled with the breakup of Yugoslavia. Milošević brought the fear of physical annihilation to a pitch; the disintegration of Yugoslavia offered a credible background to such fears. To assume that ultranationalistic paratroops armed to the teeth and encouraged by regional regimes were driven by some intrinsic, self-reproducing ethnic hatreds—cyclically reemerging from an arcane multiethnic past—is to indulge in mythmaking. It was not metaphysical past hatreds suddenly reborn that inflamed populations. It was rather an irrational but real fear of possible peril and a reawakened sense of national grievances, masking the concrete, material, present-day appetites of national regimes for territorial expansion.

The problem was that the project, particularly in the case of Bosnia-Hercegovina, involved expansion into multiethnic territories with the population so deeply intertwined—not divided—that a carve-up was virtually impossible. Had those populations lived in latent mutual hatred, the disintegration of Yugoslavia might have been less painful. It was the project of territorial expansion and the partitioning of populations, lying at the heart of the tragedy that made Yugoslavia bleed to death. The hypothesis of intrinsic, endemic Balkan hatreds is flawed on two counts. It is analytically flawed because it conflates causes and consequences. It is politically flawed because it impairs the quest for solutions. Hatred in former Yugoslavia is the consequence of the grab for territories among the Serb and Croat leadership, not its underlying foundation.

It will not be simple, once the carnage stops (and that may take years, perhaps decades), to quiet the distrust and heal the wounds. The durability of peace will depend on whether the Bosnian Muslims—who, before the end of 1993, never wanted a separate state—get the territories they now demand. It will also depend on the kinds of guarantees of autonomy and minority rights Croatia consents to granting the Croatian Serbs. Finally, the durability of peace will depend on the willingness of Serbia to grant autonomy and all minority rights to the Albanians in Kosovo. All three, in turn, hinge on the development of a robust civil society in all regions of former Yugoslavia.

It is safe to say that some form of cooperation, economic before any other, will develop soon after the war ends. Without such cooperation the regions would face insurmountable practical problems of future development and of catching up with the rest of the world. Not ideology but economic reality will render ethnically pure nation-states untenable as soon as they begin to function in peacetime as political entities. Bonds broken for the sake of the territorial carve-up will tend to form anew not because anyone has forgotten the horrors of the war but because an interrelated, unified economic system will prove to be the least costly and most profitable for all—indeed the only one viable.

The recovery will be slow, however. The physical infrastructure of industry, transportation, energy, and trade has been dismantled and much of it destroyed. Far too many homes have been razed, far too many people displaced, far too many highly qualified professionals have emigrated. All that represents a tremendous material cost. It will take, under the best of circumstances, many years to achieve the level of development of the 1990 Yugoslavia. Meanwhile, the world will have gone ahead. The place the former Yugoslavia occupied in international politics and trade has been lost and will be exceedingly hard to regain. The nations of the former Yugoslavia will gradually do better, but they will not do well for a long time.

The material necessities of everyday life will compel the populations to intermix once again. Separate states may survive, albeit not necessarily in the borders now desired by the Serb and Croat leadership. Whatever the borders, those states will soon again be multiethnic states. Their self-determination will hinge on their readiness to support a pluralistic civil society where social, political, economic, and cultural freedoms for all citizens stem from the state's commitment to minority rights. For a durable peace in Yugoslavia, nothing less will do.

NOTES

1. Slovenia was the first to establish its state in the seventh century. In the eighth century, it was overrun by a Bavarian invasion. It fell under the Hapsburgs in the thirteenth century and remained under Austro-Hungary until the end of World War I. Serbia, the largest and strongest of all South Slav medieval states, fell to the Ottoman Empire at the peak of its power in 1389. It remained under Turkish domination until after the Turkish Wars (1876–78). Croatia was an independent kingdom until the end of the eleventh century, reaching the peak of its power under Petar Kresimir (1058–74). In the last decade of the eleventh century, the territory was overrun by Hungary and remained connected with it for a full eight centuries after that. In 1097, King Kalaman of Hungary negotiated a pact granting Croatia, which had elected him king, its state rights. Bosnia, itself part of the Kingdom of Croatia at the time, refused to recognize foreign rule. Dalmatia, a southern part of Croatia, was sold in the fourteenth century by the Croatian-Hungarian King Ladislav to Venice for a hundred thousand ducats; Venice ruled it for four hundred years. In 1527, during the rule of Ferdinand of Austria, the Hapsburgs came to control Croatia. Bosnia-Hercegovina, geographically wedged between Serbia and Croatia, was until the twelfth century under either Serbian or Croatian rule. At the end of the twelfth century it became an independent state, reaching the peak of its power under King Tvrtko between 1853 and 1391. In 1463 Bosnia was overrun by Mehmet II the Conqueror; Hercegovina surrendered in 1482. In 1878 the Berlin Congress allotted Bosnia-Hercegovina to the Austro-Hungarian monarchy. The remoteness of the mountainous Montenegro region spared it from being invaded and enabled it to maintain its autonomous position in the Ottoman Empire and even to build an independent state (1860–1918). Macedonia was an independent state under the rule of King Samuilo in the tenth century but was subsequently ruled by other South Slav and non-Slav peoples well into the twentieth century. Kosovo was the seat of the expanding Serbian kingdom before the onslaught of the Turks. In the seventeenth and eighteenth century, Albanians, who had converted to Islam, began to populate the region in greater numbers. Serbia conquered Kosovo again during the Balkan Wars (1912–13), and ever since it has remained a province of Serbia.

2. At the end of the nineteenth century, Croatia and Slavonia had 209 landowners with estates of over five hundred hectares; 380 landowners had estates of between one and five hundred hectares. Branko Petranović, *Istorija Jugoslavije, 1918–1978* (History of Yugoslavia) (Belgrade: Nolit, 1978), p. 32.

3. See Anto Babić et al., eds., *Istorija naroda Jugoslavije* (The history of the peoples of Yugoslavia), vol. 1, part 4 (Belgrade: Prosveta, 1953).

4. Vojvodina was annexed to Serbia in 1919–20, as outlined in the Treaty of Versailles.

5. See Ivo Banać, *The National Question in Yugoslavia: Origin, History, Politics* (Ithaca, N.Y.: Cornell University Press, 1984), pp. 31–59.

6. Turkish invasions forced many Croats to abandon their land and migrate northward. In 1578 the Hapsburg Empire formed Vojna Kraina (the Military Frontier) in Croatia as a line of defense against the Ottoman onslaught. The Hapsburg Empire struck a deal with Serbs fleeing the Turks and settling in Croatia. The empire offered them a chance to become free owners of small plots of Croatian land, a genuine privilege within a feudal system of serfdom. Serbs were also granted religious freedoms and the rights to build their own churches. In exchange, they had to supply a certain number of foot soldiers and horsemen for military service at times of war. Wars were frequent and Serbs found themselves under arms most of the time. This prevented them from engaging in trade or artisanry; their primary occupation was military service.

Vojna Kraina served a dual defensive purpose: it was a buffer against Ottoman expansion, and it prevented the formation and consolidation of ties between different local populations that could pose a threat to the empire. Indeed, for predictable reasons, Serbs were ill received in Croatia by all relevant social groups. The Croatian feudal lords resented not being able to impose serfdom on the Serbs. The Croatian serfs held a grudge against the ethnic group of a different faith endowed with privileges the indigenous population did not enjoy. The Catholic Church saw Serbs as infidels and was quite effective in characterizing the Orthodox faith as "ungodly." These fundamental antagonisms explain why Serbs were never fully absorbed into Croatian society and why the Croats always saw them as a foreign, adversarial social element.

7. Milorad Ekmečić, *Stvaranje Jugoslavije 1790–1918* (The creation of Yugoslavia), vol. 2 (Belgrade: Prosveta, 1989), pp. 829–32.

8. It should be noted that many Croats, like the Serbs in Croatia, had no choice but to join the Hapsburg Balkanstreit Armee. The irony is that, assigned to invade Serbia in 1914, this army included 20–25 percent Serb soldiers (in addition to 50 percent Croat ones). See Dimitrije Djordjević, *The Creation of Yugoslavia 1914–1918* (Santa Barbara, Calif.: Clio Press, 1980), p. 310.

9. Prior to the nineteenth century, national consciousness was largely undeveloped among the common population. The clergy represented the only literate stratum, in addition to a scant segment of the intelligentsia. Those two social groups were the only ones maintaining national consciousness among the diverse regional populations of the same faith.

10. John Lampe, cited in Djordjević, *The Creation of Yugoslavia*, p. 343.

11. Ibid., p. 315.

12. Petranović, *Istorija Jugoslavije*, pp. 150–54.

13. Branka Prpa-Jovanović, "The Making of Yugoslavia," in Jasminka Udovički and James Ridgeway, eds., *Yugoslavia's Ethnic Nightmare* (Chicago: Lawrence Hill, 1995), p. 45.

14. For example, under Austro-Hungary the Croats and Slovenes were used to a thoroughly rationalized and predictable legal system. The legal system in the new kingdom rested on much less solid foundations, allowing for arbitrariness and corruption, which greatly irritated Croat and Slovenian elites.

15. At the very beginning of World War II Great Croatia (encompassing Croatia proper, as well as Srem—the zone between the Sava and Danube Rivers—and parts of Bosnia-Hercegovina) formed an Ustashe state under Ante Pavelić that was recognized by Hitler. Germany and Italy divided Slovenia between themselves. Italy took most of the Dalmatian coast and parts of Montenegro. Kosovo joined Albania, Bulgaria took Macedonia, and Hungary acquired a large portion of Vojvodina. Serbia, reduced to its borders preceding the Balkan Wars, was occupied by the Germans and administered by the puppet government of Milan Nedić.

16. Petranović, *Istorija Jugoslavije*, p. 198.

17. Fred Singleton, *A Short History of Yugoslav Peoples* (Washington, D.C.: Wilson Center Press, 1988), p. 177.

18. A large part of Bosnia-Hercegovina belonged to NDH during the war.

19. Draža Mihailović was appointed minister of war by the Yugoslav government in exile in 1941.

20. In the Kingdom of Yugoslavia the Communist Party was treated as a subversive organization, an agent of Moscow. Its members were persecuted and the organization was illegal, totaling in early 1941 fewer than eight thousand members.

21. See Walter Roberts and J. Tomašević, in Denison Rusinow, ed., *Yugoslavia, A Fractured Federalism* (Washington, D.C.: Wilson Center Press, 1988), p. 10.

22. Until the summer of 1943, the Allies aided the Chetniks as the representatives of the antifascist struggle in Yugoslavia. Only after a British mission led by Fitzroy Maclean arrived in September 1943 to report on the situation on the ground in Yugoslavia did it became clear that the Partisans, and not the Chetniks, represented the true patriotic, antifascist

front. The Chetniks collaborated with the Germans in their struggle against the Partisans. In 1948. Harry S. Truman awarded Draža Mihailović the Legion of Merit.

23. Denison Rusinow, *The Yugoslav Experiment 1948–1974* (Berkeley and Los Angeles: University of California Press, 1977), p. 5.

24. Petranović, *Istorija Jugoslavije*, p. 304. The wounded were carried by members of two Croat divisions: the Dalmatian division and the division of Banija.

25. Mirko Tepavac, "Tito's Yugoslavia," in Udovički and Ridgeway, *Yugoslavia's Ethnic Nightmare*, p. 68.

26. Tito, himself a Croat, was entirely unencumbered by his national origin.

27. In 1952 the name of the Yugoslav Communist Party was changed to the League of Communists of Yugoslavia (LCY).

28. Ljiljana Baćević, "Medjunacionalni odnosi" (Inter-ethnic relations) in *Istraživacki projekt CDI: Jugosloveni o drustvenoj krizi* (Research Project CDI: Yugoslavs on the social crisis) (Belgrade: Komunist, 1989), pp. 72–96. Cited in Cohen, *Broken Bonds*, p. 32.

29. Cohen, *Broken Bonds*, p. 35.

30. Gregor Tomc, "Class, Party Elites, and Ethnic Groups," in Rusinow, *Yugoslavia, A Fractured Federalism*, p. 68.

31. In 1954 that income was 48 percent of the national average; in 1975 it was 33 percent of the national average. See Gregor Tomc, *Equality and Inequality in Yugoslavia* (Ishikawa and Kawasaki, 1983), p. 83.

32. Tomc, "Class, Party Elites, and Ethnic Groups," p. 71.

33. Cohen, *Broken Bonds*, p. 35.

34. For the figures documenting the drop in interrepublic communication, see Tomc, "Class, Party Elites, and Ethnic Groups," p. 72.

35. John Burkett and Borislav Skegro, "Are Economic Fractures Widening?" in Rusinow, *Yugoslavia, A Fractured Federalism*, pp. 143–44.

36. Harold Lydall, *Yugoslavia in Crisis* (Oxford: Clarendon Press, 1989), pp. 44–45.

37. The Serb-Albanian conflict dates back to the Turkish period, when many Albanians took to Islam in order to prosper in Turkish society. In the aftermath of the First Balkan War in 1912, the European powers formed Albania with the intention of curbing the territorial ambitions of Serbia and Montenegro. Both the Albanians and the Serbs were enraged by the settlement: the Albanians because the new state included less than half of the total Albanian population, and the Serbs because a part of the territory they considered theirs went to Albania. In 1941 the Kosovo Albanians saw the Italian fascists as their liberators and collaborated with them throughout the war. A small Communist group of Kosovo Albanians joined the Partisans. In the Federative Republic of Yugoslavia, the Albanians, now a national minority, rebelled in the mid-1950s, and as a result a state of emergency was proclaimed in Kosovo. When the chief of Yugoslav police, Aleksandar Rankovic, who kept Kosovo under tight control, fell in 1966, the Albanians demanded autonomy once again and got it. Due to mismanagement, however, the region failed to achieve economic prosperity. The Kosovo Albanians remained an antagonistic social group and in the spring of 1981 demanded the status of a republic.

38. The Serb peasants expressed complaints that Albanians often burned their summer crops, killed or blinded their cattle, and repeatedly offered to purchase Serb-owned houses despite the refusal of their owners to sell. Those offers were experienced as threats, particularly because the local authorities were doing nothing to prevent the destruction of Serb property.

39. Milošević first indicated a policy shift during his visit to the town of Kosovo Polje in April 1987, when he addressed a large spontaneous rally of Kosovo Serbs and promised to protect them from oppression.

40. As early as 1967 Tudjman insisted that the official number (700,000) of those exterminated by the Ustashe in the infamous Jasenovac concentration camp between 1941 and 1945 should be divided by ten.

41. The Croatian Parliament (Sabor) debated in 1990–91 cutting off pensions for the antifascist Partisan veterans of World War II and establishing pensions for Croatian nationalists.

42. Tudjman claimed that HDZ had branches across Europe and in thirty-five U.S. cities.

43. The circumstances were advantageous. The Eastern European countries had found themselves suddenly awash with weapons and weapons-making facilities that the fall of the Berlin Wall had made obsolete. Before they could retool their industries and switch their production to civilian purposes, they needed to dispose of a huge stock of arms left over from the Cold War era. They found in Croatia, and throughout the former Yugoslavia, eager customers.

44. The elections of December 1990 in Bosnia-Hercegovina showed the body politic already divided along national lines. The three national parties, the Muslim SDA (Party of Democratic Action), the Serb SDS (Serbian Democratic Party), and the Croatian HDZ (Croatian Democratic Union), each won among their own ethnic group. An ill-fated, eight member multiethnic presidency was elected, with Alija Izetbegović as president. Hanging over the region was the question of the independence of Bosnia-Hercegovina. This was the question that led to the ultimate confrontation between the three ethnic groups and eventually to war.

45. Lidija Basta-Posavec, et al., *Inter-ethnic Conflict and the War in the Former Yugoslavia and the Possibilities for a Solution* (Belgrade: Institute for European Studies, 1992), p. 11.

46. Old hatreds are cited as the underlying causes of the war even by some serious analysts. See, for example, Cohen, *Broken Bonds*, p. 238; Mark Thompson, *A Paper House: The Ending of Yugoslavia* (New York: Pantheon Books, 1992), pp. 125–47.

47. The rate was 24 to 28 percent, depending on the region.

48. The state-controlled media in Belgrade cast the war in Croatia as a renewed genocide against the Serbs, downplaying or misrepresenting the massacres of the Croatian population and the destruction of Croatian cities like Vukovar and Dubrovnik.

49. The international community supported the Slovenian break with socialism as well. The situation in Slovenia was less complicated for geographic as well as demographic reasons. Being an ethnically homogeneous region, Slovenia did not need a war to separate from Yugoslavia.

50. The transformation is analyzed in Stipe Sikavica, "The Collapse of Tito's Army," in Udovički and Ridgeway, *Yugoslavia's Ethnic Nightmare*, pp. 133–55.

51. See Stojan Cerović, "Osveta oruzja," (The revenge of the arms) *Bahanalije* (Belgrade: Vreme knjige, 1993), pp. 23–27.

52. Television played a pivotal role in this propaganda as well as in the supernationalist buildup in the former Yugoslavia. For an analysis of the use of television as a medium of war, see Milan Milošević, "The Media Wars," in Udovički and Ridgeway, *Yugoslavia's Ethnic Nightmare*, pp. 115–32. See also Mark Thompson, *Forging War: The Media in Serbia, Croatia, and Bosnia-Hercegovina* (Article 19, International Centre against Censorship, 1994).

◻ Select Bibliography ◻

Abboushi, W. F. *The Unmaking of Palestine*. Cambridge: Middle East and North African Studies Press, 1988.

Abdel-Malek, Anouar. *Nation and Revolution*. Albany: State University of New York Press, 1981.

Abdo, Nahla. "Women of the Intifada: Gender, Class and National Liberation." *Race and Class* 32, no. 4 (1991).

Abed-Rabbo, Samir, and Doris Safie, eds. *The Palestinian Uprising*. Belmont, Mass.: Association of Arab-American University Graduates, 1990.

Abraham, Sameer Y. "The Development and Transformation of the Palestine National Movement." In Naseer H. Aruri, ed., *Occupation: Israel over Palestine*. Belmont, Mass.: Association of Arab-American University Graduates, 1983.

Abu-Lughod, Janet. "The Demographic Transformation of Palestine." In Ibrahim Abu-Lughod, ed., *The Transformation of Palestine*. Evanston, Ill.: Northwestern University Press, 1971.

Acosta, Ivonne. *La mordaza: Puerto Rico 1948–1957*. San Juan: Editorial Edil, 1987.

African National Congress. "Strategy and Tactics of the South African Revolution." In *Forward to Freedom*. London: Sechaba Publications, 1969.

Alexander, Neville. "An Approach to the National Question in South Africa." *Azania Worker* 2, no. 2 (1985).

Alexeyeva, Ludmilla. *Soviet Dissent: Contemporary Movements for National, Religious, and Human Rights*. Middletown, Conn.: Wesleyan University Press, 1985.

Alterman, Eric. "Report from the Occupied Territories." *World Policy Journal* 5, no. 3 (1988): 519–41.

Amin, Samir. *Class and Nation, Historically and in the Current Crisis*. New York: Monthly Review Press, 1980.

Anderson, Walter, and Shridhar Damle. *The Brotherhood in Saffron: The Rashtriya Swayamsevak Sangh and Hindu Revivalism*. New Delhi: Vistaar Publishers, 1987.

Apalategui, Jokin. *Nationalisme et question nationale au pays Basque, 1830–1976* (Nationalism and the national question in the Basque Country, 1830–1976). Bilbao: Edition Elkar, 1976.

———. *Los vascos de la autonomía a la independencia: Formación y desarrollo del concepto de nación vasca*. San Sebastián: Editorial Txertoa, 1985.

Arrighi, Giovanni, and John S. Saul. "Nationalism and Revolution in Sub-Saharan Africa." In Ralph Miliband and John S. Saul, eds., *The Socialist Register*. London: Merlin, 1969.

Aruri, Naseer. *The Palestine Resistance to Israeli Occupation*. Wilmette, Ill.: Medina University Press International, 1970.

———, ed. *Occupation: Israel over Palestine*. Belmont, Mass.: Association of Arab-American University Graduates, 1983.

Bagramov, E. *The CPSU's Nationalities Policy*. Moscow: Progress Publishers, 1988.

Banac, Ivo. *The National Question in Yugoslavia: Origins, History, Politics*. Ithaca, N.Y.: Cornell University Press, 1984.

Barrett, Michele. *Women's Oppression Today: Problems in Marxist Feminist Analysis*. London: Villiers Publications, 1980.

Beck, Lois, and Nikki Keddie. *Women in the Muslim World*. Cambridge, Mass.: Harvard University Press, 1978.

Beinin, Joel. "Communism in Palestine." *MERIP Reports*, no. 55 (March 1977).

Benallegue, Nora. "Algerian Women in the Struggle for Independence and Reconstruction." *International Social Science Journal* 35, no. 4 (1983).

Berberoglu, Berch. *The Internationalization of Capital: Imperialism and Capitalist Development on a World Scale*. New York: Praeger, 1987.

———. *Political Sociology: A Comparative/Historical Approach*. New York: General Hall, 1990.

———. "Nationalism and Ethnic Rivalry in the Early Twentieth Century." *Nature, Society, and Thought* 4, no. 3 (1991): 269–73.

———. *The Legacy of Empire: Economic Decline and Class Polarization in the United States*. Westport, Conn.: Praeger, 1992.

———. *The Political Economy of Development: Development Theory and the Prospects for Change in the Third World*. Albany: State University of New York Press, 1992.

———. *Class Structure and Social Transformation*. Westport, Conn.: Praeger, 1994.

———, ed. *Power and Stability in the Middle East*. London: Zed Books, 1989.

Bergad, Laird W. "Toward Puerto Rico's Grito de Lares: Coffee, Social Stratification, and Class Conflict." *Hispanic American Historical Review* 60 (November 1980).

Bernstein, Hilda. *For Their Triumphs and for Their Tears: Women in Apartheid South Africa*. London: International Defence and Aid Fund for Southern Africa, 1985.

Beşikçi, Ismail. *Devletlerarasi sömürge Kürdistan* (Kurdistan: Colony of several states). Istanbul: Alan Yayincilik, 1990.

Bhana, Surendra. *The United States and the Development of the Puerto Rican Status Question 1936–1968*. Wichita: University Press of Kansas, 1975.

Black, George. *Triumph of the People: The Sandinista Revolution in Nicaragua*. London: Zed Books, 1981.

Blaut, James M. *The National Question: Decolonising the Theory of Nationalism*. London: Zed Books, 1987.

Boismenu, Gérard, et al. *Espace régional et nation*. Montreal: Boréal Express, 1983.

Bourque, Gilles. *Classes sociales et question nationale au Québec 1760–1840* (Social classes and the national question in Quebec 1760–1840). Montreal: Parti Pris, 1970.

———. *L'Etat capitaliste et la question nationale* (The capitalist state and the national question). Montreal: Presses de l'Université de Montréal, 1977.

———. "Class, Nation, and the Parti Québécois." In Alain G. Gagnon, ed., *Quebec, State and Society*. Toronto: Methuen, 1984.

———. "Traditional Society, Political Society and Quebec Sociology, 1945–1980." *Canadian Review of Sociology and Anthropology* 26, no. 3 (May 1989).

Brenner, Johanna, and Nancy Holmstrom. "Women's Self-Organization: Theory and Strategy." *Monthly Review* 34, no. 11 (1983): 34–46.

Brunet, Michel. *Québec, Canada anglais, Deux itinéraires un affrontement* (Quebec, English Canada, Two iteneraries one confrontation). Montreal: HMH, 1968.

Bruno, Miñi Seijo. *La insurrección nacionalista en Puerto Rico—1950* (The nationalist insurrection in Puerto Rico, 1950). San Juan: Editorial Edil, 1989.

Brutents, K. N. *National Liberation Revolutions Today.* 2 vols. Moscow: Progress Publishers, 1977.

Buckland, Patrick. *A History of Northern Ireland.* New York: Holmes and Meier, 1981.

Budeiri, Musa. *The Palestinian Communist Party.* London: Ithaca Press, 1979.

Bundy, Colin. "Land and Liberation: Popular Rural Protest and the National Liberation Movements in South Africa, 1920–1960." In Shula Marks and Stanley Tarpido, eds., *The Politics of Race, Class, and Nationalism in Twentieth Century South Africa.* London: Longman, 1987.

Burchett, Wilfred. *Vietnam: Inside Story of the Guerrilla War.* New York: International Publishers, 1965.

———. 1969. *Vietnam Will Win!* New York: Monthly Review Press.

Burgos-Debray, Elisabeth, ed. *I, Rigoberta Menchú: An Indian Woman in Guatemala.* Translated by Ann Wright. London: Verso, 1983.

Cell, John. *Segregation, The Highest Stage of White Supremacy: The Origins of Segregation in South Africa and the American South.* Cambridge: Cambridge University Press, 1982.

Chaliand, Gérard. *Armed Struggle in Africa.* New York: Monthly Review Press, 1969.

———, ed. *People without a Country: The Kurds and Kurdistan.* London: Zed Books, 1980.

Chesneaux, Jean, et al. *China from the 1911 Revolution to Liberation.* Sussex: Harvester Press, 1977.

Chinchilla, Norma S. "Women in Revolutionary Movements: The Case of Nicaragua." Working paper no. 27 Michigan State University, East Lansing, Mich., June 1983.

Chorbajian, Levon, et al. *The Caucasian Knot: The History and Geopolitics of Nagorno Karabagh.* London: Zed Books, 1994.

Chu Zhihua. *Zhongguo geming yu zhongguo shehui ge jieji* (China's revolution and China's social classes). Shanghai: Lienhou Shudian, 1930.

Clark, Robert. *The Basques: The Franco Years and Beyond.* Reno: University of Nevada Press, 1979.

———. *The Basque Insurgents: ETA 1952–1980.* Madison: University of Wisconsin Press, 1984.

Clark, Truman R. *Puerto Rico and the United States, 1917–1933.* Pittsburgh, Pa.: University of Pittsburgh Press, 1975.

Cleaver, Tessa, and Marion Wallace. *Namibia: Women in War.* London: Zed Books, 1990.

Cobban, Helena. *The Palestinian Liberation Organization.* Cambridge: Cambridge University Press, 1984.

———. "The PLO and the Intifada." *Middle East Journal* 44, no. 2 (1990): 207–33.

Cohen, Leonard. *Broken Bonds: The Disintegration of Yugoslavia.* Boulder, Colo.: Westview Press, 1993.

Cohen, Leonard, and Paul Warwick. *Political Cohesion in a Fragile Mosaic: The Yugoslav Experience.* Boulder, Colo.: Westview Press, 1983.

Collinson, Helen, ed. *Women and Revolution in Nicaragua.* London: Zed Books, 1990.

Connolly, James. *Socialism and Nationalism: A Selection from the Writings of James Connolly.* With introduction and notes by Desmond Ryan. Dublin, 1948.

Danforth, Sandra. "The Social and Political Implications of Muslim Middle Eastern Women's Participation in Violent Political Conflict." *Women and Politics* 4 (Spring 1984).

Das Gupta, Jyotirindra. *Language Conflict and National Development: Group Politics and National Language Policy.* Bombay: Oxford University Press, 1970.

Davis, Horace B. *Nationalism and Socialism: Marxist and Labor Theories of Nationalism to 1917*. New York: Monthly Review Press, 1967.

———. *Toward a Marxist Theory of Nationalism*. New York: Monthly Review Press, 1978.

Davis, Miranda. *Third World—Second Sex*. London: Zed Books, 1987.

Debray, Régis. *Revolution in the Revolution?* New York: Monthly Review Press, 1967.

———. "Marxism and the National Question: Interview with Regis Debray." *New Left Review*, no. 105 (1977).

Dietz, James L. *Economic History of Puerto Rico: Institutional Changes and Capitalist Development*. Princeton, N.J.: Princeton University Press, 1986.

Dixon, R., ed. *Ireland and the Irish Question*. New York: International Publishers, 1972.

Djordjevic, Dimitrije. *The Creation of Yugoslavia, 1914–1918*. Santa Barbara, Calif.: Clio Press, 1980.

Dryer, June. *China's Forty Millions: Minority Nationalities and National Integration in the People's Republic of China*. Cambridge, Mass.: Harvard University Press, 1976.

Dubow, Saul. *Racial Segregation and the Origins of Apartheid in South Africa, 1919–1936*. New York: St. Martin's Press, 1989.

du Devoir, Dossier. *Le Québec et le lac Meech*. Montreal: Guérin, 1987.

Du Wenzhan. *Renkou zongheng tan* (On the population). Beijing: Zhongguo Qingnian Chubanshe, 1985.

Eid, N. F. *Le clergé et le pouvoir politique au Québec* (The clergy and power politics in Quebec). Montreal: HMH, 1978.

el-Rayyes, Riad, and Dunia Nahas. *Guerrillas for Palestine*. New York: St. Martin's Press, 1976.

Erwin, Alec. "The Question of Unity in Struggle." *South African Labour Bulletin* 11, no. 1 (1985).

Fanon, Frantz. *Studies in a Dying Colonialism*. New York: Monthly Review Press, 1965.

———. *Toward the African Revolution*. New York: Grove, 1967.

Fan Wenlan. "Problems of Conflict and Fusion of Nationalities in Chinese History." *Social Science in China* 1 (1980).

Farsoun, Samih. "Israel's Goal of Destroying the PLO Is Not Achievable." *Journal of Palestine Studies* 11, no. 4 (1982).

Feit, Edward. *South Africa: The Dynamics of the African National Congress*. London: Oxford University Press, 1962.

Fei Xiaotong. "Ethnic Identification in China." *Social Science in China* 1 (1980).

Ferrao, Luis Angel. *Pedro Albizu Campos y el nacionalismo puertorriqueño* (Pedro Albizu Campos and Puerto Rican nationalism). San Juan: Editorial Cultural, 1990.

Fine, Robert. "The Antinomies of Nationalism and Democracy in the South African Liberation Struggle." *Review of African Political Economy*, no. 45/46 (1989).

Flynn, P. "Women Challenge the Myth." *NACLA Report on the Americas* 14 (September–October 1980).

Fournier, Louis. *FLQ: Histoire d'un mouvement clandestin* (FLQ: The history of a clandestine movement). Montreal: Québec-Amérique, 1982.

Fournier, Pierre. *Capitalisme et politique au Québec* (Capitalism and politics in Quebec). Montreal: Albert Saint-Martin, 1981.

Fraser, Graham. *PQ: René Lévesque and the Parti Québécois in Power*. Toronto: Macmillan, 1984.

Gaffikin, Frank, and Mike Morrissey. *Northern Ireland: The Thatcher Years*. London: Zed Books, 1990.

Galib Brás, Salomé. "Ante el Congreso la batalla por la nacionalidad puertorriqueña" (The battle for Puerto Rican nationhood before Congress). *El Nuevo Día* (*New Day*), January 31, 1991.

García, Gervasio L., and Angel G. Quintero-Rivera. *Desafío y solidaridad: Breve hist-*

oria del movimiento obrero puertorriqueño (Challenge and solidarity: Brief history of the Puerto Rican workers' movement). San Juan: Ediciones Huracán, 1982.

Genet, Jean. "Four Hours in Shatila." *Journal of Palestine Studies* 12, no. 2 (1983): 3–22.

George, Vic, and Nick Manning. *Socialism, Social Welfare and the Soviet Union*. London: Routledge and Kegan Paul, 1980.

Gerhart, Gail. *Black Power in South Africa: The Evolution of an Ideology*. Berkeley: University of California Press, 1978.

Ghassemlou, Abdul Rahman. *Kurdistan and the Kurds*. London: Collets Holdings, 1965.

Giacaman, Rita, and Penny Johnson. "Palestinian Women: Breaking Barricades and Breaking Barriers." In Zachary Lockman and Joel Beinin, eds., *Intifada: The Palestinian Uprising against Israeli Occupation*. Boston: South End Press, 1989.

González Portilla, Manuel. *La formación de la sociedad capitalista en el país vasco* (The formation of capitalist society in the Basque Country). San Sebastián: Haramburu, 1981.

Gordon, David C. *Women of Algeria*. Cambridge, Mass.: Harvard University Press, 1968.

Gott, Richard. *Guerrilla Movements in Latin America*. London: Thomas Nelson, 1970.

Guelke, Adrian. *Northern Ireland: The International Perspective*. Dublin: Gill and Macmillan, 1988.

Guevara, Che. *Venceremos! The Speeches and Writings of Che Guevara*. Edited by John Gerassi. New York: Macmillan, 1968.

Gunter, Michael. *The Kurds in Turkey*. Boulder, Colo.: Westview Press, 1990.

Gupta, Dipankar. *Nativism in a Metropolis: The Shiv Sena in Bombay*. Delhi: Manohar Publishers, 1982.

Gupta, Dipankar, et al. "Punjab: Communalized beyond Politics." *Economic and Political Weekly* (Bombay) 23 (1988).

Hamelin, Jean, and Yves Roby. *Histoire économique du Québec 1851–1896* (Economic history of Quebec, 1851–1896). Montreal: Fides, 1971.

Hartmann, Heidi. "The Unhappy Marriage of Marxism and Feminism: Toward a More Progressive Union." In Alison M. Jaggar and Paula S. Rothenberg, eds., *Feminist Frameworks: Alternative Accounts of the Relations between Women and Men*. New York: McGraw-Hill, 1984.

Hassassian, M. S. *Palestine: Factionalism in the National Movement*. East Jerusalem: PASSIA, 1990.

Hay, William Rupert. *Two Years in Kurdistan: Experiences of a Political Officer, 1918–1920*. London: Sidgwick and Jackson, 1921.

Hazelkorn, Ellen. "Why Is There No Socialism in Ireland?" *Science and Society* 53, no. 2 (Summer 1989).

Heberer, Thomas. *China and Its National Minorities: Autonomy or Assimilation*. Armonk, N.Y.: M. E. Sharpe, 1989.

Heinrich, Lothar. *Die Kurdische Nationalbewegung in der Türkei* (The Kurdish national movement in Turkey). Hamburg: Deutsches Orient-Institut, 1989.

Hirson, Baruch, *Year of Fire, Year of Ash*. London: Zed Press, 1979.

Hobsbawm, Eric. *The Age of Revolution: 1789–1848*. New York: World, 1962.

———. "Some Reflections on Nationalism." In Thomas J. Nossiter et al., eds., *Imagination and Precision in the Social Sciences*. London: Faber and Faber, 1972.

———. *The Age of Capital: 1848–1875*. New York: Scribner's, 1975.

Ho Chi Minh. *Ho Chi Minh on Revolution: Selected Writings, 1920–1966*. Edited by Bernard B. Fall. New York: Signet, 1968.

Hodges, Donald C., and Robert Elias Abu Shanab, eds. *NLF: National Liberation Fronts, 1960/1970*. New York: William Morrow, 1972.

Houle, François. "Réflexions sur la restructuration de l'état au Canada" (Reflections on the restructuring of the state in Canada). *Interventions économiques*, no. 18 (1987).

Ibárruri, Dolores. *España, estado multinacional* (Spain, multinational state). Paris: Ediciones Sociales, 1971.

Ibrahim, Ferhad. *Die Kurdische Nationalbewegung im Iraq* (The Kurdish national movement in Iraq). Berlin: Schwarz, 1983.

———. "Der Golfkrieg und die Kurdische Widerstandsbewegung" (The Gulf War and the Kurdish movement of resistance). In Georg Stein, ed., *Nachgedanken zum Golfkrieg* (Reflections on the Gulf War). Heidelberg: Palmyra, 1991.

Iglesias, César Andreú. *Independencia y socialismo* (Independence and socialism). San Juan: Librería Estrella Roja, 1951.

Ismail, Tareq Y. *The Arab Left*. Syracuse, N.Y.: Syracuse University Press, 1976.

Jackson, T. A. *Ireland Her Own: An Outline History of the Irish Struggle*. New York: International Publishers, 1970.

Jayawardena, Kumari. *Feminism and Nationalism in the Third World*. London: Zed Books, 1986.

Jerusalem Media and Communications Centre. *The Intifada: An Overview*. East Jerusalem: JMCC, 1989.

Jiryis, Sabri. *Arabs in Israel*. Beirut: Institute for Palestinian Studies, 1968.

Jukes, Geoffrey. *The Soviet Union in Asia*. Berkeley: University of California Press, 1973.

Kane-Berman, John. *Soweto: Black Revolt, White Reaction*. Johannesburg: Ravan Press, 1978.

Kang, T. S. *Nationalism and the Crises of Ethnic Minorities in Asia*. Westport, Conn.: Greenwood Press, 1979.

Karis, Thomas, Gail Gerhart, and Gwendlyn Carter, eds. *From Protest to Challenge: Documentary History of African Politics in South Africa, 1882–1964*. Vol. 3. Stanford: Hoover Institution Press, 1973.

Katz, Zev, Rosemarie Rogers, and Frederic Harned, eds. *Handbook of Major Soviet Nationalities*. New York: Free Press, 1975.

Kaur, Manmohan. *Women in India's Freedom Struggle*. New Delhi: Sterling Publishers, 1985.

Kazi, Hamida. "Palestinian Women and the National Liberation Movement: A Social Perspective." In Khamsin, ed., *Women in the Middle East*. London: Zed Books, 1987.

Kelley, Kevin. *The Longest War: Northern Ireland and the IRA*. Westport, Conn.: Lawrence Hill, 1982.

Kenane, Derek. *The Kurds and Kurdistan*. London: Oxford University Press, 1964.

Khalidi, Rashid. "Palestinian Peasant Resistance to Zionism before World War I." In Edward Said and Christopher Hitchens, eds., *Blaming the Victims*. London: Verso, 1988.

Kiray, Mübeccel. "Migration und Urbanisierung in der Türkei" (Migration and urbanization in Turkey). In *Jahrbuch zur Geschchte und Gesellschaft des Vorderen Orients* (Yearbook for Middle Eastern History and Society). Berlin: Parabolis, 1987.

Knauss, Peter R. *The Persistence of Patriarchy: Class, Gender, and Ideology in Twentieth Century Algeria*. New York: Praeger, 1987.

Kothari, Rajni. "Nation Building and Political Development." In S. C. Dube, ed., *India since Independence: Social Report on India*. Delhi: Vikas, 1977.

Kuumba, Monica Bahati. "Sisters in Struggle: A Historical Materialist Analysis of Women in National Liberation Movements." Ph.D. diss., Howard University, 1993.

Lang, David Marshall. *A Modern History of Soviet Georgia*. New York: Grove Press, 1962.

Lapchick, Richard E. "The Role of Women in the Struggle against Apartheid in South

Africa." In Filomina Chioma Steady, ed., *The Black Woman Cross Culturally*. Rochester, Vt.: Schenkman Books, 1981.

Lapchick, Richard E., and Stephanie Urdang. *Opression and Resistance: The Struggle of Women in Southern Africa*. Westport, Conn.: Greenwood Press, 1982.

Laurin-Frenette, Nicole. *Production de l'état et formes de la nation* (Production of the state and forms of the nation). Montreal: Nouvelle Optique, 1978.

Le Duan. *This Nation and Socialism Are One*. Chicago: Vanguard, 1976.

Lee, Alfred McClung. *Terrorism in Northern Ireland*. New York: General Hall, 1983.

Lenin, V. I. "The Socialist Revolution and the Right of Nations to Self-Determination: Theses." In V. I. Lenin, *Collected Works*, vol. 22. Moscow: Progress Publishers, 1964.

———. "Critical Remarks on the National Question." In V. I. Lenin, *Collected Works*, vol. 20. Moscow: Progress Publishers, 1964.

———. "The Right of Nations to Self-Determination." In V. I. Lenin, *Collected Works*, vol. 20. Moscow: Progress Publishers, 1964.

———. "Preliminary Draft Theses on the National and the Colonial Questions." In V. I. Lenin, *Collected Works*, vol. 31. Moscow: Progress Publishers, 1966.

———. "The Question of Nationalities or 'Autonomisation.' " in V. I. Lenin, *Collected Works*, vol. 36. Moscow: Progress Publishers, 1966.

Lesch, Ann Mosely. *Arab Politics in Palestine*. Ithaca: Cornell University Press, 1979.

Letamendía, Francisco. *Breve historia de Euskadi, de la prehistoria a nuetros días* (Brief history of the Basque Country, from prehistory to the present day). Paris: Ruedo Ibérico, 1980.

———. *Euskadi, pueblo y nación* (The Basque Country, people and nation). 7 vols. Bilbao: Kriselu, 1991.

Lévesque, René. *La passion du Québec* (The passion of Quebec). Montreal: Québec-Amérique, 1978.

Lobao, Linda. "Women in Revolutionary Movements: Changing Patterns of Latin American Guerrilla Struggle." In Guida West and Rhoda Lois Blumberg, eds., *Women and Social Protest*. London: Oxford University Press, 1990.

Lockman, Zachary, and Joel Beinin. *Intifada: The Palestinian Uprising against Israeli Occupation*. Boston: South End Press, 1989.

Lodge, Tom. *Black Politics in South Africa since 1945*. Johannesburg: Ravan Press, 1983.

López, José A. *Puerto Rican Nationalism: A Reader*. Chicago: Editorial Coqui, 1977.

López Adán, Emilio. *Autodeterminación de los pueblos: Un reto para Euskadi y Europa* (Peoples' self-determination: A challenge for the Basque Country and Europe). Vol. 1. Bilbao: Colectivo Herria 2000 Eliza, 1985.

Löwy, Michael. "Marxism and the National Question." In Robin Blackburn, ed., *Revolution and Class Struggle: A Reader in Marxist Politics*. Glasgow: Fontana, 1977.

Lustick, Ian. *Arabs in the Jewish State*. Austin: University of Texas Press, 1980.

Luxemburg, Rosa. *The National Question: Selected Writings of Rosa Luxemburg*. Edited with an introduction by Horace B. Davis. New York: Monthly Review Press, 1976.

Lydall, Harold. *Yugoslavia in Crisis*. Oxford: Clarendon Press, 1989.

MacDonald, Michael. *Children of Wrath: Political Violence in Northern Ireland*. Cambridge: Polity Press, 1986.

Magee, John. *Northern Ireland: Crisis and Conflict*. London: Routledge and Kegan Paul, 1974.

Maldonado Denis, Manuel. *Puerto Rico: Una interpretación histórico-social* (Puerto Rico: A socio-historical interpretation). Mexico City: Siglo XXI, 1969.

———. "Prospects for Latin American Nationalism: The Case of Puerto Rico." *Latin American Perspectives* 3, no. 3 (1976).

————. *The Emigration Dialectic: Puerto Rico and the USA*. New York: International Publishers, 1980.

Malherbe, Jean Paul. *Le nationalisme basque et les transformations sociopolitiques au pays basque nord* (Basque nationalism and sociopolitical transformations in the northern Basque Country). Paris: Editions Harmattan, 1980.

Mallison, W. Thomas, and S. V. Mallison. *The Palestine Problem in International Law*. New York: Longman, 1986.

Mandel, Neville. *The Arabs and Zionism before World War I*. Berkeley: University of California Press, 1976.

Mandela, Nelson. *No Easy Walk to Freedom: Articles, Speeches, and Trial Addresses of Nelson Mandela*. London: Heinemann, 1965.

Mao Zedong. *Collected Works*. Vol. 1. Beijing: Foreign Languages Publishing House, 1968.

Marcus, Tessa. "The Women's Question and National Liberation in South Africa." In Maria van Diepen, ed., *The National Question in South Africa*. London: Zed Books, 1988.

Mari Brás, Juan. *El independentismo en Puerto Rico: Su pasado, su presente y su porvenir* (The independence movement in Puerto Rico: Its past, its present, and its future). San Juan: Editorial CEPA, 1984.

Marks, Shula, and Stanley Trapido, eds. *The Politics of Race, Class, and Nationalism in Twentieth Century South Africa*. London and New York: Longman, 1987.

Ma Yin. *China's Minority Nationalities*. Beijing: New World Press, 1985.

McBride, Sean. *Israel in Lebanon*. London: Ithaca Press, 1988.

McGarry, John, and Brendan O'Leary, eds. *The Future of Northern Ireland*. Oxford: Clarendon Press, 1990.

McRoberts, Kenneth and Dale Posgate. *Quebec: Social Change and Political Crisis*. Toronto: McClelland and Stewart, 1976.

————. *Développement et modernisation du Québec* (Development and modernization in Quebec). Montreal: Boréal Express, 1983.

Meer, Fatima. "Organizing under Apartheid." In Miranda Davis, ed., *Third World—Second Sex*. London: Zed Books, 1987.

Miller, Norman, and Roderick Aya, eds. *National Liberation: Revolution in the Third World*. New York: Free Press, 1971.

Millotte, Mike. *Communism in Modern Ireland*. Dublin: Gill and Macmillan, 1984.

Minces, Juliette. "Women in Algeria." In Lois Beck and Nikki Keddie, eds., *Women in the Muslim World*. Cambridge, Mass.: Harvard University Press, 1978.

Mohanty, Chandra Talpade. "Under Western Eyes: Feminist Scholarship and Colonial Discourses." In Chandra Talpade Mohanty, Ann Russo, and Lourdes Torres, eds. *Third World Women and the Politics of Feminism*. Bloomington: Indiana University Press, 1991.

Mondlane, Eduardo. *Struggle in Mozambique*. Baltimore: Penguin, 1969.

Motyl, Alexander J. *Sovietology, Rationality, Nationality: Coming to Grips with Nationalism in the USSR*. New York: Columbia University Press, 1990.

Muhateer. "Jixu gaige minzu jiaoyu" (Continue to reform nationality education). *Xinjiang Shehui Kexue* (Social services of Xinjiang), no. 3 (June 15, 1989).

Murray, Martin J. *South African Capitalism and Black Political Opposition*. Cambridge, Mass.: Schenkman, 1982.

————. *The Revolution Deferred: The Painful Birth of Post-Apartheid South Africa*. London and New York: Verso, 1994.

Murray, Vera. *Le Parti Québécois*. Montreal: HMH, 1976.

Nairn, Tom. "The Modern Janus." *New Left Review*, no. 94 (1975).

————. *The Break-Up of Britain*. London: New Left Books, 1977.

Nalbandian, Louise. *The Armenian Revolutionary Movement: The Development of Armenian Political Parties through the Nineteenth Century. Berkeley: University of California Press, 1963.

Nayar, Baldev Raj. Minority Politics in Punjab. Princeton, N.J.: Princeton University Press, 1966.

Nkrumah, Kwame. Neo-Colonialism: The Last Stage of Imperialism. New York: International Publishers, 1965.

———. Handbook of Revolutionary Warfare. New York: International Publishers, 1969.

No Sizwe [Neville Alexander]. One Azania, One Nation: The National Question in South Africa. London: Zed Books, 1977.

Núñez, Luis. Clases sociales en Euskadi. San Sebastián: Editorial Txertoa, 1977.

Odeh, B. J. Lebanon: Dynamics of Conflict. London: Zed Books, 1985.

Olson, Robert. The Emergence of Kurdish Nationalism and the Sheikh Said Rebellion, 1880–1925. Austin: University of Texas Press, 1989.

O'Meara, Dan. Volkskapitalisme: Class, Capital, and Ideology in the Development of Afrikaner Nationalism, 1934–1948. Cambridge: Cambridge University Press, 1983.

Omvedt, Gail. "Caste, Class and Women's Liberation in India." Bulletin of Concerned Asian Scholars 7, no. 1 (1975).

Onaindía, Mario. La lucha de clases en Euskadi (1939–1980) (Class struggle in the Basque Country, 1939–1980). San Sebastián: Hordago, 1980.

Organization of Angolan Women (OMA). Angolan Women Building the Future: From National Liberation to Women's Emancipation. Translated by Marga Holness. London: Zed Books, 1984.

Ortzi [Francisco Letamendía]. Historia de Euskadi: El nacionalismo vasco y ETA (The history of the Basque Country: Basque nationalism and ETA). Paris: Ruedo Ibérico, 1975.

Ouellet, Fernand. Histoire économique et sociale du Québec 1760–1850 (Economic and social history of Quebec, 1760–1850). Montreal: Fides, 1971.

Owen, Roger. The Middle East in the World Economy. London: Methuen, 1981.

Panitch, Leo. The Canadian State. Toronto: University of Toronto Press, 1977.

Pasapera, Germán Delgado. Puerto Rico: Sus luchas emancipadoras (Puerto Rico: Its struggles for emancipation). San Juan: Editorial Isla, 1984.

———. "Orígenes del independentismo puertorriqueño" (The origins of the Puerto Rican independence movement). Revista de Historia 1, no. 1 (January–June 1985).

Patterson, Henry. "Ireland: A New Phase in the Conflict between Nationalism and Unionism." Science and Society 53, no. 2 (Summer 1989).

Payne, Stanley G. El nacionalismo vasco, de sus orígenes a ETA (Basque nationalism, from its origins to ETA). Madrid: Dopesa, 1974.

Peng Jianqun. "A Look at China's Minorities." China Reconstructs (December 1989).

Perdue, William D. Terrorism and the State: A Critique of Domination through Fear. New York: Praeger, 1989.

Peretz, Don. Intifada. Boulder, Colo.: Westview Press, 1990.

Pérez Agote, Alfonso. El nacionalismo vasco a la salida del franquismo (Basque nationalism and the exit of Francoism). Madrid: Siglo XXI, 1987.

Perkins, Whitney T. Denial of Empire: The United States and Its Dependencies. Leiden: A. W. Sythoff, 1972.

Peteet, Julie. "Women and National Politics in the Middle East." In Berch Berberoglu, ed., Power and Stability in the Middle East. London: Zed Books, 1989.

Petry, Julia Rahib. "The Palestinian Woman: A History of Struggle." University of Dayton Review 21, no. 2 (1991).

Philipp, Thomas. "Feminism and Nationalism in Egypt." In Lois Beck and Nikki Keddie, eds., Women in the Muslim World. Cambridge, Mass.: Harvard University Press, 1980.

Probert, Belinda. *Beyond Orange and Green: The Political Economy of the Northern Ireland Crisis.* London: Zed Books, 1978.

Quigley, John. *Palestine and Israel.* Durham, N.C.: Duke University Press, 1990.

Quintero Rivera, Angel. "Background to the Emergence of Imperialist Capitalism in Puerto Rico." In Adalberto López and James Petras, eds., *Puerto Rico and Puerto Ricans.* Cambridge, Mass.: Schenkman, 1974.

———. *Conflictos de clase y política en Puerto Rico* (Class conflict and politics in Puerto Rico). San Juan: Ediciones Huracán, 1976.

———. "Imperialism and Class Struggle in Puerto Rico." *Two Thirds* 2, no. 1 (1979).

———. "Notes on Puerto Rican National Development: Class and Nation in a Colonial Context." *Marxist Perspectives* 3, no. 1 (1980).

Randall, Margaret. *Sandino's Daughters: Testimonies of Nicaraguan Women in Struggle.* Toronto: New Star Books, 1981.

Reed, Evelyn. "Women: Caste, Class, or Oppressed Sex." In Alison M. Jaggar and Paula S. Rothenberg, eds., *Feminist Frameworks: Alternative Accounts of the Relations between Women and Men.* New York: McGraw-Hill, 1984.

Rémillard, Gil. *Le fédéralisme canadien* (Canadian federalism). Montreal: Québec-Amérique, 1985.

Ricks, Thomas. "Palestinian Students Face the Future." *Commonweal* 113, no. 21 (1986): 654–58.

Rolston, Bill. "Reformism and Class Politics in Northern Ireland: The Case of the Trade Unions." *The Insurgent Sociologist* 10, no. 2 (Fall 1980).

Rowthorn, Bob, and Naomi Wayne. *Northern Ireland: The Political Economy of Conflict.* Cambridge: Polity Press, 1988.

Rusinow, Denison. *The Yugoslav Experiment 1948–1974.* Berkeley and Los Angeles: University of California Press, 1977.

Rywkin, Michael. *Moscow's Muslim Challenge.* Armonk, N.Y.: M. E. Sharpe, 1990.

Rzhanitsina, Liudmila. *Female Labor under Socialism.* Moscow: Progress Publishers, 1983.

San Sebastián, Koldo. *Historia del Partido Nacionalista Vasco* (History of the Basque Nationalist Party). San Sebastián: Editorial Txertoa, 1984.

Schultz, Victoria. "Women in Nicaragua." *NACLA Report on the Americas* 14 (March–April 1980).

See, Katherine O'Sullivan. *First World Nationalisms: Class and Ethnic Politics in Northern Ireland and Quebec.* Chicago: University of Chicago Press, 1986.

Shafir, Gershon. *Land, Labor and the Origins of the Israeli-Palestinian Conflict.* Cambridge: Cambridge University Press, 1989.

Shahmouradian, Sanval, ed. *The Sumgait Tragedy: Eyewitness Accounts.* New Rochelle, N.Y.: Caratzas Publishing Company, 1990.

Sharabi, Hisham B., ed. *Nationalism and Revolution in the Arab World.* Princeton, N.J.: Van Nostrand, 1966.

Shaw, S. J., and E. K. Shaw. *History of the Ottoman Empire and Modern Turkey.* 2 vols. Cambridge: Cambridge University Press, 1977.

Sheth, D. L. "State, Nations and Ethnicity: Experiences of Third World Countries." *Economic and Political Weekly* (Bombay) 24 (1989).

Singleton, Fred. *Twentieth Century Yugoslavia.* New York: Columbia University Press, 1976.

———. *A Short History of Yugoslav Peoples.* Washington, D.C.: Wilson Center Press, 1988.

Slovo, Joe. "South Africa: No Middle Road." In Basil Davison, Joe Slovo, and Anthony Wilkinson, *Southern Africa: The New Politics of Revolution.* London: Penguin Books, 1976.

Solé Turá, Jordi. *Nacionalidad y nacionalismos en España: Autonomía, federalismo, autodeterminación* (Nationality and nationalisms in Spain: Autonomy, federalism, self-determination). Madrid: Alianza Editorial, 1985.

Solozábal, Juan José. *El primer nacionalismo vasco* (The First Basque nationalism). Madrid: Tucar, 1975.

Stalin, Joseph. *Marxism and the National Question*. New York: International Publishers, 1934.

Suny, Ronald. "The Revenge of the Past: Socialism and Ethnic Conflict in Transcaucasia." *New Left Review*, no. 184 (October–November 1990).

———. "Incomplete Revolution: National Movements and the Collapse of the Soviet Empire." *New Left Review*, no. 189 (September–October 1991).

Szymanski, Albert. *The Capitalist State and the Politics of Class*. Cambridge, Mass.: Winthrop, 1978.

———. *The Logic of Imperialism*. New York: Praeger, 1981.

———. *Class Structure: A Critical Perspective*. New York: Praeger, 1983.

———. *Human Rights in the Soviet Union*. London: Zed Books, 1984.

Taller de Formación Política. *La cuestión nacional: El Partido Nacionalista y el movimiento obreropuertorriqueño* (The national question: The Nationalist Party and the Puerto Rican workers' movement). San Juan: Ediciones Huracán, 1982.

Tamari, Salim. "Factionalism and Class Formation in Recent Palestinian History." In Roger Owen, ed., *Studies in the Economic and Social History of Palestine in the Nineteenth and Twentieth Centuries*. Chapter 3. London: Macmillan, 1982.

Teng Xing. "Woguo shaoshu minzu diqu jiaoyu zhengti gaige guanjian" (The key to total reform of national minority education). *Qiu Shi* (Seek truth) 7 (April 1989).

Thompson, Mark. *A Paper House: The Ending of Yugoslavia*. New York: Pantheon Books, 1992.

Thorner, Daniel. *The Shaping of Modern India*. New Delhi: Allied Publishers, 1980.

Tien Hung-mao. "Sinicization of National Minorities." *Current Scene* 11 (1974).

Tolkunova, V. N., et al. *Soviet Legislation on Women's Rights*. Moscow: Progress Publishers, 1978.

Tomasevic, Jozo. *The Chetniks: War and Revolution in Yugoslavia*. Stanford: Stanford University Press, 1975.

Tong Li. "Wusi yundong yu shaoshu minzu" (The May Fourth movement and the national minorities). *Zhongyang Muinzu Xueyuan Xuebao* (Central Institute of Nationalities News), no. 1–2 (1979).

Tuñón de Lara, Manuel. *El movimiento obrero en la historia de España* (The workers' movement and the history of Spain). Madrid: Taurus, 1972.

Turok, Ben. *Revolutionary Thought in the Twentieth Century*. London: Zed Books, 1980.

Udovički, Jasminka, and James Ridgeway, eds. *Yugoslavia's Ethnic Nightmare*. Chicago: Lawrence Hill, 1994.

Unzueta, Patxo. *Sociedad vasca y política nacionalista* (Basque society and nationalist politics). Ediciones El Pais, 1987.

Urdang, Stephanie. *And Still They Dance: Women, War and the Struggle for Change in Mozambique*. New York: Monthly Review Press, 1989.

Vaillancourt, Yves. *L'évolution des politiques sociales au Québec* (The evolution of social politics in Quebec). Montreal: Presses de l'Université de Montréal, 1988.

van Bruinessen, Martin. "The Kurds in Turkey." *Middle East Report*, no. 121 (1984).

———. "Between Guerrilla War and Political Murder: The Workers Party of Kurdistan." *Middle East Report*, no. 153 (1988).

———. *Agha, Scheich und Staat: Politik und Gesellschaft Kurdistans* (Agha, Shaikh, and state: On the social and political organization of Kurdistan). Berlin: Parabolis, 1989.

van Diepen, Maria, ed. *The National Question in South Africa*. London: Zed Books, 1988.

Vanly, I. S. *Le Kurdistan irakien, entité nationale* (Iraqi Kurdistan, national entity). Neuchâtel: La Baconniere, 1970.

Van Vuuren, Nancy. *Women against Apartheid: The Fight for Freedom in South Africa, 1920–1975*. Palo Alto, Calif.: R & E Associates, 1979.

Venero García, M. *Historia del nacionalismo vasco* (History of Basque nationalism). Madrid: Editoria Nacional, 1968.

Verluise, Pierre. *Arménia: La fracture* (The breakup of Armenia). Paris: Editions Stock, 1989.

Vilar, Pierre. "On Nations and Nationalism." *Marxist Perspectives* 2, no. 1 (1979).

Vo Nguyen Giap. *People's War, People's Army*. New York: Praeger Publishers, 1962.

Walshe, Peter. *The Rise of African Nationalism in South Africa: The African National Congress, 1912–1952*. Berkeley: University of California Press, 1970.

Wang Tiezhi. "Shaoshu minzu jiaoyu de xinfazhan." (The new development of national minority education). *Jiaoyu jianxun* (Educational briefing), no. 4 (1987).

Warnock, Kitty. *Land before Honour: Palestinian Women in the Occupied Territories*. New York: Monthly Review Press, 1990.

Weiner, Myron. *Sons of the Soil: Migration and Ethnic Conflict in India*. Delhi: Oxford University Press, 1978.

Weitzer, Ronald. *Transforming Settler States: Communal Conflict and Internal Security in Northern Ireland and Zimbabwe*. Berkeley: University of California Press, 1990.

Welty, Gordon. "Progressive versus Reactive Nationalism." In Hani Faris, ed., *Arab Nationalism and the Future of the Arab World*. Belmont, Mass.: Association of Arab-American University Graduates, 1987.

West, Guida, and Rhoda L. Blumberg. *Women and Social Protest*. London: Oxford University Press, 1990.

Wheeler, Geoffrey. *The Modern History of Soviet Central Asia*. New York: Praeger, 1964.

Woods, Donald. *Asking for Trouble: The Autobiography of a Banned Journalist*. New York: Atheneum, 1981.

Workers Party of Kurdistan. *Program*. Cologne: Serxwebun, 1984.

Xian, J. "China's 1982 Constitution and the Policy toward Nationalities." *Chinese Law and Government* 16, nos. 2–3 (1983).

Zhou Enlai. "Guanyu woguo minzu zhengcede jige wenti" (A few questions concerning our country's national policy). In Gansu sheng minzu yanjiusuo (Gansu Province Institute of Nationality Studies), *Zhonghuo minzu guanxishi lunwen xuanji* (A collection of essays on the history of relations among China's nationalities). Gansu: Gansu Minzu Chubanshe, 1983.

Zubi, Nahla. "The Development of Capitalism in Palestine." *Journal of Palestine Studies* 13, no. 4 (1984): 88–109.

❒ About the Contributors ❒

ONA ALSTON DOSUNMU   is a Research Associate at the Institute for Policy Studies in Washington, D.C. She is a J.D. candidate at Georgetown University Law Center and Publications Editor for the Center's journal *Law and Policy in International Business*. She has published articles in *The Guardian*, the *Urban League Review*, and other publications. Her areas of specialization include women in Latin America and African Americans and foreign policy.

BERCH BERBEROGLU   is Professor and Chairman of the Sociology Department and Director of the Institute for International Studies at the University of Nevada, Reno. He received his Ph.D. from the University of Oregon in 1977. Dr. Berberoglu is the author of several books, including *The Internationalization of Capital, Political Sociology, The Legacy of Empire, The Political Economy of Development*, and *Class Structure and Social Transformation*, and has edited a number of volumes, including *National Liberation and Class Struggles, Power and Stability in the Middle East*, and *Class, State and Development in India*. His areas of specialization include class analysis, international political economy, development, race and ethnic relations, nationalism, and Third World studies.

GILLES BOURQUE   is Professor of Sociology at the University of Quebec at Montreal. He received his doctoral degree from the University of Paris V, Sorbonne, in 1974. Dr. Bourque is the author of numerous books, including *Classes sociales et question nationale au Québec* and *L'Etat capitaliste et la question nationale*. He has also published many articles in *Les Cahiers de recherche sociologique*, the *Canadian Review of Sociology and Anthropology*, and other journals. His areas of specialization include political sociology, the national question, and the historical sociology of Quebec and Canada.

JUAN MANUEL CARRIÓN   is Associate Professor of Sociology at the Faculty of Social Sciences, University of Puerto Rico, in Río Piedras. He received his Ph.D. from Rutgers University in 1978. He has published numerous articles on nationalism and ethnic relations in *Revista de Historia*, *El Caribe Contemporáneo*, and other scholarly journals. He has also contributed chapters to several edited volumes. His areas of interest include the national question, race and ethnic relations, development, and political economy.

LEVON CHORBAJIAN   is Professor of Sociology at the University of Massachusetts, Lowell. He received his Ph.D. from Brandeis University in 1974. Dr. Chorbajian is the editor of *Readings in Critical Sociology*. He has also published numerous articles in *Race and Class*, *Les Temps Modernes*, and other journals. A Fulbright Senior Lecturer in the USSR in 1986–87, he specializes in racial and ethnic minorities and political sociology.

DIPANKAR GUPTA   is Professor of Sociology at the Center for the Study of Social Systems, Jawaharlal Nehru University in New Delhi, India. He received his Ph.D. from Jawaharlal Nehru University in 1977. Dr. Gupta has published three books, including *Nativism in a Metropolis: The Shiv Sena in Bombay*. A forthcoming volume, titled *The Context of Ethnicity*, is due to appear in 1995. He is currently engaged in research on the farmers' movement in India.

FERHAD IBRAHIM   is Assistant Professor of Political Science in Middle East Studies at the Free University of Berlin in Germany. He received his Ph.D. from the Free University of Berlin in 1983. Dr. Ibrahim is the author and editor of a number of books, including *Die Kurdische Nationalbewegung im Irak* and *Die Kuwait-Krise*. He has also published numerous articles in *Aus Politik und Zeitgeschichte*, *Peripherie*, *Prokla*, and other journals. His areas of specialization include Middle East studies, the national question, and the Kurdish national movement.

M. BAHATI KUUMBA   is Assistant Professor of Sociology at the State University of New York, College at Buffalo. She received her Ph.D. from Howard University in Washington, D.C., in 1993. Dr. Kuumba has published numerous articles in *Feminist Issues*, *Explorations in Ethnic Studies*, and other journals. Her areas of specialization include race, class, and gender relations and social change movements.

FRANCISCO LETAMENDÍA   is Professor of Constitutional Law and Political Theory at the Universidad del País Vasco in Lejona, Vizcaya, in Spain. He received his Ph.D. from the University of Paris VIII. Dr. Letamendía is the author of several books, including *Historia de Euskadi: El nacionalismo vasco y ETA*, *El no vasco a la reforma*, and *Euskadi, pueblo y nación* (7 volumes). He has been an active participant in the Basque national movement; he served as deputy in the Spanish Parliament during the years 1977–82 and as a defense lawyer took part in the famous Burgos Trial.

MARTIN J. MURRAY is Professor of Sociology at the State University of New York at Binghamton. He received his Ph.D. from the University of Texas at Austin in 1974. Dr. Murray is the author of several books, including *The Development of Capitalism in Colonial Indochina* and *The Revolution Deferred: The Painful Birth of Post-Apartheid South Africa*. He has also published numerous articles in the *Journal of African History, Politics and Society*, the *Journal of Southern African Studies*, and other scholarly journals. His areas of specialization include political sociology, historical sociology, and South African studies.

MARTIN ORR is Assistant Professor of Sociology at Boise State University in Boise, Idaho. He received his Ph.D. from the University of Oregon in 1992, completing a doctoral dissertation titled "Social Change and Metathetoretical Shift in the Sociological Analysis of Ethnicity." His areas of specialization include social theory, class analysis, and ethnic stratification.

GERARD POSTIGLIONE is a Lecturer in the Department of Education at the University of Hong Kong. He received his Ph.D. in sociology and education from the State University of New York at Albany in 1980. Dr. Postiglione is the author of *Education and Society in Hong Kong*. He has also published numerous articles in the *Journal of Contemporary Asia, Comparative Education Review*, and other journals. His areas of specialization include the sociology of education, national minorities, and contemporary China.

JASMINKA UDOVIČKI is Professor of Critical Studies at the Massachusetts College of Arts in Boston. She received her Ph.D. from Brandeis University in 1977. Dr. Udovički is co-editor of the book *Yugoslavia's Ethnic Nightmare* and has published numerous articles in *Praxis, Philosophy and Social Criticism, Praxis International*, and other journals. Her areas of specialization include political sociology and sociology of culture. She is currently engaged in comparative research on ethnic aspects of war.

GORDON WELTY is Professor of Sociology at Wright State University in Dayton, Ohio. He received his Ph.D. from the University of Pittsburgh in 1975. Dr. Welty is the editor of *Linkages in the Middle East*. He has also published numerous articles in scholarly journals around the world, including *Antioch Review, Weltwirtschaftliches Archiv, Nature, Society, and Thought*, and *Revue Internationale de Sociologie*.